GLOBAL MODERN

D0538157

Theory, Culture & Society

Theory, Culture & Society caters for the resurgence of interest in culture within contemporary social science and the humanities. Building on the heritage of classical social theory, the book series examines ways in which this tradition has been reshaped by a new generation of theorists. It will also publish theoretically informed analyses of everyday life, popular culture and new intellectual movements.

EDITOR: Mike Featherstone, *University of Teesside*

Recent volumes include:

Sociology in Question
Pierre Bourdieu

Economies of Signs and Space
Scott Lash and John Urry

Religion and Globalization
Peter Beyer

Baroque Reason
The Aesthetics of Modernity
Christine Buci-Glucksmann

The Consuming Body
Pasi Falk

Cultural Identity and Global Process
Jonathan Friedman

The Established and the Outsiders
Norbert Elias and John L. Scotson

The Cinematic Society
The Voyeur's Gaze
Norman K. Denzin

Decentring Leisure
Rethinking Leisure Theory
Chris Rojek

GLOBAL MODERNITIES

edited by
Mike Featherstone,
Scott Lash and
Roland Robertson

SAGE Publications
London · Thousand Oaks · New Delhi

First published 1995. Reprinted 1997

 SAGE Publications Ltd
   6 Bonhill Street
   London EC2A 4PU

   SAGE Publications Inc
   2455 Teller Road
   Thousand Oaks, California 91320

   SAGE Publications India Pvt Ltd
   32, M-Block Market
   Greater Kailash – I
   New Delhi 110 048

Published in association with *Theory, Culture & Society*,
School of Human Studies, University of Teesside

British Library Cataloguing in Publication data

A catalogue record for this book is available from
the British Library.

   ISBN 0–8039–7947–9
   ISBN 0–8039–7948–7 (pbk)

Typeset by Type Study, Scarborough
Printed in Great Britain by Redwood Books, Trowbridge,
Wiltshire

CONTENTS

Contributors   vii

Preface   x

1 Globalization, Modernity and the Spatialization of Social Theory: An Introduction
Mike Featherstone and Scott Lash   1

2 Glocalization: Time–Space and Homogeneity–Heterogeneity
Roland Robertson   25

3 Globalization as Hybridization
Jan Nederveen Pieterse   45

4 Global System, Globalization and the Parameters of Modernity
Jonathan Friedman   69

5 New World Order or Neo-world Orders: Power, Politics and Ideology in Informationalizing Glocalities
Timothy W. Luke   91

6 The Times and Spaces of Modernity (or Who Needs Post-modernism?)
Anthony D. King   108

7 Routes to/through Modernity
Göran Therborn   124

8 Searching for a Centre that Holds
Zygmunt Bauman   140

9 Security, Philosophy and Politics
Michael Dillon   155

10 Normality – Exception – Counter-knowledge: On the History of a Modern Fascination
Benno Wagner   178

11 Time, Space, Memory, with Reference to Bachelard
Ann Game   192

12 The Soviet Individual: Genealogy of a Dissimulating Animal
Oleg Kharkhordin   209

13 Bio-politics and the Spectre of Incest: Sexuality and/in the Family
Vikki Bell   227

14 The Birth of Identity Politics in the 1960s: Psychoanalysis and
    the Public/Private Division
    Eli Zaretsky   244

15 The Modern Error: Or, the Unbearable Enlightenment of
    Being
    Eugene Halton   260

Index   278

CONTRIBUTORS

Zygmunt Bauman is Emeritus Professor of Sociology at the University of Leeds. He is author, among other books, of *Postmodern Ethics* and *Life in Fragments* (Blackwell, 1993, 1995).

Vikki Bell is a lecturer in the Sociology Department at Goldsmiths' College, University of London. She has published a book entitled *Interrogating Incest: Feminism, Foucault and the Law* (Routledge, 1993) and her articles have appeared, *inter alia*, in *Economy & Society, International Journal of the Sociology of Law* and *Theory, Culture & Society*.

Michael Dillon teaches Politics at Lancaster University. Author of several books in International Relations, he is now generally concerned with phenomenology and politics; and, specifically, with the question of the political at the end of metaphysics. He has written about this in *The Political Subject of Violence* (Manchester University Press, 1993) and *Politics of Security* (Routledge, forthcoming).

Mike Featherstone is Professor of Sociology at the University of Teesside. He is author of *Consumer Culture and Postmodernism* (Sage, 1991) and *Undoing Culture* (Sage, 1995). He is co-editor of *The Body: Social Process and Cultural Theory* (Sage, 1991) and editor of *Cultural Theory and Cultural Change* (Sage, 1992).

Jonathan Friedman is currently Professor of Social Anthropology at the University of Lund, Sweden. He has written on topics such as structuralism and Marxism, theories of social transformation, the imaginary and social representations, global processes, cultural formations, and the practice of identity. His books include: *Modernity and Identity* with S. Lash (eds) (Oxford: Blackwell), *System, Structure and Contradiction in the Evolution of 'Asiatic' Social Formations* (Copenhagen: National Museum, 1979), *Cultural Identity and Global Process* (London: TCS Sage, 1994) and *Consumption and Identity* (ed.), (London: Harwood).

Ann Game is Head of the School of Sociology at the University of New South Wales. She teaches and researches in the area of cultural theory and analysis. She is author of *Undoing the Social: Towards a Deconstructive Sociology* (Open University Press/Toronto University Press, 1991).

Eugene Halton teaches Sociology and Humanities at the University of Notre Dame. He is the author of *Bereft of Reason, Meaning and Modernity* (both University of Chicago Press), and co-author of *The Meaning of Things* (Cambridge University Press). He has performed blues harmonica internationally and his band is currently playing throughout the midwest region with the legendary piano player Pinetop Perkins and recording their first CD.

Oleg Kharkhordin is an Associate Member of the Institute of Sociology, Russian Academy of Sciences and is currently finishing his Ph.D dissertation in the Department of Political Science at the University of California, Berkeley. The dissertation deals with the origins of Soviet individualism. His articles on cultural aspects of current economic reform in Russia have appeared in *International Sociology* and *Europe-Asia Studies*.

Anthony D. King is Professor of Art History and of Sociology at Binghamton University, State University of New York. His recent books include *Global Cities: Post-imperialism and the Internationalisation of London*, *Urbanism, Colonialism and the World-Economy* (both Routledge, 1990) and as editor, *Culture, Globalisation and the World-System* (SUNY Binghamton/ Macmillan, 1991) and *Re-presenting the City: Ethnicity, Capital & Culture in the 21st Century Metropolis* (Macmillan, 1995).

Scott Lash is Professor of Sociology at Lancaster University. His books include *The End of Organized Capitalism* (1987), *Sociology of Postmodernism* (1990), *Economies of Signs and Space* (1994) and *Reflexive Modernization* (1994).

Timothy W. Luke is Professor of Political Science at Virginia Polytechnic Institute and State University in Blacksburg, Virginia. He is the author of *Screens of Power* (Illinois, 1989), *Social Theory and Modernity* (Sage, 1990) and *Shows of Force* (Duke, 1992).

Jan Nederveen Pieterse is author of *White on Black: Images of Africa and Blacks in Western Popular Culture* (Yale University Press, 1992) and *Empire and Emancipation* (Praeger, 1989; Pluto Press, 1990), for which he received the JC Ruigrok Award of the Netherlands Society of Sciences in 1990. He is editor of *Christianity and Hegemony* (Berg Publishers, 1992), *Emancipations, Modern and Postmodern* (Sage, 1992) and, with Bhikhu Parekh, *The Decolonization of Imagination* (Zed, forthcoming). He is at the Institute of Social Studies in The Hague.

Roland Robertson is Professor of Sociology and Religious Studies at the University of Pittsburgh. He has authored or co-authored a number of books, including *Meaning and Change, International Systems and the Modernization of Societies, The Sociological Interpretation of Religion* and *Globalization*. He has also edited or co-edited books in the areas of social theory, globality, identity and religion, as well as many articles on these and related topics.

Göran Therborn is Professor of Sociology at Göteborg University, Sweden, after holding a chair in political science at Nijmegen, Netherlands in the 1980s. His works include *The Ideology of Power and the Power of Ideology* (London: Verso, 1980) and his latest book is *European Modernity and Beyond: The Trajectory of European Societies, 1945–2000* (London: Sage, 1995). He is currently working on comparative modernities, issues of identity, and the politics of childhood, among other things.

Benno Wagner is the Program Coordinator of the Graduate School of Literature and Communication at Siegen University, where he also teaches undergraduate courses. He received his Ph.D in Comparative Literature for a book on the impact of the Green movement on the political culture and the collective imagination of Federal Germany in the late 1970s, and has published in fields like the semiotics of modern media culture, modern German literature, and intercultural communication between Aboriginal and 'European' Australians.

Eli Zaretsky is Associate Professor of History at the University of Missouri, Columbia. He is the author of *Capitalism, the Family and Personal Life* (New York: Harper and Row, 1976, 1986 revised edn); the editor of William I. Thomas and Florian Znaniecki's *The Polish Peasant in Europe and America* (Urbana, Il.: University of Illinois Press, 1985) and is currently completing a single volume history of psychoanalysis tentatively entitled 'From the Psychology of Authority to the Politics of Identity'.

PREFACE

Earlier versions of the papers in this volume were presented at the 10th Anniversary *Theory, Culture & Society* Conference held in August 1992 at the Seven Springs Mountain Resort, Champion, Pennsylvania. Special thanks are due to the University Center for International Studies at the University of Pittsburgh and the Centre for the Study of Adult Life at the University of Teesside for their generous support for the conference. In particular the conference would not have taken place without the tremendous organizational ability and hard work of Kathleen White. In addition we would like to thank Julie Roat (Pittsburgh) and Barbara Cox and Julie Chapman (Teesside) for their administrative expertise and support, as well as the assistance of Victor Roudometof and Joe Roidt (Pittsburgh). Amongst the many friends and colleagues who helped with the planning and organization of the conference and the long process of selecting and reviewing papers for this volume, those who deserve a special mention include: Stephen Barr, Josef Bleicher, Roy Boyne, Norman Denzin, Mike Hepworth, Mica Nava, Bryan S. Turner.

We would also like to thank all who attended for making the conference such an enjoyable and stimulating occasion. The success of the conference can also be gauged by the fact that we have been persuaded to hold a second conference on 'Culture and Identity: City/Nation/World', in Berlin in August 1995.

Mike Featherstone
Scott Lash
Roland Robertson

GLOBALIZATION, MODERNITY AND THE SPATIALIZATION OF SOCIAL THEORY: AN INTRODUCTION

Mike Featherstone and Scott Lash

'Globalization' has become an increasingly influential paradigm in the human sciences since the beginning of the 1990s. It has in fact in a very important sense been the successor to the debates on modernity and postmodernity in the understanding of sociocultural change and as the central thematic for social theory. The collective weight of the papers in this book suggest that globalization should be seen as now no longer emergent, but as a more fully 'emerged' theory in the social sciences. Our organizing frame of reference in this book is constructed around two major thematics. In the first the emphasis will be on social theory. Here we shall explore throughout the book the extent to which the rise of the globalization *problématique* represents the *spatialization* of social theory. This resonates with the general thrust of postmodern theory which has been to privilege the spatial over the temporal mode of analysis (Featherstone, 1991; Lash, 1990). Yet for some the postmodern is to be seen as not the end of temporal analysis, in the sense that Vattimo (1988) announced 'the end of history', but a new stage of historical development. Some postmodern theories, therefore, while emphasizing the crisis of the metanarratives, have never been sufficiently self-reflexive in recognizing their own paradigmatic and chronic foregrounding of the temporal. If their Marxist predecessors focused on a temporal metanarrative about the various transitions from feudalism to capitalism to socialism, then, for some theorists of the postmodern, history is to be conceived as a parallel set of temporal transitions from tradition to modernity to postmodernity. Here postmodernity is in effect accorded the status of being the latest stage in a master logic of historical development, notwithstanding all the obligatory homilies paid to the critique of development. In this context the concept of globalization represents an important shift in transmuting this temporality into a spatial framework. This theme is, explicitly or implicitly, addressed in many of the chapters in this book, even in those not specifically about globalization.

The second organizing theme of the book is the concern with social change. Here the question revolves around the sociocultural processes and forms of life which are emerging as the global begins to replace the nation-state as the decisive framework for social life. This is a framework in which global *flows* – in mediascapes, ethnoscapes, finanscapes and techno-scapes – are coming to assume as much, or greater, centrality than *national institutions* (Appadurai, 1990; Lash and Urry, 1994). International social, political and cultural (for example the media) organizations are standing alongside and beginning to replace their national counterparts.

This process is proving difficult to theorize, for the new global framework cannot be conceived as merely that of the nation-state writ large. Only in the most minimalist sense can one speak of a 'global society' or a 'global culture', as our conceptions of both society and culture draw heavily on a tradition which was strongly influenced by the process of nation-state formation. A central implication of the concept of globalization is that we must now embark on the project of understanding social life without the comforting term 'society'. The view that the concept of 'society' should be the basic generic unit for sociology, did not of course meet with universal approval, in particular the tradition stemming from Max Weber sought to focus upon inter- and trans-societal influences such as wars, conquest and colonialism (Tenbruck, 1994). If we move away from social change conceived as the internal development of societies to focusing on change as the outcome of struggles between the members of a figuration of interdependent and competing nation-states, then we have made an important step towards a trans-societal perspective. If we then seek to add to this an understanding of the intensification of trans-societal flows which are pushing towards a 'borderless global economy' (Ohmae, 1987) and undermining the capacity of nation-states to act, then we have moved towards the globaliz-ation perspective. One way to attempt to simplify the level of complexity which the intensification of global flows is introducing in the figuration of competing nation-states and blocs, is to regard globalization as an outcome of the universal logic of modernity. From this perspective, globalization as the triumph of the universal will introduce, on the face of it, substantial measures of abstraction, of 'disembedding', and the hollowing out of meaning in everyday life.

Such abstraction is exacerbated when the transition from the national to the global is superimposed on the change from an industrial manufacturing order to a post-industrial and informational order. In this shift from 'industrial society' to 'informational world' even the concrete labour process involves the abstraction of informationalized products and means of production that would seem further to de-situate, to hollow out meaning from forms of life. A number of authors in this book consider whether this unhappy scenario of the negation of identity will be the upshot of such change, both in the periphery of developing countries brought into the informationalized world system, and in the core itself. Others argue instead that a number of positive possibilities can be opened up. They contend that the seemingly empty and universalist signs circulating in the world informational system can be recast into different configurations of meaning. That these transformed social semantics can – in the context of traditional and self-reflexive social practices – instead inform the (re)constitution and/or creation of individual and communal identities.

It is therefore important that we become attuned to the nuances of the process of globalization and seek to develop theories which are sensitive to the different power potentials of the different players participating in the various global struggles. Different entities, such as nation-states, multi-national corporations and international organizations, approach the global field with different resources (economic and cultural) and seek to set different agendas. Not every nation-state can be fitted easily into a developmental sequence derived from Western experience of tradition–modernity–postmodernity, indeed the application of these concepts to other non-Western contexts may well be flawed and misses the politics of knowledge where a dominant particular is able to represent itself as the universal, as Japanese critics have indicated (Myoshi and Harutoonian, 1989). The Japanese case should also make us aware that nation-states possess widely differing national projects, which can themselves have global impact in the shifting power balances which attempt to define the global field (Featherstone, 1995). Today we can not only speak about Europeanization and Americanization, but also of Japanization and even Brazilianization (the latter to refer ironically to the re-emergence of fortress motifs and the spatial segregation of various social groups in global cities). The range and pluralization of responses to modernity means that it may well be preferable to refer to global modernities.

This said, the volume breaks down into four sections. The first four chapters – by Robertson, Pieterse, Friedman and Luke – are systematic enquiries into rethinking the notion of globalization. The second section includes chapters by King, Therborn and Bauman and involves the reconceptualization of modernity and modernization in the frame of the global order. The third section – comprising chapters by Dillon, Wagner and Game – is metatheoretical and works through the implications of this new spatial geopolitics for what constitutes knowledge in the human sciences. The final section – with chapters by Kharkhordin, Bell, Zaretsky and Halton – looks spatio-temporally at the construction of the individual and the grounding of subjectivity in today's world.

I

Roland Robertson opens the debates and sets the stage for much of the rest of the volume with a challenge to theorists such as Giddens (1990, 1991) for whom globalization is but 'a consequence of modernity'. This is ironic in that, for Giddens, globalization involves time–space distanciation, but at the same time his privileging of the juxtaposition of tradition and modernity tends to marginalize the spatial component of the process. For Robertson, in contrast, 'globality' is not so much a cause as a condition of modernization, and more specifically a condition of divergent modernization. There were two main contestants, as Robertson notes, in the first generation of globalization debates: 'homogenizers', including for example Giddens and a number of Marxists and functionalists, and 'heterogenizers', including such theorists of 'interculturalism' such as Edward Said (1978), Homi K. Bhabha (1990) and Stuart Hall (1992) as well as reflexive anthropologists such as Clifford and Marcus (1986). The *homogenizers* tend, ideal-typically, to subscribe to some sort of notion of world system. They look primarily at the presence of the universal in the particular, whether as commodification or as time–space distanciation. They would at least implicitly invoke a scenario of convergent development. *Heterogenizers* would tend to dispute that a system existed, will disclaim the distinction of universal and particular, and see the dominance of the West over 'the rest' as that of simply one particular over others. They will not only dispute convergence but the notion of development altogether. Finally, as 'modernists' most homogenizers will feature a scientific and realist epistemology in which the scientist as subject studies the world as object, while heterogenizers will not be realists, but hermeneuticians who see the social analyst as inseparable from his/her world, and social knowledge as involving a dialogic relation with his/her 'subjects', involving the attempt at 'intertranslatability' of the 'prejudices' of one side to the prejudices of the other. The homogenizer is most likely to be found in the social sciences and the heterogenizer, of course, in cultural studies.

It may be possible, Robertson contends, to go some way to overcoming this aporia of (modernist) homogenizers and (postmodernist) heterogenizers in the very privileging of space over (modernist and postmodernist) temporality. If globality is the condition of divergent modernization then universalism is the condition of growing particularizations. Dependency analysts such as Wallerstein would tend to understand the universal and particular to involve a contradiction – between system and anti-systemic movements, between 'McWorld' and 'Jihad world'. For Robertson there is no such necessary tension in what he sees as 'glocalization'. Other analysts such as Giddens (1991) have in effect used the concept, although not the term, glocalization in referring to 'the intersection of presence and absence' over broad stretches of time and space. This stretching of social relations over time and space involves first, the disembedding or absence of traditional and local activities and artefacts and then, the re-embedding (or 'presencing') of activities and artefacts from far away in that same local context.

What Robertson has in mind is not so much the presence of global artefacts in the local, but more a process of *institutionalization*, in which there is a global creation of locality. This takes several forms. It can be weak institutionalization in which similar processes of localization are taking place universally, without an overall guiding formal body. Examples of this are the establishment of great numbers of nationalisms with similar characteristics, or the world-wide spread of suburbanization. Or the creation of locality guided by formal international institutions, such as the International Youth

Hostel Association promoting 'particularist' back-to-nature type communalism on a world scale. Or the Pan-African movement; or the Global Forum meeting in Brazil in 1992 to organize globally the promotion of values and identities of native peoples. In each case, notes Robertson, there is the 'global institutionalization of the expectation and construction of local particularism'.

A convinced 'heterogenizer' such as Jan Nederveen Pieterse would be dubious of Robertson's arguments which he might see as representing just a more sophisticated version of universalism. Pieterse, in Chapter 3, understands globalization as '*hybridization*', 'in which forms become separated from existing practices and recombine with new form in new practices'. Pieterse would argue that globalization primarily involves neither universalization nor even 'multiculturalism', but instead *interculturalism*. For Pieterse globalization is not a condition of modernization, but instead an historical epoch, beginning from the 1960s and contemporaneous with *post*modernity. Modernity, for its part, is contemporaneous with an earlier period (1840–1960) of the hegemony of the nation-state. For him both functionalist modernization theory and Marxist dependency theory are modernist paradigms of the period of the nation-state, while true globalization theory is the postmodern analysis of hybridity.

Pieterse's special interest is cultural hybridity between enemies, involving the formation of a '*global field*' of 'global memory', circumscribed by conflictual unity – bound by common political and cultural experiences of, for example, Jew and Arab. Such conflictual hybridity is found in 'creolization', in the 'crossover culture' of European-Americans and African-Americans adopting one another's ways of life, or the 'orientalization' of Western culture through world music. But like Robertson, Pieterse urges us to understand cultural hybridity as an organizational phenomenon. Yet his idea of institutional globalization is vastly different from Robertson's. Pieterse's examples are not of the *institutionalized* pervasion of a particularism, or the initiation by institutions of particularism. Instead he refers to the appeal to a universal instance – such as the European Court of Human Rights – in a particular case; here the universal can protect the right to difference. He points more characteristically to hybrid organizational forms in which neither organization is a universal, such as the interface of transnational firms and host national government in offshore banking. Or, finally, instances in which multiculturalism becomes interculturalism, in which an individual has a choice of a plurality of ethnic organizations as a basis of multiple identity, for example in the UK a combination of British and Muslim schooling, or the north London Briton of Asian origin who plays for a local Bengali cricket club, and supports the Arsenal football club.

A wholesale challenge to the heterogenist position that Pieterse represents is launched in the 'systems-theoretical' reformulations of globalization in the interventions by Jonathan Friedman and Tim Luke. In Chapter 4 Friedman speaks not so much of globalization but of global *system*. If the theorists of 'hybridity' – Clifford, Marcus, Hall, Bhabha – are the true globalization analysts as Pieterse contends, then this, according to Friedman, is not the solution but the problem. Friedman uses his systemic approach to 'classify the classifiers', who are now widely popular if not dominant in globalization debates. He argues that Western theorists of hybridity are in fact not much of an improvement on straightforward modernization theory. Friedman contends that the notion of hybridity, like the cultural universalism of modernization theory, denies the peripheries of their own identities. That is, that implicit and integral to theories and strategies of creolization and hybridity is the *disauthentication* of Third and Fourth World identities. He claims further that the growing influence of hybridization theorists is due to the crisis of modernity in the core itself.

Friedman gives a culturalist twist to world systems theory. Here he differs from Wallerstein on two crucial counts. If a number of theorists in this book and for example Harvey (1989) and Lash and Urry (1994) see globalization as something essentially postmodern, Wallerstein sees it as having its onset with capitalism and modernity. Friedman, like Robertson (1992; Chapter 2 in this volume) understands world systems or globalization as long pre-dating the modern; as already being present millennia before the hegemony of world capitalism, in ancient civilizations, for example. In fact, for both Friedman and Robertson, globalization is fundamentally 'civilizational' in nature. Friedman's second difference from Wallerstein is that his world systems are primarily, not political-economic, but cultural phenomena. For Friedman globalization is 'a process of attribution of meaning', a process most importantly of the constitution of 'clusters of such meanings'. At a certain point of coherence and systematicity such meanings-clusters begin to comprise an 'identity-space'. For Friedman these identity-spaces are not constituted through the pervasion and transmission of ideas, but instead through the structural nature of core–periphery relations. Key here are systemic processes such as contraction, expansion, fragmentation and the like.

Although for Friedman the cultural may be dominant, it is the economy which is 'determinant'. Hence 'modernist identity' develops in 'commercial civilizations'. The abstract calculability and presumptions of formal equivalence involved in commercial transactions gives rise to what might be called a general metaphysics of equivalence. Here the concrete temporalization of the 'great chain of being' is replaced by the abstraction of modernist (meta)narrative time. As Benedict Anderson (1983) recounts in *Imagined Communities*, abstract time, abstract Cartesian space and the abstract social (in which rules and institutions replace the face-to-face relations of traditional communities) are successors to their concrete counterparts of 'tradition'. Friedman argues, however, that modernist culture and the modernist world system have entered into crisis. This crisis, like that in Daniel Bell's (1976) *Cultural Contradictions of Capitalism*, involves the decline of Western civilization. In the cultural register this is instantiated in a crisis of classificatory hegemony. Symptomatic of this is the crisis of modernist identity-space in the core. Reflexive and postmodern anthropology and cultural studies in general would be a symptom of this crisis. So, Friedman argues, is the growing 'cosmopolitanism' of Western elites, which is not so much a question of liminality as one of 'betwixt and between'.

It is also a crisis of hegemony of the West versus 'the rest' in which the 'people without history' (Wolf, 1982) can begin to use Western and indigenous symbols to construct their own identity-spaces. In this context the creolization theories of the West, this new intellectual hegemony of anti-classificatory classification, has a hidden function. It serves to 'disauthenticate' non-Western cultures as 'creole'. It serves to negate non-Western identity-space. Though pasta came originally to Italy via Marco Polo from China, notes Friedman, Italian cuisine is hardly thought of as 'creole culture'. This systemic critique of hybridity theories informs Friedman's understanding of culture, not as 'substance' but as *process*. That is, Friedman does not want to look at the hybridity of cultural artefacts – as both say Giddens (1991) and Clifford (1988) might do. Instead he wants to look at cultural practices in the creation and reproduction of identity-spaces. He wants to look not at the 'what' but at the 'how', not at disembodied artefacts, but at forms of life.

Timothy Luke, like Friedman, offers a vision of a postmodern world system, and at the same time a systemic explanation of the apparently anti-systemic. Luke's perspective, however, is not a postmodernism of core disintegration and peripheral self-identity construction, but instead one of pushing to a logical conclusion the most extreme excesses of modernist abstraction. Luke's scenario is, in short, postmodernity as dystopic hypermodernity. Also unlike Friedman, Luke paints a picture of a thoroughly informationalized world system. He speaks of a move in which the *new world order* of (modern) nation-states is replaced by a set of *neo-world orders* in today's postmodernity of global flows. Benedict Anderson's (1983) 'new world order' of nation-states was based on 'imagined communities'. These are like traditional and concrete *Gemeinschaften* in that people are willing to die for them. However, unlike 'immediate communities' which were rendered in qualitative time, full space and immediate forms of sociation, imagined communities are 'imagined' in the sense of their very abstraction – of abstract time, space and the social. Luke's postmodern 'neo-world orders' give us not imagined, but *virtual* communities, involving such levels of hyperabstraction that time destroys history, space destroys reality and the image/information flows destroy the social.

Luke's interest lies not in the social, however, but in the political form of the nation-state. Thus modernity's new world order of neutralized, historical time is a 'chronotext' – featuring the origins of the *ethnie* in which the state itself is narrator. The key to Luke's thesis lies in his analytics of, not time but space. His thesis is that there is a shift from a 'realist' new world order of nation-states to hyperrealist 'neo-world orders' of global flows. That there is a shift from 'real politics' carried out by nation-states in 'historical space', to one of hyperreal politics carried out by sub- and supra-national collective actors in post-historical 'cyberspace'. The argument about realism should be taken very seriously here. Paradigmatic for Luke in the modern nation-state order is not epistemological, but aesthetic realism, that is, Renaissance perspectival space and single point perspective. Luke's point is that it is the state who is doing the painting (see also Dillon in Chapter 9). That is, that the state as 'illustrator' paints in the sovereignty in the 'new world order'. The state as collective subject creates the 'object', 'instating' the 'new geographies' through 'inscribing writs of difference' of 'friend versus foe' in money, language, religion, ideology. This nation-state instated geopolitics 'exogenizes conflict' at the same time as 'endogenizing discipline', replacing the 'theo-dictive' *ancien régime* with the 'juris-dictive' new order.

For Luke the new world order followed an 'organizational logic' of nation-states, in which 'realist hoods' (!) created sovereign nationhood. And the informationalized neo-world orders consist of the replacement of national organizations by global flows in the familiar set of media, 'techno', 'info' and finanscapes. This new global and eminently disorganized capitalism should, argues Luke, be understood in terms of Baudrillard's hyper-realism. Unlike the Heideggerian tradition, Baudrillard does not 'destruct' the Cartesian subject–object thinking involved in realism in order hermeneutically to retrieve being-in-the-world. Instead he pushes what Heidegger would understand as 'technology' to its furthest extreme. For Baudrillard and Luke hyperrealism is much much *more* real than realism and therefore much more serious in its implications.

In modernity, realism for Luke (and Baudrillard) was based in a 'system of equivalence', in exchange and pre-eminently in representation. Realist representation meant that the subject (or proposition or idea or concept or painting) was adequate to the object that it represented. What hyperrealism presumes is that the system of equivalence is no longer a matter of representation, but that it enters into the *generation* of objects, subjects, thought and ultimately life itself. It does so through the systems of equivalence which are the basis of informational systems in, for example, micro-electronics and biotechnology. For Heidegger (see Chapter 9 by Dillon) 'technology' is above all understood in terms of systems of equivalences. What Luke (and Baudrillard) are insisting is that these systems of equivalence are that much more pervasive, and thus more totalitarian in the postmodern global order than in the mere representational realism of modernity. That is, if 'technology' (or metaphysics of presence, instrumental rationality, etc.) was confined to representational space in modernity, in global postmodernity it has shifted to the more totalitarian colonization of generational (or productive) space. Or, if in modernity technology involves the representation of the real, in post-modernity it involves the production or (pro)creation of the real. This postmodern real is moreover more real than the real. It is hyperreal.

The question then is what sort of 'technology', what sort of system of equivalences generates the hyperreality of global flows. The hyperreality of flows is generated through a process of *simulation*. What is meant by 'simulation' is not mimesis or figural (iconic) representation but instead the generation of the hyperreal by 'models'. Simulation involves in turn the 'precession of simulacra'. This is not a matter of say exchange value being a second order, more abstract semiotic transformation of use-value, and sign-value a representation of exchange-value. It is literally a *precession*, and is a process not of representation or semiotic transformation at all but instead is a process of generation, in which the 'model' precedes the hyperreal and the hyperreal precedes and then 'nullifies' the real, or 'liquidates the referent'. In this the hyperreal is the informationalized bit-streams of global flows of images, voice, data and the like.

But what are these models, 'recurrently orbiting' in an 'atmosphereless hyperspace', that precede everything else? The models are the loci of the systems of equivalence. The *langue* which produces the parole of the hyperreal flows. They are 'combinatory models', comprising 'informational units'. The models are 'systems' (systems also in Luhmann's sense). But they are 'systems of signs', 'miniaturized units', they form 'matrices', 'memory banks'. They are 'genetic miniaturizations' that lend themselves to 'systems of equivalence' which are more 'ductile' than meaning, or the adequation of signifier and signified. That is, the 'representational logic of meaning' is replaced by the 'genetic sphere of the programmed signal'.

At issue is very much what Castells (1989) calls the 'informational mode of production', as instantiated in micro-electronics and biotechnology. In the informational mode of production the system of equivalences is displaced and radicalized from representation to (generation and) production. The system of equivalences here is 'genetic', it 'acts operationally'; it 'synthesizes'. The new system of equivalences is more 'ductile' than the old mode of equivalence. If the old representational mode of equivalence saw the shift of the gift of creation from God to 'man', the new mode sees a shift to the technogenesis of the model.

What then is being generated by the model as mode of equivalence? What is generated in simulation are 'hyperreal objects' such as images, signals and 'graphemes' which flow in the 'scapes'. But these flows of such objects are 'coded', the encoding taking place in the generating. If power is invested in the nation-state in the new world order then where do we look for power in the neo-world orders? Power is often lodged in transnational capital which tends to create neo-worlds. As the real world becomes saturated with commodities, competition shifts to the 'techno-regions' of the neo-worlds. Whereas the traditional world order was 'theo-dictive', and the 'man-made' social code of the new world order is 'juris-dictive', the 'micro-molecular' codes of the neo-world orders are 'polydictive'. The polydictive codes of the neo-worlds, that is the 'virtual communities', include thus not just finance and commerce but gender, ethnicity and ecology. Access to these, not imagined but virtual communities, to these neo-worlds constituted by the 'iconic/symbolic' and 'graphic/dictive' flows is exclusive. It is based on the power and ability to decode (and encode) the signals in the flows. Such decoding/encoding ability depends on the possession of particular, virtual-community-specific types of cultural capital.

And such cultural struggles over the power to encode and decode involve a lot more than the institutions of education. They involve rights in and the ability to control intellectual property. Think for example of Microsoft's sustained hegemony in micro-electronics. The battle for markets in the informational neo-world orders is very importantly a matter of power in regard to intellectual property. For Luke the whole issue of security in the post-national global order becomes closely intertwined with intellectual property. Security, he argues, previously a problem of battles for 'real estate' by the realist hoods of the nation-state now becomes increasingly a matter of struggles for intellectual property, that is, for 'hyperreal estate' by the newer set of 'hyperrealist hoods'.

II

The chapters by King, Therborn and Bauman involve reconceptualizing modernity in the context of globalization. Anthony King in Chapter 6 thus uses globalization to spatialize modernity in two senses. First he notes that the globalization *problématique* 'finally enunciates' that about which the previous temporal notion of modernity was suspiciously silent, that it is 'spatial, Western and white'. Like Friedman, King's modernity is not about the spread of idea but is fundamentally structural and world-systemic. The latter for King, however, is not primarily 'regimes of meaning', but is instead general processes of exchange and world-wide division of labour in the 'colonial mode of production'. King's modernity is also spatial in that it happens in cities and especially in global cities. Yet these cities are at the same time spaces of flows: they are, as King notes, embedded in flows and give rise to them.

Urban and global modernity, for King, is not so much the space of metanarratives, but that where 'all that is solid melts into air'. And what is doing the melting is the cosmopolitanism of the flows. If modernity came first to late nineteenth-century Paris, and subsequently travelled to *fin de siècle* Vienna, 1920s Berlin and post-war New York, now it is no longer, King tells us, in metropolitan but in colonial space – such as São Paulo and Delhi – where the solid is melting into air at the greatest speed. In colonial space, he reminds us, take place the most frantic development of migrant and finance flows. Further, the global colonial cities have long ago under-gone – with their *bidonvilles*, etc. – the sort of class polarization that core global cities have just begun to experience. There is no need for a concept of postmodernity, King concludes, when *modernization* on a world scale (and global colonial cities) has only been with us in the last quarter-century.

Göran Therborn in Chapter 7 wants to speak of, not modernization but 'modernizations', or of a 'plurality of routes to and through modernity'. He traces four 'gates of entry' to modernity: (1) the European; (2) the New

World: in which modernity took the shape of a denial of the *ancien régime* in Europe; (3) External Threat: nationalist modernization from above as in Japan and arguably nineteenth-century Germany; (4) Colonial Zone: in which the metropole heteronomously modernizes the colony. For Therborn a particular national route to modernization is determined by first, the structural location in the world system and, second, by the domestic individual or collective actor – possessed with cultural and organizational resources – which is the key agent of modernization.

In Europe these social constructors of modernization were primarily the national bourgeoisie either as individuals or as a collectivity. In some cases, such as Sweden and Russia (see Kharkhordin in Chapter 12) the working class as collective actor seems to have been determinant. In the New World route, in the Americas, the nation itself, in grassroots popular nationalisms, was the pivotal collective agent. Where modernization is in response to an 'external threat', it is nationalist. But here social change is defensive and engineered from above, while trappings of traditional culture are kept on – such as the Japanese Emperor of the Junkers in Germany. Finally in the 'colonial zone' initial modernization came from exogenous sources, the agent of modernization being foreign nationalisms from the core. For Therborn, global modernization comprises processes of 'accumulation' and 'collectivization'. He notes that the prospects for either depend importantly on the 'openness' of the system at issue. In post-national modernization, the decline in boundedness of the system – and the rise of world markets – should encourage accumulation; yet this same decline in boundedness makes resource redistribution by collective actors, and hence 'collectivization' an ever more difficult task.

Zygmunt Bauman in Chapter 8 continues the explorations in spatialization of temporality in his thematization of modernity's 'search for a centre that holds'. This search, however, takes place less in the macro-spaces of globality than in the micro-space of community. A centre that holds, observed Arnold Gehlen, is eternally a problem for human beings because of their generic '*Instinktarmut*'. Whereas other creatures possess a structure of drives preventing them from, for example, killing their own species, *Homo Sapiens'* characteristic poverty of instincts leaves us searching for a centre that holds. This silencing of our instincts, Gehlen noted – as even our habituss learned, and is, probably for the worse, not 'natural' but 'cultural' – is the necessary other side of 'mankind's' being a 'bunch of possibilities'.

Bauman thus presents what may be the basic contradiction at the heart of human existence. This contradiction comprises on the one hand, '*systemness*' as a set of ersatz instincts for our species, whether as custom, religious ritual and precepts or legal-rational norms. It comprises, on the other hand, '*contingency*', the open-ended more 'existential' side of *la condition humaine*. Gehlen, and following him Peter Berger, believed that systemness or the resurgence of order is always inevitable. Bauman disagrees and propounds that any sort of contemporary ethical thought must champion neither systemness nor contingency, but recognize that 'man' is a complex amalgam of both, and must instead learn to live with this 'ambivalence'. It should be noted that this may be a major departure from Bauman's previous formulations. In, for example, *Modernity and the Holocaust* (1989) and *Modernity and Ambivalence* (1991), Bauman raised a challenge to 'system' from the standpoint of contingency. Indeed, in his previous work 'ambivalence' was very much understood as contingency.

It was in response to this need for a 'centre' – the need to fill the void left by our *Instinktarmut* in an age of rapid change – that the notion of 'identity' as a characteristic of the self initially emerged in the seventeenth century. 'Identity', Bauman observes, was, for Early Modern bourgeois elites whose very medium was that of contingency, something that was not yet attained, while for the masses it was what was being lost. The rise of national identity can in this context be understood as an attempt to instate contingency as system. Thus nineteenth-century elites tried to 'provide a centre that held for all', based on individualism, choice and democracy and incorporated in the nation-state. Such was Durkheim's idea of nation, and a *société* comprised of abstract norms which would achieve the amalgam of liberal individualism and system integration. Here the nation-state would guide the masses, and make them into individuals, through education into the value consensus of these norms. The nation-state would lead the masses from the systemness of particularistic traditionalism to the new systemness of universalistic modernity.

But what are the implications, Bauman asks, of the imminent demise of the nation and its supersession by the new global order? What will happen now that the state is decisively weakened as a 'centre that holds'? It is in this context that he understands the turn to community in postmodernity, and our contemporary shift towards an ethos in which 'constraint is not an unmitigated disaster'. Communities now, Bauman argues, are primarily '*bestowers* of identity' through the invention of tradition. This is exemplified in the new, post-Communist nationalisms of the 1990s. These are not for him, as Friedman (Chapter 4) and Luke (Chapter 5) contend hyperreal or simulacral nationalism, but 'imaginary centres made real' by the new nations as identity bestowers. Whereas modern nationalism would be made in the name of the universal against the particular, postmodern nationalisms would be constituted in the name of the particular against the empty and unhappy shell of an old universal.

III

Chapters 9, 10 and 11 by Dillon, Wagner and Game each in their way takes up Bauman's question of a 'centre that holds', only now the terrain of debate is shifted to the spatial contextualization of modern knowledge. Hence Michael Dillon argues in Chapter 9 that there is an 'alliance' between, on the one hand, modern knowledge as the subject–object thinking of the 'metaphysics of presence' and, on the other, the 'politics of security' of the national state. In this both 'philosophy' and 'politics' are dedicated to the stabilization of 'security' in the face of an actually existing environment of contingency, flux and more generalized insecurity. This alliance is for Dillon longstanding. For the Ancients, in Plato and in early Christianity, a supersensible universe controlled the insecurity of Heraclitean flux, first by the 'idea' and then institutionally, through the Church as the condition of human salvation. In early modernity secular de-legitimation of the Church led to a new locus of control. Now in philosophy, the ideas of rationalism and empiricism, in their 'mirror-of-nature' assumptions, helped control 'epistemological insecurity'. In politics, for its part, chaos is exogenized by the institution of the Machiavellian and Hobbesian nation-state.

But what form does this alliance take in our late-modern, contemporary era of 'technology', in which the philosophy and politics of representation, whether in philosophy or the nation-state, comes under challenge? What sort of alliance takes place in our age in which the 'calculation of equivalences' colonizes all spheres of life, an age which witnesses the ultimate retreat of the last 'finalities'? What sort of politics of security is entailed in our era when nature itself becomes understood as systems of equivalence, in for example the human genome project? Dillon considers possible politics/knowledge configurations in the context of our late-modern assumptions, in which nature becomes no longer a world of entities available to beings for transformation in respect to 'its finalities', but instead 'becomes a stock of raw material' for our own ends. Here even the calibration of human beings themselves – in, for example, reproductive technologies – becomes a matter of the calculation of equivalences.

Dillon thus develops, in a different register, themes enunciated by Tim Luke in Chapter 5. Yet whereas Luke's own methodology was systems-theoretical and perhaps ultimately realist, Dillon is sceptical of system and realism as new iterations of the politics of security. Also, Luke seems to see no way out from the neo-worlds of global technological systems that replace the nation-state as locus of security. Dillon, however, argues that the 'recovery of the question of the political' lies in our very grasp of the historical power/knowledge complex of security. It lies in our very power to recognize security as merely a 'limit' and at the same time come to terms with the 'limits of the politics of (in)security'. In both Luke and Dillon we see that 'technology' as a system of equivalences and post-national forms of cultural control are a lot more than a 'metaphysics of presence' to be deconstructed by post-structural theorists. We see that technology itself has for some time already been doing this deconstructing, as systems of equivalence and cultural control move from the space of representation to the space of generation and (re)production. We see that the global technology of the flows has already deconstructed both nation-state and the old metaphysics of presence. The problem is that at the same time it has created an altogether new apparatus of (in)security.

Benno Wagner in Chapter 10 begins where Dillon ends, that is with the question of the possibility of a 'counter-knowledge' in the face of modernity's normalizing trends. He attempts to make inroads on this through a critique of the thought of Carl Schmitt. He compares Schmitt with Gehlen, both of whom were appalled by the machine-line nature of the social. But whereas Gehlen thought there was no alternative, Schmitt thought that there was, namely in the counterposition of the state to the social. Schmitt's notion of the social was modern, his idea of the state was pre-modern – it was classical and 'exceptional'. In this sense Schmitt – famously a Hobbesian – can be understood via Weber and Foucault. Schmitt's notion of the state as exceptional is influenced by Weber's counterposition of 'charisma' to the iron cage of bureaucratic rationalization. As classical, Schmitt's state was comprised of ideal and not everyday contours, and, as in Foucault's era of the classical, it was the 'body of the king' which was possessed with sovereignty before its transfer to the social.

Schmitt, following Ronan, disagreed with the modern idea that truth lay in the suffering caused by the sovereign to the masses, but instead held the 'classical' idea that truth inheres in the 'narratives of magnificence of the sovereign'. Appalled by the modern 'humiliation' of the classical state to the status of a mere function of the social, Schmitt wanted to reinstate such a power/knowledge of the exceptional. Opposing the modern ethos in which the sovereign is replaced by a set of normalizing functions, Schmitt recalls us to the classical distinctions of 'friend and foe', 'peace and war'.

The problem is, Wagner argues, that this sort of exceptionalism, and the counter-knowledge it implies, is not possible in modernity. This is because the modern chronically displaces the friend/foe logic of the classical onto the modern opposition of 'the normal' versus 'the pathological', and because of this the exceptional can only appear as pathological. This is true Wagner notes, drawing on Canguilhem, of the entire modern episteme. Disease, for example, which had previously been primarily an 'object of fear', becomes in modernity a focus for scientific research. This is also true of the transplant of the organicist heuristic from biology into sociology. Canguilhem noted that only in the social organism is there a distinction between 'rules' and 'regulations', that is, only here is there the possibility for transgression. However, as Canguilhem, who had clearly read his Durkheim, also understood, in modernity the exceptional comes to take the form of the pathological and, as such, becomes merely the 'supplement' of normality. Canguilhem argued this modern reduction of the exceptional to normal/pathological was true not only of positivist sociology but of its vitalist and *lebensphilosophisch* opponents (Bergson, Dilthey, Nietzsche). As in Bichat's biological vitalism, life becomes the 'sum of functions that resist death' and again the exceptional is the pathological.

Schmitt's own friend/foe vitalism counterposed instead life to life, or the *Lebensart* of one people with the way of life of another. For Schmitt the 'life of a people' as a 'nation' emerges when the people 'experience the state as *their* state', and this is only possible in the 'exceptional' 'state of war' with 'the enemy'. The sovereign, also as the exceptional, for his part is 'he who is able to decide on and deal with this state of emergency'. Arnold Gehlen, in his perhaps belated critique of the Third Reich, unlike Schmitt, identified with Canguilhem's and Foucault's pessimism. For Gehlen we are doomed to a 'set of specialized practices and technical languages . . . of the scientific "culture encadre" of the "supermachine"', while the classical and the exceptional can only survive as 'empty models'. Thus for Gehlen, Schmitt's attempt to impose the exceptional in modernity could only lead to conflagration and death. The characteristic systemness of modernity (see Bauman in Chapter 8) would not allow for it.

Ann Game in Chapter 11 points to a 'non-exceptional' mode of counter-knowledge for the human sciences with sources in Gaston Bachelard and the poetics of the imagination. Drawing on Bachelard's poetics of space, she argues for a sort of knowledge that passes through, not the mediation and publicity of the Kantian categories, but instead through the immediacy and privacy of memory traces. This idea of knowledge through memory traces involves temporalizing knowledge-creation, instead of understanding it through the static categories. In this Game counterposes to Durkheim's scientific and abstract notions of time and space, Henri Bergson's *lebensphilosophisch* critique of abstract and dead time. For Bergson time (and memory) is instead a qualitative experience, which dissolves the subject–object assumptions of abstract time into *durée*. Durée means not living in time, but lived time, which is experienced intimately (as in Freud) through 'body images'.

Game then turns to draw on the work of Bachelard in the *Poetics of Space* (1969), in which the problem of knowledge is reconceived through a phenomenology of the imagination. In this the imagination is understood as a *spatially* constituted complex of memory traces. Bachelard's imagination is spatial, in the first place because the spatial complex of memory traces constitutes a sort of architectonic. Second, it is spatial in its assumptions of privacy, of intimate space. Most important it is spatial in that memory is like a 'dwelling place'; it is a 'house of memory', in which lived time is lived space. Memory for Bachelard is constituted through childhood experiences. These experiences in the first instance are not of 'abstract' childhood sexual relations but of the lived space of childhood. We often metaphorically conceive of memory, Game notes, as a 'dwelling place', through a house image of the material spaces of our most intimate being. This Proustian spatiality of memory is often derived through the traces of the first house we dwelt in as children. Memory, as the private (housed) space of childhood daydreams, as the intimate space of memory is (as in Proust) experienced as a shelter and as a place for the well-being of the self. It provides a 'spatio-temporal continuity' as against the 'tendencies to dispersion of the subject'. We should note the similarities with object-relations psychoanalytic theory in which the unconscious is constituted as a sort of 'system' through memory traces structured by object relations, which on the one hand staves off the 'ontological insecurity' of total dispersion, and on the other (in, for example, Deleuze and Guattari) preserves the principle of creativity against the abstract positivism of the ego.

Bachelard, Game observes, is indeed critical of classical psychoanalysis for its assumptions that bodily traces are constitutive of the unconscious only when mediated through the abstraction of symbols. He opposes this 'overinterpretation' in favour of a far more immediate and intimate unconscious. The refusal of abstraction also informs how the poetic imagination operates. The poetic imagination is a 'fibred space traversed by the simple impetus of words that have been experienced. . .'. These words are experienced not as representations but as 'reverberations'. That is, what passes through the imagination, through this resonating fibred space, is neither 'discursive' nor 'figural' but it is *signal*, the most motivated and last mediated type of semiotic transformation. Of Peirce's triumvirate of semiotic, mimetic (or iconic) and signal, surely Bachelard's reverberations, experienced as 'sound' refers to the last of these. Poetry for him is thus conceived on models, neither of literature (discourse), nor of the visual arts (figure), but on the lines of music as signal or sound. This holds for both the 'reception side' and the 'production side' of the poetic imagination. Let us recall the description of the displacement of technology in postmodern, global culture in the chapters by Luke and Dillon. Here 'sociocultural control' is displaced and becomes a process, no longer of representation, but of generation (of the flows). And as the process of cultural control changes so does its semiotic means. That is, for Luke (and Baudrillard) the *parole* of the hyperspace flows is indeed neither discourse, nor figure but (like in television and in the increasingly digitized means of information and communication) signal. But Luke and Baudrillard have offered us no way out from this new, far more insidious mode of normalizing security of the technology of signals and flows. Friedman (in Chapter 4) pointed us perhaps in the direction of one, looking at how the signalled flows could be transformed into other constellations of Third and Fourth World identities. Ann Game gives us an idea of how this might work in her invocation of an imagination transforming the 'reverberations' of the coded flows through the 'fibred space of memory' into an intimate and poetic form of knowledge and experience.

IV

Game's treatment of intimacy and the private leads to considerations of the nature of individualization and subjectivity in today's globalized regimes of power. The book's final chapters by Kharkhordin, Bell, Zaretsky and Halton address these issues. Oleg Kharkhordin shows in Chapter 12 how the characteristically Russian route 'to and through modernity' (see Therborn in Chapter 7) produced not the Western sort of 'confessing subject', but instead a '*dissimulating*' form of individualism. Mainstream political science had often documented behaviour in the Eastern bloc countries, in which formal politics is ignored and a belief in communism 'dissimulated', while everyday practice involves instead a covert political participation narrowly benefiting the self in a system of personal networks, bribes and the like.

This, and a more general sort of dissimulating individualism, can be understood, Kharkhordin demonstrates, first in the Russian route to, and then its route through, modernity. The Russian gate *to* modernity is closest to Therborn's ideal-type of response to external threat, instantiated in the eighteenth- and nineteenth-century modernization from above by enlightened despotic czars in response to the threat of democratic modernization from the West. The result was that 'the below' did not really modernize and a 'dual Russia' developed in which the way of life of the still fully traditional peasantry was quite opaque to both modernized elites and the state. This opacity of peasant life betrayed not a dissimulating individualism but no individualism at all. In the traditional Russian village *skhod* decisions were taken collectively by the village gathering in a democratic centralism *avant la lettre*. In the Russian language there is indeed no indigenous word for privacy, as families lived in one room, and little could be concealed from family or other villagers. Religion itself was a question of ritual. Modern individualism, including Protestantism and Catholicism, is grounded in a notion of belief. Yet Russian orthodoxy did not presume the modern differentiation between action and belief, and there was in fact little interest in what people 'believed'. In sexuality, again, individualism presupposes a private sphere and modernist differentiation of thoughts, feelings, intentions and actions. In the Russian village, in the absence of a private, there was instead communal control of sexual actions and little interest in thoughts, feelings and intentions.

Kharkhordin's arguments point to a *civilizational* explanation of the various routes to modernity, and to the importance Talcott Parsons underlined of the difference between Western and Eastern Christendom as civilizations. In a Cold War setting this was often a basis for arguments over why Poles and, say, Croatians 'naturally' belonged on the Western side of the NATO/Comecon divide while Greeks, Russians, Ukrainians, Romanians, Serbs, Bulgarians and Albanians were more 'naturally' Communists. The point at issue here though is that the twin triumphs of modernity and capitalism were also the triumphs of Western Civilization (and Western Christendom). It is that Western Civilization has been based on a confessional sort of individualism in the 'self-identical' subject. Eastern individualism was delayed, and instead the route to modernity in the East, and particularly in Russia, was grounded in a dualism, a modernizing state and a 'dissimulating collectivism' of the traditional peasantry.

The Russian route *through* modernity did bring the individualization of the masses, but only in the form, as Kharkhordin notes, not of self-identity, but self-difference. The Communist drive to industrialization of the 1930s brought first an effective ruralization of the cities. Now the small pockets of Western-individualized elites were marginalized as families of workers moved into barracks. With one family per bed and dozens of families to a single large dormitory room, there was again little space for private sexuality or any sort of a private life. As mass migration to the cities slowed and families moved into their own small apartments, some measure of privacy became increasingly possible. Now an intimate sphere, with the separation of beliefs and intentions from actions could, Kharkhordin observes, begin to emerge. This was encouraged for its part by the Communist state, in which surveillance now moved into a far more totalitarian register. If the Church and the *ancien régime* wanted only to control actions the modernist Communist state wanted also to control beliefs and intentions. This attempt to control the intimate was exemplified in the public obloquy associated with sexual misdemeanours, in which offenders were shamed in the public press.

Thus the new Communist power attempted to overcome the old dual Russia through its own construction and attempted control of private space. The result, however, was to constitute a new dualism, now of state and dissimulating individual. But even in post-Communist Russia of the mid-1990s there is a paucity of even this dissimulating individualism. That is, the state as present in the mentalities of the masses has been far more successful than the political scientists of the 1970s and 1980s had realized. Even now the masses continue in ritual support of a no longer existent system, in search of the old 'centre that held', and the dissimulating individualism of the various marginal and creative individuals is still very much persecuted.

Vikki Bell in Chapter 13 also considers the sexual construction of the subject in the route to modernity. Bell like Kharkhordin wants to contest *idées reçues* on the temporality of subject constitution. She does this through consideration of Foucault on sexuality, for whom power, which in the pre-modern, as 'Classical' power, operated through the 'deployment of alliances', now in modernity operates via the 'deployment of sexuality'. The pre-modern 'system of alliances' is part of the 'great chain of being' of traditional concrete and immediate forms of sociation, intended to repro-duce the 'body of the king' at the top of the hierarchy of the chain as well as the hierarchical chain itself. In modernity the abstract social is reproduced through the deployment of sexuality and the obsession that Foucault notes with population and demographics in order that a labour force and army can be provided.

Bell, however, focusing specifically on the incest taboo, finds this now widely accepted periodization to be wanting. She argues instead that the case of incest shows the concurrent deployment today of strategies of both alliances and sexuality, and further that we should see the contemporary family in terms of such concurrent deployment. On the accepted argument, the incest taboo is the principle of the pre-modern system of alliances, while the modern deployment of sexuality threatens this same system of alliances through the colonization of the family by sexual discourse. This is above all exemplified in Freudian sexual discourse, in which the family is threatened by child sexuality, the Oedipus complex and the like. There is an important grain of truth in this in the sense that the 'continual extension of the area of control under the deployment of sexuality' has led to the very recent entry into (public) discourse of child sexual abuse.

Yet, Bell notes, even the Freudian discourse of sexuality is double-edged.

On the one hand it constructs the incest taboo as universal, conveniently ignoring the fact that incest was probably more widespread in pre-modern and even modern peasant and working-class families who were least affected by the discourse of sexuality. So the construction of the incest taboo in modernity does tend to make safe the continued deployment of alliances. Yet at the same time the continued colonization by sex discourse tends to 'saturate' these same alliances with 'desire'.

Like Bell and Kharkhordin, Zaretsky in Chapter 14 deals with subject constitution, in this case with the emergence of 'identity politics' since the late 1960s. Zaretsky is concerned with charting the shift away from the endorsement of the production of a coherent and consistent identity, to an emphasis upon non-identity in which a positive valuation is placed on fragmentation and difference. The emphasis upon the politics of identity, he argues, has been long dominant in the psychoanalytical tradition. Although psychoanalysis acknowledged that we may well be different in different contexts, it maintained the key assumption that there is an underlying personal identity which persists throughout. Psychoanalysis thus regarded the individual as abstracted from social relations, a perspective which attained a dominant cultural position because it reflected the illusory, or imaginary way in which people lived their personal lives as separate disconnected individuals in modern society.

For theorists such as Erik Erikson, who was writing about identity in the 1940s and 1950s, the main problem was conceived as preserving ego ideals and a strong identity in the wake of weakening social institutions and the massification of culture. This was similar to one strand of Frankfurt School thought, with its lament for 'the end of the individual' and the dominance of 'pseudo-individuality' through the extension of instrumental rationality to produce a 'totally administrated world'. A second strand is found most clearly in the writings of Adorno with his emphasis upon 'non-identity thinking', and also in those of Marcuse. The latter provided a blend of Freudo-Marxism which sought to go beyond genital sexuality as well as exploring the potential for new agents of critique and praxis. Marcuse's conception of human nature is close to many of the ideas which were influential in the subsequent feminist, gay liberation and ecology movements which were to emerge in the late 1960s. *Eros and Civilization*, for example, was crucial to Denis Altman's early writings on gay identity. Altman argued that 'procreative sexuality' was linked to what Marcuse referred to as 'the performance principle', and that 'perversions' were really incipient rebellions. In both the emergent gay and lesbian identity politics there was, therefore, a move beyond demands for the tolerance of private sexual preferences to the thematization of public group identities and the construction of alternative lifestyles.

Likewise in the women's movement in the 1970s there was a movement away from concerns with equality and rights towards an 'anti-essentialist' position which argued against simpler identity notions that a person could, or should, exclusively be a woman, lesbian or black person. Influenced by post-structualist theories the emphasis shifted away from identity to the various cultural 'codes', which were continually remade into different discourses which interpellated different subjectivities. The writings of Lacan, Derrida, Deleuze, Irigaray and Foucault were used to shift the emphasis away from bounded identity towards ambiguity and difference. Hence what some members of the Frankfurt School had taken to be signs of decay (the loss of fixed identities), was now taken by others to be the harbinger of a new form of society.

Zaretsky is careful to separate the identity politics of gays, lesbians and women from those of racial and ethnic groups such as African-Americans, Hispanics and Native Americans which have promoted a politics of racial and ethnic exclusion. It is only the former group which has sought to change the structure of the family and personal life that has developed the 'politics of difference' influenced by post-structuralist theories. In reconstructing the genealogy of identity politics, Zaretsky's chapter is a timely reminder of one of the major challenges facing contemporary critical theory. This is how to combine a multiculturalist 'politics of recognition', based upon the respect of differences, with a capacity to judge between culture and barbarism, where culture is more than some arbitrary imposition of particularity and can be made compatible with a form of universalism (see Taylor, 1992).

If Kharkhordin, Bell and Zaretsky speak of an individualized and de-situated subject in modernity, Eugene Halton in Chapter 15 points tendentially to a possible re-situation. Halton's starting point is effectively Gehlen's unhappy paradox of modernity (see Bauman, Chapter 8 and Wagner, Chapter 10). In this there are two sides to (post)modernity: on the one hand there is 'technology', now extending control through the global information and communications networks, and on the other hand is 'man's' characteristic *Instinktarmut*, whose upshot is the hubristic and aggressive ego of the Faustian individual. Halton has some scores to settle with the many varieties of modernist and postmodernist theories which celebrate the hubris of this 'modernist and postmodernist rationalization', whether as 'objective' in the neo-worlds of generative information technology, or as 'subjective' in the unbounded desire of a Raskolnikov or Ahab. Halton agrees with Wagner's and Gehlen's view that the exceptional is now impossible except as this unconstrained Faustian ego, consecrated in the popular mind by works from Frankenstein to *Jurassic Park*.

Note that Halton's (and Gehlen's) explanation of the Holocaust and modernity would run counter to the views of Horkheimer and Adorno, or of Bauman. For Gehlen it is not so much the iron cage of bureaucratic rationalization that made the Holocaust possible. It is instead the disappearance of constraining myths that allowed the unconstrained hubristic individualism of Hitler to come to power at all. That is, Gehlen also sees the Holocaust not in terms of the primitive but instead in terms of modernity. And it is the individualistic, not the bureaucratic, side of modernity which for him is at its root. In this vein Halton can argue that Berman's (1982) *All That is Solid Melts Into Air* presents, not the solution but the root of the problem of this Faustian individualism. And this problem for Halton has its roots in the Enlightenment's assumptions of 'philosophical nominalism', in which the 'monism of a generating, incarnate mind' is disregarded in favour 'of the dualism of objective mechanism and subjective incorporeal spirit'.

Halton (like Alasdair MacIntyre) makes it clear that these abstract and dualist assumptions are not only true of the mirror-of-nature, subject–object epistemologies of Descartes, Locke and Kant, but also of fashionable aesthetic modernists and aesthetically informed sociologists like Simmel. The only difference is that for Simmel and aesthetic modernism the subject has freed itself from the object, resulting in an even less foundational and more hubristic individualism. Thus should be understood Simmel's counter-position of 'life' to 'form' and the abstract social; his counterposition of the realm of (subjective) value to that of (objective) fact. This Simmelian and modernist irresponsible and hubristic freeing of the subject is only exacerbated, observes Halton, in postmodernist celebrations of contingency and desire in Rorty, Derrida and Deleuze.

Halton then asks, given all this, where are we to look for some direction in how to lead our lives in such a globalized informational order? His answer is in the philosophy of pragmatism of James, Peirce and Dewey. Halton's pragmatism is vastly different from that of Rorty through his focus on the character of meaning in modernity. Halton opposes social constructionism, especially prevalent in the sociology of science, in which social reality is constructed via a sort of Husserlian intentionality beginning from assumptions of some sort of *tabula rasa*. Such constructionism is also present, he notes, in the grounding of meaning in intentionality in the classical sociology of Weber and Simmel. In his neo-Kantian theory of social action, Weber begins from an atomized and abstracted subject who '*bestows* meaning' in social action. In this view 'meaning comes from subjective intention' or 'intentionality creates meaning'. Similarly in Simmel's sociological expressionism, 'beauty is *bestowed* by subjective human perception'. Here Halton notes that the classical sociologists only reiterate the old dualism of the bestowal of meaning by spirit, except that for the neo-Kantian Weber and Simmel subjective 'value' imparts meaning to 'objective fact'.

For Halton meaning does not come from such an intentionality of the abstract social actor. For him, as in philosophical pragmatism and hermeneutics, such meaning is *always already there*. For Halton, 'the passionate and "intending" self is continuous with the communicative signs of the social medium'. Similarly aesthetic beauty is not bestowed by a subject on nature, but stems from 'a transaction between . . . nature and a human perceiver'. And knowledge is neither a priori nor socially constituted but as 'tempered achievements of creatures who evolved in transaction with the inherent forms of nature'. For Halton, meaning and reason are to be grounded above all in the *emotions*. In this claim he understands the emotions as not counterposed to but foundational of reason. He does not want to reify the passions but to consider them as 'inherently social modalities of signification embedded in, but not reducible to, conventionalized signification'. Halton follows Peirce in his understanding of the emotions as '*biosemiotic* capacities' and argues for a recasting of modern rationality as grounded in the 'extra-rational biosemiotic sources of concrete reasonableness'. These sources of the human emotions are biological in that they are rooted in the 'mammalian characteristics of mother–infant nurturance, in play and in dreaming'; they are grounded in mammalian feelings of 'the joys and sufferings of life'. Unlike Gehlen, Halton does not consider the human *Instinktarmut* to be immutable. He believes that these passions and emotions can atrophy, both 'individually and institutionally', and can 'range from fleeting sensations to instinctive proclivities'.

But human emotions for Halton are also semiotic. The human *differentia specifica* is our 'bio*semiotic* capacities' which 'transmute feeling into communicable form'. 'Through these biosemiotic capacities passions are ritually codified', especially in the form of *myths*. And it is such communal myths that are the answer to the problem of modernist hubris because they 'become limitations on human conduct'. Myth not only provides a foundation to reason, but can ground the subject also in community and nature. Myth, says Halton, is the basis of the 'inner community of passions', necessary for the 'passional relationship' to the 'outer world of nature and experience'. Myth is the basis of our 'non-rational reasonableness', which is a 'hybrid compost of organic intelligence' from 'pre-Western, non-Western and pre-historical sources'. Halton quotes Vaclav Havel, like Gehlen fundamentally influenced by Heidegger. Havel noted that myth lent a 'kind of order to the dark regions of our mind'. 'With the burial of myth', he observed, 'the barn in which the mysterious animals of the human unconscious had been housed in has been abandoned and the animals turned loose on the tragically mistaken assumption that they were phantoms – and now they are devastating the countryside'.

V

Is it, then, the retrieval and reconstitution of myth which will inform the poetic imagination of everyday life in the face of the new normalizing technologies of the 'neo-worlds', of the global flows of information and communication? Is it myth that will help constitute new, local spatialized forms of more immediate sociation in which collective identities can be fashioned via the transformation of the raw materials of these same circulating economies of signs and space? Can such collective identity formation be a basis for social movements poised to challenge the domination of the now global 'system' in the furthering of the boundaries of the (now also global) 'life-world?' In the context of globalization the notion of 'world' takes on a new significance. Now the global 'neo-worlds' technologically generating the normalizing flows are counterposed to the possibility of constitution of situated 'worlds' in Heidegger's sense of mythically constructed collective memory. These situated worlds are not necessarily neo-tribes, but themselves can be international or inter-cultural.

This book and the paradigm of globalization, as Robertson notes in Chapter 2, involve a spatializing of the previously dominant temporality in Western social theory. This sort of spatial understanding imparts a different sense to the arguable 'disorganization' of contemporary capitalism. On this view 'disorganized capitalism' should not be understood primarily as temporally succeeding organized capitalism. It ought instead to be understood as a *global system*, which is systemically disorganized, that is, based in a global structuration of disorganization. This is disorganization in the sense that a logic of organizations, and especially the nation-state, is replaced by a logic of flows, in which sociation through networks of semantic exchange are increasingly extra-institutional and decreasingly based on organizational rules of strongly normativized mutual expectations. But it may also be disorganized in the sense of a crisis of the world system. This is perhaps less an economic crisis of capitalism, which continues to accumulate approximately as sporadically as before, than a cultural crisis of modernity. Such a decentring of the world system involves a possible shattering of the cultural hegemony of the Western core. And in as much as the Western core has been rooted in the age-old victory of Western Civilization, the crisis of the core – the disorganization of capitalism on a world scale – might at the same time be the crisis of Western Civilization.

Western Civilization, Daniel Bell (1976) argued some two decades ago, is under challenge both from the outside and the inside. From the outside there is the challenge of 'the rest' to the West in the hybridization of Western culture through the movement of people and symbols from African, Asian and other 'Oriental' sources. From the inside there is the crisis of modernity in Western thought and also the challenge to Western reason of the globally flowing signs of consumer culture. Perhaps this challenge to Western Civilization is no bad thing. Perhaps, as Halton instructs us, Western reason needs to be (re)grounded in 'non-Western', 'pre-Western' and 'prehistoric sources'. Perhaps only this will save the West from its (hubristic) excesses and (normalizing) deficits. In another context we have discussed the 'aestheticization of everyday life' (Featherstone, 1991). The significance of such aestheticization has never been more significant than in today's globalized informational order of flows. But aestheticization can cut two ways. On the one hand it is a matter of the flows of signs, symbols, images and signals of today's electronic consumer society. On the other, it is the recombination of these images in the form of myth, as a sort of 'poetic unconscious', and the aesthetic refraction of these sounds and images in the identity-practices of conduct in the life-world.

We have now come full circle in our considerations of Robertson's thesis concerning the various spatializations of the temporal. It is to his more detailed arguments in Chapter 2 that we must now turn.

References

Anderson, B. (1983) *Imagined Communities*. London: Verso.
Appadurai, A. (1990) 'Disjuncture and difference in the global cultural economy', in M. Featherstone (ed.), *Global Culture*. London: Sage.
Bachelard, G. (1969) *The Poetics of Space*, trans. M. Jolas. Boston: Beacon Press.
Bauman, Z. (1989) *Modernity and the Holocaust*. Oxford: Polity.
Bauman, Z. (1991) *Modernity and Ambivalence*. Oxford: Polity.
Bell, D. (1976) *The Cultural Contradictions of Capitalism*. London: Heinemann.
Berman, M. (1982) *All That is Solid Melts Into Air*. New York: Simon & Schuster.
Bhabha, H. (ed.) (1990) *Nation and Narration*. London: Routledge.
Castells, M. (1989) *The Informational City*. Oxford: Blackwell.
Clifford, J. (1988) *The Predicament of Culture*. Cambridge: Harvard University Press.
Clifford, J. and Marcus, G. (eds) (1986) *Writing Culture*. Berkeley: University of California Press.
Featherstone, M. (1991) 'The aestheticization of everyday life', in *Consumer Culture and Postmodernism*. London: Sage.
Featherstone, M. (1995) 'Localism, globalism and cultural identity', in W. Dissanayake and Rob Wilson (eds), *Global/Local: Cultural Production and the Transnational Imaginary*. Durham: Duke University Press. Reprinted in M. Featherstone (1995) *Undoing Culture*. London: Sage, forthcoming.
Giddens, A. (1990) *The Consequences of Modernity*. Oxford: Polity.
Giddens, A. (1991) *Modernity and Self-Identity*. Oxford: Polity.
Hall, S. (1992) 'The question of cultural identity', in S. Hall, D. Held and T. McGrew (eds), *Modernity and its Futures*. Oxford: Polity.
Harvey, D. (1989) *The Condition of Postmodernity*. Oxford: Blackwell.
Lash, S. (1990) *Sociology of Postmodernism*. London: Routledge.
Lash, S. and Urry, J. (1994) *Economies of Signs and Space*. London: Sage.
Myoshi, M. and Harootunian, H. (eds) (1989) *Postmodernism and Japan*. Durham: Duke University Press.
Ohmae, K. (1987) *Beyond National Borders: Reflections on Japan and the World*. Tokyo: Kodansha.
Robertson, R. (1992) *Globalization*. London: Sage.
Said, E. (1978) *Orientalism*. Harmondsworth: Penguin.
Taylor, C. (1992) *Multiculturalism and 'the Politics of Recognition'*. Princeton: Princeton University Press.
Tenbruck, F. (1994) 'Internal history of society or universal history', *Theory, Culture & Society* 11(1).
Vattimo, G. (1988) *The End of History*. Oxford: Polity.
Wolf, E.R. (1982) *Europe and the People without History*. Berkeley: California University Press.

2

GLOCALIZATION: TIME–SPACE AND HOMOGENEITY–HETEROGENEITY

Roland Robertson

The problem

As the general topic of globalization grows in importance in sociology and in social and cultural theory generally, and as the perspectives generated in the debates about globalization impact upon various intellectual fields, it becomes increasingly necessary to attend to some very basic issues. One such issue, probably the most central one, is discussed here. This is the meaning to be attributed to the very idea of globalization.

There is an evident tendency to think of globalization in a rather casual way as referring to very large-scale phenomena – as being, for example, the preoccupation of sociologists who are interested in big macrosociological problems, in contrast to those who have microsociological or, perhaps, local perspectives. I consider this to be very misleading. It is part of the 'mythology about globalization' (Ferguson, 1992) which sees this concept as referring to developments that involve the triumph of culturally homogenizing forces over all others. This view of globalization often involves other equally doubtful attributions, such as the view that 'bigger is better', that locality – even history – is being obliterated and so on. There are numerous dangers that such conceptions of globalization will in fact become part of 'disciplinary wisdom' – that, for example, when sociology textbooks generally come to reflect the current interest in globalization they will give the impression that globalization designates a special field of sociological interest – that it is but one sort of interest that sociologists may have, and that that interest involves lack of concern with microsociological or local issues.

In all of this there is already an issue of considerable confusion, which arises in part from the quite numerous attempts to 'internationalize' – to extend culturally and anti-ethnocentrically – the curriculum of sociology. Some such attempts go further and propose a global sociology, conceived of as a universal sociology which makes the practice of the discipline increasingly viable on a global scale. Actually some of these ventures in the direction of global sociology make the theme of incorporating indigenous sociologies into a global sociology an imperative. Indeed, the problem of global sociology as a sociology which confirms and includes 'native' sociologies parallels the more directly analytical issue to which I have already referred. This is the problem of the relationship between homogenizing and heterogenizing thrusts in globalization theory. Many sociologists are happy – or at least not unwilling – to agree that sociology ought to be 'internationalized' and 'de-ethnocentrized', but they are apparently much less inclined to engage in direct and serious study of the empirical, historically formed, global field *per se* (Robertson, 1992b, 1993).

The need to introduce the concept of glocalization firmly into social theory arises from the following considerations. Much of the talk about globalization has tended to assume that it is a process which overrides locality, including large-scale locality such as is exhibited in the various ethnic nationalisms which have seemingly arisen in various parts of the world in recent years. This interpretation neglects two things. First, it neglects the extent to which what is called local is in large degree constructed on a trans- or super-local basis. In other words, much of the promotion of locality is in fact done from above or outside. Much of what is often declared to be local is in fact the local expressed in terms of generalized recipes of locality. Even in cases where there is apparently no concrete recipe at work – as in the case of some of the more aggressive forms of contemporary nationalism – there is still, or so I would claim, a translocal factor at work. Here I am simply maintaining that the contemporary assertion of ethnicity and/or nationality is made within the global terms of identity and particularity (Handler, 1994).

Second, while there has been increasing interest in spatial considerations and expanding attention to the intimate links between temporal and spatial dimensions of human life, these considerations have made relatively little impact as yet on the discussion of globalization and related matters. In particular there has been little attempt to connect the discussion of time-and-space to the thorny issue of universalism-and-particularism. Interest in the theme of postmodernity has involved much attention to the supposed weaknesses of mainstream concern with 'universal time' and advancement of the claim that 'particularistic space' be given much greater attention; but in spite of a few serious efforts to resist the tendency, universalism has been persistently counterposed to particularism (in line with characterizations in the old debate about societal modernization in the 1950s and 1960s). At this time the emphasis on space is frequently expressed as a diminution of temporal considerations.

To be sure, 'time–space' has been given much attention by Giddens and in debates about his structuration theory, but for the most part this discussion has been conducted in abstract terms, with relatively little attention to concrete issues. Nonetheless, an important aspect of the problematic which is under consideration here has been delineated by Giddens. Giddens (1991: 21) argues that 'in a general way, the concept of globalisation is best understood as expressing fundamental aspects of time–space distanciation. Globalisation concerns the intersection of presence and absence, the interlacing of social events and social relations "at distance" with local contextualities'. Giddens (1991: 22) goes on to say that 'globalisation has to be understood as a dialectical phenomenon, in which events at one pole of a distanciated relation often produce divergent or even contrary occurrences at another'. While the idea that globalization involves the 'intersection of presence and absence' is insightful and helpful, my view is that Giddens to some extent remains captive of old ways of thinking when he speaks of the production of 'divergent or even contrary occurrences'. This seems to imply an 'action–reaction' relationship which does not fully capture the complexities of the 'global–local' theme.

Some of the ambiguity here may arise from the tendency to use the term 'globalization' instead of the term '*globality*' – as in the idea of globalization as a consequence of modernity (Giddens, 1990). In fact the conjunction modernity–globalization in itself suggests a processual and temporal outcome of a social and psychological circumstance, whereas the juxtaposition of the notion of globality with that of modernity raises directly the problem of the relationship between two sets of conditions which are apparently different. In this perspective the issue of space is more specifically and independently raised via the concept of globality. The idea of modernity usually suggests a general homogenization of institutions and basic experiences in a temporal, historical mode. But there is increasing recognition that there have been a number of specific areas where modernity has developed.

Elsewhere in this volume Therborn identifies three major sites other than Europe where modernity developed relatively autonomously: the New World, where modernity developed as the result of the decimation of existing peoples; East Asia, where modernity arose as a response to a threatening external challenge; and much of Africa, where modernity was largely imposed by colonization or imperialism. The perspective involved in such a 'deconstruction' of modernity – or at least its conceptual and empirical differentiation – leads to definite recognition of the relatively independent significance of space and geography under the rubric of globality. Emphasis on globality enables us to avoid the weaknesses of the proposition that globalization is simply a consequence of modernity. Specifically, globality is the general condition which has *facilitated* the diffusion of 'general modernity', globality at this point being viewed in terms of the interpenetration of geographically distinct 'civilizations'.

The leading argument in this discussion is thus centred on the claim that the debate about global homogenization versus heterogenization should be transcended. It is not a question of *either* homogenization or heterogenization, but rather of the ways in which both of these two tendencies have become features of life across much of the late-twentieth-century world. In this perspective the problem becomes that of spelling out the ways in which homogenizing and heterogenizing tendencies are mutually implicative. This is in fact much more of an empirical problem than might at first be thought. In various areas of contemporary life – some of which are discussed in the following pages – there are ongoing, calculated attempts to combine homogeneity with heterogeneity and universalism with particularism.

In this respect we may well speak of the way in which academic disciplines have lagged behind 'real life'. At the same time, we need, of course, to provide analyses and interpretations of these features of 'reality' (recognizing that the distinction between theory and reality is extremely problematic and, I believe, ultimately untenable). I hope to show that outside academic/intellectual discourse there are many who take it for granted that the universal and particular can and *should* be combined. The question for them is: how and in what form should these be synthesized? It is not whether they *can* be interrelated. In order to comprehend the 'how' rather than the 'whether' we need to attend more directly to the question as to what is actually 'going on'. Asking that question does not, as some might well think, involve a disinterest in issues of a 'critical' nature concerning, for example, the interests served by strategies of what I here call glocalization; not least because, as I will intermittently emphasize, strategies of glocalization are – at least at this historical moment and for the foreseeable future – themselves grounded in particularistic frames of reference. There is no viable and practical Archimedean point from which strategies of glocalization can be fully maintained. Nevertheless, we appear to live in a world in which the expectation of uniqueness has become increasingly institutionalized and globally widespread.

Glocalization

According to *The Oxford Dictionary of New Words* (1991: 134) the term 'glocal' and the process noun 'glocalization' are 'formed by telescoping *global* and *local* to make a blend'. Also according to the *Dictionary* that idea has been 'modelled on Japanese *dochakuka* (deriving from *dochaku* "living on one's own land"), originally the agricultural principle of adapting one's farming techniques to local conditions, but also adopted in Japanese business for *global localization*, a global outlook adapted to local conditions' (emphasis in original). More specifically, the terms 'glocal' and 'glocalization' became aspects of business jargon during the 1980s, but their major locus of origin was in fact Japan, a country which has for a very long time strongly cultivated the spatio-cultural significance of Japan itself and where the general issue of the relationship between the particular and the universal has historically received almost obsessive attention (Miyoshi and Harootunian, 1989). By now it has become, again in the words of *The Oxford Dictionary of New Words* (1991: 134), 'one of the main marketing buzzwords of the beginning of the nineties'.

The idea of glocalization in its business sense is closely related to what in some contexts is called, in more straightforwardly economic terms, micro-marketing: the tailoring and advertising of goods and services on a global or near-global basis to increasingly differentiated local and particular markets. Almost needless to say, in the world of capitalistic production for increasingly global markets the adaptation to local and other particular conditions is not simply a case of business responses to existing global variety – to civilizational, regional, societal, ethnic, gender and still other types of differentiated consumers – as if such variety or heterogeneity existed simply 'in itself'. To a considerable extent micromarketing – or, in the more comprehensive phrase, glocalization – involves *the construction* of increasingly differentiated consumers, the 'invention' of 'consumer traditions' (of which tourism, arguably the biggest 'industry' of the contemporary world, is undoubtedly the most clear-cut example). To put it very simply, diversity sells. From the consumer's point of view it can be a significant basis of cultural capital formation (Bourdieu, 1984). This, it should be emphasized, is not its only function. The proliferation of, for example, 'ethnic' supermarkets in California and elsewhere does to a large extent cater not so much to difference for the sake of difference, but to the desire for the familiar and/or to nostalgic wishes. On the other hand, these too can also be bases of cultural capital formation.

It is not my purpose here to delve into the comparative history of capitalistic business practices. Thus the accuracy of the etymology concerning 'glocalization' provided by *The Oxford Dictionary of New Words* is not a crucial issue.[1] Rather I want to use the general idea of glocalization to make a number of points about the global–local problematic. There is a widespread tendency to regard this problematic as straightforwardly involving a polarity, which assumes its most acute form in the claim that we live in a world of local assertions *against* globalizing trends, a world in which the very idea of locality is sometimes cast as a form of opposition or resistance to the hegemonically global (or one in which the assertion of 'locality' or *Gemeinschaft* is seen as the pitting of subaltern 'universals' against the 'hegemonic universal' of dominant cultures and/or classes). An interesting variant of this general view is to be found in the replication of the German culture–civilization distinction at the global level: the old notion of ('good') culture is pitted against the ('bad') notion of civilization. In this traditional German perspective local culture becomes, in effect, national culture, while civilization is given a distinctively global, world-wide colouring.

We have, in my judgement, to be much more subtle about the dynamics of the production and reproduction of difference and, in the broadest sense, locality. Speaking in reference to the local–cosmopolitan distinction, Hannerz (1990: 250) has remarked that for locals diversity 'happens to be the principle which allows all locals to stick to their respective cultures'. At the same time, cosmopolitans largely depend on 'other people' carving out 'special niches' for their cultures. Thus 'there can be no cosmopolitans without locals'. This point has some bearing on the particular nature of the intellectual interest in and the approach to the local–global issue. In relation to Hannerz's general argument, however, we should note that in the contemporary world, or at least in the West, the current counter-urbanization trend (Champion, 1989), much of which in the USA is producing 'fortress communities', proceeds in terms of the standardization of locality, rather than straightforwardly in terms of 'the principle of difference'.[2]

In any case, we should become much more historically conscious of the various ways in which the deceptively modern, or postmodern, problem of the relationship between the global and the local, the universal and the particular, and so on, is not by any means as unique to the second half of the twentieth century as many would have us believe. This is clearly shown in Greenfeld's (1992) recent study of the origins of nationalism in England, France, Germany, Russia and America. With the notable exception of English nationalism, she shows that the emergence of all national identities – such constituting 'the most common and salient form of particularism in the modern world' (Greenfeld, 1992: 8) – developed as a part of an 'essentially international process' (Greenfeld, 1992: 14).

The more extreme or adamant claims concerning the contemporary uniqueness of these alleged opposites is a refraction of what some have called the nostalgic paradigm in Western social science (Phillips, 1993; Robertson, 1990; Turner, 1987). It is a manifestation of the not always implicit world view that suggests that we – the global we – once lived in and were distributed not so long ago across a multitude of ontologically secure, collective 'homes'. Now, according to this narrative – or, perhaps, a metanarrative – our sense of home is rapidly being destroyed by waves of (Western?) 'globalization'. In contrast I maintain – although I can present here only part of my overall argument – that globalization has involved the reconstruction, in a sense the production, of 'home', 'community' and 'locality' (cf. J. Abu-Lughod, 1994). To that extent the local is not best seen, at least as an analytic or interpretative departure point, as a counterpoint to the global. Indeed it can be regarded, subject to some qualifications, as *an aspect* of globalization. One part of my argument which must remain underdeveloped in the immediate context is that we are being led into the polar-opposite way of thinking by the thesis that globalization is a direct 'consequence of modernity' (Giddens, 1990; cf. Robertson, 1992a). In this perspective Weber's 'iron cage' is globalized. Moreover, in this view there could never have been any kind of globalization without the instrumental rationality often taken to be the hallmark of modernity (a rationality which, it is readily conceded, Giddens sees as carrying both disabling *and* reflexive enabling possibilities).

Thus the notion of glocalization actually conveys much of what I myself have previously written about globalization. From my own analytic and interpretative standpoint the concept of globalization has involved the simultaneity and the interpenetration of what are conventionally called the global and the local, or – in more abstract vein – the universal and the particular. (Talking strictly of my own position in the current debate about and the discourse of globalization, it may even become necessary to substitute the term 'glocalization' for the contested term 'globalization' in order to make my argument more precise.) I certainly do not wish to fall victim, cognitive or otherwise, to a particular brand of current marketing terminology. Insofar as we regard the idea of glocalization as simply a capitalistic business term (of apparent Japanese origin) then I would of course reject it as, *inter alia*, not having sufficient analytic-interpretative leverage. On the other hand, we are surely coming to recognize that seemingly autonomous economic terms frequently have deep cultural roots (for example, Sahlins, 1976). In the Japanese and other societal cases the cognitive and moral 'struggle' even to recognize the economic domain as relatively autonomous has never really been 'won'. In any case, we live in a world which increasingly acknowledges the quotidian conflation of the economic and the cultural. But we inherited from classical social theory, particularly in its German version in the decades from about 1880 to about 1920, a view that talk of 'culture' and 'cultivation' was distinctly at odds with 'materialism' and the rhetoric of economics and instrumental rationality.

My deliberations in this chapter on the local–global problematic hinge upon the view that contemporary conceptions of locality are largely produced in something like global terms, but this certainly does not mean that all forms of locality are thus substantively homogenized (notwithstanding the standardization, for example, of relatively new suburban, fortress communities). An important thing to recognize in this connection is that there is an increasingly globe-wide discourse of locality, community, home and the like. One of the ways of considering the idea of *global culture* is in terms of its being constituted by the increasing interconnectedness of many local cultures both large and small (Hannerz, 1990), although I certainly do not myself think that global culture is entirely constituted by such interconnectedness. In any case we should be careful *not to equate the communicative and interactional connecting of such cultures* – including very asymmetrical forms of such communication and interaction, as well as 'third cultures' of mediation – *with the notion of homogenization of all cultures*.

I have in mind the rapid, recent development of a relatively autonomous discourse of 'intercultural communication'. This discourse is being promoted by a growing number of professionals, along the lines of an older genre of 'how to' literature. So it is not simply a question of social and cultural theorists talking about cultural difference and countervailing forces of homogenization. One of the 'proper objects' of study here is the phenomenon of 'experts' who specialize in the 'instrumentally rational' promotion of intercultural communication. These 'experts' have in fact a vested interest in the promotion and protection of variety and diversity. Their jobs and their profession depend upon the expansion and reproduction of heterogeneity. The same seems to apply to strong themes in modern American business practice (Rhinesmith, 1993; Simons et al., 1993).

We should also be more interested in the conditions for the production of cultural pluralism (Moore, 1989) – as well as geographical pluralism. Let me also say that the idea of locality, indeed of globality, is very relative. In spatial terms a village community is of course local relative to a region of a society, while a society is local relative to a civilizational area, and so on.

Relativity also arises in temporal terms. Contrasting the well-known pair consisting of locals and cosmopolitans, Hannerz (1990: 236) has written that 'what was cosmopolitan in the early 1940s may be counted as a moderate form of localism by now'. I do not in the present context get explicitly involved in the problem of relativity (or relativism). But sensitivity to the problem does inform much of what I say.

There are certain conditions that are currently promoting the production of concern with the local–global problematic within the academy. King (1991: 420) has addressed an important aspect of this. In talking specifically of the spatial compression dimension of globalization he remarks on the increasing numbers of 'protoprofessionals from so-called "Third World" societies' who are travelling to 'the core' for professional education. The educational sector of 'core' countries 'depends increasingly on this input of students from the global periphery'. It is the experience of 'flying round the world and needing schemata to make sense of what they see' on the one hand, and encountering students from all over the world in the classroom on the other, which forms an important experiential basis for academics of what King (1991: 401–2) calls totalizing and global theories. I would maintain, however, that it is interest in 'the local' as much as the 'totally global' which is promoted in this way.[3]

The local in the global? The global in the local?

In one way or another the issue of the relationship between the 'local' and the 'global' has become increasingly salient in a wide variety of intellectual and practical contexts. In some respects this development hinges upon the increasing recognition of the significance of space, as opposed to time, in a number of fields of academic and practical endeavour. The general interest in the idea of postmodernity, whatever its limitations, is probably the most intellectually tangible manifestation of this. The most well known maxim – virtually a cliché – proclaimed in the diagnosis of 'the postmodern condition' is of course that 'grand narratives' have come to an end, and that we are now in a circumstance of proliferating and often competing narratives. In this perspective there are no longer any stable accounts of dominant change in the world. This view itself has developed, on the other hand, at precisely the same time that there has crystallized an increasing interest in the world as a whole as a single place. (Robbins [1993: 187] also notes this, in specific reference to geographers.) As the sense of temporal unidirectionality has faded so, on the other hand, has the sense of 'representational' space within which all kinds of narratives may be inserted expanded. This of course has increasingly raised in recent years the vital question as to whether the apparent collapse – and the 'deconstruction' – of the heretofore dominant social-evolutionist accounts of implicit or explicit world history are leading rapidly to a situation of chaos or one in which, to quote Giddens (1990: 6), 'an infinite number of purely idiosyncratic "histories" can be written'.

Giddens claims in fact that we *can* make generalizations about 'definite
episodes of historical transition'. However, since he also maintains that
'modernity' on a global scale has amounted to a rupture with virtually all prior
forms of life he provides no guidance as to how history or histories might
actually be done.

In numerous contemporary accounts, then, globalizing trends are regarded
as in tension with 'local' assertions of identity and culture. Thus ideas such as
the global *versus* the local, the global *versus* the 'tribal', the international
versus the national, and the universal *versus* the particular are widely
promoted. For some, these alleged oppositions are simply puzzles, while for
others the second part of each opposition is seen as a reaction against the first.
For still others they are contradictions. In the perspective of contradiction the
tension between, for example, the universal and the particular may be seen
either in the dynamic sense of being a relatively progressive source of overall
change or as a modality which preserves an existing global system in its present
state. We find both views in Wallerstein's argument that the relation between
the universal and the particular is basically a product of expanding
world-systemic capitalism (Wallerstein, 1991b). Only what Wallerstein
(1991a) calls anti-systemic movements – and then only those which effectively
challenge its 'metaphysical presuppositions' – can move the world beyond the
presuppositions of its present (capitalist) condition. In that light we may
regard the contemporary proliferation of 'minority discourses' (Jan-
Mohamed and Lloyd, 1990) as being encouraged by the presentation of a
'world-system'. Indeed, there is much to suggest that adherents to minority
discourses have, somewhat paradoxically, a special liking for Wallersteinian
or other 'totalistic' forms of world-systems theory. But it must also be noted
that many of the enthusiastic participants in the discourse of 'minorities'
describe their intellectual practice in terms of the *singular*, minority discourse
(JanMohamed and Lloyd, 1990). This suggests that there is indeed a
potentially *global* mode of writing and talking on behalf of, or at least about,
minorities (cf. Handler, 1994; McGrane, 1989).

Barber (1992) argues that 'tribalism' and 'globalism' have become what he
describes as the two axial principles of our time. In this he echoes a very
widespread view of 'the new world (dis)order'. I chose to consider his position
because it is succinctly stated and has been quite widely disseminated. Barber
sees these two principles as inevitably in tension – a 'McWorld' of
homogenizing globalization *versus* a 'Jihad world' of particularizing
'lebanonization'. (He might well now say 'balkanization'.) Barber is
primarily interested in the bearing which each of these supposedly clashing
principles have on the prospects for democracy. That is certainly a very
important matter, but I am here only directly concerned with the global–local
debate.

Like many others, Barber defines globalization as the opposite of
localization. He argues that 'four imperatives make up the dynamic of
McWorld: a market imperative, a resource imperative, an information-
technology imperative, and an ecological imperative' (Barber, 1992: 54).

Each of these contributes to 'shrinking the world and diminishing the salience of national borders' and together they have 'achieved a considerable victory over factiousness and particularism, and not least over their most virulent traditional form – nationalism' (Barber, 1992: 54; cf. Miyoshi, 1993). Remarking that 'the Enlightenment dream of a universal rational society has to a remarkable degree been realized', Barber (1992: 59) emphasizes that that achievement has, however, been realized in commercialized, bureaucratized, homogenized and what he calls 'depoliticized' form. Moreover, he argues that it is a very incomplete achievement because it is 'in competition with forces of global breakdown, national dissolution, and centrifugal corruption' (cf. Kaplan, 1994). While notions of localism, locality and locale do not figure explicitly in Barber's essay they certainly diffusely inform it.

There is no good reason, other than recently established convention in some quarters, to define globalization largely in terms of homogenization. Of course, anyone is at liberty to so define globalization, but I think that there is a great deal to be said against such a procedure. Indeed, while each of the imperatives of Barber's McWorld appear superficially to suggest homogenization, when one considers them more closely, they each have a local, diversifying aspect. I maintain also that it makes no good sense to define the global as if the global excludes the local. In somewhat technical terms, defining the global in such a way suggests that the global lies beyond all localities, as having systemic properties over and beyond the attributes of units within a global system. This way of talking flows along the lines suggested by the macro–micro distinction, which has held much sway in the discipline of economics and has recently become a popular theme in sociology and other social sciences.

Without denying that the world-as-a-whole has some systemic properties beyond those of the 'units' within it, it must be emphasized, on the other hand, that such units themselves are to a large degree constructed in terms of extra-unit processes and actions, in terms of increasingly global dynamics. For example, nationally organized societies – and the 'local' aspirations for establishing yet more nationally organized societies – are not simply units within a global context or texts within a context or intertext. Both their existence, and particularly the form of their existence, is largely the result of extra-societal – more generally, extra-local – processes and actions. If we grant with Wallerstein (1991b: 92) and Greenfeld (1992) that 'the national' is a 'prototype of the particular' we must, on the other hand, also recognize that the nation-state – more generally, the national society – is in a crucial respect a *cultural idea* (as Greenfeld herself seems to acknowledge). Much of the apparatus of contemporary nations, of the national-state organization of societies, including *the form* of their particularities – the construction of their unique identities – is very similar across the entire world (Meyer, 1980; Robertson, 1991), in spite of much variation in levels of 'development'. This is, perhaps, the most tangible of contemporary sites of the interpenetration of particularism and universalism (Robertson, 1992b).

Before coming directly to the contemporary circumstance, it is necessary to say a few words about globalization in a longer, historical perspective. One can undoubtedly trace far back into human history developments involving the expansion of chains of connectedness across wide expanses of the earth. In that sense 'world formation' has been proceeding for many hundreds, indeed thousands, of years. At the same time, we can undoubtedly trace through human history periods during which the consciousness of the potential for world 'unity' was in one way or another particularly acute. One of the major tasks of students of globalization is, as I have said, to comprehend *the form* in which the present, seemingly rapid shifts towards a highly interdependent world was structured. I have specifically argued that that form has been centred upon four main elements of the global-human condition: societies, individuals, the international system of societies, and humankind (Robertson, 1992b). It is around the changing relationships between, different emphases upon and often conflicting interpretations of these aspects of human life that the contemporary world as a whole has crystallized. So in my perspective the issue of what is to be included under the notion of the global is treated very comprehensively. The global is not in and of itself counterposed to the local. Rather, what is often referred to as the local is essentially included within the global.

In this respect globalization, defined in its most general sense as the compression of the world as a whole, involves the linking of localities. But it also involves the 'invention' of locality, in the same general sense as the idea of the invention of tradition (Hobsbawm and Ranger, 1983), as well as its 'imagination' (cf. Anderson, 1983).[4] There is indeed currently something like an 'ideology of home' which has in fact come into being partly in response to the constant repetition and global diffusion of the claim that we now live in a condition of homelessness or rootlessness; as if in prior periods of history the vast majority of people lived in 'secure' and homogenized locales.[5] Two things, among others, must be said in objection to such ideas. First, the form of globalization has involved considerable emphasis, at least until now, on the cultural homogenization of nationally constituted societies; but, on the other hand, prior to that emphasis, which began to develop at the end of the eighteenth century, what McNeill (1985) calls polyethnicity was normal. Second, the phenomenological diagnosis of the generalized homelessness of modern man and woman has been developed as if 'the same people are behaving and interpreting at the same time in the same broad social process' (Meyer, 1992: 11); whereas there is in fact much to suggest that it is increasingly global expectations concerning the relationship between individual and society that have produced both routinized and 'existential' selves. On top of that, the very ability to identify 'home', directly or indirectly, is contingent upon the (contested) construction and organization of interlaced categories of space and time.

But it is not my purpose here to go over this ground again, but rather to emphasize the significance of certain periods prior to the second half of the twentieth century when the possibilities for a single world seemed at the time to be considerable, but also problematic. Developing research along such lines will undoubtedly emphasize a variety of areas of the world and different periods. But as far as relatively recent times are concerned, I would draw attention to two arguments, both of which draw attention to rapid extension of communication across the world as a whole and thematize the central issue of changing conceptions of time-and-space. Johnson (1991) has in his book, *The Birth of the Modern*, argued that 'world society' – or 'international society in its totality' (1991: xviii) – largely crystallized in the period 1815–30. Here the emphasis is upon the crucial significance of the Congress of Vienna which was assembled following Bonaparte's first abdication in 1814. According to Johnson, the peace settlement in Vienna, following what was in effect the first world war (Fregosi, 1990), was 'reinforced by the powerful currents of romanticism sweeping through the world . . .'. Thus was established 'an international order which, in most respects, endured for a century' (Johnson, 1991: xix). Regardless of its particular ideological bent, Johnson's book is important because he does attempt not merely to cover all continents of the world but also to range freely over many aspects of life generally, not just world politics or international relations. He raises significant issues concerning the development of consciousness of the world as a whole, which was largely made possible by the industrial and communicative revolution on the one hand, and the Enlightenment on the other.

Second (and, regardless of the issue of the periodization of globalization, more important), Kern (1983) has drawn attention to the crucial period of 1880–1918, in a way that is particularly relevant to the present set of issues. In his study of the *Culture of Time and Space* Kern's most basic point is that in the last two decades of the nineteenth century and the first twenty years or so of the twentieth century very consequential shifts took place with respect to both our sense of space and time. There occurred, through international negotiations and technological innovations, a standardization of time–space which was inevitably both universal and particular: world time organized in terms of particularistic space, in a sense the co-ordination of objectiveness and subjectiveness. In other words, homogenization went hand in hand with heterogenization. They made each other possible. It was in this period that 'the world' became locked into a particular *form* of a strong shift to unicity. It was during this time that the four major 'components' of globalization which I have previously specified were given formidable concreteness. Moreover, it was in the late-nineteenth century that there occurred a big spurt in the organized attempts to link localities on an international or ecumenical basis.

An immediate precursor of such was the beginning of international exhibitions in the mid-nineteenth century, involving the internationally organized display of particular national 'glories' and achievements. The last two decades of the century witnessed many more such international or cross-cultural ventures, among them the beginnings of the modern religious ecumenical movement, which at one and the same time celebrated difference and searched for commonality within the framew/ emergent culture for 'doing' the relationship between the particul. certainly not uncontested, universal. An interesting example of the latte provided by the International Youth Hostel movement, which spread quite rapidly and not only in the northern hemisphere. This movement attempted on an organized international, or global, basis to promote the cultivation of communal, 'back to nature' values. Thus at one and the same time particularity was valorized but this was done on an increasingly globe-wide, pan-local basis.

The present century has seen a remarkable proliferation with respect to the 'international' organization and promotion of locality. A very pertinent example is provided by the current attempts to organize globally the promotion of the rights and identities of native, or indigenous, peoples (Charles, 1993; Chartrand, 1991).[6] This was a strong feature, for example, of the Global Forum in Brazil in 1992, which, so to say, surrounded the official United Nations 'Earth Summit'. Another is the attempt by the World Health Organization to promote 'world health' by the reactivation and, if need be, the invention of 'indigenous' local medicine. It should be stressed that these are only a few examples taken from a multifaceted trend.

Glocalization and the cultural imperialism thesis

Some of the issues which I have been raising are considered from a very different angle in Appiah's work on the viability of Pan-Africanism (1992). Appiah's primary theme is 'the question of how we are to think about Africa's contemporary cultures in the light of the two main external determinants of her recent history – European and Afro-New World conceptions of Africa – and of her own endogenous cultural traditions' (Appiah, 1992: ix–x). His contention is that the 'ideological decolonization' which he seeks to effect can only be made possible by what he calls finding a 'negotiable middle way' between endogenous 'tradition' and 'Western' ideas, both of the latter designations being placed within quotation marks by Appiah himself (Appiah, 1992: x). He objects strongly to what he calls the racial and racist thrusts of much of the Pan-American idea, pointing out that insofar as Pan-Africanism makes assumptions about the racial unity of all Africans, then this derives in large part from the experience and memory of non-African ideas about Africa and Africans which were prevalent in Europe and the USA during the latter part of the nineteenth century. Speaking specifically of the idea of the 'decolonization' of African literature, Appiah insists, I think correctly, that in much of the talk about decolonization we find what Appiah himself calls (again within quotation marks) a 'reverse discourse':

> The pose of repudiation actually presupposes the cultural institutions of the West and the ideological matrix in which they, in turn, are imbricated. Railing against the cultural hegemony of the West, the nativists are of its party without knowing it . . . . (D)efiance is determined less by 'indigenous' notions of resistance than

by the dictates of the West's own Herderian legacy – its highly elaborated ideologies of national autonomy, of language and literature as their cultural substrate. Native nostalgia, in short is largely fueled by that Western sentimentalism so familiar after Rousseau; few things, then, are less native than nativism in its current form. (Appiah, 1992: 60)

Appiah's statement facilitates the explication of a particularly important point. It helps to demonstrate that much of the conception of contemporary locality and indigeneity is itself historically contingent upon *encounters* between one civilizational region and another (cf. Nelson, 1981). Within such interactions, many of them historically imperialistic, has developed a sense of particularistic locality. But the latter is in large part a consequence of the increasingly global 'institutionalization' of the expectation and construction of local particularism. Not merely is variety continuously produced and reproduced in the contemporary world, that variety is *largely an aspect of the very dynamics which a considerable number of commentators interpret as homogenization*. So in this light we are again required to come up with a more subtle interpretation than is usually offered in the general debate about locality and globality.

Some important aspects of the local–global issue are manifested in the general and growing debate about and the discourse of cultural imperialism (Tomlinson, 1991). There is of course a quite popular intellectual view which would have it that the entire world is being swamped by Western – more specifically, American – culture. This view has undoubtedly exacerbated recent French political complaints about American cultural imperialism, particularly within the context of GATT negotiations. There are, on the other hand, more probing discussions of and research on this matter. For starters, it should be emphasized that the virtually overwhelming evidence is that even 'cultural messages' which emanate directly from 'the USA' are *differentially* received and interpreted; that 'local' groups 'absorb' communication from the 'centre' in a great variety of ways (Tomlinson, 1991). Second, we have to realize that the major alleged producers of 'global culture' – such as those in Atlanta (CNN) and Los Angeles (Hollywood) – increasingly tailor their products to a differentiated global market (which they partly construct). For example, Hollywood attempts to employ mixed, 'multinational' casts of actors and a variety of 'local' settings when it is particularly concerned, as it increasingly is, to get a global audience. Third, there is much to suggest that seemingly 'national' symbolic resources are in fact increasingly available for differentiated global interpretation and consumption. For example, in a recent discussion of the staging of Shakespeare's plays, Billington (1992) notes that in recent years Shakespeare has been subject to wide-ranging cultural interpretation and staging. Shakespeare no longer belongs to England. Shakespeare has assumed a universalistic significance; and we have to distinguish in this respect between Shakespeare as representing Englishness and Shakespeare as of 'local-cum-global' relevance. Fourth, clearly many have seriously underestimated the flow of ideas and practices from the so-called Third World to the seemingly dominant societies and regions of the world (J. Abu-Lughod, 1991; Hall, 1991a, 1991b).

Much of global 'mass culture' is in fact impregnated with ideas, styles and genres concerning religion, music, art, cooking, and so on. In fact the whole question of what will 'fly' globally and what will not is a very important question in the present global situation. We know of course that the question of what 'flies' is in part contingent upon issues of power; but we would be very ill-advised to think of this simply as a matter of the hegemonic extension of Western modernity. As Tomlinson (1991) has argued, 'local cultures' are, in Sartre's phrase, *condemned to freedom*. And their global participation has been greatly (and politically) underestimated. At this time 'freedom' is manifested particularly in terms of the social construction of identity-and-tradition, by the appropriation of cultural traditions (Habermas, 1994: 22). Although, as I have emphasized, this reflexiveness is typically undertaken along relatively standardized global-cultural lines. (For example, in 1982 the UN fully recognized the existence of indigenous peoples. In so doing it effectively established *criteria* in terms of which indigenous groups could and should identify themselves and be recognized formally. There are national parallels to this, in the sense that some societies have legal criteria for ethnic groups and cultural traditions.)

Then there is the question of diversity at the local level. This issue has been raised in a particularly salient way by Balibar (1991), who talks of *world spaces*. The latter are places in which the world-as-a-whole is potentially inserted. The general idea of world-space suggests that we should consider the local as a 'micro' manifestation of the global – in opposition, *inter alia*, to the implication that the local indicates enclaves of cultural, ethnic, or racial homogeneity. Where, in other words, is *home* in the late-twentieth century? Balibar's analysis – which is centred on contemporary Europe – suggests that in the present situation of global complexity, the idea of home has to be divorced analytically from the idea of locality. There may well be groups and categories which equate the two, but that doesn't entitle them or their representatives to project their perspective onto humanity as a whole. In fact there is much to suggest that the senses of home and locality are contingent upon alienation from home and/or locale. How else could one have (reflexive) consciousness of such? We talk of the mixing of cultures, of polyethnicity, but we also often underestimate the significance of what Lila Abu Lughod (1991) calls 'halfies'. As Geertz (1986: 114) has said, 'like nostalgia, diversity is not what it used to be'. One of the most significant aspects of contemporary diversity is indeed the complication it raises for conventional notions of culture. We must be careful not to remain in thrall to the old and rather well established view that cultures are organically binding and sharply bounded. In fact Lila Abu-Lughod opposes the very idea of culture because it seems to her to deny the importance of 'halfies', those who combine in themselves as individuals a number of cultural, ethnic and genderal features (cf. Tsing, 1993). This issue is closely related to the frequently addressed theme of global hybridization, even more closely to the idea of creolization (Hannerz, 1992: 217–67).

Conclusion: sameness and difference

My emphasis upon the significance of the concept of glocalization has arisen mainly from what I perceive to be major weaknesses in much of the employment of the term 'globalization'. In particular, I have tried to transcend the tendency to cast the idea of globalization as inevitably in tension with the idea of localization. I have instead maintained that globalization – in the broadest sense, the compression of the world – has involved and increasingly involves the creation and the incorporation of locality, processes which themselves largely shape, in turn, the compression of the world as a whole. Even though we are, for various reasons, likely to continue to use the concept of globalization, it might well be preferable to replace it for certain purposes with the concept of glocalization. The latter concept has the definite advantage of making the concern with space as important as the focus upon temporal issues. At the same time emphasis upon the global condition – that is, upon globality – further constrains us to make our analysis and interpretation of the contemporary world both spatial and temporal, geographical as well as historical (Soja, 1989).

Systematic incorporation of the concept of glocalization into the current debate about globalization is of assistance with respect to the issue of what I have called form. The form of globalization has specifically to do with the way in which the compression of the world is, in the broadest sense, structured. This means that the issue of the form of globalization is related to the ideologically laden notion of world order. However, I want to emphasize strongly that insofar as this is indeed the case, my own effort here has been directed only at making sense of two *seemingly* opposing trends: homogenization and heterogenization. These simultaneous trends are, in the last instance, complementary and interpenetrative; even though they certainly can and do collide in concrete situations. Moreover, glocalization can be – in fact, is – used strategically, as in the strategies of glocalization employed by contemporary TV enterprises seeking global markets (MTV, then CNN, and now others). Thus we should realize that in arguing that the current form of globalization involves what is best described as glocalization I fully acknowledge that there are many different modes of practical glocalization. Thus, even though much of what I said in this chapter has been hinged upon the Japanese conception of glocalization, I have in fact generalized that concept so as, in principle, to encompass the world as a whole. In this latter perspective the Japanese notion of glocalization appears as a *particular version* of a very general phenomenon.

An important issue which arises from my overall discussion has to do with the ways in which, since the era of the nation-state began in the late eighteenth century, the nation-state itself has been a major agency for the production of diversity and hybridization. Again, it happens to be the case that Japan provides the most well-known example of what Westney (1987) calls cross-societal emulation, most clearly during the early Meiji period. I would, however, prefer the term, selective incorporation in order to describe the very widespread tendency for nation-states to 'copy' ideas and practices from other societies – to engage, in varying degrees of systematicity, in projects of importation and hybridization. So, even though I have emphasized that the cultural idea of the nation-state is a 'global fact', we also should recognize that nation-states have, particularly since the late nineteenth century (Westney, 1987: 11–12), been engaged in selective learning from other societies, each nation-state thus incorporating a different mixture of 'alien' ideas.

There is still another factor in this brief consideration of 'hybridized national cultures'. This is the phenomenon of cultural nationalism. Yet again, this concept has emerged in particular reference to Japan. On the basis of a discussion of *nihonjinron* (the discourse on and of Japanese uniqueness), Yoshino (1992) argues that *nihonjinron* has, in varying degrees, been a common practice. Specifically, modern nations have tended to promote discourses concerning their own unique difference, a practice much encouraged in and by the great globalizing thrusts of the late nineteenth and early twentieth centuries. In this respect what is sometimes these days called strategic essentialism – mainly in reference to liberation movements of various kinds – is much older than some may think. It is in fact an extension and generalization of a long drawn-out process.

Finally, in returning to the issue of form, I would argue that no matter how much we may speak of global disorder, uncertainty and the like, generalizations and theorizations of such are inevitable. We should not entirely conflate the empirical issues with the interpretative-analytical ones. Speaking in the latter vein we can conclude that the form of globalization is currently being reflexively reshaped in such a way as to increasingly make projects of glocalization the constitutive features of contemporary globalization.

Notes

This chapter is a revised and expanded version of presentations at the Second International Conference on Global History, Technical University, Darmstadt, Germany, 1992 and the annual meetings of the American Sociological Association, Miami Beach, 1993. Parts of the present chapter have appeared in my 'Globalization or glocalization?' in the *Journal of International Communication* 1 (1), 1994. At different stages I have received helpful comments from Scott Lash, Ingrid Volkmer, Raymond Grew, Gayatri Spivak, Seyla Benhabib, Juliana Martinez and Frank Chang.

1. My colleague, Akiko Hashimoto, informs me that in 'non-business' Japanese *dochakuka* conveys the idea of 'making something indigenous'. For some provocative comments on the connections between multiculturalism (especially in debates about the university curriculum), consumer culture and current trends in commodification and product diversification in contemporary capitalism, see Rieff (1993).

2. This trend is, of course, partly facilitated by the 'electronic cottage' phenomenon, which increasingly enables those who can afford it to be vicinally distant from urban centres, but

communicationally close to increasingly large numbers of people. Various aspects of geographic dispersal in relation to financial globalization and centralization are explored at length in Sassen (1991).

3. Robbins (1993) has addressed issues of this kind at some length in reference to the universalism–particularism theme. See, in particular, his chapter, 'Comparative Cosmopolitans' (Robbins, 1993: 180–211).

4. Habermas (1994: 22) succinctly expresses this way of thinking when he says that 'nationalism is a form of collective consciousness which both presupposes a reflexive appropriation of cultural traditions that has been filtered through historiography and spreads only via the channels of modern mass communication'. However, the notion of reflexive appropriation suggests that the construction of tradition is primarily an *internal* matter, whereas I argue that the construction or reconstruction of tradition is closely tied to globalization (Robertson, 1992b: 146–63).

5. This contemporary ideology of home (or homelessness), as I have called it, actually involves the overlap of two, heretofore distinct discourses. On the one hand, there is the diffuse discourse which has found its clearest expression in the phenomenological notion of homelessness and which has clearly filtered into the public domain and has seemingly acquired a near-global significance (cf. Berger et al., 1973). On the other hand, there is the more specific discourse of homelessness which deals with inadequate shelter (cf. Glasser, 1994).

6. For numerous insights into the current interest in indigenous peoples, see Tsing (1993).

References

Abu-Lughod, J. (1991) 'Going beyond global babble', in A.D. King (ed.), *Culture, Globalization and the World-System*. London: Macmillan.

Abu-Lughod, J. (1994) 'Diversity, democracy, and self-determination in an urban neighborhood: the East Village of Manhattan', *Social Research,* 61 (1).

Abu-Lughod, L. (1991) 'Writing against culture', in R.G. Fox (ed.), *Recapturing Anthropology*. Sante Fe, NM: School of America Research Press.

Aeter, P. (1985) *Nationalism*. London: Verso.

Anderson, B. (1983) *Imagined Communities*. London: Verso.

Appiah, K.A. (1992) *In My Father's House: Africa in the Philosophy of Culture*. New York: Oxford University Press.

Balibar, E. (1991) 'Es Gibt keinan staat in Europa: racism and politics in Europe today', *New Left Review*, 186 (March/April).

Barber, B.R. (1992) 'Jihad vs. McWorld', *The Atlantic*, 269 (3).

Berger, P.L., Berger, B. and Kellner, H. (1973) *The Homeless Mind: Modernization and Consciousness*. New York: Random House.

Billington, M. (1992) 'The reinvention of William Shakespeare', *World Press Review* (July).

Bourdieu, P. (1984) *Distinction: A Social Critique of the Judgment of Taste*. Cambridge, MA: Harvard University Press.

Champion, A.G. (ed.) (1989) *Counterurbanization: The Changing Pace and Nature of Population Deconcentration*. London: Edward Arnold.

Charles, G. (1993) 'Hobson's choice for indigenous peoples', in R.D. Jackson (ed.), *Global Issues 93/94*. Guilford, CT: Dushkin.

Chartrand, L. (1991) 'A new solidarity among native peoples', *World Press Review* (August).

Ferguson, M. (1992) 'The mythology about globalization', *European Journal of Communication*, 7.

Fregosi, P. (1990) *Dreams of Empire: Napoleon and the First World War*. New York: Brick Lane Press.

Geertz, C. (1986) 'The uses of diversity', *Michigan Quarterly*, 5 (1).

Giddens, A. (1990) *The Consequences of Modernity*. Stanford, CA: Stanford University Press.

Giddens, A. (1991) *Modernity and Self-Identity*. Oxford: Polity.

Glasser, I. (1994) *Homelessness in Global Perspective*. New York: G.K. Hall.

Greenfeld, L. (1992) *Nationalism: Five Roads to Modernity*. Cambridge, MA: Harvard University Press.

Habermas, J. (1994) 'Citizenship and national identity', in B. van Steenbergen (ed.), *The Condition of Citizenship*. London: Sage.

Hall, S. (1991a) 'The local and the global: globalization and ethnicity', in A.D. King (ed.), *Culture, Globalization and the World-System*. London: Macmillan.

Hall, S. (1991b) 'Old and new identities, old and new ethnicities', in A.D. King (ed.), *Culture, Globalization and the World-System*. London: Macmillan.

Handler, R. (1994) 'Is "identity" a useful cross-cultural concept?', in J.R. Gillis (ed.), *Commemorations: The Politics of National Identity*. Princeton, NJ: Princeton University Press.

Hannerz, U. (1990) 'Cosmopolitans and locals in world culture', in M. Featherstone (ed.), *Global Culture*. London: Sage.

Hannerz, U. (1992) *Cultural Complexity: Studies in the Social Organization of Meaning*. New York: Columbia University Press.

Hobsbawm, F. and Ranger, T. (eds) (1983) *The Invention of Tradition*. Cambridge: Cambridge University Press.

JanMohamed, A.R. and Lloyd, D. (eds) (1990) *The Nature and Context of Minority Discourse*. Oxford: Oxford University Press.

Johnson, P. (1991) *The Birth of the Modern: World Society 1815–30*. New York: Harper-Collins.

Kaplan, R.D. (1994) 'The coming anarchy', *Atlantic Monthly*, 273 (2).

Kern, S. (1983) *The Culture of Time and Space, 1880–1918*. Cambridge, MA: Harvard University Press.

King, A.D. (1991) 'Introduction: spaces of culture, spaces of knowledge', in A.D. King (ed.), *Culture, Globalization and the World-System*. London: Macmillan.

Masden, R. (1993) 'Global monoculture, multiculture, and polyculture', *Social Research*, 60 (3).

McGrane, B. (1989) *Beyond Anthropology: Society and the Other*. New York: Columbia University Press.

McNeill, W.H. (1985) *Polyethnicity and National Unity in World History*. Toronto: University of Toronto Press.

Meyer, W.J. (1980) 'The world polity and the authority of the nation state', in A. Bergesen (ed.), *Studies of the Modern World System*. New York: Academic Press.

Meyer, W.J. (1992) 'From constructionism to neo-institutionalism: reflections on Berger and Luckmann', *Perspectives* (ASA Theory Section) 15 (2).

Miyoshi, M. (1993) 'A borderless world: from colonialism to transnationalism and the decline of the nation-state', *Critical Inquiry*, 19 (4).

Miyoshi, M. and Harootunian, H.D. (eds) (1989) *Postmodernism and Japan*. Durham: Duke University Press.

Moore, S.F. (1989) 'The production of cultural pluralism as a process', *Public Culture*, 1 (2).

Nelson, B. (1981) 'Civilizational complexes and intercivilizational encounters', in T.H. Huff (ed.), *On the Roads to Modernity*. Totowa, NJ: Rowman & Littlefield.

Oxford Dictionary of New Words, compiled by Sara Tulloch (1991) Oxford: Oxford University Press.

Phillips, D.L. (1993) *Looking Backward: A Critical Appraisal of Communitarian Thought*. Princeton, NJ: Princeton University Press.

Rhinesmith, S.H. (1993) *A Manager's Guide to Globalization*. Alexandria, VA: American Society for Training and Development.

Rieff, D. (1993) 'Multiculturalism's silent partner: it's the economy, stupid', *Harper's*, 287.

Robbins, B. (1993) *Secular Vocations: Intellectuals, Professionalism, Culture*. London: Verso.

Robertson, R. (1990) 'After nostalgia? Wilful nostalgia and the phases of globalization', in B.S. Turner (ed.), *Theories of Modernity and Postmodernity*. London: Sage.

Robertson, R. (1991) 'Social theory, cultural relativity and the problem of globality', in A.D. King (ed.), *Culture, Globalization and the World-System*. London: Macmillan.

Robertson, R. (1992a) 'Globality and modernity', *Theory, Culture & Society*, 9 (2).

Robertson, R. (1992b) *Globalization: Social Theory and Global Culture*. London: Sage.

Robertson, R. (1993) 'Globalization and sociological theory', in H. Martins (ed.), *Knowledge and Passion: Essays in Honour of John Rex*. London: Tauris.

Robertson, R. (1995) 'Theory, specificity, change: emulation, selective incorporation and modernization', in B. Grancelli (ed.), *Social Change and Modernization: Lessons from Eastern Europe*. Berlin: Walter de Gruyter.

Sahlins, M. (1976) *Culture and Practical Reason*. Chicago: Chicago University Press.

Sassen, S. (1991) *The Global City: New York, London, Tokyo*. Princeton: Princeton University Press.

Simons, G.F., Vázquez, C. and Harris, P.R. (1993) *Transcultural Leadership*. Houston: Gulf.

Soja, E.W. (1989) *Postmodern Geographies: The Reassertion of Space in Critical Social Theory*. London: Verso.

Tomlinson, J. (1991) *Cultural Imperialism*. Baltimore: Johns Hopkins University Press.

Tsing, A.L. (1993) *In the Realm of the Diamond Queen*. Princeton, NJ: Princeton University Press.

Turner, B.S. (1987) 'A note on nostalgia', *Theory, Culture & Society*, 4 (1).

Wallerstein, I. (1991a) *Unthinking Social Science: The Limits of Nineteenth-Century Paradigms*. Oxford: Polity Press.

Wallerstein, I. (1991b) 'The national and the universal: can there be such a thing as world culture?', in A.D. King (ed.), *Culture, Globalization and the World-System*. London: Macmillan.

Westney, D.E. (1987) *Imitation and Innovation: The Transfer of Western Organizational Patterns to Meiji Japan*. Cambridge, MA: Harvard University Press.

Yoshino, K. (1992) *Cultural Nationalism in Contemporary Japan: A Sociological Enquiry*. London: Routledge.

3

GLOBALIZATION AS HYBRIDIZATION

Jan Nederveen Pieterse

The most common interpretations of globalization are the ideas that the world is becoming more uniform and standardized, through a technological, commercial and cultural synchronization emanating from the West, and that globalization is tied up with modernity. These perspectives are interrelated, if only in that they are both variations on an underlying theme of globalization as Westernization. The former is critical in intent while the latter is ambiguous. My argument takes issue with both these interpretations as narrow assessments of globalization and instead argues for viewing globalization as a process of hybridization which gives rise to a global mélange.

Globalizations in the plural

Globalization, according to Albrow, 'refers to all those processes by which the peoples of the world are incorporated into a single world society, global society' (1990: 9). Since these processes are plural we may as well conceive of globalizations in the plural. Thus in social science there are as many conceptualizations of globalization as there are disciplines. In economics, globalization refers to economic internationalization and the spread of capitalist market relations. 'The global economy is the system generated by globalising production and global finance' (Cox, 1992: 30). In international relations, the focus is on the increasing density of interstate relations and the development of global politics. In sociology, the concern is with increasing world-wide social densities and the emergence of 'world society'. In cultural studies, the focus is on global communications and world-wide cultural standardization, as in CocaColonization and McDonaldization, and on postcolonial culture. In history, the concern is with conceptualizing 'global history' (Mazlish and Buultjens, 1993).

All these approaches and themes are relevant if we view globalization as a multidimensional process which, like all significant social processes, unfolds in multiple realms of existence simultaneously. Accordingly, globalization may be understood in terms of an open-ended synthesis of several disciplinary approaches. This extends beyond social science, for instance to ecological concerns, technology (Henderson, 1989) and agricultural techniques (for example, green revolution).

Another way to conceive of globalizations plural is that there are as many modes of globalization as there are globalizing agents and dynamics or impulses. Historically these range from long-distance cross-cultural trade, religious organizations and knowledge networks to contemporary multi-national corporations, transnational banks, international institutions, technological exchange and transnational networks of social movements. We can further differentiate between globalization as policy and project – as in the case of Amnesty International which is concerned with internationalizing human rights standards – or as unintended consequence – as in the case of the 'globalizing panic' of AIDS. *Globalism* is the policy of furthering or managing (a particular mode of) globalization. In political economy it refers to policies furthering or accommodating economic internationalization (Petras and Brill, 1985); or to the corporate globalism of transnational enterprises (Gurtov, 1988); and in foreign affairs, to the global stance in US foreign policy, in its initial post-war posture (Ambrose, 1971) and its post Cold War stance.

These varied dimensions all point to the inherent fluidity, indeterminacy and open-endedness of globalizations. If this is the point of departure it becomes less obvious to think of globalizations in terms of standardization and less likely that globalizations can be one-directional processes, either structurally or culturally.

Globalization and modernity

Modernity is a keynote in reflections on globalization in sociology. In several prominent conceptualizations, globalization is the corollary of modernity (Giddens, 1990).[1] It's not difficult to understand this trend. In conjunction with globalization, modernity provides a structure and periodization. In addition, this move reflects the general thematization of modernity in social science from Habermas to Berman. Together globalization and modernity make up a ready-made package. Ready-made because it closely resembles the earlier, well-established conceptualization of globalization: the Marxist theme of the spread of the world market. The timing and pace are the same in both interpretations: the process starts in the 1500s and experiences its high tide from the late nineteenth century. The structures are the same: the nation-state and individualization – vehicles of modernity or, in the Marxist paradigm, corollaries of the spread of the world market. In one conceptualization universalism refers to the logic of the market and the law of value, and in the other to modern values of achievement. World-system theory is the most well-known conceptualization of globalization in the Marxist lineage; its achievement has been to make 'society' as the unit of analysis appear as a narrow focus, while on the other hand it has faithfully replicated the familiar constraints of Marxist determinism (Nederveen Pieterse, 1987).

There are several problems associated with the modernity/globalization approach. In either conceptualization, whether centred on capitalism or modernity, globalization begins in and emanates from Europe and the West.

In effect it is a theory of Westernization by another name, which replicates all the problems associated with Eurocentrism: a narrow window on the world, historically and culturally. With this agenda it should be called Westernization and not globalization. Another problem is that globalization theory turns into or becomes an annex of modernization theory. While modernization theory is a passed station in sociology and development theory, it is making a comeback under the name of globalization – the 1950s and 1960s revisited under a large global umbrella. Robertson (1992: 138–45) takes issue with the prioritization of modernity, notably in Giddens' work. Robertson's approach to globalization is multidimensional with an emphasis on sociocultural processes. At the same time, his preoccupation with themes such as 'global order' is, according to Arnason, 'indicative of a Parsonian approach, transferred from an artificially isolated and unified society to the global condition' (1990: 222). Neo-modernization theory (Tiryakian, 1991) and the contemporary re-thematization of modernity indicate the continuing appeal of modernization thinking, but the problems remain.

The tendency to focus on social structure produces an account from which the dark side of modernity is omitted. What of modernity in the light of Bauman's *Modernity and the Holocaust* (1989)? While the Marxist perspective involves a critical agenda, the thematization of modernity, whether or not it serves as a stand-in for capitalism, does not.

> . . . the ambiguities involved in this discourse are such that it is possible, within it, to lose any sense of cultural domination: to speak of modernity can be to speak of cultural change as 'cultural fate' in the strong sense of historical . . . inevitability. This would be to abandon any project of rational cultural critique. (Tomlinson, 1991: 141)

Generally, questions of power are marginalized in both the capitalism and modernity perspectives. Another dimension which tends to be conspicuously absent from modernity accounts is imperialism. Modernity accounts tend to be societally inward looking, in a rarefied sociological narrative, as if modernity precedes and conditions globalization, and not the other way round: globalization constituting one of the conditions for modernity. The implication of the modernity/globalization view is that the history of globalization begins with the history of the West. But is not precisely the point of globalization as a perspective that globalization begins with world history? The modernity/globalization view is not only geographically narrow (Westernization) but also historically shallow (1500 plus). The timeframe of some of the perspectives relevant to globalization is as follows.

Table 3.1 *Timing of globalization*

Author	Start	Theme
Marx	1500s	modern capitalism
Wallerstein	1500s	modern world-system
Robertson	1500s, 1870–1920s	multidimensional
Giddens	1800s	modernity
Tomlinson	1960s	cultural planetarization

Apparently the broad heading of globalization accommodates some very different views. The basic understanding is usually a neutral formulation, such as 'Globalization can thus be defined as the intensification of worldwide social relations which link distant localities in such a way that local happenings are shaped by events occurring many miles away and vice versa' (Giddens, 1990: 64). The 'intensification of worldwide social relations' can be thought of as a long-term process which finds its beginnings in the first migrations of peoples and long-distance trade connections, and subsequently accelerates under particular conditions (the spread of technologies, religions, literacy, empires, capitalism). Or, it can be thought of as consisting only of the later stages of this process, from the time of the accelerating formation of global social relations, and as a specifically global momentum associated with particular conditions (the development of a world market, Western imperialism, modernity). It can be narrowed down further by regarding globalization as a particular epoch and formation – as in Tomlinson's view of globalization as the successor to imperialism (rather than imperialism being a mode of globalization), Jameson's view of the new cultural space created by late capitalism, and Harvey's argument where globalization is associated with the postmodern condition of time–space compression and flexible accumulation.

But, whichever the emphasis, globalization as the 'intensification of worldwide social relations' presumes the prior existence of 'worldwide social relations', so that globalization is the conceptualization of a *phase* following an existing condition of *globality* and part of an ongoing process of the formation of world-wide social relations. This recognition of historical depth brings globalization back to world history and beyond the radius of modernity/Westernization.

One way around the problem of modernization/Westernization is the notion of multiple *paths* of modernization, which avoids the onus of Eurocentrism and provides an angle for reproblematizing Western development. This has been advanced by Benjamin Nelson as part of his concern with 'intercivilizational encounters' (1981) and taken up by others (e.g. Therborn, 1992). The idea that 'all societies create their own modernity' also forms part of development discourse analysis, along with the theme of 'reworking modernity' in the context of popular culture and memory (Pred and Watts, 1992; Rowe and Schelling, 1991).

The modernizations plural approach matches the notion of the *historicity* of modernization common in Southeast and East Asia (Singh, 1989). That Japanese modernization has followed a different path from that of the West is a cliché in Japanese sociology (Tominaga, 1990) and well established in Taiwan and China (Li, 1989; Sonoda, 1990). It results in an outlook that resembles the argument of polycentrism and multiple paths of development (Amin, 1990). But this remains a static and one-dimensional representation: the multiplication of centres still hinges on centrism. It's not much use to make up for Eurocentrism and occidental narcissism by opting for other centrisms such as Afrocentrism, Indocentrism, Sinocentrism or polycentrism. In effect, it echoes the turn of the century pan-movements: pan-Slavism, pan-Islamism, pan-Arabism, pan-Turkism, pan-Europeanism, pan-Africanism etc, in which the logic of nineteenth-century racial classifications is carried further under the heading of civilizational provinces turned into political projects. This may be the substitution of one centrism and parochialism for another and miss the fundamental point of the 'globalization of diversity', of the mélange effect pervading everywhere, from the heartlands to the extremities and vice versa.

Structural hybridization

With respect to cultural forms, hybridization is defined as 'the ways in which forms become separated from existing practices and recombine with new forms in new practices' (Rowe and Schelling, 1991: 231). This principle can be extended to structural forms of social organization.

It is by now a familiar argument that nation-state formation is an expression and function of globalization and not a process contrary to it (Robertson, 1992; Greenfeld, 1992). At the same time it is apparent that the present phase of globalization involves the relative weakening of nation-states – as in the weakening of the 'national economy' in the context of economic globalism and, culturally, the decline of patriotism. But this too is not simply a one-directional process. Thus the migration movements which make up demographic globalization can engender absentee patriotism and long-distance nationalism, as in the political affinities of Irish, Jewish and Palestinian diasporas and emigré or exiled Sikhs in Toronto, Tamils in London, Kurds in Germany, Tibetans in India (Anderson, 1992).

Globalization can mean the reinforcement of or go together with localism, as in 'Think globally, act locally'. This kind of tandem operation of local/global dynamics, global localization or *glocalization*, is at work in the case of minorities who appeal to transnational human rights standards beyond state authorities, or indigenous peoples who find support for local demands from transnational networks. The upsurge of ethnic identity politics and religious revival movements can also be viewed in the light of globalization. 'Identity patterns are becoming more complex, as people assert local loyalties but want to share in global values and lifestyles' (Ken Booth quoted in Lipschutz, 1992: 396). Particularity, notes Robertson, is a *global* value and what is taking place is a 'universalization of particularism' or 'the global valorization of particular identities' (1992: 130).

Global dynamics such as the fluctuations of commodity prices on the world market can result in the reconstruction of ethnic identities, as occurred in Africa in the 1980s (Shaw, 1986). State development policies can engender a backlash of ethnic movements (Kothari, 1988). Thus, 'globalisation can generate forces of both fragmentation and unification . . . globalisation can engender an awareness of political difference as much as an awareness of common identity; enhanced international communications can highlight conflicts of interest and ideology, and not merely remove obstacles to mutual understanding' (Held, 1992: 32).

Globalization can mean the reinforcement of both supranational and sub-national regionalism. The European Union is a case in point. Formed in response to economic challenges from Japan and the United States, it represents more than the internal market and is in the process of becoming an administrative, legal, political and cultural formation, involving multiple Europes: the Europe of the nations, regions, 'European civilization', Christianities, etc. The dialectics of unification mean, for instance, that constituencies in Northern Ireland can appeal to the European Court of Human Rights in Strasbourg on decisions of the British courts, or that Catalonia can outflank Madrid and Brittany outmanoeuvre Paris by appealing to Brussels or by establishing links with other regions (for example, between Catalonia and the Ruhr area). Again there is a ongoing flow or cascade of globalization – regionalism – sub-regionalism. Or, 'Globalization encourages macro-regionalism, which, in turn, encourages micro-regionalism' (Cox, 1992: 34).

> Micro-regionalism in poor areas will be a means not only of affirming cultural identities but of claiming pay-offs at the macro-regional level for maintaining political stability and economic good behaviour. The issues of redistribution are thereby raised from the sovereign state level to the macro-regional level, while the manner in which redistributed wealth is used becomes decentralised to the micro-regional level. (Cox, 1992: 35)

What globalization means in structural terms, then, is the *increase in the available modes of organization*: transnational, international, macro-regional, national, micro-regional, municipal, local. This ladder of administrative levels is being crisscrossed by *functional networks* of corporations, international organizations and non-governmental organizations, as well as by professionals and computer users. Part of this is what has been termed the 'internationalization of the state' as states are 'increasingly engaged in multilateral forms of international governance' (Held and McGrew, 1993: 271). This approximates Rosenau's conceptualization of the structure of *'post-international politics'* made up of two interactive worlds with overlapping memberships: a state-centric world, in which the primary actors are national, and a multi-centric world of diverse actors such as corporations, international organizations, ethnic groups, churches (1990). These multi-centric functional networks in turn are nested within broader sprawling 'scapes', such as finanscapes and ethnoscapes (Appadurai, 1990).

Furthermore, not only these modes of organization are important but also the informal spaces that are created in between, in the interstices. Inhabited by diasporas, migrants, exiles, refugees, nomads, these are sites of what Michael Mann (1986) calls 'interstitial emergence' and identifies as important sources of social renewal.

Also in political economy we can identify a range of hybrid formations. The notion of articulation of modes of production may be viewed as a principle of hybridization. The dual economy argument saw neatly divided economic sectors while the articulation argument sees interactive sectors giving rise to mélange effects, such as 'semi-proletarians' who have one foot in the agrarian subsistence sector. Counterposed to the idea of the dual economy split in traditional/modern and feudal/capitalist sectors, the articulation argument holds that what has been taking place is an inter-penetration of modes of production. Uneven articulation has, in turn, given rise to phenomena such as asymmetric integration (Terhal, 1987). Dependency theory may be read as a theory of structural hybridization in which dependent capitalism is a mélange category in which the logics of capitalism and imperialism have merged. Recognition of this hybrid condition is what distinguishes neo-Marxism from classical Marxism (in which capital was regarded as a 'permanently revolutionizing force'): that is, regular capitalism makes for development, but dependent capitalism makes for the 'development of underdevelopment'. The contested notion of semiperiphery may also be viewed as a hybrid formation.[2] In a wider context, the mixed economy, the informal sector, and the 'third sector' of the 'social economy', comprising co-operative and non-profit organizations (Defourny and Monzón Campos, 1992), may be viewed as hybrid economic formations.

Hybrid formations constituted by the interpenetration of diverse logics manifest themselves in hybrid sites and spaces. Thus, urbanization in the context of the fusion of pre-capitalist and capitalist modes of production, as in parts of Latin America, may give rise to 'cities of peasants' (Roberts, 1978). Border zones are the meeting places of different organizational modes – such as Free Enterprise Zones and offshore banking facilities (hybrid meeting places of state sovereignty and transnational enterprise), overseas military facilities and surveillance stations (Enloe, 1989). Border lands generally have become a significant topos (Anzaldúa, 1987). The blurring and reworking of public and private spaces is a familiar theme (for example, Helly and Reverby, 1992). Global cities (Sassen, 1991) and ethnic mélange neighbourhoods within them (such as Jackson Heights in Queens, New York) are other hybrid spaces in the global landscape. The use of information technology in supranational financial transactions (Wachtel, 1990) has given rise to a hyperspace of capital.

Another dimension of hybridity concerns the experience of time, as in the notion of mixed times (tiempos mixtos) common in Latin America, where it refers to the coexistence and interspersion of premodernity, modernity and postmodernity (Calderón, 1988; Vargas, 1992). A similar point is that 'intrinsic asynchrony' is a 'general characteristic of Third World cultures' (Hösle, 1992: 237).

Globalization, then, increases the range of organizational options, all of which are in operation simultaneously. Each or a combination of these may be relevant in specific social, institutional, legal, political, economic or cultural spheres. What matters is that no single mode has a necessary overall priority or monopoly. This is one of the salient differences between the present phase of globalization and the preceding era from the 1840s to the 1960s, the great age of nationalism when by and large the nation-state was the single dominant organizational option (Harris, 1990). While the spread of the nation-state has been an expression of globalization, the dynamic has not stopped there.

The overall tendency towards increasing global density and interdependence, or globalization, translates, then, into the pluralization of organizational forms. Structural hybridization and the mélange of diverse modes of organization give rise to a pluralization of forms of co-operation and competition as well as to novel mixed forms of co-operation. This is the structural corollary to flexible specialization and just-in-time capitalism and, on the other hand, to cultural hybridization and multiple identities. Multiple identities and the decentring of the social subject are grounded in the ability of individuals to avail themselves of several organizational options at the same time. Thus globalization is the framework for the amplification and diversification of 'sources of the self'.

A different concern is the scope and depth of the historical field. The Westernization/modernity views on globalization only permit a global momentum with a short memory. Globalization taken widely, however, refers to the formation of a world-wide historical field and involves the development of global memory, arising from shared global experiences. Such shared global experiences range from various intercivilizational encounters such as long-distance trade and migration to slavery, conquest, war, imperialism, colonialism. It has been argued that the latter would be irrelevant to global culture:

> Unlike national cultures, a global culture is essentially memoryless. When the 'nation' can be constructed so as to draw upon and revive latent popular experiences and needs, a 'global culture' answers to no living needs, no identity-in-the-making . . . . There are no 'world memories' that can be used to *unite* humanity; the most global experiences to date – colonialism and the World Wars – can only serve to remind us of our historic cleavages. (Smith, 1990: 180)

If, however, conflict, conquest and oppression would *only* divide people, then nations themselves would merely be artefacts of division for they too were mostly born out of conflict (for example, Hechter, 1975). Likewise, on the larger canvas, it would be shallow and erroneous to argue that the experiences of conflict merely divide humanity: they also unite humankind, even if in painful ways and producing an ambivalent kind of unity (Abdel-Malek, 1981; Nederveen Pieterse, 1990). Unity emerging out of antagonism and conflict is the a, b, c of dialectics. It's a recurrent theme in postcolonial literature, for example *The Intimate Enemy* (Nandy, 1983). The intimacy constituted by repression and resistance is not an uncommon notion either, as hinted in the title of the Israeli author Uri Avneri's book about Palestinians, *My Friend the Enemy* (1986). A conflictual unity bonded by common political and cultural experiences, including the experience of domination, has been part of the make-up of hybrid postcolonial cultures. Thus the former British Empire remains in many ways a unitary space featuring a common language, common elements in legal and political systems, infrastructure, traffic rules, an imperial architecture which is in many ways the same in India as in South Africa, along with the legacy of the Commonwealth (King, 1991).

Robertson makes reference to the deep history of globality, particularly in relation to the spread of world religions, but reserves the notion of globalization for later periods, starting in the 1500s, considering that what changes over time is 'the scope and depth of consciousness of the world as a single place'. In his view 'contemporary globalization' also refers to 'cultural and subjective matters' and involves *awareness* of the global human condition, a global consciousness that carries reflexive connotations (1992: 183). No doubt this reflexivity is significant, also because it signals the potential capability of humanity to act upon the global human condition. On the other hand, there is no reason why such reflexivity should halt at the gates of the West and not also arise from and be cognizant of the deep history of intercivilizational connections including, for instance, the influence of the world religions.

Global mélange: windows for research on globalization

How do we come to terms with phenomena such as Thai boxing by Moroccan girls in Amsterdam, Asian rap in London, Irish bagels, Chinese tacos and Mardi Gras Indians in the United States, or 'Mexican schoolgirls dressed in Greek togas dancing in the style of Isidora Duncan' (Rowe and Schelling, 1991: 161)? How do we interpret Peter Brook directing the Mahabharata, or Ariane Mânouchkine staging a Shakespeare play in Japanese Kabuki style for a Paris audience in the Théâtre Soleil? Cultural experiences, past or present, have not been simply moving in the direction of cultural uniformity and standardization. This is not to say that the notion of global cultural synchronization (Hamelink, 1983; Schiller, 1989) is irrelevant – on the contrary – but it is fundamentally incomplete. It overlooks the countercurrents – the impact non-Western cultures have been making on the West. It downplays the ambivalence of the globalizing momentum and ignores the role of local reception of Western culture – for example the indigenization of Western elements. It fails to see the influence non-Western cultures have been exercising on one another. It has no room for crossover culture – as in the development of 'third cultures' such as world music. It overrates the homogeneity of Western culture and overlooks the fact that many of the standards exported by the West and its cultural industries themselves turn out to be of culturally mixed character if we examine their cultural lineages. Centuries of South–North cultural osmosis have resulted in an intercontinental crossover culture. European and Western culture are *part* of this global mélange. This is an obvious case if we reckon that Europe until the fourteenth century was invariably the recipient of cultural influences from 'the Orient'.[3] The hegemony of the West dates only from very recent times, from around 1800, and, arguably, from industrialization.

One of the terms offered to describe this interplay is the *creolization* of global culture (Friedman, 1990; Hannerz, 1987). This approach is derived from creole languages and linguistics. 'Creolization' itself is an odd, hybrid term. In the Caribbean and North America it stands for the mixture of African and European (the Creole *cuisine* of New Orleans, etc.), while in Hispanic America *'criollo'* originally denotes those of European descent born in the continent.[4] 'Creolization' means a Caribbean window on the world. Part of its appeal is that it goes against the grain of nineteenth-century racism and the accompanying abhorrence of *métissage* as miscegenation, as in Comte de Gobineau's view that race mixture leads to decadence and decay for in every mixture the lower element is bound to predominate. The doctrine of racial purity involves the fear of and *dédain* for the half-caste. By stressing and foregrounding the *mestizo* factor, the mixed and in-between, creolization highlights what has been hidden and valorizes boundary crossing. It also implies an argument with Westernization: the West itself may be viewed as a mixture and Western culture as a creole culture.

The Latin American term *mestizaje* also refers to boundary-crossing mixture. Since the early part of the century, however, this has served as a hegemonic élite ideology, which, in effect, refers to 'whitening' or Euro-peanization as the overall project for Latin American countries: while the European element is supposed to maintain the upper hand, through the gradual 'whitening' of the population and culture, Latin America is supposed to achieve modernity (Graham, 1990; Whitten and Torres, 1992). A limitation of both creolization and *mestizaje* is that they are confined to the experience of the post-sixteenth-century Americas.

Another terminology is the 'orientalization of the world', which has been referred to as 'a distinct global process' (Featherstone, 1990). In Duke Ellington's words, 'We are all becoming a little Oriental' (quoted in Fischer, 1992: 32). It is reminiscent of the theme of 'East wind prevailing over West wind', which runs through Sultan Galiev, Mao and Abdel-Malek. In the setting of the 'Japanese challenge' and the development model of East Asian Newly Industrialized Countries, it evokes the Pacific Century and the twenty-first century as the 'Asian century' (Park, 1985).

Each of these terms – 'creolization', *'mestizaje'*, 'orientalization' – opens a different window on the global mélange. In the United States 'crossover culture' denotes the adoption of black cultural characteristics by European-Americans and of white elements by African-Americans. As a general notion, this may aptly describe global intercultural osmosis and interplay. Global 'crossover culture' may be an appropriate characterization of the long-term global North–South mélange. Still, what is not clarified are the *terms* under which cultural interplay and crossover take place. Likewise in terms such as 'global mélange', what is missing is acknowledgement of the actual unevenness, asymmetry and inequality in global relations.

Politics of hybridity

Given the backdrop of nineteenth-century discourse, it's no wonder that arguments that acknowledge hybridity often do so on a note of regret and

loss – loss of purity, wholeness, authenticity. Thus, according to Hisham
Sharabi (1988: 4), neo-patriarchical society in the contemporary Arab world
is 'a new, hybrid sort of society/culture', 'neither modern nor traditional'.
The 'neopatriarchal petty bourgeoisie' is likewise characterized as a 'hybrid
class' (1988: 6). This argument is based on an analysis of 'the political and
economic conditions of distorted, dependent capitalism' in the Arab world
(1988: 5), in other words, it is derived from the framework of dependency
theory.

In arguments such as these hybridity functions as a negative trope, in line
with the nineteenth-century paradigm according to which hybridity, mixture, mutation are regarded as negative developments which detract from
prelapsarian purity – in society and culture, as in biology. Since the
development of Mendelian genetics in the 1870s and its subsequent adoption
in early twentieth-century biology, however, a revaluation has taken place
according to which crossbreeding and polygenic inheritance have come to be
positively valued as enrichments of gene pools. Gradually this then has been
seeping through to wider circles; the work of Bateson (1972), as one of the
few to reconnect the natural sciences and social sciences, has been influential
in this regard.

In post-structuralist and postmodern analysis, hybridity and syncretism
have become keywords. Thus hybridity is the antidote to essentialist notions
of identity and ethnicity (Lowe, 1991). Cultural syncretism refers to the
methodology of montage and collage, to 'cross-cultural plots of music,
clothing, behaviour, advertising, theatre, body language, or . . . visual
communication, spreading multi-ethnic and multi-centric patterns'
(Canevacci, 1992; 1993: 3). Interculturalism, rather than multiculturalism,
is the keynote of this kind of perspective. But it also raises different
problems. What is the political *portée* of the celebration of hybridity? Is it
merely another sign of perplexity turned into virtue by those grouped on the
consumer end of social change? According to Ella Shohat (1992: 109), 'A
celebration of syncretism and hybridity per se, if not articulated in
conjunction with questions of hegemony and neo-colonial power relations,
runs the risk of appearing to sanctify the *fait accompli* of colonial violence'.
Hence a further step would be not merely to celebrate but to theorize
hybridity.

A theory of hybridity would be attractive. We are so used to theories that
are concerned with establishing boundaries and demarcations among
phenomena – units or processes that are as neatly as possible set apart from
other units or processes – that a theory which instead would focus on
fuzziness and mélange, cut-and-mix, crisscross and crossover, might well be
a relief in itself. Yet, ironically, of course, it would have to prove itself by
giving as neat as possible a version of messiness, or an unhybrid categorization of hybridities.

By what yardstick would we differentiate hybridities? One consideration
is in what context hybridity functions. At a general level hybridity concerns
the mixture of phenomena which are held to be different, separate;

hybridization then refers to a *cross-category* process. Thus with Bakhtin (1968) hybridization refers to sites, such as fairs, which bring together the exotic and the familiar, villagers and townsmen, performers and observers. The categories can also be cultures, nations, ethnicities, status groups, classes, genres, and hybridity, by its very existence, blurs the distinctions among them. Hybridity functions, next, as part of a power relationship between centre and margin, hegemony and minority, and indicates a blurring, destabilization or subversion of that hierarchical relationship.

One of the original notions of hybridity is *syncretism*, the fusion of religious forms. Here we can distinguish, on the one hand, syncretism as *mimicry* – as in Santería, Candomblé, Vodûn, in which Catholic saints are adapted to serve as masks behind which non-Christian forms of worship are practised (for example, Thompson, 1984). The Virgin of Guadeloupe as a mask for Pacha Mama is another example. On the other hand, we find syncretism as a mélange not only of forms but also of beliefs, a merger in which *both* religions, Christian and native, have changed and a 'third religion' has developed (as in Kimbangism in the Congo).

Another phenomenon is hybridity as migration mélange. A common observation is that second-generation immigrants, in the West and else-where, display mixed cultural patterns – for example, a separation between and, next, a mix of a home culture and language (matching the culture of origin) and an outdoor culture (matching the culture of residence), as in the combination 'Muslim in the daytime, disco in the evening' (Feddema, 1992).

In postcolonial studies hybridity is a familiar and ambivalent trope. Homi Bhabha (1990) refers to hybrids as intercultural brokers in the interstices between nation and empire, producing counter-narratives from the nation's margins to the 'totalizing boundaries' of the nation. At the same time, refusing nostalgic models of precolonial purity, hybrids, by way of mimicry, may conform to the 'hegemonized rewriting of the Eurocentre'. Hybridity, in this perspective, can be a condition tantamount to alienation, a state of homelessness. Smadar Lavie comments: 'This is a response-oriented model of hybridity. It lacks agency, by not empowering the hybrid. The result is a fragmented Otherness in the hybrid' (1992: 92). In the work of Gloria Anzaldúa and others, she recognizes, on the other hand, a community-oriented mode of hybridity, and notes that 'reworking the past exposes its hybridity, and to recognize and acknowledge this hybrid past in terms of the present empowers the community and gives it agency' (1992: 92).

An ironical case of hybridity as intercultural crossover is mentioned by Michael Bérubé, interviewing the African American literary critic Houston Baker, Jr: 'That reminds me of your article in *Technoculture*, where you write that when a bunch of Columbia-graduate white boys known as Third Bass attack Hammer for not being black enough or strong enough . . . *that's* the moment of hybridity' (1992: 551).

Taking in these lines of thought, we can construct a *continuum of hybridities*: on one end, an assimilationist hybridity that leans over towards the centre, adopts the canon and mimics the hegemony, and, at the other end, a destabilizing hybridity that blurs the canon, reverses the current, subverts the centre. Hybridities, then, may be differentiated according to the components in the mélange. On the one hand, an assimilationist hybridity in which the centre predominates – as in V.S. Naipaul, known for his trenchant observations such as there's no decent cup of coffee to be had in Trinidad. A posture which has given rise to the term Naipaulitis. And on the other hand, an hybridity that blurs (passive) or destabilizes (active) the canon and its categories. Perhaps this spectrum of hybridities can be summed up as ranging from Naipaul to Salman Rushdie (cf. Brennan, 1989), Edward Said, Gayatri Spivak. Still, what does it mean to destabilize the canon? It's worth reflecting on the politics of hybridity.

Politics of hybridity: towards political theory on a global scale

Relations of power and hegemony are inscribed and reproduced *within* hybridity for wherever we look closely enough we find the traces of asymmetry in culture, place, descent. Hence hybridity raises the question of the *terms* of mixture, the conditions of mixing and mélange. At the same time it's important to note the ways in which hegemony is not merely reproduced but *refigured* in the process of hybridization. Generally, what is the bearing of hybridization in relation to political engagement?

> At times, the anti-essentialist emphasis on hybrid identities comes dangerously close to dismissing all searches for communitarian origins as an archaeological excavation of an idealized, irretrievable past. Yet, on another level, while avoiding any nostalgia for a prelapsarian community, or for any unitary and transparent identity predating the 'fall', we must also ask whether it is possible to forge a collective resistance without inscribing a communal past. (Shohat, 1992: 109)

Isn't there a close relationship between political mobilization and collective memory? Isn't the remembrance of deeds past, the commemoration of collective itineraries, victories and defeats – such as the Matanza for the FMLN in El Salvador, Katipunan for the NPA in the Philippines, Heroes Day for the ANC – fundamental to the symbolism of resistance and the moral economy of mobilization? Still, this line of argument involves several problems. While there may be a link, there is no necessary symmetry between communal past/collective resistance. What is the basis of bonding in collective action – past or future, memory or project? While communal symbolism may be important, collective symbolism and discourse merging a heterogeneous collectivity in a common project may be more important. Thus, while Heroes Day is significant to the ANC (16 December is the founding day of Umkhonto we Sizwe), the Freedom Charter, and more specifically, the project of non-racial democracy (non-sexism has been added later) has been of much greater importance. These projects are not of a 'communal' nature: part of their strength is precisely that they transcend communal boundaries. Generally, emancipations may be thought of in the plural, as a project or ensemble of projects that in itself is diverse, heterogeneous, multivocal.[5] The argument linking communal past/collective resistance imposes a unity and transparency which in effect reduces the space for *critical* resistance, for plurality *within* the movement, diversity within the process of emancipation. It privileges a communal view of collective action, a primordialist view of identity, and ignores or downplays the importance of *intra*group differences and conflicts over group representation, demands and tactics, including reconstructions of the past. It argues as if the questions of whether demands should be for autonomy or inclusion, whether the group should be inward or outward looking, have already been settled, while in reality these are political dilemmas. The nexus between communal past/collective engagement is one strand in political mobilization, but so are the hybrid past/plural projects, and in actual everyday politics the point is how to negotiate these strands in round-table politics. This involves going beyond a past to a future orientation – for what is the point of collective action without a future? The lure of community, powerful and prevalent in left as well as right politics, has been questioned often enough. In contrast, hybridity when thought of as a politics may be subversive of essentialism and homogeneity, disruptive of static spatial and political categories of centre and periphery, high and low, class and ethnos, and in recognizing multiple identities, widen the space for critical engagement. Thus the nostalgia paradigm of community politics has been contrasted to the landscape of the city, along with a reading of 'politics as relations among strangers' (Young, 1990).

What is the significance of this outlook in the context of global inequities and politics? Political theory on a global scale is relatively undeveloped. Traditionally political theory is concerned with the relations between sovereign and people, state and society. It's of little help to turn to the 'great political theorists' from Locke to Mill for they are all essentially concerned with the state–society framework. International relations theory extrapolates from this core preoccupation with concepts such as national interest and balance of power. Strictly speaking international relations theory, at any rate neo-realist theory, precludes global political theory. In the absence of a concept of 'world society', how can there be a notion of a world-wide social contract or global democracy? This frontier has opened up through concepts such as global civil society, referring to the transnational networks and activities of voluntary and non-governmental organizations: 'the growth of global civil society represents an ongoing project of civil society to reconstruct, re-imagine, or re-map world politics' (Lipschutz, 1992: 391). Global society and postinternational politics are other relevant notions (Shaw, 1992; Rosenau, 1990). A limitation to these reconceptualizations remains the absence of legal provisions that are globally binding rather than merely in interstate relations.

The question remains as to what kind of conceptual tools we can develop to address questions such as the double standards prevailing in global politics: perennial issues such as Western countries practising democracy at home and imperialism abroad; the edifying use of terms such as self-determination and sovereignty while the United States are invading Panama or Grenada. The term 'imperialism' may no longer be adequate to address the present situation. It may be adequate in relation to US actions in Panama or Grenada, but less so to describe the Gulf War. Imperialism is the policy of establishing or maintaining an empire, and empire is the control exercised by a state over the domestic and foreign policy of another political society (Doyle, 1986: 45). This is not an adequate terminology to characterize the Gulf War episode. If we consider that major actors in today's global circumstance are the IMF and World Bank, transnational corporations and regional investment banks, it is easy to acknowledge their influence on the domestic policies of countries from Brazil to the Philippines, but the situation differs from imperialism in two ways: the actors are not states and the foreign policy of the countries involved is not necessarily affected. The casual use of terms such as recolonization or neocolonialism to describe the impact of IMF conditionalities on African countries remains just that, casual. The situation has changed also since the emergence of regional blocs which can potentially exercise joint foreign policy (for example, the European Community) or which within themselves contain two or more 'worlds' (for example, NAFTA, APEC). Both these situations differ from imperialism in the old sense. Current literature on international political economy shows a shift from 'imperialism' to 'globalization'. The latter may be used with critical intent (for example, Miliband and Panitch, 1992) but is more often used in an open-ended sense. I've used the term 'critical globalism' as an approach to current configurations (Nederveen Pieterse, 1993). According to Tomlinson (1991: 175),

> the distribution of global power that we know as 'imperialism' . . . characterised the modern period up to, say, the 1960s. What replaces 'imperialism' is 'globalisation'. Globalisation may be distinguished from imperialism in that it is a far less coherent or culturally directed process. . . . The idea of 'globalisation' suggests interconnection and interdependency of all global areas which happens in a less purposeful way.

This is a particularly narrow interpretation in which globalization matches the epoch of late capitalism and flexible accumulation; still, what is interesting is the observation that the present phase of globalization is less coherent and less purposeful than imperialism. That does not mean the end of inequality and domination, although domination may be more dispersed, less orchestrated, more heterogeneous. To address global inequalities and develop global political theory a different kind of conceptualization is needed. We are not without points of reference but we lack a theory of global political action. Melucci has discussed the 'planetarization' of collective action (1989; Hegedus, 1989). Some of the implications of globalization for democracy have been examined by Held (1992). As regards the basics of a global political consensus, the UN Declaration of Human Rights, and its subsequent amendments by the Movement of Non-Aligned Countries, may be a point of reference (Parekh, 1992).

Post-hybridity?

Cultural hybridization refers to the mixing of Asian, African, American, European cultures: hybridization is the making of global culture as a global mélange. As a category hybridity serves a purpose on the basis of the assumption of *difference* between the categories, forms, beliefs that go into the mixture. Yet the very process of hybridization shows the difference to be relative and, with a slight shift of perspective, the relationship can also be described in terms of an affirmation of *similarity*. Thus, the Catholic saints can be taken as icons of Christianity, but can also be viewed as holdovers of pre-Christian paganism inscribed in the Christian canon. In that light, their use as masks for non-Christian gods is less quaint and rather intimates transcultural pagan affinities.

Ariane Mânouchkine's use of Kabuki style to stage a Shakespeare play leads to the question, which Shakespeare play? The play is Henry IV, which is set in the context of European high feudalism. In that light, the use of Japanese feudal Samurai style to portray European feudalism (Kreidt, 1987: 255) makes a point about transcultural historical affinities.

'Mexican schoolgirls dressed in Greek togas dancing in the style of Isidora Duncan', mentioned before, reflects transnational bourgeois class affinities, mirroring themselves in classical European culture. Chinese tacos and Irish bagels reflect ethnic crossover in employment patterns in the American fast food sector. Asian rap refers to cross-cultural stylistic convergence in popular youth culture.

An episode that can serve to probe this more deeply is the influence of Japanese art on European painting. The impact of *Japonisme* is well known: it inspired impressionism which in turn set the stage for modernism. The colour woodcuts that made such a profound impression on Seurat, Manet, Van Gogh, Toulouse Lautrec, Whistler belonged to the Ukiyo school – a bourgeois genre that flourished in Japan between the seventeenth and nineteenth centuries, sponsored by the merchant class. Ukiyo-e typically depicted urban scenes of ephemeral character, such as streetlife, enter-tainments, theatre, or prostitution, and also landscapes. It was a popular art form which, unlike the high art of aristocracy, was readily available at reasonable prices in book stores (rather than cloistered in courts or monasteries) and therefore also accessible to Europeans (Budde, 1993). This episode, then, is not so much an exotic irruption in European culture, but rather reflects the fact that bourgeois sensibilities had found iconogra-phic expression in Japan earlier than in Europe. In other words, Japanese popular art was modern before European art was. Thus what from one angle appears as hybridity to the point of exoticism, from another angle, again, reflects transcultural class affinities in sensibilities *vis à vis* urban life and nature. In other words, the other side of cultural hybridity is transcultural convergence.

What makes it difficult to discuss these issues is that two quite distinct concepts of *culture* are generally being used indiscriminately. The first

concept of culture (culture 1) views culture as essentially territorial; it assumes that culture stems from a learning process that is, in the main, localized. This is culture in the sense of *a culture*, that is the culture of a society or
social group. A notion that goes back to nineteenth-century romanticism
and that has been elaborated in twentieth-century anthropology, in particular cultural relativism – with the notion of cultures as a whole, a Gestalt,
configuration. A related idea is the organic or 'tree' model of culture.

A wider understanding of culture (culture 2) views culture as a general
human 'software' (Banuri, 1990: 77), as in nature/culture arguments. This
notion has been implicit in theories of evolution and diffusion, in which culture is viewed as, in the main, a *translocal* learning process. These understandings are not incompatible: culture 2 finds expression in culture 1,
cultures are the vehicle of culture. But they do reflect different emphases in
relation to historical processes of culture formation and hence generate
markedly different assessments of cultural relations. Divergent meta-
assumptions about culture underlie the varied vocabularies in which cultural
relations are discussed.

Assumptions about culture

Territorial culture	Translocal culture
endogenous	exogenous
orthogenetic	heterogenetic
societies, nations, empires	diasporas, migrations
locales, regions	crossroads, borders, interstices
community-based	networks, brokers, strangers
organic, unitary	diffusion, heterogeneity
authenticity	translation
inward looking	outward looking
community linguistics	contact linguistics[6]
race	half-caste, mixed-breed, métis
ethnicity	new ethnicity
identity	identification, new identity

Culture 2 or translocal culture is not without place (there is no culture
without place), but it involves an *outward-looking* sense of place, whereas
culture 1 is based on an *inward-looking* sense of place. Culture 2 involves
what Doreen Massey calls 'a global sense of place': 'the specificity of place
which derives from the fact that each place is the focus of a distinct *mixture* of
wider and more local social relations' (1993: 240).

The general terminology of cultural pluralism, multicultural society, intercultural relations, etc. does not clarify whether it refers to culture 1 or
culture 2. Thus, relations among cultures can be viewed in a static fashion (in
which cultures retain their separateness in interaction) or a fluid fashion (in
which cultures interpenetrate).

Cultural relations

Static	Fluid
plural society (Furnivall)	pluralism, melting pot
multiculturalism (static)	multiculturalism (fluid), interculturalism

| global mosaic | cultural flow in space (Hannerz) |
| clash of civilizations | third cultures |

Hybridization as a perspective belongs to the fluid end of relations between cultures: it's the mixing of cultures and not their separateness that is emphasized. At the same time, the underlying assumption about culture is that of culture/place. Cultural forms are called hybrid/syncretic/mixed/creolized because the elements in the mix derive from different cultural contexts. Thus Ulf Hannerz defines creole cultures as follows: 'creole cultures like creole languages are those which draw in some way on two or more historical sources, often originally widely different. They have had some time to develop and integrate, and to become elaborate and pervasive' (1987: 552). But, in this sense, would not every culture be a creole culture? Can we identify any culture that is *not* creole in the sense of drawing on one or more different historical sources?[7] A scholar of music makes a similar point about world music: 'all music is essentially world music' (Bor, 1994: 2).

A further question is: are cultural elements different merely because they originate from different cultures? More often what may be at issue, as argued above, is the *similarity* of cultural elements when viewed from the point of class, status group, life-style sensibilities or function. Hence, at some stage, towards the end of the story, the notion of cultural hybridity itself unravels or, at least, needs reworking.

To explore what this means in the context of globalization, we can contrast the vocabularies and connotations of globalization-as-homogenization and globalization-as-hybridization.

Globalization/homogenization	*Globalization/diversification*
cultural imperialism	cultural planetarization
cultural dependence	cultural interdependence
cultural hegemony	cultural interpenetration
autonomy	syncretism, synthesis, hybridity
modernization	modernizations
Westernization	global mélange
cultural synchronization	creolization, crossover
world civilization	global ecumene

What is common to some perspectives on both sides of the globalization/homogenization/heterogenization axis is a territorial view of culture. The territoriality of culture, however, itself is not constant over time. For some time we have entered a period of accelerated globalization and cultural mixing. This also involves an overall tendency towards the 'deterritorialization' of culture, or an overall shift in orientation from culture 1 to culture 2. Introverted cultures, which have been prominent over a long stretch of history and which overshadowed translocal culture, are gradually receding into the background, while translocal culture made up of diverse elements is coming into the foreground. This transition and the hybridization processes themselves unleash intense and dramatic nostalgia politics, of which ethnic upsurges, ethnicization of nations, and religious revivalism form part.

Hybridization refers not only to the crisscrossing of cultures (culture 1) but also and by the same token to a transition from the provenance of culture 1 to culture 2. Another aspect of this transition is that due to advancing information technology and biotechnology, different *modes* of hybridity emerge on the horizon: in the light of hybrid forms, such as cyborgs, virtual reality and electronic simulation, intercultural differences may begin to pale to relative insignificance – although of great local intensity. Biotechnology opens up the perspective of 'merged evolution', in the sense of the merger of the evolutionary streams of genetics, cultural evolution and information technology, and the near prospect of humans intervening in genetic evolution, through the matrix of cultural evolution and information technologies (Goonatilake, 1994).

Conclusion: towards a global sociology

Globalization/hybridization makes, first, an empirical case: that processes of globalization, past and present, can be adequately described as processes of hybridization. Secondly, it is a critical argument: against viewing globalization in terms of homogenization, or of modernization/ Westernization, as empirically narrow and historically flat.

The career of sociology has been coterminous with the career of nation-state formation and nationalism, and from this followed the consti- tution of the object of sociology as society and the equation of society with the nation. Culminating in structural functionalism and modernization theory, this career in the context of globalization is in for retooling. A global sociology is taking shape, around notions such as social networks (rather than 'societies'), border zones, boundary crossing and global society. In other words, a sociology conceived within the framework of nations/ societies is making place for a post-inter/national sociology of hybrid formations, times and spaces.

Structural hybridization, or the increase in the range of organizational options, and cultural hybridization, or the doors of erstwhile imagined communities opening up, are signs of an age of boundary crossing. Not, surely, of the erasure of boundaries. Thus, state power remains extremely strategic, but it is no longer the only game in town. The tide of globalization reduces the room of manoeuvre for states, while international institutions, transnational transactions, regional co-operation, sub-national dynamics and non-governmental organizations expand in impact and scope (Griffin and Khan, 1992; Walker, 1988).

In historical terms, this perspective may be deepened by writing diaspora histories of global culture. Due to nationalism as the dominant paradigm since the nineteenth century, cultural achievements have been routinely claimed for 'nations' – that is, culture has been 'nationalized', territoria- lized. A different historical record can be constructed on the basis of the contributions to culture formation and diffusion by diasporas, migrations, strangers, brokers. A related project would be histories of the hybridization of metropolitan cultures, that is a counter-history to the narrative of imperial history. Such historical inquiries may show that hybridization has been taking place all along but over time has been concealed by religious, national, imperial and civilizational chauvinism. Moreover, they may deepen our understanding of the temporalities of hybridization: how certain junctures witness downturns or upswings of hybridization, slowdowns or speed-ups. At the same time it follows that, if we accept that cultures have been hybrid *all along*, hybridization is in effect a tautology: contemporary accelerated globalization means the hybridization of hybrid cultures.

As such, the hybridization perspective remains meaningful only as a critique of essentialism. Essentialism will remain strategic as a mobilizational device as long as the units of nation, state, region, civilization, ethnicity remain strategic: and for just as long hybridization remains a relevant approach. Hybridity unsettles the introverted concept of culture which underlies romantic nationalism, racism, ethnicism, religious revivalism, civilizational chauvinism, and culturalist essentialism. Hybridization, then, is a perspective that is meaningful as a counterweight to the introverted notion of culture; at the same time, the very process of hybridization unsettles the introverted gaze, and accordingly, hybridization eventually ushers in post-hybridity, or transcultural cut and mix.

Hybridization is a factor in the reorganization of social spaces. Structural hybridization, or the emergence of new practices of social co-operation and competition, and cultural hybridization, or new translocal cultural expressions, are interdependent: new forms of co-operation require and evoke new cultural imaginaries. Hybridization is a contribution to a sociology of the in-between, a sociology from the interstices. This involves merging endogenous/exogenous understandings of culture. This parallels the attempt in international relations theory to overcome the dualism between the nation-state and international system perspectives. Other significant perspectives are Hannerz' macro-anthropology and his concern with mapping micro-macro linkages (1992) and contemporary work in geography and cultural studies (for example, Bird et al., 1993).

In relation to the global human condition of inequality, the hybridization perspective releases reflection and engagement from the boundaries of nation, community, ethnicity, or class. Fixities have become fragments as the kaleidoscope of collective experience is in motion. It has been in motion all along and the fixities of nation, community, ethnicity and class have been grids superimposed upon experiences more complex and subtle than reflexivity and organization could accommodate.

Notes

1. An equivalent view in international relations is Morse, 1976. After having argued for globalizations in the plural, I will still continue to use globalization singular in this text

because it matches conventional usage and because there's no need to stress the point by way of inelegant grammar.

2. The mélange element comes across for instance in the definition of semiperiphery of Chase-Dunn and Hall (1993: 865–6): '(1) a semiperipheral region may be one that mixes both core and peripheral forms of organization; (2) a semiperipheral region may be spatially located between core and peripheral regions; (3) mediating activities between core and peripheral regions may be carried out in semiperipheral regions; (4) a semiperipheral area may be one in which institutional features are in some ways intermediate between those forms found in core and periphery'. Interestingly, Chase-Dunn and Hall also destabilize the notions of core and periphery, pointing for instance to situations 'in which the "periphery" systematically exploits the "core"' (1993: 864). I am indebted to an anonymous reviewer of *International Sociology* for alerting me to this source and to the relevance of semiperiphery in this context.

3. Elsewhere I've argued this case extensively (Nederveen Pieterse, 1994; also 1990: Ch. 15).

4. As against *peninsulares*, born in the Iberian peninsula, *indigenes*, or native Americans, and *ladinos* and *cholos*, straddled betwixt those of European and native American descent.

5. In *Pour Rushdie* (1993), a collection of essays by Arab and Islamic intellectuals in support of freedom of expression, Paris is referred to as a 'capitale arabe'. This evokes another notion of hybridity, one that claims a collective ground and is based on multiple subjectivities in the name of a universal value.

6. Mary Louise Pratt distinguishes between a linguistics of community and a linguistics of contact (quoted in Hannerz, 1989: 210–11).

7. Several of the 'primitive isolates', the traditional study objects of anthropology, may be possible exceptions, although even this may be questioned in the context of the long stretch of time.

References

Abdel-Malek, A. (1981) *Civilizations and Social Theory*, 2 vols. London: Macmillan.

Albrow, M. (1990) 'Introduction', in M. Albrow and E. King (eds), *Globalization, Knowledge and Society*. London: Sage.

Ambrose, S. E. (1971) *Rise to Globalism: American Foreign Policy since 1938*. London: Allen Lane.

Amin, S. (1990) *Delinking: Towards a Polycentric World*. London: Zed. (Orig. French edn 1985.)

Anderson, B. (1992) 'The new world disorder', *New Left Review*, 190: 3–14.

Anzaldúa, G. (1987) *Borderland/La Frontera*. San Francisco: Spinsters/Ann Lute.

Appadurai, A. (1990) 'Disjuncture and difference in the global political economy', in M. Featherstone (ed.), *Global Culture: Nationalism, Globalization and Modernity*. London: Sage. pp. 295–310.

Arnason, J.P. (1990) 'Nationalism, globalization and modernity', in M. Featherstone (ed.), *Global Culture: Nationalism, Globalization and Modernity*. London: Sage. pp. 207–36.

Avneri, U. (1986) *My Friend the Enemy*. London: Zed.

Bakhtin, M. (1968) *Rabelais and his World*. Cambridge, MA: MIT Press.

Banuri, T. (1990) 'Modernization and its Discontents: a cultural perspective on theories of development', in F. Appfel Marglin and S.A. Marglin (eds), *Dominating Knowledge*. Oxford: Clarendon Press. pp.73–101.

Bateson, G. (1972) *Steps to an Ecology of Mind*. San Francisco: Chandler.

Bauman, Z. (1989) *Modernity and the Holocaust*. Ithaca, NY: Cornell University Press.

Bérubé, M. (1992) 'Hybridity in the center: an interview with Houston A. Baker, Jr', *African American Review*, 26 (4): 547–64.

Bhabha, H.K. (1990) 'DissemiNation: time, narrative and the margins of the modern nation', in H.K. Bhabha (ed.), *Nation and Narration*. London: Routledge.

Bird, J. et al. (eds) (1993) *Mapping the Futures: Local Cultures, Global Change*. London: Routledge.

Bor, J. (1994) 'Studying world music: the next phase', unpublished paper.

Brennan, T. (1989) *Salman Rushdie and the Third World: Myths of the Nation*. New York: St Martin's Press.

Budde, H. (1993) 'Japanische Farbholzschnitte und europäische Kunst: Maler und Sammler im 19. Jahrhundert', in D. Croissant et al. (eds), *Japan und Europa 1543–1929*. Berlin: Berliner Festspiele/Argon.

Caldéron, F. (1988) 'América Latina, identitad y tiempos mixtos, o cómo pensar la modernidad sin dejar de ser boliviano', in *Imágenes desconocidas*. Buenos Aires: Ed CLACSO. pp. 225–9.

Canevacci, M. (1993) 'Fragmented identity, governmental policy and cultural syncretism', unpublished paper.

Canevacci, M. (1992) 'Image accumulation and cultural syncretism', *Theory, Culture & Society*, 9 (3): 95–110.

Chase-Dunn, C. and Hall, T.D. (1993) 'Comparing world-systems: concepts and working hypotheses', *Social Forces*, 72 (1): 851–86.

Cox, R.W. (1992) 'Global perestroika', in R. Miliband and L. Panitch (eds), *New World Order? Socialist Register 1992*. London: Merlin Press. pp. 26–43.

Curtin, P.D. (1984) *Cross-cultural Trade in World History*. Cambridge: Cambridge University Press.

Defourny, J. and Monzón Campos, J.L. (eds) (1992) *The Third Sector: Cooperative, Mutual and Nonprofit Organizations*. Brussels: De Boeck.

Doyle, M.W. (1986) *Empires*. Ithaca, NY: Cornell University Press.

Enloe, C. (1989) *Bananas Beaches and Bases: Making Feminist Sense of International Politics*. Berkeley: University of California Press.

Featherstone, M. (ed.) (1990) *Global Culture: Nationalism, Globalization and Modernity*. London: Sage.

Feddema, R. (1992) 'Op weg tussen hoop en vrees: de levensoriëntatie van jonge Turken en Marokkanen in Nederland'. Utrecht University, Ph.D dissertation.

Fischer, M.M.J. (1992) 'Orientalizing America: beginnings and middle passages', *Middle East Report*, 22 (5): 32–7.

Friedman, J. (1990) 'Being in the World: globalization and localization', in M. Featherstone (ed.), *Global Culture: Nationalism, Globalization and Modernity*. London: Sage. pp. 311–28.

Giddens, A. (1990) *The Consequences of Modernity*. Stanford, CA: Stanford University Press.

Goonatilake, S. (1994) 'Merged evolution: the long term implications of biotechnology and information technology', unpublished manuscript.

Graham, R. (ed.) (1990) *The Idea of Race in Latin America 1870–1940*. Austin: University of Texas Press.

Greenfeld, L. (1992) *Nationalism: Five Roads to Modernity*. Cambridge, MA: Harvard University Press.

Griffin, K. and Khan, A.R. (1992) *Globalization and the Developing World*. Geneva: UNRISD.

Gurtov, M. (1988) *Global Politics in the Human Interest*. Boulder, CO and London: Lynne Rienner.

Hamelink, C.J. (1983) *Cultural Autonomy in Global Communications*. New York: Longman.

Hannerz, U. (1987) 'The world in Creolisation', *Africa*, 57 (4): 546–59.

Hannerz, U. (1989) 'Culture between center and periphery: toward a macro-anthropology', *Ethnos*, 54: 200–16.

Hannerz, U. (1992) *Cultural Complexity*. New York: Columbia University Press.

Harris, N. (1990) *National Liberation*. London: Tauris.

Hechter, M. (1975) *Internal Colonialism: The Celtic Fringe in British National Development, 1536–1966*. London: Routledge & Kegan Paul.

Hegedus, Z. (1989) 'Social movements and social change in self-creative society: new civil initiatives in the international arena', *International Sociology*, 4 (1): 19–36.

Held, D. (1992) 'Democracy: from city-states to a cosmopolitan order?', in D. Held (ed.), *Prospects for Democracy*. Cambridge: Polity Press. pp. 13–52.

Held, D. and McGrew, A. (1993) 'Globalization and the liberal democratic state', *Government and Opposition*, 28 (2): 261–88.

Helly, D. O. and Reverby, S.M. (eds) (1992) *Gendered Domains: Rethinking Public and Private in Women's History*. Ithaca, NY: Cornell University Press.

Henderson, J. (1989) *The Globalization of High Technology Production*. New York: Routledge.

Hösle, V. (1992) 'The Third World as a philosophical problem', *Social Research*, 59 (2): 227–62.

King, A.D. (ed.) (1991) *Culture, Globalization and the World-System: Contemporary Conditions for the Representation of Identity*. London: Macmillan.

Kothari, R. (1988) *Rethinking Development*. Delhi: Ajanta.

Kreidt, D. (1987) '"Kann uns zum Vaterland die Fremde werden?" Exotismus im Schauspieltheater', in *Exotische Welten, Europäische Phantasien*. Wurttemberg: Cantz. pp. 248–55.

Lavie, S. (1992) 'Blow-ups in the borderzones: Third World Israeli authors' gropings for home', *New Formations*, 18: 84–106.

Li, L. (1989) 'Theoretical theses on "social modernization"', *International Sociology*, 4 (4): 365–78.

Lipschutz, R.D. (1992) 'Reconstructing world politics: the emergence of global civil society', *Millennium*, 21 (3): 389–420.

Lowe, L. (1991) 'Heterogeneity, hybridity, multiplicity: marking Asian American differences', *Diaspora*, 1 (1): 24–44.

Mann, M. (1986) *The Sources of Social Power*. Cambridge: Cambridge University Press.

Massey, D. (1993) 'A global sense of place', in A. Gray and J. McGuigan (eds), *Studying Culture*. London: Edward Arnold. pp. 232–40.

Mazlish, B. and Buultjens, R. (eds) (1993) *Conceptualizing Global History*. Boulder, CO: Westview.

McGrew, A.G. and Lewis, P.G. (eds) (1992) *Global Politics*. Cambridge: Polity Press.

Melucci, A. (1989) *Nomads of the Present*. London: Hutchinson Radius.

Miliband, R. and Panitch, L. (eds) (1992) *New World Order? Socialist Register 1992*. London: Merlin Press.

Morse, E.L. (1976) *Modernization and the Transformation of International Relations*. New York: Free Press.

Nandy, A. (1983) *The Intimate Enemy: Loss and Recovery of Self under Colonialism*. New Delhi: Oxford University Press.

Nederveen Pieterse, J.P. (1987) 'A critique of world-system theory', *International Sociology*, 3 (3): 251–66.

Nederveen Pieterse, J.P. (1990) *Empire and Emancipation: Power and Liberation on a World Scale*. London: Pluto Press.

Nederveen Pieterse, J.P. (1993) 'The development of development theory: towards critical globalism', *Tidskriftet Grus*, 13 (38): 5–22 (Danish translation).

Nederveen Pieterse, J.P. (1994) 'Unpacking the West: how European is Europe?', in A. Rattansi and S. Westwood (eds), *Racism, Modernity, Identity: On the Western Front*. Cambridge: Polity Press. pp. 129–49.

Nelson, B. (1981) *On the Roads to Modernity* (ed. T. E. Huff). Totowa, NJ: Rowman and Littlefield.

Parekh, B. (1992) 'The cultural particularity of liberal democracy', in D. Held (ed.), *Prospects for Democracy*. Cambridge: Polity Press. pp. 156–75.

Park, Sung-Jo (ed.) (1985) *The 21st Century – the Asian Century?* Berlin: EXpress Edition.

Petras, J. and Brill, H. (1985) 'The tyranny of globalism', *Journal of Contemporary Asia*, 15 (4): 403–20.

Pour Rushdie (1993). Paris: Eds La Découverte/Carrefour des littératures/Colibri.

Pred, A. and Watts, M.J. (1992) *Reworking Modernity: Capitalisms and Symbolic Discontent*. New Brunswick, NJ: Rutgers University Press.

Roberts, B. (1978) *Cities of Peasants: The Political Economy of Urbanization in the Third World*. London: Edward Arnold.

Robertson, R. (1992) *Globalization*. London: Sage.

Robertson, R. (1994) 'Glocalization: space, time and social theory', *Journal of International Communication*, 1 (1).

Rosenau, J.N. (1990) *Turbulence in World Politics*. Brighton: Harvester.

Rowe, W. and Schelling, V. (1991) *Memory and Modernity: popular culture in Latin America*. London: Verso.

Sassen, S. (1991) *The Global City: New York, London, Tokyo*. Princeton, NJ: Princeton UP.

Schiller, H.I. (1989) *Culture Inc*. New York: Oxford University Press.

Sharabi, H. (1988) *Neopatriarchy: A Theory of Distorted Change in Arab Society*. New York: Oxford University Press.

Shaw, M. (1992) 'Global society and global responsibility: the theoretical, historical and political limits of "international society"', *Millenium*, 21 (3): 421–34.

Shaw, T. (1986) 'Ethnicity as the resilient paradigm for Africa: from the 1960s to the 1980s', *Development and Change*, 17 (4): 587–606.

Shohat, E. (1992) 'Notes on the "post-colonial"', *Social Text*, 31/32: 99–113.

Singh, Y. (1989) *Essays on Modernization in India*. New Delhi: Manohar.

Smith, A.D. (1990) 'Towards a global culture?', in M. Featherstone (ed.), *Global Culture: Nationalism, Globalization and Modernity*. London: Sage. pp. 171–92.

Sonoda, S. (1990) 'Modernization of Asian countries as a process of "overcoming their backwardness": the case of modernization in China', paper presented to 12th World Congress of Sociology, Madrid.

Terhal, P.H.J.J. (1987) *World Inequality and Evolutionary Convergence*. Delft: Eburon.

Therborn, G. (1992) 'Routes to/through modernity', unpublished paper.

Thompson, R.F. (1984) *Flash of the Spirit: African and Afro-American Art and Philosophy*. New York: Vintage.

Tiryakian, E.A. (1991) 'Modernization: Exhumetur in Pace', *International Sociology*, 6 (2): 165–80.

Tominaga, K. (1990) 'A theory of modernization of non-Western societies: toward a generalization from historical experiences of Japan', paper presented to 12th World Congress of Sociology, Madrid.

Tomlinson, J. (1991) *Cultural Imperialism*. Baltimore: Johns Hopkins University Press.

Vargas, V. (1992) 'The feminist movement in Latin America: between hope and disenchantment', in J.P. Nederveen Pieterse (ed.), *Emancipations, Modern and Postmodern*. London: Sage. pp. 195–214.

Wachtel, H.M. (1990) *The Money Mandarins: The Making of a Supranational Economic Order*. Armonk, NY: M.E. Sharpe.

Walker, R.B.J. (1988) *One World, Many Worlds*. Boulder, CO: Lynne Rienner.

Whitten, Jr, N.E. and Torres, A. (1992) 'Blackness in the Americas', *Report on the Americas*, 25 (4): 16–22.

Willets, P. (ed.) (1982) *Pressure Groups in the Global System*. London: Pinter.

Young, I.M. (1990) *Justice and the Politics of Difference*. Princeton, NJ: Princeton University Press.

4

GLOBAL SYSTEM, GLOBALIZATION AND THE PARAMETERS OF MODERNITY

Jonathan Friedman

Two versions of the global

There are today many versions of global theorizing and analysis and there is all too often a tendency to conflate them, even where they represent virtually opposing views of the nature of the 'global'. Below I should like to distinguish two very different approaches to global process. The first is a rather recent development combining interests from literary studies, Birmingham inspired cultural sociology,[1] which has focused on globalization as a recognition of what is conceived as increasing world-wide interconnections, interchanges and movements of people, images and commodities. The second is what I shall refer to as the global systems approach, which developed somewhat earlier as a kind of global historical political economy and which has more recently begun to tackle questions of culture and identity in global systemic terms. There is, of course, some overlap in these very broad approaches, but there has often been a critique levelled by the former at the latter, one that is less argued than asserted. Researchers such as Robertson (1992) and, to a lesser degree, Hannerz (1987) have complained of the lack of culture in the analyses of world system researchers, often as if to imply that the point of departure of such analyses was somehow wrong. While it is surely the case that world system theorists have been primarily concerned with political economic phenomena, this does not exclude an adequate approach to so-called issues of culture in such a framework, nor even a unified approach in which cultural specificity is an aspect of other social phenomena. We shall be arguing that many of the categories of globalization discourse are ideological products of a specific form of identity space, often referred to as 'modernity', which is itself a product of the modern world system.

(1) Globalization

In recent years there has developed a relatively large literature dealing with globalization. Much of this discussion has centred on what at first appeared to be an aspect of the hierarchical nature of imperialism, that is, the increasing hegemony of particular central cultures, the diffusion of American values, consumer goods and lifestyles. In some of the earliest discussions it was referred to as 'cultural imperialism' and there was great alarm concerning the obliteration of cultural differences in the world, not just in the official 'economic' periphery but in Western Europe where, in the late 1950s and 1960s, there was a genuine fear, at least among the cultural elites, of the *défi americain* and the hegemony of Coca Cola culture. Today this theme has been developed primarily in the work of cultural sociologists and, more recently, among anthropologists, into a more complex understanding of cultural processes that span large regions of the world. Robertson has recently formulated the question of globality as a duality of objective and subjective processes. 'Globalization refers both to the compression of the world and to the intensification of the consciousness of the world as a whole' (1992: 8).

He refers here to both an increase in global interdependence and the awareness of that interdependence. He goes so far as to suggest, contrary to his earlier articles (for example, 1991), that this compression has been going on for more than merely the past century, even for a millennium or more, although it did not always have the same character. Now, in fact, the reference to compression is not unpacked with respect to the actual processes that might be involved, and Robertson is almost wholly concerned with the problem of consciousness and culture. The very notion of compression refers to diminished distance among parts, to implosion, to the kinds of phenomena detailed among proponents of the 'global village'. Such mechanisms are related to technological speed-up and what Harvey in more precise terms has called time–space compression, referring to the rate of transport of people, sound, pictures and any other forms of information, including, of course, money. In his analysis they do not just happen because of scientific development or some neutral technological evolution. They are driven by the process of capital accumulation, that is, the specific social form of those strategies that organize the world economy. For Robertson, however, the fact of global interdependence is the exclusive aspect of the global system relevant to his argument, and it enables him to relegate all other system properties, not least the economic, political and social structural, to the sidelines of his more restricted interest in globalization as awareness of the fact.

The essential character of globalization resides here in the consciousness of the global, that is, individual consciousness of the global situation, specifically that the world is an arena in which we all participate. There are numerous aspects of this awareness. That to which Robertson addresses himself is simply the universal as a more or less concrete experienced representation, an understanding that we are all part of something bigger. Of course this might as well be God or the Absolute Spirit, as the world of humankind. And the awareness of the universal existence of 'humankind' can hardly be dated to what he has described as the twentieth-century

GLOBALIZATION AS A PROBLEM

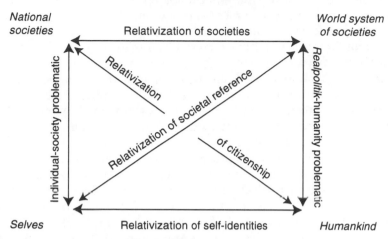

Figure 4.1 *Robertson's model of globalization*

emergence of the world system. His discussion, following Parsons, concentrates on the interplay of particularism and universalism, contrasting a globalization in the total sense, the idea of humanity as such and a universalization of particularisms as in nationalism. This latter phenomenon is not understood as fragmentation but as diffusion of an idea, that is, the social circumstances of the emergence of local identities are treated very much as an intellectual or cognitive globalization.

Robertson posits four distinct yet related elements that form the framework of global processes. These are: selves (individuals), nation-states, humankind and the world system of nation-states. These emergent forms are linked in the period 1870–1920 by means of a series of relations that is shown in Figure 4.1.

This diagram is concerned to illustrate essential processes of relativization involved in the progression toward the experience of globality. The top of the diagram, the relativization of societies is, as I understand it, the awareness of the larger field of interaction among states, where the bottom concerns the expansion of individual identity to include all of humankind. The hypothesis is, in any case, that the world is becoming more of a single unity. He does not predict the withering away of the state, of course, and stresses that the emergence of the nation-state is itself a product of global diffusion that organizes the global field. All of the linkages between the terms are cognitive or discursive in nature. I would place these terms in the framework of what I shall refer to later as the identity space of modernity, which is itself a product of developing global systems, but not equivalent to the global as such. The relativizations are expressions of processes of differentiation/separation in modernity.[2] Thus the notion of 'humankind' is not so much an awareness of the larger world as a universalized vision of that world dependent upon the process of individualization itself. The organization of the world into ethno-species or races is an alternative form of identification of 'the other' in the same system. The recognition of a larger arena of politics and economics among state units, of course, can take several different forms, from imperial hierarchy to world competition. Robertson's diagram says nothing about the nature of the relativization process, nor about the way it might change over time. On the contrary it details a mere recognition, one that is not discovered in the world, but merely posited, that is, Robertson's own recognition of the globalized state of the world, the cognition of the cosmopolitan intellectual.

Robertson does not, as I have underscored, maintain that we are all becoming identical to one another. On the contrary, he argues for two interpenetrating processes: the universalization of particularism (as in the nation-state) and the particularization of universalism (the appropriation of the universal in local contexts, that is, nationalized modernism, Japanese Buddhism). This fundamental cultural dynamic of the global is paralleled in other discussions of globalization (Appadurai, 1990; Friedman, 1991; Hannerz, 1991) in slightly different ways. Here there is also another kind of reasoning, one that cannot easily be reduced to questions of meaning and interpretation. In a more recent discussion he stresses the way in which the local is itself a global product, in which the particular is an aspect of globalization rather than its complementary opposite. A whole series of local and localizing phenomena – ethnicity, nationalism, indigenous movements – can be understood as global products. Localizing strategies are themselves inherently global. Here I feel that Robertson may have overemphasized the mental or semantic aspect of such phenomena. He stresses, for example, the 'standardization' of locality, as if the latter were an exported plan or idea rather than a social situation or context. In our own approach, such localized similarities are the result of the global social forces and conditions that provoke similar reactions and articulations. While Robertson is not always clear, it would appear that global culture is the basis of a carbon-copy spread of nation-states in this century. 'The proliferation of – in many ways similar – nation states in the twentieth century has, in this view, to be explained in reference to the crystallization of global political culture' (Robertson, 1992: 69).

This process, neatly summarized by the expression 'crystallization of global political culture', is, in fact, a process involving the global institutionalization of political structures directly related to colonial and postcolonial hierarchy and the formation of international organs of regulation such as the United Nations, aid organizations, etc. Robertson also seems to argue that the global is very much a question of competing interpretations of 'global circumstances' and that the latter are constituting aspects of the system itself, but he provides no alternative to the political-economy models on their own ground. Awareness of the globe, communication between its regions, competing interpretations of the globe are not specific enough, it seems to me, to provide a dynamic understanding of global processes. The fact that fundamentalisms, for example, provide alternative visions of the global situation, does not explain their emergence and power, nor the more interesting temporal parallel between such movements and other ethnic, indigenous and communal movements.

In my own terms, globalization is very much about global awarenesses but also about the way in which they are established in definite periods of the history of already existing global systems. Globalization is about processes of attribution of meaning that are of a global nature. This should not be conflated with global processes of attribution that are local, such as nationalisms, ethnicities, balkanizations, which are in fact localizations rather than globalizations.[3] Robertson's universal religions establish transnational identities, but they can only do so if those who participate in them actually identify as such. Buddhism, for example, is very local in Sri Lanka, where it is strongly tied to the constitution of the state itself. Its more ecumenical versions in California and elsewhere, as global movements, have a very different focus. The fact that Nigerians watch *Dallas* might be a very localized phenomenon among actual viewers who, even while they are aware of the imported (that is, global) status of the programme, may use such status to define a set of local hierarchical relations that bear little resemblance to the society that produced the programme. But the cosmopolitan who chuckles at this fact is the true representative of globalization since the meaning that he attributes to the appearance of *Dallas* in Africa *is* global in nature, the meaning of the cosmopolitan, equivalent, I would argue, to the meaning of the modern. The formation of ethnicities and nations, while a global product, cannot be understood in terms of cultural diffusion. While Robertson apparently agrees with Wallerstein's characterization of nationalism as a global phenomenon, the latter sees it in terms of global forces and relations themselves and not the spread of an idea. Particularization is a product of the global system in particular phases of its 'development' and not a general characteristic of the 'global field'. For example, the appearance of Fourth World movements for the re-establishment of cultural-political autonomy among indigenous peoples is a global process in social terms. It is a change in identification that has accompanied the decline of modernist identity in the hegemonic centres of the world system. Yet the forum offered by the World Council of Indigenous Peoples, the large number of media reports, Hollywood films such as *Dancing with Wolves* have all heightened the representability of Fourth World peoples as such. The latter phenomenon is globalization, but here too, its appearance now is a determinate product of the global system in a phase of decentralization and de-hegemonization.

(2) Global system

Globalization refers to processes that are usually designated as cultural, that is, concerned with the attribution of meaning in the global arena. The global arena is the precondition for globalization. It is, for example, the precondition for the formation of local identities such as nation-states, Third and Fourth Worlds, ethnicities, religious movements. While the latter are localizing strategies, they are globally generated (though not in the sense of 'globalization'). The global arena is a product of a definite set of dynamic properties, including the formation of centre/periphery structures, their expansion, contraction, fragmentation and re-establishment throughout cycles of shifting hegemony. This set of dynamic properties, which have been discussed in some detail in other publications (Ekholm, 1975; Ekholm and Friedman, 1980; Friedman, 1992), are what we refer to as the global system, or global process. There are numerous cultural processes that are directly generated in global systems. These are the processes of identity formation and fragmentation referred to above. There are other phenomena that are less systemic, such as Marco Polo's gift of pasta from China. Marco Polo's voyages were certainly part of a systemic process, but the fact of pasta as opposed to other products is more difficult to argue for in systemic terms. The introduction of pasta into the cuisine of the Italian peninsula is a process of globalization, and the final elaboration of a pasta-based Italian cuisine is, in metaphorical terms, a process of cultural syncretism, or perhaps creolization. But such mixture is only interesting in terms of the practice of local identity, and not in terms of the cosmopolitan's identification of the origins of specific elements. Thus the fact that pasta became Italian, and that its Chinese origin became irrelevant is the essential culture-producing process in this case. Whether origins are maintained or obliterated is a question of the practice of identity. The nature of the culture of a territory is reducible to the question of identification and thus of identity. I would argue here that the practice of identification is properly a question of global systems and not of globalization. The latter is the product of the former. The practice of identity constitutes and transforms the actors in the system and is the dynamic behind the creation of specific configurations of meaning. This implies that the above discussion of globalization is more properly about the global systemic mechanisms of globalization.

Global systems include globalization processes. They include the establishment of global institutional forms and global processes of identification and their cultural products. But global processes have also been the major forces of social transformation of large parts of the world even without the establishment of regular institutional networks. The collapse and transformation of great empires in both the Old and New World, the metamorphosis of 'tribal' social systems as the result of the reorientation of trade, the formation of colonial societies, the production of hunters and gatherers and chiefdoms as well as pluralism, lumpenproletariats and state classes are all part and parcel of the global system, that is, engendered by global processes. I have argued for many years that the world investigated by anthropologists is a world already transformed structurally by its integration into the global system (Ekholm and Friedman, 1980). Most of our research in what we have called global systemic anthropology has focused on the integrative transformational processes that have generated the 'ethnographic present' that ethnography, also a global system product, has translated into discourses on Western identity, the discourses of evolutionism, relativism, of society as a self-contained organism, of culture as substance. The global system has pervaded the real transformation of the world's societies as well as the centre's representations of the results of that transformation. Now it ought not be necessary to. insist that social transformation is also cultural transformation. The emergence of cannibalism, large scale witchcraft, Frazerian sacred kings, and new clan structures in late nineteenth-century Central Africa is a product of a catastrophic transformation of the entire region. The latter are major cultural changes, novelties in important respects, discontinuities even if there are clear transformational continuities (Ekholm-Friedman, 1991).

The global system involves the articulation between expanding/contracting central 'sectors' and their emergent/disappearing peripheries. This articulation is one of decisive transformation of life forms in the broadest sense of the word. It is, moreover, a long-term historical process that can only be adequately understood as such. The historical processes of global systems possess specific properties, such as expansion/contraction, hegemonization/fragmentation, that inform and limit the conditions of existence, reactions and cultural strategies of those who participate in them. We shall be arguing that there is an immediate relation between the life conditions that tend to differentially emerge in such systems and the generation of what we refer to below as 'identity spaces' from which culturally specific institutional/representational forms are produced. Such forms include the way central powers classify the world, and how these classifications change over time, how, when and where such notions as modernism, primitivism, traditionalism emerge, but also the variety of colonial regimes, postcolonial states, and social and cultural movements. In such terms, the identity spaces of the global system are the source for much of the content of 'globalization'.

'Globalization' refers in this context to the formation of global institutional structures, that is, structures that organize the already existing global field, and global cultural forms, that is forms that are either produced by or transformed into globally accessible objects and representations. The fact that Western intellectuals interpret the world as a single place is not in itself a fact of globalization unless it becomes a prevailing interpretation for the rest of the world system. The fact that the nation-state has become a global phenomenon is not a fact of globalization, but a global system phenomenon.[4] Balkanization is not globalization, but it is certainly a global phenomenon. Its dynamics are not about the establishment of organizations that span larger regions or even the globe, but about a transformation of the relations of self-identification in the world at a specific historic conjuncture.

Globalization in global systems: institutional process Global relations have always been most easily identifiable in terms of visible institutions, such as colonial administrations, transnational corporations, world banking, labour organizations but also international religious structures of Christianity and Islam, the media corporations, etc. One might refer to such phenomena as 'globalization' as opposed to 'global systemic processes', because they are constructed within already existing global fields. Colonial administrations reinforce and institutionalize already existent global hierarchy. Multinationals are an historically generated product of a given phase of global relations. World banking, labour organizations, religious structures, etc. are the products of projects of consolidation in already existing world orders. To clarify what is meant here we can take the example of the tourist industry, one of the largest if not *the* largest, multinational economic activity in the world. The existence of large-scale tourism has to do with emergent trends in consumption. It might be said to have emerged in the interplay of changing income structures in the centre of the system as well as changing conditions of transportation. It is, as such, a global systemic phenomenon. But the elaboration of the tourist industry as such, the construction of fantasy worlds away from home, the form of advertising, the very organizational structure of tourism is, in our terms, a question of globalization, the express creation of global social structures. Globalized structures are not new to the present global system. The mercantile companies from the fifteenth to the eighteenth centuries were globally institutionalized structures. The existence of such structures, including virtual diasporas of trade colonies set up by single companies is, furthermore, a characteristic of most commercial civilizations dating back far into the ancient world. The great empires of the past were powerful globalized organizations and just as often powerful globalizing cultures. Even in the absence of obvious imperial structures, the trade systems of the Indian Ocean and Southeast Asia produced immense institutional and cultural globalization in what is usually referred to as the Hinduization of Southeast Asia and Indonesia, and the Islamization of the Indian Ocean. Cable News Network, CNN, is a global organization producing reality for viewers in most of the world today. One of its own advertisements romantically depicts examples of its viewers from various parts of the world, here using different cultures and physical appearances in an imaged argument for the unity of mankind under CNN. Robertson's 'humankind' is also the underlying identity of the world news network itself. The socialization of the global arena in terms of regularly reproduced praxis, is the core of the institutional process of globalization.

Globalization in global systems: cultural process   It is, of course, incorrect to distinguish categorically between institutional and cultural processes, since they are simultaneous aspects of the global, thoroughly intertwined and interpenetrating. The representation of other worlds, other scenes, the primal fantasies of world travel, are embedded in the institutional organization of the tourist industry and motivate much of its activity. Mercantilist representations saturate both the practice and the self-interpretation of the great trade companies. However, I think it is necessary to make an analytical distinction here, one of aspects rather than of levels of reality. This is in order to illuminate more clearly the specific structures involved in such processes. As the writings on globalization have been self-consciously culturalist, this is even more important, since I have been arguing that globalization is a sub-set of global systemic processes.

The awareness of the global, the consciousness of an imploding world, a global village and all representations of the global, whether in fragments or wholes, from world music to world maps, are globalized products rather than merely our representations of the larger world *only* if they participate in or are otherwise part of a global arena of identification.

We can try here to specify the domain to which the term globalization, in the cultural sense, might apply:

1 What is required here is a stable frame of global reference, one that allows access from different parts of the global system to the same set of expressions or representations. This can apply to any kind of expression or representation, be it in the form of an object or an attribute.
2 In order for the globalization to be homogenizing it is also necessary for the frames of attribution of meaning to belong to the same frame as the place where the 'thing' was first produced.

The first of these requisites refers to a weak globalization. It refers merely to the existence of a global field of reference, to access beyond local communities, territories, states and regions to a wider arena. The second is the stronger form. It implies that the mechanisms of appropriation of the global have themselves become globalized, that is, that we all understand the objects and representations that circulate in the larger arena in the same way. The basis of the first form consists in all means that communicate and mediate representations in the global system and which guarantee reception of that which is produced and transported. The basis of the second lies in the creation of subjects on a global scale that interpret the world similarly. There is a continuum of possibilities here, some of whose points can be exemplified in concrete form.

For the existence of devices such as radios and televisions, able to pick up waves from various points of transmission gives rise to the following possibilities.

1 These devices need not be used as means of communication of the content of the signals they contain, but may be simply prestige items to be exchanged at marriages and funerals, or given away to clients.
2 These devices may be used in the context of communication, but in a way restricted as follows:
   (a) the language of the communication may not be understood;
   (b) the images might be understood but interpreted in terms of local context;
   (c) the images might be understood in terms of more familiar ranges of meaning attribution, that is, identifiable types of clothing, vehicles, houses, etc., and the activities of the persons represented might also

be interpreted on the basis of these more generally accessible meaningful images, but, as the language is not understood, a very wide range of interpretation on the basis of local resonances may have little or nothing to do with the original meaning attributed to the image set.

3 These devices may be used in the context of communication but in a way restricted as follows:
   (a) the language of the communication may be understood, but the context of meaning attribution might be different, that is, Shakespeare in the bush syndrome;
   (b) the images might be understood in relation to the language used and the local range of attributable meaning, but that range might also be only meaningful in terms of local contexts. X may understand that *Dallas* is about millionaires and their problems with family relations and personal ambitions, and may see analogies to their own situations, but the luxury might be so crucial for the local practice of identity and status that the themes of the story become irrelevant.

The prerequisite for strong globalization is the homogenization of local contexts, so that subjects in different positions in the system have a disposition to attribute the same meaning to the same globalized objects, images, representations, etc. Weak globalization entails that the local assimilates the global into its own realm of practised meaning. Strong globalization requires the production of similar kinds of subjects on a global scale. In order to comprehend the differences in kinds of globalization it is necessary to understand the nature of the global process itself, that is, as a social process that transforms social conditions of the production of meaning attribution.

Globalization and disillusioned cosmopolitanism   Can there be cases of transcultural, transnational meaning attribution, identity or culture? In this approach, the latter is only possible where the identification process is explicitly transcultural, that is, mixed or supranational, that is, not in between, but above. This kind of identification, we would argue, is positional in global terms, being typical of the cosmopolitan position itself. Cosmopolitan is, in identity terms, betwixt and between without being liminal. It is shifting, participating in many worlds without becoming part of them. It is the position and identity of an intellectual self situated outside of the local arenas among which he or she moves. The practice of cosmopolitanism, common to the self-styled global ethnographer of culture, is predicated on maintaining distance, often a superiority to the local. By their very self-definition, cosmopolitans are unauthentic and quintessentially 'modern', as we shall see below. By means of the installation of a continuous alterity with respect to other identities, cosmopolitans can only play roles, participate superficially in other people's realities, but can have no reality of their own other than alterity itself. Thus the opposition between cosmopolitan and local is a simple deduction from the meaning of cosmopolitan itself, a notion that presupposes the existence of at least two local cultures. The anthropologist of globalization is engaged in self-identification as he or she identifies his or her object. Now there was a time when cosmopolitans, as anthropologists, could pass themselves off as masters of otherness. This was in a world of discrete cultures, the classical mosaic of relativism. From the global systemic point of view, this was itself an illusion, the product of the imperial order of Western hegemony. As that order has collapsed, the discreteness of cultural boundaries has dissolved. The world has become, for the weary exoticist, 'a gradual spectrum of mixed-up differences' (Geertz, 1980: 147). This is, as we have argued, a symptom of disorder in power relations and not the emergence of a new truth. Anthropologists can survive in their old identity by redefining their 'object'. By identifying globalized products they become the major locus of global identification, experts on global culture. Global cultural anthropologists join the ranks of global art curators, art and literary critics . . . once monopolists of otherness, now recouping their monopoly by redefining the object as creolized, mixed up otherness – otherness at home, and home among the others. The self-reflexivity of the anthropologist might already be the expression of a cosmopolitanism that opens the way to an understanding of the conditions of globalization. For it is the transnational structures and organizations themselves that are the locus of the transcultural. The question, however, is why and when such self-reflexivity appears, because it is patently the case that the consciousness is no mere response to the existence of global institutions and even less so to the existence of global processes which have been here all the time. On the contrary, as we shall suggest below, it has everything to do with the conditions of self-identification among the occupants of such institutions.

Global system, global institution, globalization   Our argument has been that there is a relation of encompassment between global systems and the processes of globalization. Global systems develop internal organizations of a trans-state character. These are often of a political nature. They include alliance organizations, whether political or military, cultural organizations, the media, diplomatic and aid organizations, etc. At the base level there are the multinational economic organizations, global investment and specu-lation machines. I have suggested that these structures are not new, nor do they necessarily produce a cultural globalization process. The latter requires the development of a global awareness, not least among the personnel involved in globalized or globalizing institutions, from World Bank economists and diplomats to anthropologists. This is an awareness that is produced quite generally in certain quarters of the world system where declining hegemony and disorder combined with increasing intensity of communication have pressed the global upon everyday consciousness. But one might also suggest that there has emerged a global class structure, an international elite made up of top diplomats, government ministers, aid officials and representatives of international organizations such as the

United Nations, who play golf, dine, take cocktails with one another, forming a kind of cultural cohort. This grouping overlaps with an international cultural elite of art dealers, publishing and media representatives, the culture industry VIPs who are directly involved in media representations and events, producing images of the world and images for the world. The news is made by them, very much about them and communicates their visions of reality. This does not imply hegemonic homogeneity. Nor does it imply that their identities are entirely the product of their location in the system. On the contrary the visions are products of the more general state of global processes of identification and self-identification which are not to be confused with the existence of global institutions and networks. Global fragmentation thus implies a proliferation of interpretations of the world, and it is this proliferation that is the historically specific content of global discourses. The World Bank can shift from all-out developmentalism to a serious support for tribal alternatives and ecosystem maintenance. It is not the Bank itself that is the source of either of these positions, which must be traced back, I would claim, to the specific identity space of 'modernity' and its historical vacillations. But there are also certain shared properties here that are attributable to the common positions of such elites. It is from these quarters that much of the globalization discussion has emerged, from the economic 'global reach' to the cultural 'global village'.

Global processes contain and transform their own internal boundaries and articulate dialectically with the local structures that together constitute them. In this perspective, the suggestion that such processes are somehow organized by states, markets, movements and everyday life (Hannerz, 1992b: 217–97) is an impractical one, insofar as the latter are themselves generated, and very variously so, within the larger global process. African states do not 'manage meaning' the way Southeast Asian or European states do. Cargo cults organize their worlds in very different ways from the Green Movement in the West. I might suggest, on the contrary, that the analysis of global phenomena should focus precisely on the way such institutional-cultural forms: states, markets, moments and everyday life, are produced and reproduced in the global local articulations of the world system.[5]

Reformulating culture: return to the verb

If cultural globalization is, as we have argued, a product of the global system, we might also suggest that the concept of culture is itself generated in the transformation of the centres of such systems. From the global point of view, culture is a typical product of Western modernity that consists in transforming difference into essence (Friedman, 1987, 1988, 1991). Its starting point is the awareness of specificity, that is, of difference, of different ways of doing similar things. Where difference can be attributed to demarcated populations we have culture or cultures. From here it is easy enough to convert difference into essence, race, text, paradigm, code, structure, without ever needing to examine the actual process by which specificity comes to be and is reproduced. Culture, a modern tool, applied to the global context in which it emerged, generates an essentialization of the world, the formation of a configuration of different cultures, ethnic groups or races, depending upon the historical period, and the professional identities of the identifiers.

People do specific things and they attribute specific meanings, and the latter is also a specific form of practice. Now, if such specificities can be found in a population, one ought then to ask how they arise. How does the specific practice or meaning become more or less homogeneous in the population, and to what degree? Here the functions of socialization, of authority and identity play crucial roles.

From this point of view, culture is always problematic. Its constitution and reproduction are contested issues. We do, of course, readily admit that much of the specificity of practice is relatively automatic and/or habitual, but here, also, we have to enquire as to how the habitual is organized in the larger social context, how it becomes 'naturalized'. We must account for its role. All of this highlights the fact that cultural specificity can never be accounted for in terms of itself. It can never be understood as an autonomous domain that can account for the organization of behaviour.

If the practice of meaning and of interaction are both elaborated out of historically specific (objective) conditions of subjective existence, as Bourdieu might have it, then we have a model for the production of specificity that does not need to rely on a prior notion of culture as the organization of meaning.

In other words, culture is practised and constituted out of practice. It is not a code or a paradigm unless it is socially employed as such, that is, to socialize or otherwise transmit a set of rules abstracted from the context of their production. The force of culture is the force of the social relations that transfer propositions-about-the-world from one person or position to another.

The most dangerously misleading quality of the notion of culture is that it literally flattens out the extremely varied ways in which the production of meaning occurs in the contested field of social existence. Most atrociously, it conflates the identification of specificity by the anthropologist with the creation and institutionalization of semantic schemes by those under study. It confuses our identification with theirs and trivializes other people's experience by reducing it to our cognitive categories. Geertz is explicit about this in insisting that rituals, social formations and power structures are all of the same order, that is, cultural texts, specificities for our cultural catalogues (Geertz, 1980: 135).

Culture as the anthropological textualization of otherness, in other words, does not correctly represent the way in which the specificity of otherness is generated and maintained. It consists merely in the *translation of the identification of specificity into the specification of identity and ultimately the speciation of identity*. Its usefulness resides entirely in its classificatory properties, but these are highly suspect. Its weakness resides in the fact that it says virtually nothing about that which is classified, being a kind of metacommunication about difference itself. In global terms, the culturalization of the world is about how a certain group of professionals located at central positions identify the larger world and order it according to a central scheme of things. The following note on 'creolization' is an example of precisely such textualization in the context noted above of disillusioned cosmopolitanism. Creolization was once something that happened to the colonial others of the world. Now, in this age of fragmenting hierarchies, when there is no longer an exemplary centre from which to view the other, we must literally take the bird's eye view, position ourselves above the world or perhaps in the space of the jetplane. But the concept remains logically predicated on the notion of culture as text, as substance; that is, having properties that can be mixed or blended with other cultures.

Creolization as confused essentialism

Creolization is an unavoidable consequence of the use of the notion of culture that we have criticized above. It refers to the meeting and mixing of meanings from disparate sources in a single place, a situation that has apparently arisen on a global scale only quite recently.

> The notion of creolization . . . fairly neatly summarizes a cultural process of a type widespread in the world today. The concept refers to a process where meanings and meaningful forms from different historical sources, originally separated from one another in space, come to mingle extensively. Creole cultures in their pure form [sic!] are, to put it paradoxically, intrinsically impure; I note this as a matter of ethnographic fact, certainly without perjorative intent. The typical context of creolization is a social structure where the bearers of some of these traditions somehow count for more than others as do consequently their respective traditions. (Hannerz, 1992a: 96)

This mingling of cultures, the fusion that leads to supposedly new products, is a metaphor that can only succeed in terms of a previous metaphor, that of culture as matter, in this case, apparently, a fluid. In strictly formal terms this substantialization of culture also leads to an understanding of the latter in terms of products rather than production. Thus, while allusion is made to the 'social organization of meaning', the social organization as such all but disappears in references to *flows* of meaning, from the centre to periphery and back. But the metaphor of substance is further compounded by the implicit political connotations of the notion of creolization, connotations that are ignored in the objectivist language of culturalism. The use of the concept of creole in linguistics is quite clear, if heavily debated. It has usually been taken to refer to a situation or sometimes phase in which a secondary and often rudimentary language used to communicate between different groups, either in trade or in colonial situations, becomes assimilated to first language status by a new generation of speakers. The more rudimentary secondary language is often referred to as 'pidgin'. The latter incorporates elements of at least two languages which is where the concept of mixture might be introduced. And 'creolization' refers then to the process whereby pidgins acquire native speakers with an implied complexification of both grammatical and lexical components. The categories of pidgin and creole have recently been under attack and it has been suggested by some that they are not useful theoretical terms. It has been argued cogently that many of the world's major 'natural' languages are themselves products of similar processes, thus greatly reducing the specificity of the pidgin and creole categories. While there are clear structural differences between so-called natural languages and pidgins, at least where the latter are defined more or less formally as secondary forms of communication, there are no adequate linguistic criteria for distinguishing between creole and 'natural' languages. On the contrary, what is left of the category 'creole' is its purely cultural status in relation to more 'primary' or natural languages. In the sense of mixture, it might further be argued that all languages are creole, which implies that the concept has no distinctive linguistic value. When the term creole is transferred to the essentialist notion of culture it can only express the idea of mixture, the mixture of two or more 'pure' cultures, that is, pure black + pure white + pure indian. Now in fact such classification of others is a product of colonial contexts of plantation labour based on various combinations of imported and 'indigenous' labour. These classifications were undertaken, furthermore, by the dominant elites and it is only in special conditions of socialization that creole became a form of self-characterization. Our argument here is that creole is a form of identification of others, a form stabilized by hegemonic arrangements that emerged in the global system. The mixed nature of other people's cultures is only made real by means of establishing, even institutionalizing, social identities. Thus it would not be quite as simple to convince the English and French that they also were speakers of creoles or had creolized cultures. Italians have debated, needless to say, the origins of pasta, some arguing that it pre-dated Marco Polo's voyages. But for most, the Chinese connection is today quite irrelevant for the cultural definition of spaghetti. The establishment and maintenance of creole identity is a social act rather than a cultural fact. That is, the definition of creole implies the recognition of disparate origins, a recognition that must be maintained as part of the identity of the bearers of this 'objectively' mixed culture in order for the creole category to have any validity over time.[6] The use of the concept 'creole' in colonial contexts was a stable mechanism of identification based on an essentialized view of culture. If the world is understood as largely creolized today this expresses the identity of the classifier who experiences the transgression of cultural, that is, ethnic, national, boundaries as a global phenomenon. The problem is not that we have suddenly been confronted with cultural flows on a world scale comparable to those which occurred in a more restricted way in the plantation sectors of the Caribbean or Southeast Asia. The problem is that conditions of identification of both self and other have changed. Cultures don't flow together and mix with each other.

Rather, certain actors, often strategically positioned actors, identify the world in such terms as part of their own self-identification. Cultural mixture is the effect of the practice of mixed origins.[7]

Globalization as disjuncture

Appadurai's approach to the global is more similar to that that I have advocated insofar as it attempts to maintain a vision of a global system *within which* cultural processes occur. But a substantialized view of culture, and even of a global cultural system, is introduced and it produces a vision of cultural confusion, even cultural chaos (Appadurai, 1990: 20), which disturbs a much more fertile potential that is contained in this work. He divides the world, somewhat arbitrarily, into ethnoscapes, mediascapes, technoscapes, finanscapes and ideoscapes. Here we are free of the entanglements of the culture concept. Instead we have a series of flows or topoi in which peoples, money, technology, representations and political identities move around the world, congealing at specific points into specific configurations of regional, national and local structures. It is the increasing disjuncture among these flows that is characteristic of today, producing the mixed-up differences that others might describe as creolization. Here it is not only culture that is mixed up, but practically everything else as well: India exporting computer experts to the US and waiters to Dubai. The flowering of ethnic diasporas throughout the world is seen to be the major source of new fundamentalisms. But this de-territorialization is also the source of new consumer tastes in India and of fears in Los Angeles of Japanese take-overs. The major theme of his discussion is that globalization consists in a cannibalizing dialectic between tendencies to homogeneity and tendencies to heterogeneity, a theme which runs parallel to discussions of particularization/universalization, and localization/globalization. I find myself in agreement with much of what Appadurai writes, but I fail to see the disjunctures to which he refers. In global systemic terms, there is a logical connection between the decentralization of world accumulation and the fragmentation of identities, the emergence of new conditions of local accumulation and of survival in the world arena. The fact that India can produce high-tech engineers and that much of southern California was bought up by Japanese investors during the 1980s are not matters of disjuncture but of conjuncture, a quite systematic process of decentralization in the world arena. The globalization of fundamentalisms and of powerful nationalisms is part of the same process, the violent eruption of cultural identities in the wake of declining modernist identity. The concept of disjuncture appears to suggest a certain turmoil attributed to a formerly more systematic world. But what appears as disorganization and often real disorder is not any the less systemic and systematic. I might venture to suggest that the disorder is not about the introduction of randomness or chaos into the global arena, but a combination of two processes: first a fragmentation of the global system and the consequent multiplication of

local projects and localizing strategies and, second, a simultaneous globalization of political institutions, class associations and common media of
representation. If Brooklyn-born Polynesian dancers represent the
Hawaiian Hula to tourists by putting on a Tahitian fire dance on a Waikiki
stage (though this no longer occurs in today's world of monitored
authenticity), this need not be understood as postmodern chaos. On the
contrary, it is surely one of the constants of global cultural history. It is only
chaotic for the culture expert whose identification of origins is disturbed by
the global processes of changing identities, a disturbance that is, consequently, translated into a de-authentification of other people's 'actually
existing' cultures. The problem can only arise on the basis of the notion of
culture as essence or substance.

The leaky mosaic

Common to the anthropological vision, and to Western essentialism in
general, is the notion that culture is somehow the major actor in the global
arena. This, I have argued, is a reflex of Western modernity itself. Even
among those most concerned to criticize the ideal that the world is made up
of discrete cultures, even, where culture is defined as the social organization
of meaning, it is still seen to flow from one geographical area to another,
either in the form of ethnic migration, media transmissions, or the global
movement of products and services. For these anthropologists of globalization, the latter process is quite new, apparently related to the general
globalization of capital that has occurred in the past two decades, and to the
obvious awareness that people have of their access to the goings on of the
larger world. This can be expressed in terms of the classical categorization of
approaches to ethnographic reality. These approaches have usually been
contrasted as two: 'the ladder' and 'the mosaic'. The first refers to the notion
that cultures (in this case social types) can be ordered in evolutionary time, a
time that translates the distribution of societies in space into a temporal
progression. This is the anthropology of hegemony, first the classical
evolutionary scheme of the British hegemony, then the neo-evolutionism of
the American hegemony. The mosaic is the relativist version of the above,
re-transposing time into space and maintaining the vision of a world divided
into well defined bounded units all of equal value or perhaps even
incommensurable. The globalized vision of the ethnographic universe,
which is the map of the 'peoples' of the world, is one that is aware of the
mixtures existing at any one point in the larger world, that no culture is pure,
that all contain elements from other places in the larger system (if 'system' is
the right word). In other words, this is a vision of a leaky mosaic in which
cultures run over their edges and flow into one another, channelled, to some
extent, by the remaining political and economic hierarchies of the world
system. The popularity of this understanding of the world is, I think, related
precisely to the continuity that it expresses with respect to an older cultural
relativism, even more its resonance with a practice of essentializing identity

that is the pervasive foundation of relativism. But if, as we have argued, the mosaic never existed, and if culture is truly the social organization of meaning, then what appears as globalization cannot be explained in terms of cultural overflows in a previously well formed ethno-cultural map of the world.

From culture to the practice of identity: the parameters of modernity

The issue of creolization, mixture, postmodern pastiche and what others have referred to as 'cultural hybridization' is clearly a central problem for a good many intellectuals whose profession is to identify the world. The discussions of globalization owe most of their impetus to this experience. It is noteworthy that both creolization and hybridization employ an image of the mixing of pure or original strains to produce a new form. The image itself belongs to a more basic view of culture that derives from the notion of race. It equates the notions of population with specific practices and ways of life, in terms of a notion of common substance. This culture is simply there, like an object, to be investigated and understood. And it is this essentialist notion that I have criticized, a notion that, as I shall argue, is not easy to shed, simply because it is very strongly implicated in our own modern identity and in the way that we configure our world.

The practice of identity is not a question of identity possessed by an individual or group, that is, as a label or title. Nor is it about the identity defined by the psychologist, attributed to others, although the activity of the psychologist is very much part of what I am trying to get at here. The practice of identity is about the identification of an existential world, the attribution of meaning to the world, to objects, persons and relations. This practice identifies the self as it identifies the world. It is not the application of a code to the organization of the world by a methodological individual or actor. It is a highly motivated practice rooted in the way immediate experience is structured in definite social contexts. Where codes are involved, it is because they have been actively included in such practices, that is, because they are socialized into the process of identification. I have referred to this in terms of identity spaces, and I have in other contexts discussed the identity space of modernity. I would argue here that the terms of the globalization discussion are all derivative of the identity space of modernity. The very essentialism of culture as substance, of meaning that flows, is one of a plethora of metaphors that are generated by such a space. Globalization is a flow of meaningful objects and ideas that retain their meaning in their movement. Behind such a notion are a number of assumptions:

1 The individual is separate from culture in the sense that he partakes of it, consumes it, uses it in various ways. This is a relation of externality.
2 Even where culture is a code that organizes society, it stands as a separate text, a relation of externality.
3 The relation between subject and culture here is a relation between subject and role, between an empty subject and alternative identities.

4 All identities, no matter what their cultural content, have the same form. They are texts of or for practice, for particular scenarios and social rules, rituals, forms of symbolism. But there is no difference in the mode of existence of these rules, rituals and forms.

It is in such terms that a Mayan or Hawaiian nationalist represents a hybrid culture, because the very idea of nationalism is a Western import. This banality does not afford us any insight into what Mayan and Hawaiian nationalists are doing, or how they construe the world, but merely that they participate in the modern universe of political language.

Until relatively recently, African cloth was made primarily in Holland and Germany. The production was targeted to specific 'tribes', that is, based on specific patterns, and the cloth was not obtainable in Europe. The production of local difference on a global scale is proof of a global relation in production and consumption. It is not, of course, the globalization of culture, of meaning, but of the global control over local consumption via product differentiation. This is clearly a global systemic relation, but is it also globalization? It is certainly not a globalization of 'meaning', except for the observer of the phenomenon, that is, for the global researcher.

In several previous publications I have discussed a phenomenon called *la sape*, whereby young men from the Congo and Zaire, usually from more impoverished urban areas, systematically accumulate designer clothing, moving up the ranks of finery until moving to Paris, *l'aventure*, in order to engage in becoming *un grand*. The emergence of a kind of cult group surrounding this process is well documented, with clearly defined age classes and competitive cat-walking, organized by returning to Brazzaville, centre in the periphery, sewing the accumulated labels into a single jacket and performing *la danse des griffes* at the local *sape* club. Now in one sense this process is about globalization, the globalization of people, or garments, a veritable traffic in people and goods, sometimes including drugs and often resulting in the re-import of low-end jeans and t-shirts to be sold in the African markets. What is not occurring, however, is a mixture of culture, not unless the notion is confined to the museological definition of ethnographic objects. A lumpenproletarian Congolese who flaunts his Versace suit and Westin crocodile shoes is not, in my view, a Westernized African, nor is he something 'betwixt and between'. This is because he is engaged in a specific practice of accumulation of 'life-force' that assimilates the Western goods to an expression of a process that is entirely African. The Western is encompassed by the practice of *la sape*. The clothes are contained within a different project, and the properties of the clothes do not alter those of the project. The content does not shape the container. On the other hand, his entire project, as a social practice, is in its turn encompassed by the larger global processes upon which it is, in its global specificity, entirely dependent.

Thus, instead of falling back on a model of cultural flows or other similar metaphors, I think it better to conceive of such global cultural processes in terms of positioned practices such as assimilation, encompassment and integration in the context of social interaction. This is a relation between container and contained in the sense of the variable forms of incorporation of the products of a global field of interaction into the practice of local strategies, and the relation of these processes to the practice of identification, that is, of meaning attribution.

From the point of view of identification as an ongoing practice, the concept of culture upon which the notion of globalization is based is a product of the identity space of modernity. I have argued throughout this chapter for a shift from the vocabulary of culture to that of identification precisely in order to avoid the essentialization and substantialization that are such powerful reflexes of modernity. In several other works (for example, Friedman, 1992) I have argued that commercial global systems have a structural propensity to produce the kinds of identity spaces that we refer to as 'modernities'. Such spaces emerge in the commercial centres of global systems to varying degrees, depending upon the extent of dissolution of former kin and generally 'holistic' sodalities. The latter leads in its turn to a process of individualization, the emergence of a self-regulating subject. Self-regulation implies self-identification, an experiential separation between subject and social role. This separation is the essence of modern alterity, and it defines a space of subjective movement among alternative identities, a movement among differences. The latter, coupled to the hierarchy of power, produces the notion of self-development and, abstracted, of development in general, in a universe where all identity, all position, is achieved, by whatever means. If this latter is the core of modernism, it is dependent upon real movement, real change and mobility. Where such is impossible the other possible formulation is simply movement between difference, the mosaic. Culture is an abstract form of the way the world is identified in this kind of universe. It is the abstraction of and essentialization of difference, either in the safe form of text or in the more volatile form of essence. In one sense the textual form, the liberal notion of culture as code or programme, maintains the separation of peoplehood from what they do, but it essentializes the 'what they do' into a fixed corpus, as close as one can get to 'substance'.[8] The identity space of modernity contains a continuum of variation from specificity as text to specificity as essence, but it is always a substance that is at issue.

It is in this sense that globalization 'theory' is a product of the parameters of modernity, that is, of the way in which modern subjects identify the world. It is in such terms that the metaphors of hybridization, creolization, mixture, etc. find their resonance. It is also in such terms that Robertson's 'relativizations' of globality can be understood. His four terms separating self as national from self as humankind, society as specific from society as integral part of the larger world, are not products of a recent awareness of the shrinking world, but fundamental aspects of modern identity. Humankind is merely the 'universal' referent whose opposite pole is the modern individual. It is implicit in such pre-twentieth-century concepts as 'human rights', 'humanity', the 'universal'. The globalized relativizations of which

Robertson speaks are simply expressions of these fundamental separations of modern identity.

Notes

1. Parsons should also be included here in the case of Robertson, Wuthnow and several other researchers.

2. In the following discussion of modernity as an identity space I underscore the implicit connection between individualization, alterity and the abstraction of social identity. This process generates the possibility of a notion of a generalized humanity stripped of its historical and cultural particulars.

3. The fact that such particularizations are global phenomena does not qualify them as 'globalization' in this view, because they are practices that fragment the larger field of power. That local power occurs in a world arena at a specific point in time qualifies it as a global systemic phenomenon, but one that is not equivalent to the diffusion of the practice of local power.

4. It should be noted that the use of the term nation-state conceals the fact that many nation-states in the Third World, while using the vocabulary of Western institutions, are organized in entirely different ways. The nation-state terminology has everything to do with the organization of economic and political power in the global arena. Here we may speak of an institutional tendency to globalization, but it is not the concrete national states that are globalized, merely the terminology and rhetoric. Globalized also are the relations of access to capital on a world scale, although there has been increasing decentralization here. The relation between the nation-state terminology, the rhetoric of development or modernization, and the desire for international funding and support are all elements in the formation of new elites and elite identities. But these, I would argue, are clearly dependent on the contours of the world system itself. In other words, globalization is a dependent aspect of the world system.

5. It is true that there are numerous activities carried out by states that might appear to be quite common, certainly in the use of violence and in the rhetoric of power and democracy. There are even certain aspects to the national project of creating a common history that can be shown to be quite global. But I do not think that these commonalities are the result of a common recipe that has been passed around the world. Rather I think it would be more profitable to look at the relations of force involved, the conditions of legitimation and the historical similarities, often the result of previous globalized structures such as colonial regimes. To exemplify this more concretely, the nation-state (see note 3), Papua New Guinea, has all the trappings of a modern state and it carries on many activities similar to those found in other parts of the world, including a project of national homogenization called pan-melanesianism. But the actual relation between governmental categories and the strategies of gaining and maintaining power, the immediate understanding of the function of the state and of democracy are vastly different from anything that might enable us to classify this state with others just because it is referred to as a nation-state. A similar argument has been made for Africa by Bayart (1989).

6. To make matters even worse, work by linguists such as Labov has demonstrated that extreme dialect variations can result from immediate social differentiation without the introduction of other languages, i.e. without mixture, thus, for example, producing language divergence (Labov and Harris, 1986) that can later be the source of new recombinations which can appear in formal terms as creoles. Many linguists have argued that creolization is a general aspect of all language change and not a more specific historical phenomenon.

7. Now, of course, the practice of mixed identity is not the privilege of anthropologists and other cultural classifiers. It sometimes becomes central to local representations of trans-ethnic identity in the lumpenized quarters of 'world cities', often expressed in world art, music and literature where it is also transformed into global representations of the world media. But the trans-ethnic is often a weak identity, supported by cultural classifiers, in a more serious context of stronger separate ethnicities in conflict.

8. Even here there is a tendency to stick culture on to people in an essentializing way, as

when Geertz (1980) claims that there is no universal human nature underneath the specificity of cultures.

References

Appadurai, A. (1990) 'Disjuncture and difference in the global cultural economy', in M. Featherstone (ed.), *Global Culture. Nationalism, Globalization and Modernity*. London: Sage. pp. 293–310.

Bayart, J.F. (1989) *L'État en Afrique: la politique du ventre*. Paris: Fayard.

Ekholm, K. (1975) 'On the limits of civilization: the dynamics of global systems', *Dialectical Anthropology*, 5 (2): 155–66.

Ekholm, K. and Friedman, J. (1980) 'Towards a global anthropology' in L. Blussé, H. Wesseling and G. D. Winius (eds), *History and Underdevelopment*. Leiden/Paris: Centre for the History of European Expansion/Maison de Science de l'Homme.

Ekholm-Friedman, K. (1991) *Catastrophe and Continuity: The Transformation of an African Culture*. London: Harwood Academic.

Friedman, J. (1976) 'Marxist theory and systems of total reproduction', *Critique of Anthropology*, 2 (7): 3–16.

Friedman, J. (1987) 'Prolegomena to the Adventures of Phallus in Blunderland', *Culture and History*, 1.

Friedman, J. (1988) 'Cultural logics of the global system', *Theory, Culture & Society*, 5 (2/3): 447–60.

Friedman, J. (1991) 'Further notes on the Adventures of Phallus in Blunderland', in L. Nencel and P. Pels (eds), *Constructing Knowledge*. London: Sage. pp. 96–113.

Friedman, J. (1992) 'General historical and culturally specific properties of global systems', in *Review*, 15 (3): 335–72.

Geertz, C. (1980) *Negara*. Princeton: Princeton University Press.

Hannerz, U. (1987) 'The world in creolization', *Africa*, 57: 546–59.

Hannerz, U. (1991) 'Cosmopolitans and locals in world culture', in M. Featherstone (ed.), *Global Culture. Nationalism, Globalization and Modernity*. London: Sage. pp. 237–51.

Hannerz, U. (1992a) 'Stockholm: double creolizing', in Å. Daun, B. Ehn and B. Klein (eds), *To Make the World Safe for Diversity: Towards an Understanding of Multicultural Societies*. Stockholm: Swedish Immigration Institute and Museum & Ethnology Institute, Stockholm University.

Hannerz, U. (1992b) *Cultural Complexity: Studies in the Social Organization of Meaning*. New York: Columbia University Press.

Labov, W. and Harris, W. (1986) 'De facto segregation of black and white vernaculars', in D. Sankoff (ed.), *Diversity and Diachrony*, Current Issues in Linguistic Theory 53. Amsterdam: John Benjamins.

Robertson, R. (1991) 'Social theory, cultural relativity and the problem of globality', in A.D. King (ed.), *Culture, Globalization and the World-System: Contemporary Conditions for the Representation of Identity*. Binghamton/London: State University of New York/Macmillan.

Robertson, R. (1992) *Globalization. Social Theory and Global Culture*. London: Sage.

5

NEW WORLD ORDER OR NEO-WORLD ORDERS: POWER, POLITICS AND IDEOLOGY IN INFORMATIONALIZING GLOCALITIES

Timothy W. Luke

On glocality

The celebrated new world order of sovereign nation-states, jointly collaborating within the framework of the United Nations to pursue truth, justice and the American way, did not last much longer than the victory parades after the Gulf War. Something else has begun to fill the void left after the end of the Cold War, and it does not look like the international harmonization of interests promised by President Bush after the UN coalition's victory over Iraq. This chapter deals with tendencies, suggesting that at least one kind of post-national and transnational order is gradually evolving out of the informational modes of production emerging above and below the realms of the modern nation-state. Characterizing these changes is difficult, but this study provides a start towards interpretation. Arguably, the workings of power, politics and ideology in these new transnational flows of capital, people, commodities, information and culture are generating a cybersphere/ telesphere that is coextensive with, but different from, first nature in the natural biosphere and second nature in the industrial technosphere. This new 'third nature' of cyberspatial/televisual/informational glocality fuses the local and the global in new everyday life-worlds. And, it is the hyperreal estate of these glocal territories which now anchors many social struggles, political organizations, economic competitions and cultural creolizations in most regions of the existing capitalist world system.

Fukuyama's strange but convenient division of all the world's nation-states into the 'historical world', or those areas where what he regards as liberal democracy, capitalism and scientific secularism are not yet in command, and the 'post-historical world', or those areas where he believes liberal democracy's hegemony and capitalist economic progress may have seen History end, is problematic but perhaps still promising as a conceptual distinction. It essentially reaffirms the old Cold War schemas of the First World nation-states setting the directions taken by the so-called Second,

Third and Fourth World countries (Fukuyama, 1992: xii–xiv), but it trips over some new wrinkles that may indicate what is developing today.

Perhaps glocality tends to assume two different forms. In Fukuyama's post-historical world, for example, it is coextensive with the core informationalizing capitalist industrial regions of the planet, which are fairly 'tame zones' of political/economic/cultural viability. However, in the historical world, it is a range of 'wild zones' encompassing the larger mass of the world system's pre-informational, agricultural, quasi-industrial semi-peripheries and peripheries (Attali, 1991; Luke, 1989). These spreading 'wild zones' increasingly are slipping out of the prevailing currents of global technology, information and capital flows (O'Brien, 1992). True, some goods and services are still produced there, and life continues to go on. Yet, the jungle, the mountains and the desert today are reclaiming roads, cities and fields, such as we see across large swathes of Albania, Afghanistan, Armenia, Bosnia, Burma, Cambodia, Georgia, Moldova, Peru, Somalia or Zaire as well as Newark, Los Angeles, Miami, while their human populations struggle with each other more and more over less and less. Once more 'civilized' life-worlds are decaying as the entire social order becomes a heavily 'historical' wild zone where humans physically fight, like Hobbes' uncivil beasts, over food, shelter, recognition or power. Wild zones lack certain and secure access to the global flow of post-historical change; tame zones mark the certainty and security of access in core regions, while perhaps actually sustaining these destructive patterns toward wild zoning elsewhere. Yet, in both spaces, the nation-state and its realist discourses about power, politics and ideology appear to be disintegrating. Here, then, perhaps we should map out the apparent shift from realism in 'historical settings' to hyperrealism in 'post-historical settings' as codes of simulation displace logics of representation.

The corrosion of industrial modernity's structure and substance can be traced to the 'informationalization' of the social means of production, consumption and administration, during and after the 1960s when the global impact of mass telecommunications, electronic computerization, cybernetic automation and rapid transportation began to be experienced broadly around the world (Luke, 1983: 59–73). This shift also marks the coming of 'late' or 'disorganized capitalism' with all of its postmodernist trappings. As Jameson claims, this is a change 'which is somehow decisive but incomparable with the older convulsions of modernization and industrialization, less perceptible and dramatic somehow, but more permanent precisely because it is more thorough going and all-pervasive' (1991: xxi).

Informationalization changes structures of social action as well as institutional sites of cultural process in several different ways. Castells, for example, argues 'what is facilitated by information technologies is the interconnection of activities, providing the basis for the increasing complexity of service industries, which exchange information relentlessly and ubiquitously. . . . Whatever becomes organizationally and legally possible can be technologically implemented because of the versatility of the technological medium' (1989: 142). In appraising today's global economic changes, Reich (1991: 172) asserts that national prosperity depends upon

> the functions that Americans perform – the value they add – within the global economy. Other nations are undergoing precisely the same transformation, some more slowly than the United States, but most are caught up essentially in the same transnational trend. Barriers to cross-border flows of knowledge, money, and tangible products are crumbling; groups of people in every nation are joining global webs.

Reich (1991: 131) also contrasts the 'nominal nationality' professed by many modern major corporations with their 'actual transnationality' as global parts-sourcing, foreign markets, expatriate management, multinational labour recruiting and world-wide financial dealings increasingly typify their operations. As the networks of informational exchange unfold in the cybernetic spaces of informationalized processes, many new questions arise. Again, as Castells (1989: 142) asserts,

> there is a shift, in fact, away from the centrality of the organizational unit to the network of information and decision. In other words, *flows, rather than organizations*, become the units of work, decision, and output accounting. Is the same trend developing in relation to the spatial dimension of organizations? Are flows substituting for localities in the information economy? Under the impact of information systems, are organizations not timeless but also placeless?

The depth and direction of these flows constitutes a new dimension of thought and action. Partly local, partly global, such glocal flows are a telesphere/cybersphere of artificial spaces created by streams of data, audio and video. In this third nature, there are innumerable new regions of action, developing their own agendas, interests and values beyond, beside and beneath the nation-state.

Power in context and chrontext

Always essentially fictive constructs of linear space in real time, the jurisdiction of nation-states, as institutionalized in-statements of power, are discursive fields of state authorship inscribed upon individuals and groups, whose attributes and behaviours are continuously remanufactured by the coercive gaze or normalizing hand of jurisdictive state power (or, literally, 'law speech' speaking). As containers of modernity, modern realist states presume the existence and acceptance of elaborate discourses of instrumental action, rational reflection, linear causality, natural objectivity, complex hierarchy, inert matter, universal materialism and human subjectivity to ground its treatment of space as perspectival and time as neutral. 'Nationality' is its organizing and valorizing logic.

Reduced to its bare first principles, realist discourses for defining international relations in terms of nationality are wholly invested in cartographies cued on the sovereignty of states (Morgenthau, 1985). The modern state's leadership in-states itself as a national author(ity), and its in-statement forms boundaries, delimits territories, inscribes orders on individuals, societies and environments. These writs of sovereignty are locational, directional, perspectival in their graphic impact. They de-emphasize the local and demonize the global in order to legitimize their own national-statist construction of economic, political and social action. The national sovereign(ty) of this type of state is its own author(ity), empowering it allegedly to inscribe order across anarchy, as it scrolls its powers graphically over some particular culture, people, territory and power usually represented as a country. These ethno-graphies define oppositions of us/them, same/other, friend/foe, in a country's cultural codes. These demo-graphies set categories of more/less, growth/stagnation and elite/commoner in a country's population pools. These geo-graphies delineate boundaries of inside/outside, foreign/domestic, ours/theirs in a country's territorial terminologies. And, these poli-graphies sound out barriers of access/exclusion, power/powerlessness, order/disorder in a country's political processes.

Fabricating national order/fomenting national disorder

While it is a resilient structure, the modern nation-state does not have a timeless and enduring history as a permanent constituent fixture of human political life. It is, at best, an unstable historical construct, fabricated first in Europe during the aftermath of the Thirty Years War, where it was used as an economic, linguistic, political and geographical container of modernity in Europe (Hobsbawm, 1990). After 1918, it began to be imposed more globally as peoples colonized by Europe sought to recreate European nation-stateness in their own Third World post-imperial settings. As Toulmin (1990: 7) observes, 'the modern era began with the creation of separate, independent sovereign states, each of them organized around a particular nation, with its own language and culture, maintaining a government that was legitimated as expressing the national will, or national traditions, or interests'. Yet, its universality or generality has been quite limited from the very beginning (Hobsbawm, 1990). Not every European nation-state fits this realist bill of political particulars (Gellner, 1983). Even Toulmin's essentially mainstream realist construction of the nation-state emphatically affirms how 'England and France were type examples of "national" development' (1990: 93) that provided the paragon for other nations to measure their 'nation-state' developments against. The 'modern nation-state' basically is a place-holding term that 'means' England or France, because Italy, Germany, Spain, Poland, Russia or Austria, as nation-states, all possess national state histories that are much more like Third World countries, even when you look through Toulmin's realist optics (Armstrong, 1982; Tilly, 1975).

Toulmin's citation of the standard modern historical archive, of course, simply reconfirms the modern realist narrative about the nation-state system emerging from the Peace of Westphalia. From a theodictive licence of earthly sovereignty granted to a feudal satrap, there was conferred the jurisdictive agency of secular sovereignty to the nation-state. Left free to strictly police or freely tolerate varying professions of faith, the sovereign then could foster behind its identifiable boundaries those formulas for stability, development and modernization that it preferred within the realm. Along with religion, the sovereign state also had to strictly police or freely tolerate any countercoding sub-national, supernational, a-national or anti-national social forces (or, perhaps, primordial, traditional, theological 'contra-dictions') that did not go along with this coercive construction of separate, independent sovereign states, usually organized around a particular nation, with its own 'nationalized' religion, language and culture. The sovereign's author(ity) inscribed each realm in polygraphic codes of inside/outside, same/different, right/wrong, us/them, legal/illegal as it claimed or made its juris-diction. Speaking/writing its laws, each nationalizing state drew out its own ethnography (culture writing), geography (space writing), chronography (time/tradition writing) and biography (interests writing). Thus, such governments, once so in-stated, emerged to construct their countries' collective interests, wills and traditions out of discord with these in-stated 'nations', which proved even in the ideal type models of England and France, to be very limited, fictive and artificial.

In creating their modes of sovereignty and modernity, national state structures disclaimed commitments to or discharged engagements with the pre-modern practices of oral (informal) knowledge, particular (practical) culture, local (communal) interests and timely (grounded popular) issues attached to local/regional politics in order to impose a disciplinary normalization rooted in modern theories of written (formal) knowledge, general (national) culture, universal (state) interests and timeless (abstract historical) issues tied into the national/international politics of the capitalist world system. Ultimately, however, blocs of state or national hoods, like feudal aristocrats, capitalist burghers or managerial technocrats, gave their blessing to other hoods, like Joseph Stalin, who defined nationhood as 'a historically evolved, stable community of language, territory, economic life and psychological make-up manifested in a community of culture' (1936: 8).

Subsequently, it is only one very limited local/regional elites' language, culture and economy that creates the 'national' communities of culture in most nation-states (Breuilly, 1982). One primordial identity was reinvented as 'the tradition' of an entire national territory, and then coercively universalized throughout the cultural spheres of such in-stated space (Hobsbawm and Ranger, 1983). Yet, at least since 1918, and more urgently since 1945, these foundations of the modern state have been cracking in crisis after crisis. Perspectival space and neutral time are simply slipping away into the post-perspectival vision and rhythmic time of the post-modernity. Once again, the oral, particular, local and timely agendas of extra-statist social forces, set loose in the informationalizing forces of glocality, are contesting the written, general, universal and timeless line of statist authorities. And it is becoming difficult, or even impossible, to accept the discipline of orthodox discourses about realism. The realist in-statement

of sovereign nationhood is not an ontological given; it is rather a gift of
ontology to the realist hoods behind any nation's in-stated sovereignty.

Global shift: the hyperreal

After centuries of explosive growth, Baudrillard holds that advanced
capitalist economies now are experiencing an implosive reversal in the
manner by which power circulates between the masses and organized
institutions. Obviously, modernity itself changes along with the growth of
this type of advanced capitalist society as it becomes more entwined within
the informational modes of production. A new reality logic based upon
simulation rather than representation constitutes the dominant organizing
principle of this new era. Therefore, in Baudrillard's vision of today's new
world order, 'McLuhan's formula, *the medium is the message*' appropriately
is 'the key formula of the era of simulation (the medium is the message – the
sender is the receiver – the circularity of all polls – the end of panoptic and
perspectival space – such is the alpha and omega of *our* modernity' (1983b:
101). Yet, if the masses no longer act as traditional historical subjects in their
new post-historical habitat, then what happens to that traditional context,
namely, the modern nation-state?

Baudrillard also suggests that the means of information in today's global
transnational economy unhinge ordinary metaphorical relations, because
the operative semiotic principles of this informational order are those of
simulation rather than pre-industrial counterfeit or industrial mechanical
reproduction. Abstractions can no longer be seen as 'the maps', 'the
doubles', 'the mirrors' or 'the concepts' of any terrain metaphorically
regarded as 'the real'. On the contrary, all abstract frames of the real begin
to function only as simulations. For Baudrillard (1983a: 2),

> simulation is no longer that of a territory, a referential being or a substance. It is
> the generation by models of a real without origin or a reality: a hyperreal. The
> territory no longer precedes the map, nor survives it. Henceforth, it is the map
> that precedes the territory – PRECESSION OF SIMULACRA – it is the map
> that engenders the territory . . .

In this hyperspace, something very important has disappeared, namely,
what always was the ineluctable non-identity of map and terrain. Therefore,
a provisional hyper-ontology of these flows must somehow define and
describe what now 'is' beyond realism's perspectival space and neutral time.
To characterize hyperreality, Baudrillard argues that one must see everything anew:

> No more mirror of being and appearances, of the real and its concept. No more
> imaginary coextensity: rather, genetic miniaturization is the dimension of
> simulation. The real is produced from miniaturized units, from matrices, memory
> banks and command models – and with these it can be reproduced an infinite
> number of times. It no longer has to be rational, since it is no longer measured
> against some ideal or negative instance. It is nothing more than operational. In
> fact, since it is no longer enveloped by an imaginary, it is no longer real at all. It is a

hyperreal, the product of an irradiating synthesis of combinatory models in a hyperspace without atmosphere. (1983a: 3)

Traditional notions of causality, perspective and reasoning are undercut completely by the electronic means of information, which efface the difference between cause and effect, ends and means, subject and object, active and passive. Baudrillard (1983a: 55) observes,

we must think of the media as if they were, in outer orbit, a sort of genetic code which controls the mutation of the real into the hyperreal, just as the other, micro-molecular code controls the passage of the signal from a representative sphere of meaning to the genetic sphere of the programmed signal.

Simulation in the global flow goes beyond the old realist divisions of space and time, sender and receiver, medium and message, expression and content as the world's complex webs of electronic media generate un-bound(ed)aries of new hyperspaces with 'no sense of place'.

Decentring the nation-state

Instead of being a container of modernity or reactor of progress, the twentieth-century nation-state increasingly has turned into a fetter on meaningful social transformations, serving as a containment structure against change or a deactivator of progressive initiatives. On one level, maybe the flows of power are eroding its foundations or bringing glocal sites of resistance into being. Still, on another level, maybe the persistence of nations, or the constant re-instatement of states in even greater numbers, is replaying codes of hyperreality, not a logic of rationality of realist *Realpolitik*. The Leviathan's covenants to end the *bellum omnium contra omnes* only made the war of all against all only more possible. The major core Western nation-states could pretend to enjoy 'actual nationality' prior to 1914. For those nation-states with major empires, there was even a measure of 'nominal transnationality' as imperializing nationalist evange-lizers made lame attempts to Germanize the Baltics or Balkans, make Frenchmen out of Africans or Asians, to Russify Georgians or Kazakhs, and make Americans out of Hawaiians or Filipinos. These efforts, nevertheless, were cultural/economic/political disasters even on their own terms. None-theless, more new nation-states were drawn up across the former holdings of the Ottoman, Romanov, Hohenzollern and Habsburg empires. And, after 1945, this proliferation of 'nation-states' accelerated even more rapidly until now, in 1992, still more new nation-states are forming out of the old communist Yugoslav and Soviet federations.

Yet, is their operational fabric much more hyperreal than real? How can today's Zaire, Oman, Peru, Fiji, Belize, Cambodia, Kazakhstan, Bahrain, Grenada, Moldova or Sudan seriously be seen by realists as credible nation-states? The multiplication of real nation-states from a score or so in 1914 to nearly two hundred today perhaps should be read as the precession of a hyperreal model of glocalization rather than the righting of historical oppression by peoples in-stating their own emancipation in realist national governments. As Baudrillard suggests, 'simulation is characterized by a *precession of the model*, of all models around the merest fact – models come first, and the orbital (like the bomb) circulation constitutes the genuine magnetic field of events' (Baudrillard, 1988: 175). Even though area studies experts, comparative politics savants and international relations specialists in North America or Western Europe constantly labour to certify the historical necessity and social authenticity of each one of today's almost two hundred nation-states, the nationhood and in-statedness of most of them are highly contestable.

The appearance of increasingly greater numbers of 'nation-states', as Latin America, Eastern Europe, Africa, the Middle East, the Soviet Union and Asia have experienced decolonization, suggests the disappearance of the nation-state number has already taken place. If every one of the now nearly ten score nation-states behaved like the classic examples of modern England or France, then the world would soon end in violent total war. Similarly, even if every new nation-state tried to emulate Japan, Germany or the United States, the new world order would quickly unravel, pulling apart into hundreds of petty squabbles. The central attributes of classical realist states have already evaporated, as many nation-states survive as little more than simulations of states, with their own flags, national anthems, armies and national airlines, but someone else's currency, energy grids, diplomacy, trade links, navy or food exports actually sustaining their national survival.

In the military sphere, nuclear weapons are still sought after by many nation-states as the definitive sign of real sovereignty. With nuclear weapons, it is believed in Baghdad, Pretoria, Teheran, Pyongyang, Jerusalem and Brasilia that the state becomes a superpower, a magnum force or a serious player. Yet nuclear weapons are essentially useless as anything more than a tottering sovereign's sign of national self-definition. Their possession defines their in-stated owner's will to make their citizens pay for symbolic powers with tangible resources: lives lost from radiation poisoning, innovations not enjoyed from technological talent invested in weaponry, monies mis-spent from maintaining constant deterrence patrols, policies not implemented from political authorities playing superpower games (Luke, 1989; Mueller, 1989). Ironically, even as nuclear weapons are taken as the *sine qua non* of actual national sovereignty, their potential physical powers show the transnational shredding of this myth. Nuclear weapons are post-national engines of destruction. They were originally built in an anti-fascist struggle by a united nations of scientific talent that articulated the talented sciences of national unity, but their actual use could re-instate the fascist holocaust on a global scale. If all 'nuclear devices' were 'exchanged', their destructive effects could not be contained within national borders: they would kill entire biomes, civilizations, hemispheres, in trying to simply destroy the cities and citizenries of one nation-state. Once again, this material sign of realist national power proves to be, in fact, an immaterial and extremely expensive, semiurgic generator of hyperrealist post-national powerlessness (Luke, 1991: 30–44).

In the economic sphere, most nation-states increasingly have spent their treasure since 1945 accumulating the weapons of war. Outside of this agenda, they often are little more than virtual realities imagineered on a geographic basis at a national level to in-state delivery of some mix of social services as their real virtue. Today, the attributes of 'nationality' boil down to fleeting, floating coefficients of entitlement to a basic material standard of living that now marks the collective identity of different 'national' entities as states. Varying levels of individual and collective access to goods and services from the capitalist world system, which are measured along a flexible continuum of statistical indicators, establish the essential socio-economic profiles of 'what is' a First, Second, Third or Fourth World nation-state. Americans are 'Americans' or Pakistanis are 'Pakistanis' because they have this or that covariant opportunity to own a car, have a TV, eat red meat, see a dentist, use a VCR, possess a dwelling or die after age 80. Such 'standards of living' also are little more than tactical hallucinations deployed to induce the silent majorities to 'live out [of] standards' that are endless precessions of new corporate-generated models of everyday life in neo-worlds mutating from simulation to simulation. Looking at these nation-states, *simulated differences*, driven again by copying models of meaning for which there are no originals, and *neutralized identities*, dynamicized by parallel processes of material production and consumption in each state's everyday life-world, are no more than parodies of national diversity or global community. Despite the pretexts of 'national' cultural autonomy, the transnational commodity flow of McDonald's food products in Montreal, Moscow, Manila, Munich, Melbourne and Minneapolis is the same deterrent force arrayed against real local/national specificity. A simulation of cuisine in 'fast food' creates its own models of culture, behaviour and desire within the confines of 'fast capitalism' (Agger, 1989). Now, the territorial in-statements of nations simply provide territorialized historical imaginaries to shake and sort out such transnational economic and social welfare benefits in accord with their closeness to or distance from the central post-historical currents in the global flow of capital, energy, goods and power.

Unbound(ed)aries of flow

Informationalization generates new structuralizing games, or perhaps alternate encoding dictions, nested in rapid and intense *flows* of ideas, commodities, symbols, people, images and money on a global scale, which are disjunctive and fragmenting, anarchical and disordered. Flows are unbounded by spatial borders, passing along unboundaries without frontiers in the constant flux of exchange. Plainly, a 'transnational' flow of goods, capital, people and ideas has existed for centuries; it antedates even the rise of modern nation-states. However, this historical flow, at least until the 1950s or 1960s, tended to move more slowly, move less and more narrowly than the rush of products, ideas, persons and money that develops with jet transportation, electronic telecommunication, massive decolonization and extensive computerization after 1960. It is these greater intensities, rates, densities, levels and velocities in the post-historical flow, which have transmuted it quantitatively into something qualitatively new, complex and different. Actually, in the postmodern culture of the flow, 'culture' itself 'has become a product in its own right; the market has become a substitute for itself. . . . Postmodernism is the consumption of sheer commodification as a process' (Jameson, 1991: x). Rather than acceding to a privileged geopolitical or geoeconomic reading of global power, the flow's postmodern spectra of commodification generate many different grammars across a wide band of still less well-understood 'writings' and 'readings' of planetary political processes. These other structuralizing discursive forces, or taken collectively 'polydictions', today flow more placelessly behind, between and beyond in-stated boundaries set into nationalized space as these new artifices of encoding structure and process become quite fluid, defined by the shifting networks of information carrying these flows.

Moving from place to flow, terrains to streams, introduces non-perspectival, anti-hierarchical and disorganizational elements into traditional spatial/industrial/national notions of sovereignty. Having open and unconstrained access to flows, not closed domination of places, becomes a crucial attribute of power, perhaps as vital as juridico-legal sovereignty, in informationalized societies. Likewise, a chaotic stability spins out from within the codes by maintaining dynamic equilibria of access, linkage, turnover, connection, exchange and service to accord with the diverse agendas of the various different encoders and decoders, while security slips inside concerns over the assuring integrity of codes, openness of access, extent of service, scope of linkage and increase of turnover within the flow's unbound(ed)aries. Caught in the currents of hyperreal forces moving across the mediascapes of informationalization, the nation-state – with its more traditional geopolitical concerns for policing juris-dictively its territories, populations and markets – often comes up short with nothing near complete closure over events within its boundaries. Hence, the nation-state often proves to be both resilient and fragile as it faces the erosion of global flows.

Flows are intentionally guided and socially sited at one, several or many places. Given these larger structural trends, the concrete reality of place, expressed in terms of a sociocultural context of spatial location, gradually is being displaced by the tangible imaginary of flow, understood in terms of iconic/symbolic access to, or process through, networks of informational circulation. The latter is not displacing or destroying the former, but rather they are coexisting together. Therefore, from these building contradictions within a dialectic of organizational centralization and informational decentralization 'between places and flows', one might uncover in the workings of global change 'the gradual transformation of the flows of power into the power of flows' (Castells, 1989: 171). Indeed, the flows are perhaps the basis of defining new types of core, semi-peripheral, peripheral and external areas as they restructure the market niches of cities, regions and countries as 'wild' or 'tame' zones. Most importantly, informationalization entails entirely new sociospatial and sociochronic codes that simultaneously generate the (s)pace of contemporary power, ideology and exchange dynamics. The flow is partly post-spatial, partly post-sovereign, and partly the primary networking of new kinds of international communities. The world system of transnational capitalism gains its figurations in the televisual/computational/cyberspatial conduits of the flow. This distinction can also be extended to interpret the workings of many scientific communities, cultural networks, technological innovations, telecommunication links and media markets as they create hyperreal estate out of telematic territory or cyberspatial flow that are 'actually transnational'. Nominal nationality, or geopolitical spatiality set out in a state's juris-diction, increasingly competes with actual transnationality, or chronopolitical flowality rising within a-statal polydictions.

Flows, then, are decentring, despatializing and dematerializing forces, but they work alongside and against the geopolitical codes of spatial sovereignty. The local and the global are commingling in new 'glocal' modes of production across and outside of national boundaries. Within the flow, there are new universals and new particulars being created by the networks of transnational exchange as fresh identities, unities and values emerge from sharing access to the same symbols, markets and commodities in a new pattern of glocalization. Many institutions of existing nation-states are now a fetter upon the emerging glocal modes of production.

By seeing their security and prosperity as the results of national policies, national interests or national decision-makers, contemporary consumers and producers often mistake thoroughly transnational or largely local forces as the workings of their nation-state. Similarly, xenophobic political appeals, stressing exclusively nationalistic benefit or costs, occlude how closely coupled most present-day core economies and societies have become. Borders today are highly porous, and the pressure of glocal flows of goods and services are continuously eroding them even more every day. To take only one example, consumers and producers in America depend upon oil lifted in Saudi Arabia, fast food from Canadian-owned franchise operations, credit cards from Hong Kong-controlled banks, automobiles built in Mexico by Japanese firms transplanting their output as American cars, groceries produced in Central America, South Africa or Southeast Asia sold in British-owned store chains, newspapers held by Australian multinationals but publishing in New York, televisions fabricated in Taiwan by American companies to show programmes made in Canada by Japanese-owned studios headquartered in Los Angeles, and information gathered by British wire services in Eastern Europe for broadcast on 24-hour cable news networks centred in Atlanta. The modelling of their behaviour in production and consumption is more glocal than national. Similar accounts of glocal interdependence can be adduced for virtually any 'nation-state' in the world today. The notion of 'national interest' has less and less meaning in these glocal webs of interdependence. Forcing these loosely coupled but vital connections of everyday life into the categories of realist state action results in xenophobic reactions: if something is not produced and/or consumed at home, then it allegedly must represent necessarily a weakening of 'national' power, productivity or prestige. Yet, this archaic reading of transnational flows in terms of national states misses how embedded and efficient these glocal webs of exchange actually have become.

Outside of the state, and inside shared technological goals, common ecological challenges, similar symbolic systems, parallel coding orders and comparable product meanings, the flow creates new glocal communities that are blurring the old geographics of 'them' and 'us', 'other' and 'I', or 'friend' and 'foe' in new informational modes of ideography, videography or plutography. The origins and outlets of its many component currents can still be traced back to in-stated ethnogeographic settings, or the spaces of nominal nationality; however, their effects, taken together in the streams of the global flow, are also being felt glocally, or locally and globally as actual transnationality. Beyond the realities of territorial jurisdictive statics, fixed to structured processes inside of tightly inscribed borders, there are the new hyperrealities of polydictive flow dynamics, fluctuating within coded links along loosely coupled local/global networks. These hypermodernizing transformations in the flow are not mediations of realist modernization; instead, they act as the carriers of postmodernity, because 'postmodernism is what you have when the modernization process is complete and nature is gone for good' (Jameson, 1991: ix).

'New world order' or 'neo-world orders'

Those places where glocality prevails essentially emerge from the manifold processed worlds of the flow. As a capitalist world system originally formed, the geographic codes of entrepreneurial capital gradually reinscribed the surface of the planet in terms of rational market exchange, extending outward in the fourteenth and fifteenth centuries from the initial Eurocentric core of commerce, capturing the inhabitants of numerous non-European zones of *terra incognita* in its orbit, closing every frontier and mapping all unexplored territories across the planet. Every society and bioregion from the Antarctic to Africa to the Arctic to Asia to the Antipodes was soon catalogued to its fullest extent for any economic utility or ecological possibility. The closing of this open world of Nature to an extensive mode of production, however, forced Western capitalists to begin fabricating innumerable new artificial worlds, or 'neo-worlds', out of a new intensive mode of production by generating man-made technoregions. Entrepreneurial capital met its critical limit for more growth in the encirclement of the planet and the integration of diverse pre-capitalist modes of production from various bioregions within a single system of commodity production in 'the national geographics' of the core capitalist powers' imperialism. Transnational corporate capital, on the other hand, has gradually reinscribed the economic and ecological realities in such national geographics of local consumption and regional production as transnational geographics of glocal production and consumption.

Every craft and science, each industry and trade, projects its graphic and dictive force as 'neo-worlds' generated in the intensive expansion of global exchange. These newfoundlands iterate out in the still evolving and diversifying terrains of technoregions defined by intensive modes of production used by corporate capitalism, which still delineates the main symbolic expanses and material realities composing the substance of our everyday life-worlds today. Here, transnational topographies and transcultural territories emerge in the flow from the processes of international communication, travel, commerce and transportation. No longer grounded to one planetary place, one ethno-national location or one environmental site, these semi-imaginary/semi-concrete neo-worlds form with their own diverse technoregions of socioeconomically re-engineered cultural space. Increasingly, they are also becoming the most meaningful homelands of contemporary individuals and groups. They are simulations of territory, models for behaviour, circuits of operationalization that frame thought and action glocally.

These neo-worlds are, in fact, perhaps the common ground of transnational society. Contemporary workers and modern corporations, for example, no longer set out to prosper in 'the new world' or 'the colonial world'. Instead, they labour to make their marks in the space, time and values of globalized/globalizing neo-worlds. Their models or maps precede and engender the territory being contested or claimed. These territories form in the flow, and here is where much of today's political struggle, economic competition and cultural contest occur. Hence, who sets the pace in automobile output, who controls the Earth's computer software production, who leads transnational media production, who leads international money markets or who directs world telecommunication systems is materially far more important to most individuals, households and firms than who holds the state leadership in Guatemala, Germany, Ghana or Greece.

These technoregionalizing neo-worlds all taken together form the terrains of the everyday modern life-world of contemporary individuals and society where they defy the laws of physics by coexisting simultaneously in the same time and space. Fragmented, partialled, fractionated, most human households in many existing nation-states import and export pieces and parts of them as the commodified goods and practices of a material existence that is coming to envelop late capitalism. In these international socioeconomic and cultural spaces, entire ecologies of domination and resistance, production and consumption, growth and decay, all operate in these pluripotent neo-worlds. Each new technology and discourse of modernity fabricates its own complex of technoregions to be conquered and mastered through many competing means of behavioural modelling and mapping.

The closing of the natural frontiers in the 1880s and 1890s simply saw the displacement of the colonizing impulse into new realms of social activity defined by geographies of economic, technological and social spaces rather than military and strategic ones. Global social ecology cannot be understood any longer as only the biogeography of naturally evolved bioregions in the world, it also requires immersion in a technogeography of artificially constructed technoregions in the neo-worlds. Neo-worlds are artificial spaces, built environments, coded milieux. They constitute a practical placement of economic, cultural and social interactions within glocal networks of sub-national, national and supranational exchange from which individuals and communities fabricate their shared strategies for occupying these spaces.

New social forces beyond the nation-state, working in a variety of settings like the market, science, the intelligentsia, technology, the mass consuming/ producing public, medicine or even the global ecology, find new means of agencies allowing them to write over/against/for and speak to/against/for the state in the neo-world orders. The unravelling of the national state today echoes the cacophony of such new coding games. Exclusively political poles and fundamentally geopolitical polarities are slipping out of phase. In glocality, many different voices can and do speak outside of (and within) the rational/instrumental speech settings of statist juris-diction. And, like ancient theodictions, such new dictional entities are fabricating their own codes of power, spaces of operation, frames of time and signs of authority beyond the nation-states' in-stated jurisdictions.

Other agents – beyond, beneath, behind or beside the state – are decentring, dematerializing, deconstructing conventional notions of cen-tralized state power. Since 'national security' ordinarily means the security of nation-states, this hollowing out of existing state formations also changes the nature of sovereignty, national security and autonomy discourses, raising new questions about the security problematics of the neo-worlds formed in the informational flow. Already now after the Cold War, for example, global firms are recognizing their post-statal/anti-statal security needs by generating new discourses about industrial espionage, terrorist attacks, market-segment defence and intellectual property protection in the competition over control in the global flow. Ordinary individuals have seen that ecological threats to their immediate bioregions cannot be handled by nation-states or perhaps even international organizations, so they are developing their own transnational ecological self-defence initiatives. Similarly, the telematic infrastructure of the flow itself is generating its own security problematic in new discourses about the cybernetic infrastructure's access rules, user expectations, virus infestations, data protection and hyperreal estate defence.

In each instance, some a-statist force running through these multiple channels seeks to make its own plural, parallel neo-world in speaking through codes of culture, commerce, ethnicity, finance, technology, gender, ecology or health in order to rule off some space of exclusive control, to rule as the most legitimate knowing force and to set the rules for its definitive codes of author(ity)? In more 'ideal' speech situations inside the flow, 'tame zones' emerge in the transactions made possible by these dictive systems' polyglot discourses. In less than 'ideal' speech situations outside of the flow, 'wild zones' begin growing, and they make only intermittent contacts with the ongoing exchanges of the flow. The power centres/speech communities of third nature exist, but their glocal forms of existence often float inarticulately or undetected in national statist readings of global business, international technology, transnational ecology or multinational culture. Because we now know why realists cannot read the a-statist texts of the neo-worlds, perhaps we should recognize how these new post-statal, a-statal, non-statal, anti-statal or crypto-statal neo-worlds' influences are being felt glocally above and beyond the grasp of realist nation-states in the proliferating discursive channels of hyperreal flows.

The disintegrating trends in glocality are quite clear. The nation-state no longer reigns with impunity even in realist time and space. Nuclear weapons are developed vainly by nation-states as definitive signs of national sovereignty, but they also give nation-state leaderships a capability to extinguish life in geographic space and historic time almost instantaneously by dis-instating nations thermonuclearly. Basic physical security against external threats is impossible to guarantee (Mueller, 1989). Hard currencies are viciously guarded by nation-states to signal their sovereignty. Yet, the rise of computerized financial transactions plus transnational political economies are hollowing out national currencies and economies from within, rendering them into little more than tracings of unstable commodity markets and futures contracts (McKenzie and Lee, 1991). Ordinary economic prosperity is often incapable of being assured (O'Brien, 1992; Sakaiya, 1991). Nativist nationalism valiantly redefines the purity of each nation-state's language and culture. Nonetheless, the creolizing impact of mass media culture, which is denominated in codes of permissive individualism, secular humanism, strategic rationalism and commercialized English, is imploding many nations' local cultural particularities. Fundamental linguistic/moral/ethnic/religious identity often is impossible to enforce, in spite of the hordes of border police vigilantly guarding national boundaries to enforce the nation-state's policy prerogatives. Remote-sensing surveillance satellites, floods of tourists and direct news uplinks/downlinks make domestic national discipline – in both tame/peaceful/normal or wild/strife-torn/abnormal regions – totally transparent to both domestic and foreign audiences. Thus, the primary political authority of the nation-state is imperilled as a true authoritative force with absolute finality by these glocalizing counter forces (Attali, 1991; Blackburn, 1990).

As nation-state realism now twists and turns tamely through the mazes of the hyperreal, it perhaps becomes a wild conceptual copy of a world for which there really is no longer any good original. The fixed truths of traditional realist *terra firma* – or a sovereignty-bound 'new world order' of nation-states – implode in the code flux of contemporary hyperreal *terra infirma* – or the sovereignty-free 'neo-world orders' of glocal technoregions. The third nature of cyberspatial/televisual/informational interactions exists in mappings, simulations, linkages, imageries and models that are beyond the containments of nation-states in the neo-worlds of postmodern time–space compression. The challenge for critical social and political theory, in moving on to this terrain, will be to develop new discourses of critique and caring to cope with the new forms of destruction, domination and disintegration developing with the formation of this third nature.

Note

An earlier version of this paper was presented at the *Theory, Culture & Society* Conference, 16–19 August 1992. Part of it also appears in *Alternatives*, 18 (1993).

References

Agger, Ben (1989) *Fast Capitalism*. Urbana: University of Illinois Press.

Armstrong, John (1982) *Nations Before Nationalism*. Chapel Hill: University of North Carolina Press.

Attali, Jacques (1991) *Millennium: Winners and Losers in the Coming World Order*. New York: Random House.

Blackburn, Richard James (1990) *The Vampire of Reason: An Essay in the Philosophy of History*. London: Verso.

Baudrillard, Jean (1983a) *In the Shadow of the Silent Majorities*. New York: Semiotext(e).

Baudrillard, Jean (1983b) *Simulations*. New York: Semiotext(e).

Baudrillard, Jean (1988) *Selected Writings*, ed. Mark Poster. Stanford: Stanford University Press.

Breuilly, J. (1982) *Nationalism and the State*. Manchester: Manchester University Press.

Castells, Manuel (1989) *The Informational City: Information Technology, Economic Restructuring, and the Urban-Regional Process*. Oxford: Blackwell.

Fukuyama, Francis (1992) *The End of History and the Last Man*. New York: Free Press.

Gellner, Ernest (1983) *Nations and Nationalism*. Oxford: Oxford University Press.

Hobsbawm, E.J. (1990) *Nations and Nationalism since 1780*. Cambridge: Cambridge University Press.

Hobsbawm, E.J. and Ranger, Terence (eds) (1983) *The Invention of Tradition*. Cambridge: Cambridge University Press.

Jameson, Frederic (1991) *Postmodernism, or the Cultural Logic of Late Capitalism*. Durham: Duke University Press.

Luke, Timothy W. (1983) 'Informationalism and ecology', *Telos*, 53: 59–72.

Luke, Timothy W. (1989) *Screens of Power: Ideology, Domination, and Resistance in International Society*. Urbana: University of Illinois Press.

Luke, Timothy W. (1991) 'The discourse of deterrence: national security as communicative interaction', *Journal of Social Philosophy*, 22: 30–44.

McKenzie, Richard B. and Lee, Dwight R. (1991) *Quicksilver Capital: How the Rapid Movement of Wealth Has Changed the World*. New York: Free Press.

Morgenthau, Hans J. (and Kenneth Thompson) (1985) *Politics Among Nations*, 6th edn. New York: Knopf.

Mueller, John (1989) *Retreat from Doomsday: The Obsolescence of Major War*. New York: Basic Books.

O'Brien, Richard (1992) *Global Financial Integration: The End of Geography*. New York: Council on Foreign Relations Press.

Reich, Robert B. (1991) *The Work of Nations: Preparing Ourselves for 21st-Century Capitalism*. New York: Knopf.

Sakaiya, Tachi (1991) *The Knowledge-Value Revolution, or a History of the Future*. New York: Kodansha International.

Stalin, Joseph (1936) *Marxism and the National and Colonial Question*. Moscow: Progress Publishers.

Tilly, Charles (ed.) (1975) *The Formation of National States in Western Europe*. Princeton: Princeton University Press.

Toulmin, Stephen (1990) *Cosmopolis: The Hidden Agenda of Modernity*. New York: Free Press.

6

THE TIMES AND SPACES OF MODERNITY (OR WHO NEEDS POSTMODERNISM?)

Anthony D. King

Thinking modernity

'Modern' must be one of the most common and, at the same time, unproblematized metaphors used to represent a myriad aspects of contemporary life, not least the so-called 'modern city'. Let me start by looking at its taken-for-granted meaning given in contemporary dictionaries.

According to the *Oxford English Dictionary* (1989) (and also Webster's) modern means 'characteristic of the present or recent times, as distinguished from the remote past'. We might distinguish it from 'contemporary' (which means 'right now') by saying that it 'pertains to the current age or period'. According to the *Oxford English Dictionary* (1989), it is used in contradistinction to 'ancient' and 'medieval', as in 'Modern History', the period of history after the so-called 'Middle Ages' (that is, the close of the fifteenth century to today, according to the 1864 source cited. We might remark in passing that this is an intriguing conceptualization of five centuries which have sufficient coherence and commonality to be subsumed by one concept.).

Just to destabilize our notions of the modern, we might note that its first recorded use in the sense indicated above is in 1585, and 'modernist', 1588; 'modernity', meaning the quality or character of being modern, is identified in 1627, and 'modernism', 'modernness', 'modernizer', 'modernize', are all in use by the first half of the eighteenth century. For 'modernization', meaning to make modern, cause to conform to modern ideas, we have to wait a little longer, till 1770, though there are references to aristocrats 'modernizing' their ancient homes in the mid-eighteenth century. Raymond Williams (1984) makes the point that for the earlier use of the terms, 'modern' and 'modernize', the sense is unfavourable, that is, that the alteration or change that was implied needed to be justified. Only in the nineteenth and twentieth centuries did 'modern' acquire a positive connotation, meaning improved or efficient. Hence, whereas 'modern' has generally positive connotations (though not always, as when we refer to 'modern problems') 'contemporary' is a more neutral term. It goes without saying that all these citations from the *OED* are from English literature, presumably written in England (or Britain).

The etymology of 'modern' suggests that it comes from the Latin *'modus'*, meaning 'measure'. This is an interesting insight which turns our attention to both modish (fashionable), and *à la mode*. It also prompts a useful thought which I shall insert here though it will arise again later in the chapter: that is, if we adopt Williams' point that the contemporary connotations of 'modern' are positive, by what and whose criteria is a positive notion of cultural modernity *measured*? How do we know which is a modern city? Or which is the most modern city? Who is doing the measuring? Are they female or male? Black, brown or white? Is it the Population Crisis Committee in Washington (1990) with their 'livability' indices showing degrees of air pollution, murders per thousand population and telephones per head, or the late Ayatollah Khomeinei?

The point I wish to emphasize, however, is that the criterial attributes of 'modern' in the sense in which it has been defined here are primarily temporal, not spatial. Its meaning is defined not just in relation to 'history' but to someone's very specific history. The question of space, of the place, location, society, country, nation-state, or life-space to which 'the present or recent' refers, is taken for granted and unproblematized, though it is evident from what is referred to as 'Modern History' (so capitalized, and in contradistinction to the 'Middle Ages') that that space is Western, if not European, and at least titularly Christian.

In short, because 'modern' and 'modernity', understood to mean 'as of the present', are neither temporally nor geographically grounded, because they float in space, they are empty of meaning and hence irrelevant for either description or analysis. Strictly speaking, a phrase such as 'the modern city' applies equally to Kabul, New York or Varanasi.

It is also the case that, till quite recently, scholars operating within various disciplinary discourses used these terms both selectively and differently. Many, indeed, continue to do so, and it is the distinction between what I would broadly call 'humanities' conceptualizations of modernity and those of the social sciences which is a central theme of my chapter. Like Williams (1984), I would suggest that 'modern', and especially 'modernism', 'modernity' and 'modernist', are terms and concepts especially used in the humanities to refer to particular movements and tendencies in the arts, literature and architecture, largely between 1890 and 1940, which took place principally in Europe and the USA and with very little (though some) reference to the world system as a whole (to use another metaphor, also in the 1989 edition of the *OED*). Indeed, in many humanities disciplines, the very concepts of the modern and modernity can be taken as *foundational* to the extent that they determine the nature of the knowledge produced, the temporal, spatial and conceptual boundaries which govern its construction, as well as the identity of its producers. In art history, for example, professional identities are principally defined in terms of 'periods', structured across Western concepts of time. Practitioners are either 'modernists' or 'pre-modernists' and if the latter, medievalists, or someone who 'does' 'ancient' or 'Baroque'. It is this geographically limited use of 'modern' which is the parent of the postmodern which I shall make a digression to address.

In contemporary (sociological) usage, this particular understanding of the modern is grounded in a very distinctive, industrial and monopoly phase in the development of the capitalist world economy which took place in Europe and the USA, principally in the nineteenth century and the first half of the twentieth century. If modernity and modernism can be defined by reference to the cultural practices of specific elites (which is an arguable proposition in itself), then, according to Harvey (1989), it was a cultural manifestation of early twentieth-century capitalism. This, though *premised* on relations within the world system as a whole, and particularly on those of colonialism, was nonetheless largely restricted in its manifestations to Europe and North America. I say 'largely' because it is necessary to acknowledge what Pieterse refers to as the 'upsurge of non-Western influences' on 'modernism' which were experienced in Paris, which he appropriately calls 'the cultural center of the colonial age'. He refers here to *l'art nègre*, 'via the cubism of Braque and Picasso, the fauvisme of Matisse, and the naive painting of Henri Rousseau' (1992: 371).

Yet these (humanities) concepts of modernity and modernism, as they have been utilized in Europe and North America, were never understood in this way (see, for example, the representative texts on *Modernism, 1890–1930* by Bradbury and McFarlane [1976], or Timms and Kelley's collection on *Urban Experience and Modern European Literature and Art* [1985]). Modernity was invariably defined only in relation to Europe and the USA, and not within the world system as a whole. It follows, therefore, that postmodernity operates with the same geographical restrictions, whether in terms of the Eurocentric intellectual sources on which it draws, the phenomena it purports to explain, or the areas of the world to which it supposedly relates. Lyotard himself states that 'the postmodern condition' (1984) is only a symptom of what he calls 'the most highly developed societies' and for Frederic Jameson, it is 'almost a synonymous term for American culture' (Young, 1990: 205).

In contemporary Western (and probably also in certain 'non-Western', 'non-critical') usage, 'modern' refers to 'modern industrial – and now, post-industrial – societies', which are usually though not necessarily market/capitalist. The general discussion of modernity in these societies, in the humanities especially but also in the social sciences, has conceptualized the topic historically in relation to economic, technological, social and cultural changes either within Europe, or 'the West' as a whole, or in relation to a nationally defined society. The second and, as I shall discuss below, more recent referent for 'modern' is the Enlightenment project in Europe, with its emphasis on rationality, order, the state, control and the belief in progress. In both of these particular, and essentially Eurocentric discourses, Paris, through spatial, technological, energy and architectural transformations, becomes the paradigmatic 'modern city' in the last third of the nineteenth century, with Vienna, London and Berlin following close behind (Lash, 1990). Though I could provide numerous titles in support of these propositions, particularly representative would be Marshall Berman's *All That is Solid Melts Into Air* (1983) and its citing of Baudelaire's dicta on modernity: 'By modernity, I mean the ephemeral, the contingent, the half of art whose other half is eternal and immutable' (1863, in Berman, 1983: 133) and T.J. Clark's *The Painting of Modern Life. Paris in the Art of Manet and his Followers* (1984). The factor common to both, though more pronounced in Clark, is that despite nodding reference to the French Empire or to the appearance (in Clark's account) of the black subject, the world outside Europe (or even, in some sense, outside France) hardly exists. It is a totally Eurocentric vision.

The same is true of Seed and Wolff's otherwise instructive edited collection on Manchester and *The Culture of Capital* (1988). Here, the assumption is that this immensely significant city in the history of capitalist industrialization, the city on which both Marx and Engels drew for much of their inspiration and theorization, as containing, representing and supporting a particular form of cultural capital, is somehow economically, socially and spatially autonomous, resulting from some fictitious national economy. Nowhere is it suggested that this city is the very specific economic, social, spatial and built environment outcome of processes of production, consumption and exchange which were not only world-wide and global, but which rested on a particular division of labour, a colonial mode of production, in which Manchester was at the core (King, 1984, 1990a; Spivak, 1988). The colonies are the absence, *Cotton*opolis the presence. Without making that recognition, there is no explaining the contemporary social and cultural modernity stemming from the existence of tens of thousands of Algerians or Moroccans in Paris nor Indians, Pakistanis and West Indians in Manchester. These shortcomings are the direct outcome of defining the modern and modernism by reference to a particular point in time, but without reference to space.

Modernity and 'the West'

The term 'modern', partly because of its linguistic origin in English (and later, American English) and the subsequent linguistic imperialism of colonial and international English, has become unproblematically associated with 'the West', to use a spatial and geographical metaphor, though one that is also economic, political, moral and philosophical. Thus, as I have mentioned above, from being first used as a term of abuse and then of commendation, the abstract metaphor 'modern' was, between the late nineteenth and mid-twentieth centuries, appropriated and given a very distinct and particular materialization, not only in Western literature, music and the arts, but in architecture and urban design.

The so-called 'modern city' we are speaking of was not just characteristic of 'present or recent times' *anywhere* but only in Western Europe and North America. Nor, of course, did it take the same manifestation in the various countries of those two continents, nor did its 'modern' forms occupy all of the space of the city which it touched. To speak of 'Western modernity', therefore, or of 'the modern Western city' is something of an excess, a kind of Orientalism in reverse (Said, 1978). Rather than referring in blanket fashion to 'the modern city' it would make more sense to label this form of urbanism either according to its place of origin (perhaps western Europe), the mode of production which sustained it (late capitalism), the technology, energy base and materials (high energy cement) it generated, or the social, sexual, ethnic and racial division of labour it helped to establish (the first international division of labour). Nonetheless, the notion of 'the modern' was firmly and powerfully fixed in 'the West' and then conveyed to other parts of the world through the uneven relationship of colonialism and global capitalism (see also Sardar, 1992).

In the colonies, as Hamedah (1992) points out, it was through the construction of the centred authority of the so-called 'modern city' that the indigenous settlement came to be called the 'traditional city'. As a number of studies have shown (Holston, 1989; King, 1976, 1990a; Rabinow, 1989; Wright, 1992) the urban outcome of colonialism was not simply the transplantation of a 'modern Western city' but rather a product that was the distinct outcome of colonial modernity. Though having some superficial resemblance to aspects of the city in the metropole, it was not only inherently different from it but was to a large extent politically, econ-omically, administratively, and spatially dependent on it.

Nowhere is this dependence better illustrated than in the architectural and spatial practices of what at first was called 'Modernism' and subsequently, with a similar degree of Western hubris, the 'International Style' (King, 1990a: 61, 78, 98). As applied to urban and architectural form, the term 'International Style' was coined in the early 1930s to refer, initially in Europe and North America, to the high-tech, high-energy materials, and capital-intensive building and design practices applied to high-value, often central city sites housing the institutions of monopoly capitalism (Hitchcock and Johnson, 1966) when world economic and political relations were dominated by capitalist institutions and European as well as Japanese colonialisms were at their height. It was the political space of French colonialism in the 1930s that permitted the designs of this system's most well-known practitioner, Le Corbusier, to be constructed in Algeria in the 1930s (Lamprakos, 1992) and, in a fit of postcolonial euphoria, in India's Chandigarh and (with different architects) Brazilia in the 1950s (Holston, 1989).

In this particular historical and urban thematic context, therefore, Mark Elvin's conceptualization of modernity proves useful. As a historian whose work focuses mainly on China, Elvin is concerned to find a definition of modernity that (1) 'is not based on chronology, and so escapes the confusion caused by continuous updating' and (2) one that enables him 'to see societies as varying combinations of "modern" and "non-modern" elements, sometimes mutually indifferent, sometimes mutually supportive, and sometimes mutually hostile. In this view, of course, neither present-day Western Europe nor present day North America emerges as wholly "modern" ' (1986: 209).

On these premises Elvin defines modernity as 'a complex of more or less effectively realized concerns with power'. It is a complex that contains at least three elements: first, 'power over other human beings, whether states, groups or individuals, according to the system under consideration'; second, 'practical power over nature in terms of the capacity for economic production' and, third, 'intellectual power over nature in the form of the capacity for prediction' (Elvin, 1986: 210). To this, however, we also need to add the power, under imperialism, not only to construct knowledge but also the parameters and paradigms within which that knowledge is made legitimate. It is the power to name, classify and categorize (King, 1994). It is the historical situation which Spivak refers to as 'the history of the epistemic violence of imperialism' (1988: 172).

The times of modernity

So far, my argument has stressed the essential spatialization of the Eurocentric concept of modernity; but what about what Bhabha (1991) has called its 'ambivalent temporality'? Because modernity, if it means 'as of the present or recent times, as distinguished from the remote past', not only exists everywhere, even though it may take on different nuances dependent on linguistic and cultural differences, it exists at different times: 'each repetition of the sign of modernity is different, specific to its historical and cultural conditions of enunciation' (Bhabha, 1991: 207).

Bhabha also questions both the conventional spatialization of modernity as well as its temporality. He writes, '(T)hrough Kant, Foucault traces the "ontology of the present" to the exemplary event of the French Revolution and it is there that he stages his sign of modernity. . . . The eurocentricity of Foucault's theory of cultural difference is revealed in his insistent spatializing of the time of modernity' (1991: 202).

Bhabha's particular criticism, however, is reserved for 'the ethnocentric limitations of Foucault's spatial sign of modernity (which) become(s) immediately apparent if we take our stand, in the immediate post-revolutionary period, in San Domingo with the Black Jacobins, rather than in Paris'. Here, in short, Bhabha is pointing to the sharp disjunction between a so-called 'modern disposition of mankind' (based on ideas of the Enlightenment) and the contradictory (and conveniently forgotten) colonial and slave histories.

Modernity, he suggests, is about 'the historical construction of a specific position of historical enunciation and address': there is never a 'real' modern in itself as 'modernity' comes out of a temporarily continuous and spatially comparative relational perspective.[1]

Like Bhabha, I have also argued (King, 1991: 8) that the real emergence of 'today's' modernity, as an ideology of beginning, of modernity as the new, is in colonial not metropolitan space. My own 'specific position of historical enunciation' for deciding what is modern – which has a location both in time as well as space – rests on the following two criteria.

To begin with, we take 1995 (rather than 1945 or 1895) as the 'now' of modernity. This is a modernity judged not by some elitist Eurocentric conceptions of 'modernism' grounded in literature, painting or architecture, notions which are now firmly historic and fixed in the cultural canons of the West[2] but by the present-day reality, in conditions of grossly uneven development, of the total internationalization of production, and of world interdependence in which, in theory at least, there are no Others (Giddens, 1990).

My second criterion is the existence, in a significant number of cities round the world, of ethnicities, races and peoples from virtually all parts of the planet. If we ask, on the basis of these two criteria, where the first historical occurrence was of what today we call the 'modern multicultural' city, the answer is certainly not in the European or North American 'core' cities of London, Los Angeles or New York, but probably in 'peripheral' ones of Rio, Calcutta or Mombasa. I write 'probably' because it is precisely due to the Eurocentric focus of much demographic as well as other social research, that we do not have an immediate answer to this highly important historical question. I also put quotation marks round 'core' and 'periphery' as it is evident from what I am saying that, from a social and cultural (rather than an economic and political) perspective, the core would become the periphery and the periphery the core.

Clearly, I am not speaking here of some kind of technological or architectural modernity but rather of a social and cultural modernity. The question therefore is not only *whose* version of modernity we are operating with, but *when* and *where* that version comes to be fixed as a dominant global paradigm. From then, and there, it is passively used as a reference point (a *measure* in fact, to return to the start of the chapter), from which all forms of contemporary cultural and historical critique take off. We need only imagine the intellectual and disciplinary chaos (not least in conventional interpretations of, for example, literature, or art and architectural history) were the categories of 'modernity' or 'modernism' to be withdrawn from the canon or declared obsolete. I shall return to these issues below.

'Modernization', 'postcolonialism' and the 'postmodern'

If 'modernism', 'modernist' and 'modernity' are the preferred terms, with preferred meanings, of the humanities, 'modernization', while not normally found in the vocabulary of the humanities, is nonetheless central to the social sciences. Here, I shall focus on a particular sociological understanding of 'modernization', and modernization theory, and will draw on three representative texts published at the height of that paradigm's influence in the late 1960s: Cyril Black's *The Dynamics of Modernization. A Study in Comparative History* (1966), Marion J. Levy's *Modernization and the Structure of Societies. A Setting for International Affairs* (1966) and a collection edited by Myron Weiner, *Modernization: The Dynamics of Growth* (1966).[3]

I would suggest that the principal distinction between the humanities' understanding of modernism and that of the social sciences of modernization falls along the following lines. Where 'modernity'/'modernism' are Euro-American concepts, grounded in a spatially restricted historical temporality, 'modernization' is a (largely American) term, the criterial attributes of which are both spatial and geographical, as well as temporal and historical. The meaning of the term, and the mode in which it is used, rest on an assumption that the modern is measured not only diachronically, in relation to the past of one's own (always Western, Northern) society, but synchronically, in relation to the present of someone else's (always Eastern, Southern) society. Where the humanities' 'modern' has, till quite recently, ignored what today we might refer to as the 'world system' or 'the global', the social sciences' 'modernization' attempted to address these dimensions, though within the paradigms of internationalism available in the 1960s; 'world systems' and 'globalization' paradigms, of course, emerged only from the 1970s and 1980s although Nettl and Robertson (1968) presented an argument which attempted to bridge modernization and globalization perspectives.

In Black's (1966) terms, 'modernization' refers to:

> the dynamic form that the age-old process of innovation has assumed as a result of the explosive proliferation of knowledge in recent centuries. . . . If a definition is necessary, 'modernization' may be defined as the process by which historically evolved institutions are adapted to the rapidly changing functions that reflect the unprecedented increase in man's knowledge, permitting control over his environment, that accompanied the scientific revolution. This process of adaptation had its origins and initial influences in the societies of Western Europe, but in the nineteenth and twentieth centuries these changes have been extended to all other societies and have resulted in a worldwide transformation affecting all human relationships. (1966: 7)

In regard to the realm of politics, Black continues:

> Political scientists frequently limit the term 'modernization' to the political and social changes accompanying industrialization, but a holistic definition is better suited to the complexity and interrelatedness of all aspects of the process. (1966: 7)

For Levy (1966: 11), the definition of modernization hinges on:

> the uses of inanimate sources of power and the use of tools to multiply the effect of effort. A society will be considered more or less modernized to the extent that its members use inanimate sources of power and/or use tools to multiply the effects of their efforts.

However, Levy's book is primarily addressed to an examination of the structure of 'relatively modernized' and 'relatively non-modernized' societies, to questions within these of role definition, solidarity, and economic and political allocation. Examining the organizational context of societies, he focuses on kinship and family organization, government units, armed forces and other organizational contexts such as churches and educational groups, concluding with a discussion of the common elements and lines of variation in all societies. Significantly, in this 850-page book, reference to colonies and colonialism occurs only on four pages.

To illustrate his theme, Levy addresses questions about the spatial 'spread' of modernization.

> There are of course conspicuous differences in the level of modernization. England, France and at least West Germany represent high levels of moderniz-ation. . . . Nothing in Asia would fall on the relatively modernized side of the line save for Japan. . . . No African country save South Africa and isolated portions of Algeria could qualify as being on the relatively modernized side of the line. (1966: 37)

Weiner's collection, which includes contributions from twenty-four of the leading proponents of modernization theory in the 1960s, is divided into three main sections, each dealing with the modernization of society and culture, politics and government, and the economy. The fact that none of the contributors are women or speak from Third World positions is a simple but telling commentary on Bhabha's point about the different repetitions of 'the sign of modernity'.

> Each of the social science disciplines has focused on different elements of the modernization process. Economists see modernization primarily in terms of man's application of technologies to the control of nature's resources in order to bring about a marked increase in the growth of output per head of population. Sociologists and social anthropologists have been primarily concerned with the process of differentiation that characterises modern societies. . . . They have explored the way in which new structures arise to assume new functions . . . and they give attention to the differentiations occurring within social structures as new occupations emerge. . . . [They] also study some of the disruptive features of the modernization process: rising tensions, mental illnesses, divorce . . . racial, religious, and class conflict.
>   Political scientists . . . have focused particularly on the problems of nation and government building as modernization occurs. [Those] concerned with develop-ment are interested not only in who exercises power and how . . . but how governments increase their capacity to innovate change . . . and cope with social conflict. (Weiner, 1966: 3)

It is not my object here to enter into a critique of these particular versions of modernization theory, largely displaced by later paradigms: the develop-ment of underdevelopment, dependency theory, world-systems perspec-tive, Marxist theories on the internationalization of capital, and the renewed interest in colonialism and imperialism. Rather, in resurrecting these 30-year-old extracts from a discourse on 'modernization', my aim is to demonstrate that globe-wide discourses about 'the modern', and the social science debates which both preceded and succeeded them, have a substan-tial history long before the relatively recent discovery, in the prism of the postmodern, of the world outside Europe and North America and the interconnectedness of these places with it. For at least one theme which proponents of postmodernism are concerned with, in the UK as also in North America, is a very *belated* recognition of the world outside themselves – and the decentrings, cultural relativizations and contradictions that this recognition has brought about.

One explanation for this development is to be found, first, in the migration, and subsequently, the voices of 'Third World' intellectuals, often doubly displaced from their own space (especially India, Pakistan, East and North Africa, the Caribbean, Palestine, each place subsequently reconceptualized, in the 1980s, as the postcolony), often via the post-imperial metropole, to the still globally culturally hegemonic realm of the USA. Here, the discursive space created by debates around multiculturalism, diversity, anti-racism and cultural identity has provided fertile ground for the seeds of a postcolonial critique to develop, hybridizing with the narratives of Black, Hispanic and Native American oppression. Ironically, therefore, it is the presence of Third World intellectuals in the humanities, and especially comparative literature (I refer particularly to the work of Edward Said, Gayatri Spivak, Homi Bhabha, Aijiz Ahmad and others, principally, though not wholly, in the academies of the English-speaking regions of the ideological 'West' – the UK, USA, Canada, Australasia) which has brought, in the 1980s, a new consciousness of colonialism to North America and the UK under the umbrella of the postmodern. As a central theme of cultural politics, this 'discovery' of colonialism, displacement and cultural difference has been effected by scholars in comparative literature, art history or cultural studies, on the territory of the post-imperial metropole (UK), in Australia (Ashcroft et al., 1989), Canada, or the still imperial hegemony of the USA and not, as with an earlier generation of anthropologists (Asad, 1973), sociologists (Worsley, 1963) and others, on the terrain of the postcolony itself.[4]

Thus, answering the question 'What is postmodernism?' in a recent (1989) text on the topic, the author (a scholar of English and Comparative Literature in Canada), makes the discovery that

> the postmodernist's initial concern is to de-naturalise some of the dominant features of our way of life: to point out that those entities that we experience as 'natural' (they might even include capitalism, patriarchy, liberal humanism) are in fact 'cultural'; made by us, not given to us. (Hutcheon, 1989: 2)

Similarly, in his widely circulated text, *What Is Post-Modernism?* (1986) architect Charles Jencks constructs a table delineating three types of society based on their 'major form of production': 'pre-modern 1000 BC–1450; modern 1450–1960; post-modern 1960–   ' (1986: 47). Here, the distinction between the 'modern' form of production (Industrial Revolution: factory, mass production, centralized) and its related society (capitalism: owning class of bourgeoisie, workers) and the 'postmodern' production form (Information Revolution: office, segmentation, decentralized) and its related society (global: para-class of cognitariat, office workers) provides an even better example for my argument. In designating 'postmodern' society as 'global' *only* from 1960, Jencks totally ignores the development of the capitalist world economy from the sixteenth century, as well as the emergence of global relations of production and colonialism prior to that date.[5]

In addition to the international migration of postcolonial and post-imperial scholars to the US in the 1970s and 1980s, the other factor which has inserted postcolonialism into the discourse on the postmodern is the increased awareness, by academics in the metropole, 'of the globe as such', to use Robertson's phrase. Both movements are the outcome of globalization (Robertson, 1992). The additional sophistication which various strands of literary theory has given to these theoretical developments has not only refined the larger macrosociological explanations provided for them but, in being shunted round the postcolonial intellectual world of the 1980s, has also done much to confirm such explanations.

Modernity and interconnectedness

For two centuries at least, prevailing definitions of 'modernity' have been premised on a set of values which were, as I have suggested above, predominantly Western, male, white, oriented to the individual and ecologically innocent (in fact, rapacious). The cultural de-centring of the last decade, giving the margins a form of weak power (Hall, 1991: 48), are altering these criteria. If we address ourselves to the question of the urban, and urban restructuring, we might ask whether notions of the modern, as they were typically represented between the 1930s and the 1950s, by so-called 'futuristic' exhibitions about space, skyscrapers, monorail transportation, utopian architecture and the like, have any credence whatsoever in the 1990s.

For example, were we to take New York City as the epitome of what many scholars have frequently represented as the paradigmatic example of what, through immensely powerful cinematic and photographic representations, the 'modern' city of the 1950s and 1960s was supposed to be (see Wallock, 1988, for example), and examine it by reference to what some (even US based) organizations see as appropriate contemporary criteria (Population Crisis Committee, 1990) the city would present a dismal picture of congestion, astronomical costs, air pollution, massive energy use, murder and social malaise, even though many observers might see it as having a high ranking on scales of ethnic, cultural and racial diversity.[6]

Definitions of cultural modernity which made reference to questions of equity in regard to gender, race, ethnicity, to questions of access, affirmations of identity, ecologically progressive transportation systems, security and employment, would give us a totally different set of criteria for judging which of the world's cities could be said to be the 'most modern'.

So far, I have been trying to develop connections between two phenomena: the first of these is the interconnectedness of a single world economy, a world system if we wish to represent it this way, or the idea, to use

Robertson's (1992) term, of 'the consciousness of the world as such'. It is a representation in which we need to acknowledge that the particular economic, social, material and cultural flows in which cities are embedded, and to which they also give rise, as part of a single, interconnected global system and culture which increasingly gives rise to what Appadurai (1991) has termed 'global ethnoscapes'. It is also to recognize that cultural as well as economic and social phenomena in one part of this system, which may be a 'global city' (King, 1990b), means recognizing *contemporary* cultural, economic and social phenomena in others. This is not to suggest some kind of hegemonic, totalizing cultural imperialism but rather to acknowledge the historical and cultural specificities which attach to each place, yet which simultaneously may also be linked by different flows to many places.

Equally important are the descriptive, metaphorical phenomena, the terms and concepts by which we represent 'cultural modernity', especially in relation to the present phase of urban restructuring which has been especially evident in the last quarter of a century. Contemporary cultural modernity is comprehensible only if it takes in a global conceptualization of 'the modern', which dispenses both with Eurocentric and Westerncentric criteria which link 'the modern' to the distinctive Western notion of industrialization, urbanization and the rest, as well as Williams' notion of the modern as evaluative and positive.

Reclaiming modernity: the contemporary metropolis

What my argument suggests, therefore, is a readjustment, a conscious chronological sliding of the terms 'modern' and 'modernity', and the conditions and places to which they refer, along the following lines.

First, we should take the 'global space' of the present as the 'now' of modernity. This would allow us to see that what till now has been called 'modern society', that is, nineteenth- and twentieth-century industrial, often capitalist societies, characterized by technology, rational bureaucracies and the rest, was a concept applied entirely to the West with little recognition that this state of modernity was premised on the West's colonized Other. This phase we should reconceptualize as the *pre-modern*.

We might then take what Occidental, generally European and American, intellectuals have conceptualized as the postmodern (using, as I have indicated, the myopic Eurocentric views of modernity suggested above) and characterized for Jencks (1986), for example, by fragmentation and irony, and which belatedly recognizes the existence of a world beyond the Western hemisphere, which (again, belatedly) is seen as forcibly impinging itself on the so-called modern, Western world in contributing to international migration, cultural and ethnic hybridization, multiculturalism, etc., and re-label this as the *modern*. As this more accurately captures the economic, social and cultural totality characterizing emerging urban formations round the globe, particularly the so-called 'world cities', this would seem a logical proposition. It is this respatialization of the modern which leads me to my conclusion.

Conclusion

Cultural modernity can hardly be addressed in the abstract, without reference to a specific, objective place, or a particular subject (or set of subjectivities). As far as large Western metropolises are concerned, the burgeoning increase in the internationalization of capital, international labour migration, and technological transformations, as well as increased dependence on tourism, are likely to lead to many of the structural characteristics identified for the global city by Sassen (1991), Zukin (1991), King (1990b) and others, though not necessarily to give rise to their particular functions. I refer to the growth of indigenous as well as multinational producer services, with their dependent component of low-level service provision, multiculturalism, the expansion of the cultural economy, the proliferation of the economy of the sign and the exacerbation of ethnic, racial and social difference such that, as Abu-Lughod (1991) has argued, New York and Cairo begin to have more in common, if only on the surface, than New York and Chicago.

Structurally, the ever-increasing growth of low-income migration combines with the expansion of top level service jobs to produce the forms of economic, social and spatial polarization that have become especially characteristic of these cities in the 1980s and 1990s.

In this way, the characteristics of cities in the 'most advanced' urban economies increasingly approximate to those of what were once called 'Third World' cities, at least in the degree of economic, social and spatial polarization, in the extent and complexity of their ethnic, social and racial mixes, in the occupational structures of their de-industrialized, or non-industrialized populations, and in the chaos of the built environment. In this sphere, a variety of competing modes of production (global capitalism, local state socialism, new forms of feudalism) produce on one hand corporate office towers, luxury apartments and hotels, state hospitals (Zukin's 'landscapes of power', 1991) alongside a variety of local vernaculars, shanties, cardboard cities and street people warming themselves at shop corners and entrances to subways, manifesting not only deep economic fissures and contradictions, but also cultural and regional heterogeneities.

If these are the characteristics of what is now the 'modern city' in the West, as we have seen it develop in the last twenty years, then it is evident that cultural modernity, understood in terms of poverty as well as riches, was prefigured much earlier, in what is generally referred to as the 'Third World' city of the 1950s and 1960s. Indeed, as I have argued elsewhere (1991), the Eurocentrically defined cultural conditions of a so-called postmodernity – irony, pastiche, the mixing of different histories, intertextuality, schizophrenia, cultural chasms, fragmentation, incoherence, disjunction of supposedly modern and pre-modern cultures (Harvey, 1989) were characteristic of colonial societies, cultures and environments on the global periphery (in Calcutta, Hong Kong, Rio or Singapore) decades, if not centuries, before they appeared in Europe or the USA. How did the local Gujarati inhabitants read the text of 'modern' Bombay in the 1870s? Or the British colonials, that of the village settlements of the Gujaratis? The same question can be put in relation to the Dutch, British and Iroquois in what was to become New York in the early seventeenth century.

What this suggests, therefore, is that what some have labelled 'post-modern' culture pre-dated what they have labelled 'modern' culture, but then that is only possible if we look at modernity in terms of space as well as time.

Notes

This is a revised version of a paper presented at the 10th Anniversary Conference of *Theory, Culture & Society*, Seven Springs, Champion, PA, in August 1992. A shorter version was given at a session on 'Urban restructuring and cultural modernity', at a Conference on 'A New Urban and Regional Hierarchy. Impacts of Modernization, Restructuring and the End of Bipolarity', sponsored by the International Sociological Association Research Committee 21, Lewis Center for Regional Policy Studies, UCLA, and the Program for Comparative Social Analysis, UCLA. UCLA, 23–25 April 1992. I would like to thank Abidin Kusno, Roland Robertson and Janet Wolff for their comments on an earlier draft.

1. I am indebted to Abidin Kusno for this sentence.
2. A recent visit to the Guggenheim Museum of Modern Art in New York was sufficient to demonstrate how historic 'modernism' has actually become. The impression arises not only from the representational absence of any artists other than 'dead white European males' but, on the brink of the twenty first century, their nineteenth-century birthdates
3. This latter has a certain irony as, long before 'voice' had entered critical discourse as a term of contestation, the volume was published as and by the 'Voice of America Forum Lectures'.
4. The relation of these discourses to critiques of colonialism in the 1960s and earlier by, for example, Ranajit Guha, Romila Thapur, Syed Alatas and others, and the geography and history in which this takes place, is the subject of another paper.
5. That the (social science) authors of books on colonialism, the outcome of their own postcolonial experience in the late 1960s, found new audiences for their works in the USA, as well as positions in the US academy, some twenty years later, further confirms my point. I refer to Talal Asad (*Anthropology and the Colonial Encounter*, 1973), moving from the University of Hull to New York's New School of Social Research in 1988, and my own *Colonial Urban Development* (1976), and a move from London's Brunel University to the State University of New York in the same year.
6. On a scale measuring public safety (murders per 100,000), food costs, living space per person, education, public health, clean air, peace and quiet, New York is listed 12th of the 14 largest metropolitan areas in the US (Seattle is the first) and 27th of the world's 100 largest (Melbourne is the first) (Population Crisis Committee, 1990).

References

Abu-Lughod, Janet (1991) 'New York and Cairo. A view from the street', *International Social Science Journal*, 125: 307–18.

Appadurai, Arjun (1991) 'Global ethnoscapes. Notes and queries for a transnational anthropology', in Richard G. Fox (ed.), *Recapturing Anthropology: Working in the Present*. Santa Fe, NM: School of American Research Press.

Asad, Talal (ed.) (1973) *Anthropology and the Colonial Encounter*. London: Ithaca Press.

Ashcroft, Bill, Griffiths, Gareth and Tiffin, Helen (1989) *The Empire Writes Back. Theory and Practice in Postcolonial Literature*. London and New York: Routledge.

Berman, Marshall (1983) *All That is Solid Melts Into Air: The Experience of Modernity*. London: Verso.

Bhabha, Homi K. (1991) '"Race", time and the revision of modernity', *Oxford Literary Review*, 13: 193–219.

Black, C. E. (1966) *The Dynamics of Modernization. A Study in Comparative History*. Evanston/London: Harper & Row.

Bradbury, M. and McFarlane, J. (1976) *Modernism, 1890–1930*. Harmondsworth: Penguin Books.

Clark, Timothy J. (1984) *The Painting of Modern Life: Paris in the Art of Manet and his Followers*. London: Thames and Hudson.

Elvin, Mark (1986) 'A working definition of "modernity"?' *Past and Present*, 113 (November): 209–13.

Giddens, Anthony (1990) *The Consequences of Modernity*. Cambridge: Polity Press.

Hall, Stuart (1991) 'The local and the global: globalisation and ethnicity', in Anthony D. King (ed.), *Culture, Globalization and the World-System. Contemporary Conditions for the Representation of Identity*. London/Binghamton: Macmillan Education/Department of Art and Art History, SUNY Binghamton .

Hamedah, Shirine (1992) 'Creating the traditional city: a French project', in Nezar AlSayyad (ed.), *Forms of Dominance: On the Architecture and Urbanism of the Colonial Enterprise*. Aldershot: Avebury. pp. 241–60.

Harvey, David (1989) *The Condition of Postmodernity. An Enquiry into the Origin of Cultural Change*. Oxford, UK and Cambridge, MA: Blackwell.

Hitchcock, H.R. and Johnson, P. (1966) *The International Style*. New York: W.W. Norton.

Holston, James (1989) *The Modernist City. An Anthropological Critique of Brazilia*. Chicago: Chicago University Press.

Hutcheon, Linda (1989) *The Politics of Postmodernism*. London/New York: Routledge.

Jencks, Charles (1986) *What is Post-Modernism?* New York: St Martin's Press.

King, Anthony D. (1976) *Colonial Urban Development. Culture, Social Power and Environment*. London/Boston: Routledge & Kegan Paul.

King, Anthony D. (1984) *The Bungalow. The Production of a Global Culture*. London/Boston: Routledge & Kegan Paul.

King, Anthony D. (1991) 'Spaces of culture, spaces of knowledge', in Anthony D. King (ed.), *Culture, Globalization and the World-System*. London: Macmillan Education.

King, Anthony D. (1990a) *Urbanism, Colonialism and the World-Economy. Cultural and Spatial Foundations of the World Urban System*. London/New York: Routledge.

King, Anthony D. (1990b) *Global Cities. Post-Imperialism and the Internationalization of London*. London/New York: Routledge.

King, Anthony D. (1994) 'Terminology and types: making sense of some types of dwellings and cities', in Karen Franck and Lynda Schneekloth (eds), *Ordering Space: Types in Architecture and Design*. New York: Van Reinhold Nostrand.

Lamprakos, Michele (1992) 'Le Corbusier and Algiers: the plan Obus as colonial urbanism', in Nezar AlSayyad (ed.), *Forms of Dominance: On the Architecture and Urbanism of the Colonial Enterprise*. Aldershot: Avebury. pp. 183–210.

Lash, Scott (1990) *Sociology of Postmodernism*. London/New York: Routledge.

Levy, Marion J. (1966) *Modernization and the Structure of Societies. A Setting for International Affairs*. Princeton, NJ: Princeton University Press.

Nettl, J.P. and Robertson, Roland (1968) *International Systems and the Modernization of Societies*. New York: Basic Books.

Oxford English Dictionary (1989) Oxford: Oxford University Press.

Pieterse, Jan Nederveen (1992) *Empire and Emancipation*. London: Verso.

Population Crisis Committee (1990) *Cities. Life in the World's Largest Metropolitan Areas*. Washington: Population Crisis Committee.

Rabinow, Paul (1989) *French Modern. Norms and Forms of the Social Environment*. Cambridge, MA: MIT Press.

Robertson, Roland (1992) *Globalization. Social Theory and Global Culture*. London: Sage.

Said, Edward (1978) *Orientalism*. Harmondsworth: Pelican.

Sardar, Ziauddin (1992) 'Terminator 2. Modernity, postmodernism and the "Other"', *Futures* 24 (5): 493–506.

Sassen, Saskia (1991) *The Global City. New York, London, Tokyo*. Princeton: Princeton University Press.

Seed, John and Wolff, Janet (eds) (1988) *The Culture of Capital*. Manchester: Manchester University Press.

Spivak, Gayatri Chakravorty (1988) 'Three women's texts and a critique of imperialism', *Critical Inquiry*, 12 (1): 243–61.

Timms, Edward and Kelley, David (eds) (1985) *Unreal City: Urban Experience and Modern European Literature and Art*. Manchester: Manchester University Press.

Wallock, Leanard (1988) 'New York City: capital of the twentieth century' in Leanard Wallock (ed.), *New York. Culture Capital of the World, 1940–1965*. New York: Rizzoli.

Webster's New Universal Unabridged Dictionary (1984) New York: Simon & Schuster.

Weiner, Myron (1966) *Modernization: The Dynamics of Growth*. Voice of America Forum Lectures.

Williams, Raymond (1984) *Keywords. A Vocabulary of Culture and Society*. London: Fontana.

Worsley, Peter (1963) *The Third World*. London: Weidenfeld & Nicolson.

Wright, Gwen (1992) *The Politics of Design in French Colonial Urbanism*. Chicago: Chicago University Press.

Young, Robert (1990) *White Mythologies. Writing History and the West*. London/New York: Routledge.

Zukin, Sharon (1991) *Landscapes of Power. From Detroit to Disney World*. Berkeley/Los Angeles: University of California Press.

7

ROUTES TO/THROUGH MODERNITY

Göran Therborn

The ironic return of the sociological master narrative

In these supposedly postmodernist times, a good deal of macrosociology has returned to the master narrative of its youth and classical maturity. That is, to the story of the two world characters, under various names, and their appearances and actions: industrial versus military society, the positive versus the religious (and the metaphysical) age, *Gemeinschaft* and *Gesellschaft*, mechanical and organic division of labour, tradition and rationality, primitive and modern or traditional and modern societies. Now it is modernity and pre-modernity (Giddens, 1990, 1991; Luhmann, 1992; Münch, 1986) or modernity/modernism and postmodernism (*Theory, Culture & Society*, 1988), or the *Bildungsroman* of the younger character, modernization (Tiryakian, 1991).

The major differences between the protosociological and the classical sociological versions, from Saint-Simon to Weber, are three. One concerns the scenography. In the long nineteenth century, the stage for the characters was primarily political and, later, economic (Therborn, 1976: Chs 3–5). Now, the story unfolds, above all, in the realm of culture (cf. Featherstone, 1990), which makes works in cultural philosophy and cultural analysis (Berman, 1982; Habermas, 1985; Lyotard, 1984) central to the current argument. Secondly, there is, so far, a shift of emphasis. The dichotomous contrast, while still a central part of the plot, has paled. Instead, the overwhelming effort is invested in depicting the present, whether modern or postmodern. Whether any of those differences constitute any intellectual advance is a moot point, on which any judgement will be withheld here. But it might be argued that a third noticeable dissimilarity of the current narrations, as compared with those of the nineteenth century, does constitute a scientific advance. The world history character of the story is now not just presupposed but argued, in terms of 'globalization' (Featherstone, 1990; Giddens, 1990: 63ff; cf. Albrow and King, 1990). Exceptionally, as in Robertson (1992), the globalization argument may even be linked to an explicit concern with the constraints of West-centredness.

The reach of this possible advance appears to be fairly limited, though. Generally, 'globally' so to speak, the globalization thesis is a blunt assertion, though one not lacking some degree of plausibility in the age of satellite communication, rather than an elaboration of modalities and powers. In face of the prevailing sweeping generalizations about (post)modernity, the pleas for a 'one world sociology' of diversity by previous (Archer, 1991; Oommen, 1990) presidents of the International Sociological Association look little more than pious hopes.

The limitation of this warmed over occidentalist 'universalism' should be obvious to any knowledgeable re-reader of what may be considered the two most brilliant pieces of classical social analysis, Marx and Engels' *The Communist Manifesto* (1848/1972) and Weber's *The Economic Ethics of the World Religions* (1920/1988). The first is probably the most influential text of secular social analysis ever written, which at least testifies to the unmatched brilliance of its argumentation. The second is arguably the greatest individual sociological contribution so far, in its unrivalled combination of analytical edge and empirical mastery.

From Marshall Berman (1982) we have learnt, that the *Communist Manifesto* can also be read as the Modern Manifesto. On its first eight pages (in the *Werke* edition) we do in fact learn about 'modern industry' (three times), 'modern bourgeois society' (twice), the 'modern bourgeois/ie' (twice), 'modern workers' (twice), 'modern state power', 'modern productive forces' and of 'modern relations of production' (Marx and Engels, 1848/1972: 462–9). Indeed, it might very well be argued that the *Communist Manifesto* is the first major sociopolitical affirmation of modernity,[1] contemporary with, albeit slightly antedated by Baudelaire's *Salon de 1846* and its final section on 'the heroism of modern life' (1992).

However, even the most sympathetic contemporary reader of the *Manifesto* will notice the dated prognosis of the following:

> National differences and antagonism between peoples are daily more and more vanishing, owing to the development of the bourgeoisie, to freedom of commerce, to the world market, to uniformity in the mode of the production and in the conditions of life corresponding thereto. (Marx and Engels, 1848/1972: 479; English translation from Kamenka, 1983: 225)

In fact, even Communist countries have gone to war against each other, like Kampuchea and Vietnam, or to the brink of it, like the USSR and China, not to speak of the hecatomb of the First World War and the Holocaust of the Second. The asphalting of the globe by the capitalist world market never quite happened. The current indisputable fact of globally simultaneous media events are hardly convincing evidence for the broad thesis of unspecified globalization.

The enormous historical erudition and perceptiveness of Max Weber still stand up very well to the standards of historians two generations later (Kocka, 1986). But the most specific guiding question of his *Economic Ethics of the World Religions* has been surpassed by world history. The 'emergence of bourgeois enterprise capitalism with its rational organization of free labour' (Weber, 1920/1988: 10, emphasis omitted) is no longer unique to the West. On the contrary, eminently successful competing models of capitalist enterprise have since Weber's time emerged in East

Asia, in Japan and among the Four Tigers (for a sober sociological analysis, see Hamilton and Biggart, 1988).

In brief, the global diffusionist and levelling perspective of Marx and Engels has materialized only in parts and patches. The West is no longer uniquely rational and successful, as it could still look to an observer as shrewd and well-read as Max Weber. Instead of being resurrected, the classical grand narrative of social science needs to be divided up.

Questionable in the overarching thematic of classical sociology is not necessarily its efforts at epochal interpretation, a topic of natural social interest which there is no reason to leave to philosophers or dilettantes. Long overdue, however, is a systematic recognition of the diversity of epochal experiences on the globe, even outside the 'core–periphery' axis of world system analysis. On the other hand, any interpretative attempt at this level of generality will leave a number of rivals, among which a first scholarly sorting by logic, empirical plausibility and investigative fertility may be made, but between which a crucial demonstration is not to be expected.

Modernity and the discovery of the future

'Modernity' has some positive attraction as an epochal label, apart from its current fashionability. Its vague generality makes it capable of wrapping up and relating a number of important economic and political phenomena, which other labels tend to dissociate: phenomena such as capitalism and socialism, industrial and other non-agrarian societies, dictatorships and democracies, bureaucratic and non-bureaucratic organizations. Its cultural connotations tend to focus on experience more than on development (Berman, 1982: 15; Jameson, 1992: 310), which leads more easily in the direction of global diversity. By contrast, 'modernization' is heavily loaded with associations of a single process – though possibly with several parallel axes – a single direction, and a given end (Parsons, 1971; Wehler, 1975). Finally, 'modernity' provides a natural link to cultural studies in the humanities, which provide both a rich source of knowledge for culturally interested sociologists and an interested qualified audience for sociological contributions on the topic.

The relative vacuity of the word, on the other hand, calls for some definitions and specification before use. Basically a time concept, 'modernus' originally developed in medieval Latin as a contrast to the ancient, and to Antiquity (Calinescu, 1987: part 1). The literal referent of 'modern' and 'modernity' is the present, but a new epoch, which we may well call modernity, is characterized by a discovery of the future more than by a valorization of the present: that is, the discovery of the future as an open, unbuilt site never visited before, but a place reachable and constructible. The present is then the beginning of the future, rather than an extension, a prolongation, a repetition or a decay of the past.

The discovery of the future as a contour on an open horizon seems to be only about 200–250 years old, at least in Christian Europe. It may have started from the Judaeo–Christian conception of irreversible time. If cosmic time or human history is cyclical, there can be no future, of course, only the turning around of the wheel. On the other hand, Judaeo–Christian eschatology held out no open vista into unknown, non-constructed futures. The end of the world, the Last Judgement, and the final division into a pre-constructed Heaven or Hell, constituted the religious perspective. Without necessarily confronting the end of the world scenario head on, secularized conceptions of an empiricist gathering of knowledge, of progress and human changeability, of enlightenment, gradually opened the window to the future, as we know it today – as something unfamiliar and non-prescribed, but something at least in principle attainable and buildable. (The variable conceptions of the future – of developmentalist anticipation, sceptical uncertainty, futurological curiosity, etc. – however interesting, are not of immediate concern in the context here.)

Detecting the future was a long and gradual process, which gathered momentum in the eighteenth-century Enlightenment and was finally realized by the French Revolution, by the American Revolution of Independence, and the effect of the latter in Britain. An important part was played by protosociology and the rise of evolutionary conceptions of society and politics, in the French line from Condorcet to Saint-Simon, and in the Scottish Enlightenment (Therborn, 1976: 150–63).

One indicator, from the field of politics, is the establishment of the current meaning of the terms 'revolution' and 'reform', that is, as designating two ways of bringing about a change resulting in something novel. As the Latin prefix 're-' shows, the original meaning of the words was rather the opposite of their contemporary sense, viz. a return to the past, or, in the case of revolution, a cyclical, 'revolving' motion, like that of celestial bodies or of the wheels of a watch (Therborn, 1989; see also Kosellek, 1985: esp. Ch. 1).

The opening up of the present to a future, to something unprecedented, has provided the epoch of the past two centuries with much of its particular timbre, be it in economic enterprise, in political organization, in scholarship, in ideological discourse or in the arts. Next year is not likely to be like this year, or like yesteryear, and should not be. 'Modernity', in this context, will refer first of all to this reorienting the present towards the open horizon of novelty, that is, towards the future.

Without here entering into a sociology-of-knowledge exercise, it is obvious that the discovery and the clear recognition of the future are related to profound social changes which gathered force in the second half of the eighteenth century, the Enlightenment (including the ideological reception of the British 1688 settlement), the beginning of industrialism, the birth of 'the first new nation', the Revolution in France and its international repercussions. From their epicentre in the North Atlantic area, the shock waves of revolutions and of wars for and against them spread rapidly to Central and South America, to Egypt and the Ottoman Empire, to the conquest of India and current Indonesia, to the building of Singapore and the white peopling of Australia. As little as the discovery of the spherical character of the Earth, was the discovery of the future confined to the unbloody serenity of the realm of ideas.

After the failure of the Great Unifiers: the structural and the cultural dialectics of modernity

In social science, sociology being no exception, concepts of time are peripheral, at best. And a social scientific interpretation of an era should pertain to characteristically epochal values on the core variables of the discipline. Otherwise, the contribution of the latter to the interpretation, and the interpretation's relevance to the discipline may appear idiosyncratically contingent. In other words, a sociological conception of modernity should (also) express the latter in terms of the sociological paradigm, if there is one.

In other contexts (Therborn, 1991, 1994) I have argued that contemporary sociology does have a major paradigm, which covers a number of competing schools and theories. In contrast to economics and to rational choice models generally, the mainstream sociological mode of explaining social action is based on the (systematic) variability of actors, instead of the variability of situations with their relative prices and incentives. Sociologists tend to conceive of social actors as crucially varying in two fundamental respects, in their *structural location*, that is, in the relative amount of resources and constraints available to them, and in their *cultural belonging*, in their internalized culture.

Structural location refers first of all to differentiated institutional endowments with resources and constraints of action, and secondly to a-institutional allocations. This variable set also includes location in a time sequence – being the first, the last or something else to something – and spatial distance/proximity. Cultural belonging involves three features, primarily. Belonging to a culture means having a certain identity, differentiated from the rest of the world, mastering a particular cognitive and symbolic code, and having internalized a special set of values and norms.

Standard sociological procedure in dealing with modernity is to assign certain values to modernity on the master variables, which may be phrased in various ways, or to fill out the system traits of it (Giddens, 1990, 1991; Levy, 1966; Luhmann, 1992; Münch, 1986; Parsons, 1971; Tiryakian, 1991 is in this respect a shining exception.) This is in line with the nineteenth-century tradition from Saint-Simon to Weber – Marx excepted, of course – and may seem to be the natural thing to do. But it is remarkably different from the ambivalence or contradictoriness of modernity stressed in many important and penetrating cultural studies (Bauman, 1990; Berman, 1982; Habermas, 1985). And the pervasiveness of conflict in modernity is now hard to forget or neglect for an observer writing in the early 1990s, having lived through or watched rather closely the ignominious end of so many celebrations of peace, order and progress: *la Belle Epoque*, the mid-1920s, the 1950s-early 1960s, and most recently the year from the fall of the Berlin Wall to the end of the Gulf War.

The persistent, recurrent discordances of the modern era render suspect a central motif of the grand epochal narrative of social science, that of the Great Unifier. In the tradition of Condorcet and Comte it was Reason and Science. To Saint-Simon and Spencer it was Industry, to the Scottish Enlightenment it was Commerce. To Marx it was Capitalism. To Weber and, as Habermas (1981: Ch. 4) has shown, the German-oriented branch of Western Marxism from Lukács to Adorno, it was Rationalization and Disenchantment. Recently, the Great Unifier has reappeared as 'the juggernaut' of modernity in a Giddensian formulation (Giddens, 1990: 139).

With due respect for the empirical longsightedness of the pure theorist, the major stumbling blocks in the way of any Great Unifier are, in fact, clearly visible. The structuration of the human population has become vastly more *unequal* since the advent of modernity. The eminent economic historian Paul Bairoch (1981: 8) has estimated the ratio of economic resources (GNP per capita) in the most developed and in the least developed parts of the world as $1:8$ in 1800, $4:5$ in 1860, $10:4$ in 1913, $17:9$ in 1950 and $25:7$ in 1970. The process of polarization is continuing. According to the World Bank's *World Development Report 1992* (here cited from the *Frankfurter Allgemeine Zeitung*, 24 April 1992: 2), the ratio of the GDP per capita of the countries having the richest 20 per cent of the world population to those harbouring the poorest 20 per cent was $30:1$ in 1960, $32:1$ in 1970, $45:1$ in 1980, and $60:1$ in 1990. A calculation in class rather than in country terms would, according to the same source, give a ratio of economic resources of the world's top 20 per cent to those of the poorest fifth of about $150:1$ in 1990. That within the most developed or the most modern countries there has taken place a process of equalization is here no more than a secondary qualification, because of the very tendency of globalization, the globalization of economic and political relations as well as of knowledge.

The other big stone in the way of any peacefully converging march of Modernization is, of course, *nationalism* and ethnic rivalries. Nationalism is, in fact, a product of the social transformations of the second half of the eighteenth century and a manifestation of the ensuing social era with the same birthright as, say, the world market and mass literacy. The rise of nationalism is intimately connected both with the uneven development of the globalized economy and with the spread of literacy and education (Anderson, 1983; Gellner, 1983; Hobsbawm, 1991).[2]

In other words, two massive empirical features of social development over the past 200 years have not been incorporated into the grand social scientific narratives of the epoch, the global increase in inequality[3] and the rise and crystallization of divisive and at least potentially mutually hostile collective identities.

Against this background, it will be worth while pondering whether the epoch of modernity, of which we have delineated above at least the beginning and a considerable stretch, may be characterized by any specific sociological dialectic or tension? Or are global polarization and the repro-duction of rival nationalisms to be taken as no more than empirical con-tingencies? The aim, then, cannot be to present an explanation of the processes of modern history, nor to try to capture the possible inner ten-sions of the modern experience. Rather, my intention is to throw a couple of beams of light into the dynamics of modern social structures and cul-tures.

First, two, as it were, global points about conflict. Other things being equal, we should expect social formations, where the actors are aware that the future may very well differ from the present and from anything that has been, to be more unstable, more tense, more full of strife and clashes, than social formations where the opposite is the dominant presumption. The rulers, the privileged, and the victors should be more fearful and less self-confident, perhaps more accommodating, alternatively more repressive. The ruled, the disadvantaged, and the defeated should be more hopeful, more restless, more likely to raise demands or to plan for revenge or escape than to submit in humility and passivity.

Second, if we drop the barely tenable assumption of the Great Unifier of Reason, Commerce, Industry, Modernization, or Modernity, it should be expected that 'globalization', *ceteris paribus*, should increase the chances of friction, tension and clashes, and that it should amplify them. The multi-plication of the number of social and cultural contacts should lead to more, rather than less conflict – unless overwhelmingly counteracted by some Great Unifier. The hopes for and the candidacies to the latter have been plenty, but they have all failed, at least so far.

Increasingly inequality is also understandable as an inherent tendency of modernity. Any open-ended accumulation of social resources that takes place in an *aggregate*, rather than in a bounded *collectivity* of people should be expected to exhibit a tendency towards increasing inequality. Without the mechanisms of redress and redistribution possible in a collectivity, the success at utilizing available resources in round one, should be expected to constitute an advantage in round two, and so on. Global accumulation and global aggregation have outpaced global collectivization. The result are the figures recorded by Bairoch and of the World Bank.

Modern social structures and modern cultures also have certain intrinsic conflicts. The most central seems to be between two different sides of the open future of modernity, the *openness of social constructions and of their 'objective' weight*, on the one hand, and *the openness of the social con-structors and the possible range of their subjectivity*, on the other. This unity of opposites or dialectical contradiction may be found in the field of struc-turation as well as in the world of culture. Structurally, the non-fenced hor-izon of social constructions means the boundless possibilities of organizational aims, demands, monitoring, surveillance, repression in the allocation, deployment and generation of resources and constraints of social action. But at the same time, modernity has meant the opening of the world to the intentions, options and demands of subjects of action, of free citizens, workers and individuals.

Culturally, the same contradiction takes at least two major forms. One concerns cognition, with the simultaneous development of the social construction of accumulated knowledge – of science and technology – and of the valorization of subjective experience. A variant is the typically modernist combination of the invention (Hobsbawm and Ranger, 1983) and the debunking of tradition, another the parallel development of Big Science/High-Tech with the personalization of politics and the 'personal interest' of the mass media generally. It can, secondly, be spotted in the realm of values, in the tension between the construction of enlightenment and progress and the underpinning of subjective doubt and scepticism.

In the modernity of cultural identity there is also an important dialectic of *individualism* and *collectivism*. Modernity means an opening in the mould of the traditional identity, a possibility of escape from the handed down identity of the family, the locality and social rank. This aperture has two sides. One, leading to an internal patio of individual effort, individual education, occupational choice, romantic love and mobility, geographical and social. The other is turned towards the street of society, to the collectivity of a nation, a class, of a body of citizens, of associational membership. Modern individualism and modern collectivism condition each other, depend upon each other, as well as clash against each other. Only an individual who has emancipated him or herself from the bonds of tradition can function as a full-blown patriot, citizen, militant. On the other hand, it is the collective movements which open the doors of the compounds of tradition. At the same time, between being an individualist and being a collectivist there is no stable mid-point.

Four passes of entry

Once we have discarded the belief in a Great Unifier, even the most basic outline of the development of modernity becomes an empirical question. For my own part, I am just embarking on a research project about it. So what I might offer at this point is no more than some lines of investigation and hypotheses which appear promising on the basis of some previous research (Therborn, 1992), reactions to some earlier formulations (Therborn, 1990) and, of course, from atop a giant body of other people's work.

Taking the globe as an area of comparative empirical research, we may distinguish four major entries into modernity.[4] One is the *European* gate *of revolution or reform*, that is, of endogenous change, the pioneering route, the reasons for which so fascinated Max Weber and have thrilled the Weberian tradition ever since. The French Revolution and the British process from the mid-seventeenth century to 1832 constituted the first major unlockings of this gate.[5] It might be argued that the first gate to modernity thrown wide open was not the European one at all, but indisputably the very first *brèche* was burst open there.

More important, though, is the fact, often forgotten or by-passed, that *resistance* to modernity was also generated within Europe, which is the scene of the most protracted, principled and well-organized battles for and against. Europe was the birthplace not only of liberalism and socialism, but also of legitimism, ultramontanism, conservatism and Fascism (which embraced both anti-modernity and modernity). Only through the fall of the Romanovs, Habsburgs and Hohenzollerns was the victory of the modern forces made final, but significant rearguard action continued up to the end of the Spanish Civil War, in which the outright enemies of modernity formed a significant, though not dominant part of the victorious Franco coalition.

The second pass was located in the *New Worlds* of the Americas, a product of transcontinental migration and genocide, and it was the entrance through *independence*, first of a major part of North America, soon followed by that of the South and Central parts of the hemisphere. In this case, tradition was basically external, the European empires, which were literally thrown into the ocean.[6] Instead of being between progress and reaction, New Worlds conflicts have centred on non-territorial ethnic relations and on federalism and centralism. Alternatively, the more open sociopolitical order led to more complex configurations of politics than the European blocs of reform versus resistance, for example, with rival lower class *caudillos* or political machine bosses pitted against socially *insouciant* advocates of enlightenment, as well as against traditional conservatives. The United States, rather than any part of Europe, might claim to have been the vanguard of victorious modernity, but I am more interested in the location, the shape and the shadows of the entry passes, than in identifying who was the first to enter, or in clocking in this country or that.

Third, modernity could appear as a sudden external threat, as in Bonaparte's expedition to Egypt in 1798 or in Commodore Perry's ships outside Edo in 1853. From such a foreign menace followed attempts at drastic, defensive change from above, according to the Japanese slogan of the Meiji Restoration, 'enrich the country, strengthen the army' and move towards 'civilization and enlightenment' (Beasley, 1972: 241, 352). This pattern of *imposed* or *externally induced modernization* started with Muhammed Ali in Egypt early in the nineteenth century and the somewhat later Tanzimat reforms at the centre of the Ottoman Empire, was most successful in Japan, which provided a not very successfully followed example to China.

This third route of entry, which also includes Iran, Siam/Thailand and a few others, was made up of *external threat and selective imports*. Popular rights were here typically granted from above as an instrument of strengthening a regime under acute external pressure, and a good deal of resistance to modernizing change came from below, from large sections of the people itself. A lasting problem along this route has been to find and keep two moving equilibria at the same time: between the trappings of traditional domestic power and the imported instruments of development, and between accumulation and popular acquiescence. The Japanese rulers have been eminently successful in both tasks, with some crucial help from the US after 1945. The Shah of Iran ultimately failed, and currently bets are being taken on how long the Chinese leadership can keep playing a Sino-Communist variant of the same game.

Finally, there is a vast area from Northwestern Africa via the Indian subcontinent to the Archipelago of Southeast Asia, where modernity arrived by *conquest, subjection and appropriation*, the gate of the *colonial zone*. The Nigerian writer Chinua Achebe (1958/1965) captured the arrival of colonial modernity using a theme from the modern Irish poet W.B. Yeats and his poem 'The second coming': 'Things fall apart: the centre cannot hold/Mere anarchy is loosed upon the world'. Here the road to modernity began as a massive defeat, from which the structuration of the conquerors had to be accepted and their culture learnt, which then could be turned against the conqueror himself and used as means to independence. Pre-modernity was indigenous but defeated, and became discredited by that defeat. Modernity was foreign, but could not be selectively imported and had to be assimilated. Attempts at assimilation, however assiduous, did not remove the barrier between conqueror and conquered, and therefore led to new struggles. The trauma of ex-colonial national emancipation and the issues of national identity, national unity and national development have been of enduringly central significance.

The four routes to modernity distinguished here correspond, *mutatis mutandis*, to the seven patterns of modernization identified by Cyril Black (1966) in one of the most perceptive contributions to 1960s modernization literature. The additional three patterns of Black derive from his temporal and cultural dichotomization of what we have here called the European, the New Worlds and the Colonial Zone routes. Though explicitly based on five considerations (p. 96), Black's ordering is primarily chronological (1966: 90–4), and is part of a largely North America–Western Europe-centred conception of modernization as a sequence of three stages, 'Consolidation of Modernizing Leadership', 'Economic and Social Transformation' and 'Integration of Society'. Only North America and Northwestern Europe had reached this final stage, although Black expected a number of countries to do so 'in the course of the next generation' (1966: 82).

The very different perspective of my interest in routes to and through modernity from the unilinear schema of Black's *Dynamics of Modernization* will be evident, even if any polemic about the framework and its application to countries and dates is abstained from here.

Before leaving, for the time being, our four routes of entry to modernity, a couple of remarks should be added. Though meant to constitute 'real' historical types, the four gates may also be used as ideal types, and individual societies may confront combinations and mutations of them. The history of Egypt, for instance, has features both of externally induced but domestically led entry, and of colonial experiences. Nineteenth- early twentieth-century Russia I think belongs basically to the endogenous European pattern – which is here certainly not meant to consist of a set of social units without significant contacts between and influence upon each other – but from the earlier tradition of Peter and Catherine and on, there is also a non-negligible external element. In modern Latin American history, the colonization of the Indians – as well as their killing and marginalization – is a persistent counterpoint in many countries to the de facto mostly dominant New Worlds song.

The implication of the above is that the route to modernity of the peoples of Europe who have created nation-states far into the modern epoch, from the Balkan peoples to, most recently, the Slovaks and the Macedonians, is largely different from that of the Colonial Zone. How and to what extent remains to be spelt out, although one dissimilarity obviously relates to the much smaller gap in resources and culture between the subjects and the empire in the former case. But it is not to be assumed from the outset that there are no similarities to take notice of.

The four entries singled out here are open to further subdivision. But a considerable amount of abstract generality is deliberate, because the distinction has not been made primarily for purposes of description but for explanation. The hypothesis is that these passes of entry into the modern epoch have weighed upon subsequent social structuration and cultural developments. This has occurred in ways, surely more general and indeterminate but not fundamentally different from the way in which Stein Rokkan (1970: 131) argued that twentieth-century Western European party systems had been shaped by the layered divisions and experiences ensuing from what Rokkan regarded as the 'four critical junctures' of modern European history: the Reformation and Counter-reformation, the Democratic Revolution of 1789 and, after, the Industrial Revolution and the Russian Revolution.

One implication of this is that it is the structural location rather than the cultural carpeting of the entry which has more effects upon later events and patterns. It is the location, internally or externally, of the forces for and against new social transformations which is assumed to matter most here, not, for example, their religious belonging or background. However, that is no more than a hypothesis, which so far has proved fruitful, but which might turn out to require revision.

Without in any way belittling the greatness of his contribution, this perspective entails, then, a rupture with Max Weber's problematic. The latter is now superseded by history in one sense at least, viz. in the sense that there are now undeniably modern societies with different religions. How far the perspective adopted here will hold remains to be demonstrated, but as modernity in the sense defined above entails a breaking out of the time perspective of all religions – none of which has explicitly embraced an open secular future – and modernity then is the direct emanation of no particular religion, some structural, non-emanationist account for the rise of modern society is inescapable. On the other hand, the analytical script used here does not exclude a major role for religion (see p. 136).

The notion of modernization as one (set of) process(es) has to be discarded. Instead, we need to conceptualize trajectories through a terrain of modernity. In this sense, a topology of modernity, of its structural as well as its cultural landscape, is called for, with regard to which routes and trajectories from the different passes of entry can be hypothesized and investigated. Classical sociology and contemporary historiography have left a large number of signposts for this job. But the map itself remains to be drawn. I shall save my still very provisional ideas on the lay-out of the global terrain of modernity for another occasion.

Vehicles of modernity, plus luggage and connections

Modern social action may be summarized in two fundamental forms, which we might label *individualist* and *associative* action. Both can refer to different kinds of acting units, to corporate bodies and to physical individuals, as well as to any number of concrete activities. As analytical categories, they are then capable of relating a wide range of phenomena. Both are based on possibilities of choice and, as such, stand in common distinction to prescribed forms of action, whether individual or collective. Put more lyrically, individualist action and associative action are both manifestations of modern freedom.

The two kinds of action can also capture the basic variation of modern conceptions and practices of social change. There is one line of thought and practice in terms of individual enlightenment, education, choice, competition, achievement, the aggregates of which are also assumed to provide the best chances for the freedom/prosperity/happiness/development/ welfare, etc. of all. And there is another one couched in terms of association, collectivity, unity, co-operation, solidarity and organization as the best road to freedom, justice, strength and development.

Therefore, we may here talk of two main (types of) *vehicles through modernity*, individualism and association. They manifest themselves in the everyday behaviour of individuals and groups, in the operation of enterprises, in sociopolitical programmes and in public policies. But their use varies enormously across modern societies and over time, in relation to pre-written social scripts, in their meaning, in the relative importance of one or the other, in their application to different social spheres, in their combinations, mutations and concrete manifestations.

It is this variation of the forms of modern social action, and of political and intellectual discourses about them, which makes up the main object of my project about modernities, in their relations to the structural routes to and through modernity identified above. Two social spheres, where the confrontations and conflicts of prescription, individualism and association have been especially acute and protracted, will be in focus: the economy and the family. That is, the individualist and the associative forms of action carried out by structurally defined class members and other economic agents, and those of men and women, parents and children, in family relationships.

As problems and as remedies, the basic forms of modern social action also form the core of the three major ideologies or value systems and political programmes of the modern era, of Liberalism, Socialism and Nationalism. Their designs of action constitute, so to speak, the main ideological luggage of modern travellers through history. On the basis of the programmatic sources and targets of action we may get at their interrelationship in the following manner.

Table 7.1 *Modern programmes of social action*

| Recommended action | Target of action | |
	Universal aggregate	Bounded collectivity
Individualist	Liberalism	(Populism?)
Associative	Socialism	Nationalism

Socialism and Liberalism have both universalistic targets of programmatic action, although more often explicit in the former – 'everybody' – more implicit or indirect in the latter, 'anybody'. Whereas socialists strive to organize class members and possible class affiliates, nationalists set out to associate nation members, although usually less comprehensively than the socialists of the Second International. Both clubs, the nation and the class, are social constructions, by nationalists and socialists, respectively, even though the latter is much more amenable to systematic definition.

On the level of elaborate -isms, there is hardly any modern world view of a scope comparable to those of Liberalism, Socialism and Nationalism. But the logic of the fourfold table propels us to look a little harder. And clearly, a network of clientelistic relationships, aggregating people for help from some patron or leader, rather than associating them for justice or unity, would fit into the upper right-hand corner of the table. Some such characterization seems to apply to several tendencies known as 'populism'.

However, the major discourses on modern social action cannot be captured solely by Table 7.1. Rather, the modern -isms should be understood as built upon, sometimes firmly and impressively, sometimes shakily and sporadically, a plinth of cultures of pre-modern origin, above all of *religion*. Indeed, a very important aspect of journeys through modernity has consisted of reinterpretations and reorganizations – and, occasionally (especially in colonial Africa, but also in current Central America), of reinvigorated diffusion – of religion, from the Vedantic Reformation in India and the Islamic Salafiyya movement to the Catholic and Calvinist 'pillarization' of early twentieth-century Europe and post-Second World War Christian Democracy. Though the forces of all religions have formed major battalions of anti-modernity, cultural modernity should not be equated with anti-clericalism, atheism or religious indifference. On the other hand, conservatism – with a small c – constitutes, of course, a constant contrast and opposition to modernity.

One final additional consideration: the interpretation, the evaluation and the application of individualist and associative forms of action have to be studied not only in relation to the gates of entry into modernity and to the subsequent structurations of first-hand travelling experience. The opening up of the world has also meant the development of a still barely systematically researched system of cultural channels, connections of contact and modes of perception. This system of influences is certainly not reducible to 'Westernization'; consider the political and economic influence of Japan from the Meiji period and on, the hopes invested in and the model of the USSR, or the literary and educational impact of Egypt throughout the Islamic world, from providing Indonesian writers in the 1930s with exemplars of prose fiction to providing Afghan political leaders in the 1990s with an Islamic education.

Nor is the international cultural system of modern connectedness to be approached from an assumption of diffusion. What happens at the receiving end is an empirical question, and the hypothesis of syncretism and 'creolization' will often hold more promise than the one of diffusion (see Hannerz, 1987; Vasantkumar, 1992).

Towards a de-centred conception of the global

'Globalization', then, must not imply any Great Unifier of the globe. The analysis of modernity and postmodernity need not resurrect the master narrative of nineteenth-century sociology. Modern historical social development cannot be encapsulated in 'the West and the rest' formula. New means and forms of global communication, new patterns of global interdependence, call for corresponding forms of analytical attention.

However, there is another global challenge, a challenge to comparative studies, to a de-Westernized, de-centred conception of the global, to grasp the diversity of the modern world. To get a handle on diversity means, also, to simplify it, to find something between the endless undulations of the sea and the one asphalted highway. It is in that perspective, that this chapter has provided an outline of the four major gates of entry to modernity, a topology of the terrain it travels, the two main vehicles of modern social action and an inventory of modern travellers' heaviest pieces of cultural luggage. The travels themselves remain to be researched, and their stories to be written.

Notes

The research project from which this paper has emerged is financed by the Swedish National Bank Tercentenary Fund and by the Swedish Humanities and Social Science Research Council. I want to thank my panel chairman Roland Robertson and other participants for general encouragement to go on with this paper, and Jan Nederveen Pieterse for helpful comments.

1. Marx's 'ultimate purpose' (*lezte Endzweck*) with *Capital* was to 'disclose the economic law of motion of modern society', as he put it in his preface to the first edition of the first volume. (The translation is mine from the German original, Marx, 1867/1921: viii.)

2. Roland Robertson's (1992: 58) formulation 'that the prevalence of national society in the twentieth century is an aspect of globalization . . . the diffusion of *the idea* of the national society . . .' aptly expresses a paradox, but evades confronting the issues of nationalism and national conflict head on.

3. Marx did, of course, predict an economic polarization, but in class terms which are not immediately transposable onto a global plane, because within the most developed territories of capitalism a class de-polarization has taken place.

4. The empirical ground for this bold assertion is a study of the development of the right to vote in all the major areas of the earth (Therborn, 1992).

5. A Scandinavian reform route developed quietly almost simultaneous with the revolutionary upheavals in France (Therborn, 1989).

6. True, in Mexico, in Peru and, especially, in Brazil the original, early nineteenth-century line-up was more entangled than that, before being straightened out in a not too dissimilar way. A noteworthy difference from the very beginning, though, was that whereas eighteenth- and nineteenth-century Britain in North America represented the Old World, in the South it stood, with France, for progress, against the anachronistic traditions of Spain and Portugal, see Bushnell and Macaulay, 1988; Lynch, 1973; Romero, 1981. This perspective on Ibero-America differs from a current of twentieth-century Latin American thought emphasizing the Latinity, Catholicism and general Iberian tradition of Latin America, first elaborated by José Enrique Rodó in 1900 and continued more recently in the work of Leopolodo Zea (1992). But at issue here is not whether the latter traditions persist – they do – nor whether they are good or bad, a question upon which my answer would be of little interest. It is whether the New Worlds' perspective of local advance towards the future in contrast to the backwardness of the mother country has been the dominant one among the tone-setting groups in Latin America. In my understanding it has (see Merquior, 1991).

References

Achebe, C. (1958/1965) *Things Fall Apart*. London: Heinemann.

Albrow, M. and King, E. (1990) *Globalization, Knowledge and Society*. London: Sage.

Anderson, B. (1983) *Imagined Communities*. London: Verso.

Archer, M. (1991) 'Sociology for one world: unity and diversity', *International Sociology*, 6: 131–47.

Bairoch, P. (1981) 'The main trends in national economic disparities since the Industrial Revolution', in P. Bairoch and M. Lévy-Leboyer (eds), *Disparities in Economic Development since the Industrial Revolution*. London: Macmillan. pp. 3–17.

Baudelaire, C. (1992) *Selected Writings in Art and Literature*, trans. P.E. Charvet. Harmondsworth: Penguin.

Bauman, Z. (1990) 'Modernity and ambivalence', *Theory, Culture & Society*, 7: 143–69.

Beasley, W. (1972) *The Meiji Restoration*. Stanford, CA: Stanford University Press.

Berman, M. (1982) *All That Is Solid Melts Into Air*. New York: Simon and Schuster.

Black, C. (1966) *The Dynamics of Modernization*. New York: Harper & Row.

Bushnell, D. and Macaulay, N. (1988) *The Emergence of Latin America in the Nineteenth Century*. New York/Oxford: Oxford University Press.

Calinescu, M. (1987) *Five Faces of Modernity*. Durham: Duke University Press.

Featherstone, M. (ed.) (1990) *Global Culture*. London: Sage.

Gellner, E. (1983) *Nations and Nationalism*. Ithaca: Cornell University Press.

Giddens, A. (1990) *The Consequences of Modernity*. Stanford, CA: Stanford University Press.

Giddens, A. (1991) *Modernity and Self-Identity*. Cambridge: Polity Press.

Habermas, J. (1981) *Theorie des kommunikativen Handelns*, 2 vols. Frankfurt: Suhrkamp.

Habermas, J. (1985) *Der philosophische Diskurs der Moderne*. Frankfurt: Suhrkamp.

Hamilton, G. and Biggart, N.W. (1988) 'Market, culture and authority: a comparative analysis of management and organization in the Far East', *American Journal of Sociology*, 94, Supplement: S52–S94.

Hannerz, U. (1987) 'The world in creolization', *Africa*, 57 (4): 547–59.

Hobsbawm, E. (1991) *Nations and Nationalism since 1780*. Cambridge: Cambridge University Press.

Hobsbawm, E. and Ranger, T. (eds) (1983) *The Invention of Tradition*. Cambridge: Cambridge University Press.

Jameson, F. (1992) *Postmodernism, or, the Cultural Logic of Late Capitalism*. Durham: Duke University Press.

Kamenka, E. (ed.) (1983) *The Portable Karl Marx*. New York: Viking Press.

Kocka, J. (ed.) (1986) *Max Weber, der Historiker*. Göttingen: Vandenhoeck & Ruprecht.

Koselleck, R. (1985) *Futures Past*. Cambridge, MA: MIT Press.

Levy, M. (1966) *Modernization and the Structure of Societies: A Setting for International Affairs*, 2 vols. Princeton: Princeton University Press.

Luhmann, N. (1992) *Beobachtungen der Moderne*. Opladen: Westdeutscher Verlag.

Lynch, J. (1973) *The Spanish American Revolutions, 1808–1826*. London: Weidenfeld & Nicolson.

Lyotard, J.F. (1984) *The Postmodern Condition*. Mancester: Manchester University Press.

Marx, K. (1867/1921) *Das Kapital*, vol. 1. Hamburg: Otto Meissner.

Marx, K. and Engels, F. (1848/1972) 'Manifest der Kommunistischen Partei', *Werke*, vol. 4. East Berlin: Dietz. pp. 461–93.

Merquior, J.G. (1991) 'The other West: on the historical position of Latin America', *International Sociology*, 6 (2): 149–64.

Münch, R. (1986) *Die Kultur der Moderne*, 2 vols. Frankfurt: Suhrkamp.

Oommen, T.K. (1990) 'Sociology for one world: a plea for an authentic sociology', *Sociological Bulletin*, 29 (1–2): 1–13.

Parsons, T. (1971) *The System of Modern Societies*. Englewood Cliffs, NJ: Prentice-Hall.

Robertson, R. (1992) *Globalization*. London: Sage.

Rokkan, S. (1970) 'Nation-building, cleavage formation and the structuring of mass politics', in S. Rokkan with A. Campbell (eds), *Citizens, Elections, Parties*. Oslo: Universitetsforlaget.

Romero, J.L. (1981) *Situaciones e ideologías en Latinoamérica*. México: UNAM.

Theory, Culture & Society (1988) *Special Issue on Postmodernism*, vol. 5 (2–3).

Therborn, G. (1976) *Science, Class and Society*. London: Verso.

Therborn, G. (1989) 'Revolution and reform: reflexions on their linkages through the great French Revolution', in J. Bohlin, Bertil Fridén, Urban Herlitz, Åke Kihlström, Anders Molander and Martti Rantanen (eds), *Samhällsvetenskap, ekonomi, historia*. Göteborg: Daidalos. pp. 197–220.

Therborn, G. (1990) 'Vías a través de la modernidad', lecture to the Mexican Chamber of Deputies, 26 November, *Relaciones*, 4: 3–11.

Therborn, G. (1991) 'Cultural belonging, structural location and human action', *Acta Sociologica*, 34: 177–91.

Therborn, G. (1992) 'The right to vote and the four world routes to/through modernity', in R. Torstendahl (ed.), *State Theory and State History*. London: Sage. pp. 62–92.

Therborn, G. (1994) 'Sociology as a discipline of disagreements and as a paradigm of competing explanations: culture, structure, and the variability of actors and situations', in P. Sztompka (ed.), *Agency and Structure: Re-orienting Social Theory*. Philadelphia: Gordon & Breach.

Tiryakian, E. (1991) 'Modernisation: *exhumetur in pace* (rethinking macrosociology in the 1990s)', *International Sociology*, 6 (2): 165–80.

Vasantkumar, N.J. (1992) 'Syncretism and globalization', paper read at the *Theory, Culture & Society* 10th Anniversary Conference, at Seven Springs, PA, August 1992.

Weber, M. (1920/1988) *Gesammelte Aufsätze zur Religionssoziologie*, 3 vols. Tübingen: J.C.B. Mohr.

Wehler, H.-U. (1975) *Modernisierungstheorie und Geschichte*. Göttingen: Vandenhoeck & Ruprecht.

8

SEARCHING FOR A CENTRE THAT HOLDS

Zygmunt Bauman

We are desperate to work our way out of the maelstrom.
(Benjamin Nelson, 1981)

All truly decisive departures this century took us, sociologists, and our kindred experts on history and its works, unawares. Like weather forecasters, we are at our best when prognosticating more of the same; it is the change, the radical change, change in the rules of the game and thus in the game itself, that defies our imagination, shackled as it has been since the beginning of the modern age to continuous time and monotoneity of institutional reproduction. A Hebrew sage of the third century said that three things come unexpected: the Messiah, a found article and a scorpion; on the strength of our shared experience, we may add a fourth one: changes in social mentality and cultural transformations in general.

All the more remarkable was Peter Berger's feat, who as long ago as 1970 presaged that 'the contemporary mood of anti-institutionalism is unlikely to last. . . . Man's fundamental constitution is such that, just about inevitably, he will once more construct institutions to provide an ordered reality for himself' (Berger, 1970). At the time these words were entrusted to newsprint, the message they carried raised quite a few sociological eyebrows. And little wonder – as virtually all the so-called 'empirical evidence' pointed in exactly the opposite direction. That was, as the older among us may still remember, the time of the 'greening of America', of the end of all and any establishment, of rule-breaking being the only rule salvaged from the universal rule-massacre and of the final liberation from everything, including liberation itself, its commitments and its chores. In the caustic verdict of one mortified yet witty observer, the only disagreement which still divided the progressive sociological opinion of the time was that between the action faction and the praxis axis.

Berger wrote what he did not as a challenge to determinism, as it were, but out of conviction that the world is exactly of the regular and orderly kind that modern sociology wanted it to be. The return of institutions that Berger intuited was not to be another feat of free experimentation, but a return to normality. It was the anti-institutionalism which in Berger's view was an aberration, a break in the routine which would soon, as it must, re-establish itself with a vengeance. However unexpected and improbable in the light of current experience, the imminent shift of the cultural pendulum would be but a manifestation of the essential prerequisite of the human condition – one that cannot be altered even if, for a brief moment, it might be neglected and thus seem suspended; a prerequisite which can be precisely calculated, known in detail and hence serve as the ground for a reasonably safe prediction.

That permanent and unalterable human condition (in Berger's own words 'man's fundamental constitution') which makes it impossible for the snubbing, disavowing and disobeying of institutions to last, Berger gleaned from Arnold Gehlen's work (at that time inaccessible to English readers) – a debt he was to acknowledge later in the preface to the English translation of *Die Seele im technischen Zeitalter* (Gehlen, 1980). In Gehlen's rendition, that condition derives from the *Instinktarmut* – the dearth of instinctual equipment – bequeathed to the human species by the biological evolution. *Instinktarmut*, the incurable affliction of the human subject, rebounds in *Weltoffenheit* – the curious 'openness' of its object, the human world. The underdetermination, underdefinition of the human being, robbed of the instincts nature so lavishly bestowed on other species, makes that being into a 'bunch of possibilities' which need to be sorted out so that some of them might solidify into the reality of existence; it also makes the habitus of the human being into a cistern full of fluid chances that need to be inventoried, examined, evaluated and classified according to the interest they may attract and their potential utility. Acting on this need is not easy, and is a source of constant tension and anxiety.

The anxiety would be lessened, tensions allayed, the total situation made more comfortable, were the stunning profusion of possibilities somewhat reduced; were the world a bit more regular, its occurrences more repetitive, its parts better marked and separated; in other words – were the events of the world more predictable, and the utility or uselessness of things more immediately evident. One may say that because of their 'fundamental constitution' human beings have inborn (hereditary) vested interests in an orderly, structured world free of mysteries and surprises. They also have similar vested interests in being more clearly defined themselves, and having their inner possibilities pre-selected for them, turned into the source of orientation rather than being a cause of confusion and distress.

Society may be seen then as an ingenious, though by no means deliberately designed contraption, meant to service such vested interests; whilst the institutions and strict cultural codes, habitualized traditions and coercive norms, are the services rendered. Gehlen could have drawn an additional argument in favour of his thesis from Norbert Wiener's cybernetic vision of human condition; since the void left by the evolutionary silencing of the instincts can be only filled by *learnt* skills and inclinations, and since the ways of acting which have been habitualized through learning stay useful and effective only as long as the world goes on responding in the habitual way – the humans, doomed to rely on what they learn, can only thrive (indeed, survive) in an *organized* (structured, regular) environment; that is, in a setting in which entities are clearly demarcated, while probabilities of events are sharply differentiated, tightly managed and calculable.

Humanity's 'fundamental constitution' as seen by Wiener, Gehlen or Berger privileges structure, power hierarchy and power-assisted definitions of social locations and rules of social interaction. It privileges, one may say, a setting in which essences precede existence; a setting in which the externally supplied, a priori identity is unfolded a posteriori in the life of the individual, rather than being laboriously constructed from scratch in the course of that life. When viewed in the light of that conception, existentialist philosophies of the last half century appear to be both symptoms and auxiliary causes of a temporary, and in the end abortive, deviation from the norm; one may even say: a case of the blatant and potentially morbid violation of 'human essence'. An unfounded existence, or an existence which deems itself unfounded, or one which is carried as if it was unfounded, or one which strives to get free of its foundation – is an aberration, a sign of diseased existence and an inexhaustible fount of social and psychical pathology.

This is one view of the consequences of the notorious paucity of instinctual armament in man. It is not the only one, though. And it is not the only alternative to the existentialist strategy, which proposes (particularly in its most influential, folkloristic versions) to take a full stock and squeeze every potential benefit of the chance offered by the absence of anterior determination, and thus to lift the labour of self-construction from its modality of a blind fate up to the more agreeable status of a consciously embraced destiny. Indeed, one can think also of a third position, which centres on the fact that the endemic underdetermination of human beings is an intrinsically ambivalent attribute: neither an unambiguous curse, nor an unmixed blessing; a source of constant misery, but also of a never fading glory. Most importantly, it is that very ambivalence, the duality rather than singularity of human fate, that makes the 'essence' of humanity; the essence which can be only spoken of in inverted commas, since it is a kind of essence that denies essence, that fails to do what essences are admittedly for, that is prominent mostly for the irreducible ambiguity of its effects, neither of which can be diagnosed without qualification as 'healthy' or 'pathological'.

It is such a third, intermediate position which can be gleaned from the most recent writings of Jean-François Lyotard (1991: 2–7). 'Shorn of speech, incapable of standing upright, hesitating over the objects of its interest, not able to calculate its advantages, not sensitive to common reason, the child is eminently the human because its distress heralds and promises things possible'. Humanity is in a state of perpetual childhood, undying promise and never fully foreclosed possibility – though all the efforts that mark human existence, that are viewed as making that existence meaningful, and classified as attributes of 'maturation', are aimed at leaving childhood behind, standing upright, shedding hesitations, calculating advantages and losses, making common reason rule, and altogether substituting a solid reality for vague and elusive possibility.

> What is proper to humankind is its absence of defining property, its nothingness, or its transcendence. . . . As if reason had no doubt that its vocation is to draw on the indeterminate to give it form, and that it cannot fail to succeed in this. Yet it is only at the price of this doubt that reason reasons.

Because of this property it cannot shed, humanity is bound to implement itself in the perpetual effort to run away from its predicament. But this implementation is its denial; success is its defeat, search for tranquillity brings more misery. Duality is the human fate, and human existence will stay dual, bound to recognize itself simultaneously in two utterly dissimilar images of systemness and contingency. No monistic 'solutions', whether practical or theoretical, will either extirpate that duality from existence or theorize it out and away. No selection, however wisely or cleverly made, will ever exhaust the infinity of possibilities which human 'underdetermination' opens up. Each order is in the end a selection, but each selection just because it is a selection will therefore arouse anger and prompt rebellion, though rebellion against a selection can only be made in the name of another selection . . .

This is the paradox never to be resolved: the endemic indetermination renders man free to choose, yet this freedom is invariably deployed in frenzied efforts to foreclose the choice. Were humans at the start not formless and open to many forms, the formative labour of education would be unthinkable; neither would culture, that set of channels in which the flow of human activity is directed, be conceivable. But education or culture are effective as far as they make choices for their human objects, and preclude other choices which, from the perspective they set, turn wayward and aberrant. The result is the *system*, which in Lyotard's words 'has the consequence of causing the forgetting of what escapes it'. And what escapes it is the other aspect of human condition, at least some part of it that avoided harnessing and resisted obliteration. No system has ever completely disposed of that residue. But what remains in that residue is itself fraught with system-building zeal. When striking back, it may topple this system here and now, one that looms currently over its horizon as the embodiment of all oppressive constraint, of constraint as such; but only to start erecting another system, that will set aside its own residue. It is solely the period of *interregnum*, when the forces of order and the anti-systemic forces are finely balanced, which creates the illusion of the 'end of a system'. But the human condition is such that in one fell swoop it spawns systems and the rebellions against them: anti-systemic protest and system-building zeal.

One is tempted (many theorists indeed have been) to view modernity (that unique form of life which gestated imperceptibly through most of the middle ages, came into philosophers' view around three centuries ago, emerged as consciously self-propelling and self-monitoring a century and a half later, and reached its culmination in the last half century, in Europe and its many offshoots) as a period in which human inherent in-determination has finally come into its own. Perched as we are today at the peak of modernity's achievement, we are inclined – when looking down on the up-hill path that brought us here – to see mostly the story of a breathtaking, obsessive surge up and forward, of unstoppable *transcendence*: barriers being jumped over or kicked aside, new ridges climbed which but yesterday seemed beyond reach, ever new limits declared, and made null and void. This view has been given an updated rendering by the French historian Krzysztof Pomian, who came to define the unique European civilization, that locally conceived civilization which in its global hubris and ecumenical ambition called itself 'modernity', as one 'qui pose comme possible, parfois même comme souhaitable, un déplacement, voire une abolition de chaque frontière et inspire des comportements individuels et collectifs en vue d'y arriver' (1992). This is, writes Pomian, a civilization which has the 'manière d'être qui consiste en un déplacement perpétuel des frontières', and hence 'une diminution du respect pour les barrières, les obstacles, voire les interdits' (1992) – *all* barriers, obstacles and prohibitions – as its most decisive distinguishing marks. The urge to transgress, kept at bay elsewhere or at other times, here had been set loose and virtually went on the rampage. Mechanisms emerged that make transgression self-propelling, needing no purpose. Compulsively, we go on breaking ever new boundaries though we would rather not pay the price of the breakthrough (the pursuit of economic growth, in full consciousness of waste piling up and ecological damage, being the most salient example of such compulsion). Having become the mode of modern existence, transgression also turned into its own goal, needing no justification or apology. Hillary climbed Mount Everest 'because it was there'; we break the barriers because we do not respect them, do not acknowledge their right to be there, and thus see each one of them as an insult and a challenge.

What this account leaves out of sight is that the amazing compulsion and ability to transgress was all along, paradoxically, the by-product – one is tempted to say an *unanticipated consequence* – of the frantic search for a new order, a new level of stability. The corrosive substance of transgression was, so to speak, the waste of the order industry. It was the seductive image of the omelette which sealed the fate of the eggs. Present ridges were abandoned because new ridges up there seemed to promise more safety and stability; barriers were broken because the land behind them seemed more fertile for a life free of tensions which made people restless in the first place. Modernity, indeed, proved to be the time of transgression. But it has been such a time because it cannot stop seeking an order, indeed 'building' an order which 'nature', most blatantly, could not secure. Modern history ran under the sign of the conviction that only under the rule of human reason would the world, and the fate of humans in it, be in safe-keeping. Descartes called to unmask tradition so that men can become 'mâitres et possesseurs de la nature'; a manifesto, if there ever was one, of what Maritain called the 'anthropocentric optimism of thought': what humans needed but nature failed to provide, humans most certainly will. Modern utopias and revolutionary ideologies inspired their readers or followers to transgress in the name of the end to all future transgression; they all painted an alluring image of a new order of things which will put paid to transgression, and all the discomforts that come with it, by banishing everything the humans might conceivably wish to be transgressed.

You need what you miss. It was modernity's organic inability to secure a system that works which made modernity the most restless of known forms of human life. It was modernity's conscious preoccupation with order, the ceaseless experimenting with ever new orders, which left each specific order too little time to muzzle or tame that multifinality which brought the indeterminacy of human condition fully into the open; but that preoccupation itself was a response to the underdetermination already revealed and suffered. Order and freedom surged forth together, to become the two poles between which modern existence was plotted, two hubs of the axis around which modern mentality rotated.

Gehlen wrote of the pre-scientific view of the world as 'caught in a rhythmic, self-sustaining, circular process of motion, thus constituting an animated *automatism*' (1980: 13). That view, later dismissed and derisively dubbed as *pre*-scientific, was, as all views are, a mental reprocessing of practice. It was existence itself which was modelled after the automation, with its regular cycles of activity fitted tightly into nature's seasons; so regular, that they inspired the philosophers still at the threshold of the modern, 'scientific' era, to describe God as clockmaker, and His creation as clockwork. Plausibly, the image of God, itself a personification of the idea of preordination, a powerful force hovering high above the vale of tears and definitely out of reach of ordinary mortals, summed up the experience of life as a process which human enterprise may influence but little, if at all. Plausibly as well, the absence of the idea of infanthood as a separate human condition, so strikingly documented by Philippe Ariès, reflected the practice of undisturbed and unchallenged continuity between the earliest and the latest stages of individual life, at no point reaching the crossroads with its choice of itineraries; in such a practice no room was left for the childhood as a state of acute indeterminacy.

Not that identity was *experienced* in that bygone world as given once and for all and immutable, or *theorized* as 'ascriptive status', as it has been construed, with ex-post-facto insight, by Sir Henry Maine and the generations of social scientists who followed him. The researchers of the *OED* located the first ever application of 'identity' to the human individual and his/her personality only in the middle of the seventeenth century. The concept of individual identity was coined when the tension between possibility and determination was already lived as the axis of life experience. It would be incorrect to say that at the early stage of the modern era the openness of individual identity was discovered, and replaced the former conviction that identities are given at birth and for life. Neither the first nor the second image could emerge or exist on its own. What was truly acutely experienced and avidly theorized about was the *opposition* between openness and closure, indeterminacy and determination, possibility and inevitability – between what humans could and should do and that which they needed to accept in humility as irreparably beyond their power. The image of identity emerged, one may say, at the interface between doing and suffering.

And it emerged not as liberation, but as bereavement: identity appeared in human view first as the need to *fill a void*. Less and less could one confine one's concerns to living 'up to the standard' – since less and less could one say with certainty what was *the standard* one had to live up to. Standards started to shift, and then there were many of them. The authority of each one came to be cast in doubt, ridiculed or otherwise sapped by another, finding its own indignance reciprocated. A yawning hollowness now spread where once was a centre that held the world, and all its segments, in place. Order was not something to be obeyed and observed – as there was no order which could be observed without conflict and singeing one's fingers. If there was to be an order at all, one had to think of it as something to be constructed and defended, in all its fragility and precocity. It was not that here and there the unexpected, the irregular or the anomalous threatened the order of human universe: anomalies fill the modern stage wall to wall, anomalies are the universe. As Benjamin Nelson (1981: 208) put it in his usual pithy mode,

> the apparent anomalies of our time are general, universal, they are also deliberate. Everything undergoes the kind of shifting that one would expect in a society which, as Kierkegaard saw, has this inexhaustible capacity to absorb any sort of dissenting innovation and turn it into some kind of form of impersonation, new life-style, new stage setting, new points of departure for spectacle, business, or busy work.

No longer do things carry their sense written all over their face. Now they must be made sense of. There is as much order in the world, and no more, as we manage to put into it.

It was the mind-boggling competition of standards cancelling each other's authority, which sedimented 'the individual' as the experience of rupture between the 'doing' and the 'suffering'. For the individual, as Gehlen (1980: 41) remarked, 'there is no longer a close correspondence between his view of what he is doing, and his view of what happens to him'; I propose that this disconnection, this glaring dearth of correspondence, is what made modern life into an *individual* life. The individual was born with a task for which he or she was ill-equipped. He or she had to blaze a life-trail through a land marked with more crossroads than roads. As there were few signposts to guide him or her, each turn could not but leave in its wake a gnawing doubt and harrowing suspicion of error.

Individuality was, of course, as still is, a matter of degree. If, as Anthony Giddens made clear, self-constitution of individuality (self-actualization, the ongoing process of identity-sustenance) as a 'reflexively organized endeavour' is a universal predicament of the modern person – then it is also true that in modern society:

> class divisions and other fundamental lines of inequality, such as those connected with gender or ethnicity, can be partly *defined* in terms of differential access to forms of self-actualization and empowerment. . . . Holding out the possibility of emancipation, modern institutions at the same time create mechanisms of suppression, rather than actualization, of self. (Giddens, 1991: 6)

With the advent of modernity some people, the elite, were cast into the choosing mode first, and in a more radical fashion than others. These 'others' – the 'masses' – were spared the choice, as the choice was made for them before they knew it. The masses differed from the elite precisely in not being individuals; neither in the shape of their life-predicament, nor in the resources without which no choice can be contemplated, nor in the achievements expected of them. The difference between the elite and the masses was not a mere opposition; it stood for an active relationship of domination and dependency, for a split between the subject and the object of action. The elite – the free, the individuals – faced a twofold task. They needed guidance for their own choices, but not *any* guidance; they required a formula which at the same time would help them to direct their own lives and demonstrate beyond reasonable doubt why others are not fit to direct theirs.

The formula was to be good for both the elites' and the masses' consumption; what it was to promote in the first case, it was to deny in the second. These contrary demands involved it from the start in a contradiction it struggled to overcome without ever definitely succeeding. Intellectually, modernity was to remain incurably two-faced. *Liberalism* was one face: humanity as individualism, the sacred right of the individual to his body, person, property, mode of life, the sacred duty of the individual to pursue happiness, personal improvement and self-fulfilment. Also, inevitably, this view included the criminality of all constraints imposed on individual choice, emptiness of common causes unless the 'common' means shared gains and joint action to avoid losses; togetherness as a contract between self-interested partners. The second face was *communalism*: belonging as the only right, loyalty as the supreme duty; dignity as basking in collective glory; self-interest as partaking of collective welfare; and seeking the place that has-been-allotted-already, making the best of it without looking sideways, as the recipe for honest life. The first face was meant for the elite who could afford it; the second for the masses, who could not. To the *freischwebende* intellectuals, who tried to make sense of both, the two-facedness was all along the cause of a headache no mental antics were able to allay. Their co-presence defied logic and denied the rational coherence of the kind modernity claimed and illegitimately boasted of. Explaining either of the two likenesses away (as a diseased distortion, not the 'proper' face of modernity), not to mention trying to conjure it out in practice, could only incapacitate modernity as a viable form of life. Perhaps instead of two faces, one should speak of the two legs on which modernity stood. It could move only using both.

Modernity, which invented and proudly promoted individualism, also spawned nationalism, communism and fascism. All in equal measure were its legitimate children; all were equally at home in the family house of modernity, as were the elites and the masses, which modern society sedimented at its poles. Nationalism, communism and fascism were tools of the elites' hegemony over the masses: nets in which the masses were held once the elites set themselves apart as members of superior culture designing rules all of their own; mechanisms that helped to reforge political and economic domination into a cultural hegemony; pins holding together the split and potentially conflict-ridden society. Individualism and collectivist ideologies alike were responses to the modern identity crisis. All offered identity as a *choice*; individualism offered it to the minority who could choose; the ideologies of 'belonging' offered it, as a sort of consolation prize, to the majority that could not. There was a constant demand for both kinds of offers. Their co-presence might have seemed incongruent to the devotees of reason. The abstract contradiction notwithstanding, the two formulae reveal complementarity once set against the sociopsychological logic of the inherently two-tier society. The resourceful find the choice exhilarating. To the resourceless, the inability to exercise in practice the choice apparently open in theory brings humiliation and an acute need for psychic compensation which only the collectively supplied identity can bring.

Complementarity does not necessarily mean peaceful cohabitation. The culture of identity-choice, being the culture of the dominant, tends to become the dominant culture. In modern society, which has dismantled or radically weakened the non-reflective automatism of the orderly reproduction of order, it is the job of the dominant to provide the centre that holds society together. The dominant culture tends, therefore, to become a *hegemonic* culture; a proselytizing culture, a culture of conversion and assimilation, a culture that represents its privilege as the pattern for all, and its standards as universal; a culture that demands not only respect but also emulation. The dominant culture of modern society being what it is – a culture of choice and self-constitution – its hegemony cannot but constantly undermine the compensatory capacity of collectivist ideologies and collective identities they offer. It cannot but sap the authority of everything short of the 'universally human', that is everything that sets limits to individual self-creation. The impact depends on the condition of the affected. As Berger indicated, 'what to one will appear as a profound loss will be seen by another as the prelude to liberation' (1970). But contrary to Berger, the difference *does not* depend 'on one's basic assumptions about man'. It is a philosopher's fallacy to imagine that – by adopting a different philosophy – men and women (all people, including those who have little possibility of choice) can reforge the loss into a gain. The fallacy itself is an organic part of the hegemonic drive; it also makes manifest that drive's organic weakness.

The modern elite of the already-liberated despises herd instinct, crowd behaviour, the faceless mass. More than anything else, it scorns ascription, pre-determination, wing-clipping. It respects only such identity as can be said to have been freely chosen: it even demands (as Sartre did) that *serial fate* be embraced as self-made *destiny*. What has been chosen is of lesser importance, when compared to the *opportunity* to choose. Getting out of the herd is the condition of humanity, insofar as the already-liberated cannot conceive of humanity in any other way but that of an extrapolation of their consciously embraced modality. The humanizing function of the elite boils down, therefore, to spreading the gospel of opportunity. To be human is to choose. Choice is human. Humanity thus circumscribed leaves out, however, a good many of such people as may desire to be human, and to be human in the form the choosers' classes have stamped on humanity. The *opportunity* to choose does not always, does not for all, follow the *gospel* of choice – and then the outcome is disillusionment, disaffection and anger.

One by one, all obstacles to free choice have been discredited, disavowed and disempowered. Ours, says Baudrillard, 'is the state after the orgy. . . . All finalities of liberation are already behind us . . . we are now accelerating in the void' (1990: 4). Not all find the void a comfortable place; not all can move freely there, let alone accelerate. Some *choose* the void as the habitat they prefer; some feel rather that they are *thrown in* the void without having been asked, let alone consulted. For them, the dismantling of constraints is not experienced as liberation, but as a loss: and what has been lost reveals itself, in retrospect, as identity. If, for some, identity is 'what is not yet', for others identity means 'what is no more'. In the 'state after the orgy', there are no identities in the present. For some, they loom in the future, as an exhilarating challenge and a pleasurable task; for others, they lie in the past ever more distant and beyond reach: the case for nostalgia, sorrow and wrath.

The two aspects of modern existence sediment as two forms of life, two tiers of society. Each tier has its reason to be disenchanted, but the reasons neither coincide nor add up. What one tier needs, the other has in excess and in supply greater than it bargained for. One tier suspects in the form of life of the other a remedy for the discomforts of its own. This is precisely what the theoretical efforts to build unified, coherent and universally valid models of modern condition attempt to forget or neglect to remember. It is for this reason that each is found sooner or later unsatisfactory; each leaves too much out, unexplained and inconceivable – only to be forcefully reminded of what has been left out by realities which can no more be theorized away as relics, anomalies or transitory ailments. Hence the pendulum-like restlessness of intellectual moods. Hence the constant tussle between the extremes. Hence the habit of replacing a worn-out, shown-to-be-useless formula, with its exact opposite – only too often mistaken for a change in public sensibility or in the social condition of humanity.

For the vision of modern condition as one lived by the lonely individual busily experimenting with their own identity, while playfully assembling and disassembling a variety of colourful, seductive cultural tokens – the voracious and evidently insatiable appetite of modern men and women for collectivist shelters is bound to remain a mystery. To the subscribers to alternative visions, which take stock of the condition of the other, disempowered half, and logically conclude that a prospect of a *collective* redemption is what that other half must need – the deep-seated fear of the 'I will put you in the place you deserve' promise comes as an unpleasant surprise and can be only construed as conspiracy of unreason.

Two phenomena have come into prominence in recent years, which barely tolerate (or so it seems) a logically coherent account. One is the rise of new tribalism, xenophobia, intolerance to otherness. This has been decried by politicians as germination of the not-fully-wiped-out racist virus; by social theorists, keen to unravel lawfulness in every turn reality may take, this has been classified as the resurgence of community, the comeback of tradition and prematurely buried historical roots, resurrection of nationhood and the primacy of natural belonging. The other phenomenon is systematic rejection, by one country after another, of any political offer redolent of collectivist solutions to individual troubles. Country by country, elections are won by politicians careful not to expound on any vision except the vision of radical absence of visions; politicians who promise to interfere the least with the solitude of individual struggles. The well-nigh universal applause with which the systematic tendency to shift the burden of taxation from direct to indirect taxes is greeted provides an illuminating aspect of this phenomenon: shifting the burden does not cut the sum total of taxes, and thus does not augment the sum total of resources that serve individual freedom, but it offers a brief interlude – between cashing a cheque and writing one – in which mastery over fate can be played out gratifyingly and the individual may assert oneself as he who chooses and identifies oneself through the choices made.

The apparently rampant collectivism of the first phenomenon, the ostensibly rugged individualism of the second; can they both be accommodated in one coherent model of modern condition? Current theoretical responses seem to suggest that they cannot. One response that is rapidly rising in authority and popularity is that which makes Berger's theoretical guess into a prophecy come true: the communalist response, clamouring to vindicate the community, tradition, commonality of fate and culture – whose obituaries, penned by the adherents of the system-individual syndrome, it declares premature. Once seen as the major obstacle to full humanity, community ties and a culturally confined horizon are here recast into humanity's natural domicile.

It is not very difficult to understand why such a plea on behalf of the reputedly neglected community should inflame the sociologists' imagination. For the duration of the modern era, the hopes of the sociologists were, for better or worse, vested with the managers of the society and locked in their control room – the state. This remained a rational investment, as long as the state (aptly described as the 'nation-state', though only in retrospect – for orthodox sociology the territory circumscribed by that state was too evident to require a name of its own; the name 'society' would do) took it upon itself to pin together the potentially contradictory tasks of individual liberation and systemic integration of those who could not, or would not be made into individuals – each task, and both of them, seen as a matter for societal legislation, norm-setting, institution-building, value-promoting, social engineering. Such a tight, neat and compact arrangement seems to be increasingly frayed at its dual – the 'systemic' and the 'individual actor' – projections, however. More importantly still, this impression itself comes from the fast weakening (some would even say disappearing) centre: the nation-state loses or gives up its real, or assumed central role of the control room, where systemic performances and individual actions were co-ordinated and the value-clusters holding them together composed and issued forth. Without the centre to hold it, the system appears much less systemic – hardly systemic at all; and disparate individual deeds and motivations must be referred elsewhere in search of their co-ordinating principle.

This 'elsewhere' is, by the overwhelming sociologists' choice, the community; an entity much softer and looser than the nation-state ever was or dreamed to be, an entity with fluid frontiers, a petering out and waning periphery around anything but a unified core, and a but vaguely defined membership. Communities come in many sorts. Yet the ethnic ones are in the forefront, serving as a model by which all others are measured or imagined. It is after their pattern that the religious, gender, political or taste-cultural communities or quasi-communities are conceived. Instead of the prerequisite-function connection which was assigned the integrating task in the nation-state based systems, the two-directional link of cultural determination and allegiance is accredited with producing and reproducing the living tissue of community.

Communities are theorized as first and foremost *cultural* formations. And culture is an activity in which we, the knowledge class, are by common agreement particularly good. No wonder that, evicted from the service of the state which lost its interest in grand ideological formulae once the monotonous reproduction of social order came to be secured by means other than political legitimation, we, the culture-makers, culture-brokers and cultural missionaries, look to community in hopeful anticipation of useful, prestigious and rewarding employment.

As has been the case so many times in the past, sociological imagination has followed the shifting realities of sociologists' social placement. Now, as always in the past, it tends to represent our current experience as true social reality, and spin a 'new and improved' ontological vision out of the yarn of our current concerns and anxieties. In doing this, we follow today the example of the nocturnal moth from Karl Marx's doctoral dissertation, which – 'when the universal sun has gone down', 'seeks the lamplight of a private world'.

Postmodernity is a swarming time for nocturnal moths, being as it is the sunset time of universality. But is it, really, the sunset time as so many would swear? Universality as dreamt of by modern mind had two faces which could not be set apart. One turned toward human habitat, the other towards the interior of the human actor: a universal context for human life set and supervised by one and only human reason; and the purely human 'nothing but human' actor, stripped free of all local garbs that hid and belied his humanity. The two universalities were fastened together in and by the nation-state: that truly unique, wondrous contraption which worked with some success to wed what never before nor since has been brought together – the supreme authority of legislative reason, and the supreme moral allegiance of men and women subjected to that authority. The marriage could hardly survive the slow, yet relentless erosion of the nation-state, simultaneously skimmed from above and sapped from below.

From above, the nation-state's economic sovereignty is thinned, followed closely by its capacity for independent policy-making. The nation-state no longer presides over anything approximating the concept of 'national economy'. Assets of many a supranational corporation exceed today the GNP of an average nation-state; with capital moving freely through boundaries that look tight only in world atlases, multinationals find it easy to blackmail nation-states into submission to whatever they define as the interest of the economy. Indeed, of Albert Hirschman's two strategies, the Voice needs seldom to be used – the threat of the Exit will usually do. In Harold Perkin's estimation:

> the corporations, either individually or collectively, can bring influence to bear on the politicians and bureaucrats, who cannot afford to ignore their wishes, and can, with supreme irony, capture the state itself for their ideology and so use it to ensure freedom from state intervention. (1992: 57)

From below, the state-endorsed nationhood is increasingly contested as the principal frame of cultural identity, by smaller-scale allegiances – territorial or non-territorial, claimed to be natural or self-admittedly contrived. The *état*-ized nation's integrative capacity becomes ineffective and in the end redundant. The role of the moral community, one that sets norms and monitors conformity, is increasingly fragmented and pluralized. But unlike the state, moral communities that take over this role have only their shaky powers of persuasion with which to promote conformity (and, indeed, moral consensus). Gaining converts to the norms they preach, raising the numbers of those who adhere, is a task identical to creating morality, itself a task identical in its turn with bringing the community into being (Walzer, 1971: 8). It is open to doubt whether the nation-state, with all its accomplishment in bringing the economy, politics and morality, coercion and education, within the domain of the same legislative authority, has ever attained more than a remote likeness to the integrated, self-equilibrating system drawn by its court painters. Most certainly, however, communities are not nation-states in miniature.

An odd thing happened on the road from nation-state to community: without a centre wishing and able to hold, it is now the scattered peripheries that have to conjure up, by efforts all of their own and divided as they are, centres to be held by. To acquire the power to bestow identities, communities must talk themselves into reality, whilst silencing the talk about this reality being but the reality of their talking. Boundaries of 'our language' must be drawn, to include as dialects what the competitors would promote as languages and exclude as foreign languages what their speakers would claim to be just dialects. Traditions must be invented that contest the competitors' view of what in the past was united and what was disparate, and assign prime importance to what the competitors would rather marginalize or better still make forgotten. Loyalties must be negotiated anew and priorities within multiple allegiances rearranged. All this is to be done loud and clear, in a world in which public attention is the scarcest of commodities, and in which to be of consequence is to be heard and seen. If the survival of the nation-state requires beating off the enemies outside and incapacitating the strangers inside, the self-gestation of a community requires shouting down the competitors and numbing the dissidents. It requires rather a lot of militancy, belligerence and aggression. It leaves little time for tolerance and compromise, still less for solidarity. It favours war-cries over arguments, effigy-burning over contemplating the diversity of human ways.

In the world of nation-states identities were felt often as a burden rather than the gift of freedom; frequently they came together with the experience of constraint and oppression. In these circumstances, radical liberation took the form of universalism: there were too many centres and each held too fast. Liberation meant shaking off the grip of the centres. It was the nation-state itself, with its drive toward uniformity, the substance of the nation-building effort, that first raised the banner of universalism; but there was no clear reason why that banner should not beckon the troops beyond the state-guarded boundaries. Nationalism's war against parochiality spawned willy-nilly, as its logical extension, a cosmopolitan disdain for the parochiality of nationalism; nationalism itself became vulnerable to the charge which it used to such effect in promoting its own brand of universality. The drive to replace centres which *should not* hold with a centre that *should* led to a situation without a centre that *could*.

Thus universalism, the sign under which nation-states won, only to find themselves robbed of the fruits of their victory – seems to have lost a large part of its attraction. It made identities too nebulous, immaterial, and altogether weightless for comfort, not to mention security. It made individuality feel like bereavement rather than freedom. In the time we call postmodernity the stern and paternal centre stands less unambiguously for oppression, and constraint seems less of an unmitigated disaster. Today, civil wars – also, and most prominently, the wars waged in the name of liberation – are fought to gain the recognition of the communal right to endow identity. In such wars, imaginary centres are made real, or made to look real, so that they may behave as centres do: so that they may *hold*. Since the centres have now little more than the soldierly dedication of the periphery to rely on for the strength of their grip, the chances of a lasting peace are dim.

References

Baudrillard, Jean (1990) *La Transparence du mal: essai sur les phénomêmes extrêmes*. Paris: Gallimard.

Bauman, Zygmunt (1992) *Intimations of Postmodernity*. London: Routledge.

Berger, Peter (1970) 'On the obsolescence of the concept of honour', *European Journal of Sociology*, 11: 339–47.

Gehlen, Arnold (1980) *Man in the Age of Technology*, trans. Patricia Lipscomb. New York: Columbia University Press.

Giddens, Anthony (1991) *Modernity and Self-Identity: Self and Society in the Late Modern Age*. Cambridge: Polity Press.

Lyotard, Jean François (1991) *The Inhuman: Reflections on Time*, trans. Geoffrey Bennington and Rachel Bowlby. Cambridge: Polity Press.

Nelson, Benjamin (1981) *On the Road to Modernity: Conscience, Science and Civilization. Selected Writings*, edited by Toby E. Huff. Totowa: Rowman & Littlefield.

Perkin, Harold (1992) 'The enterprise culture in historical perspective: birth, life, death – and resurrection?', in Paul Heelas and Paul Morris (eds), *The Values of the Enterprise Culture: The Moral Debate*. London: Routledge.

Pomian, Krzysztof (1992) 'L'Europe et ses frontières', *Le Débat*, 68: 28–47.

Walzer, Michael (1971) *Obligations: Essays on Disobedience, War, and Citizenship*. Cambridge, MA: Harvard University Press.

9

SECURITY, PHILOSOPHY AND POLITICS

Michael Dillon

What might be called a society's threshold of modernity has been reached
when the life of the species is wagered on its own political strategies.
(Michel Foucault, 1987: 143)

Security and modernity

Here, deliberately juxtaposed because there is an intimate link between
them, are two of the most emblematic as well as problematic terms of our
times, elementary words that now seem indispensable for human being.
Modernity is a self-defining historical location – these are modern times and
we are moderns – security specifies the pre-condition for the self, and for
that taking charge of ourselves and the world, which is the defining project of
the other. A secure self and a secure world. A secure self seeking security in
the secure self-knowledge by which it secures the world, and itself, for itself.

In order to establish its version of the truth about these words, modern
thinking would either have us define and refine security and modernity in all
their particulars so as to measure, evaluate and exhaust their meaning; and
us in relation to them. This is the rationalist response (Oakeshott, 1991;
Taylor, 1993). Or, it would have us cultivate and refine the technologies of
individual reflexivity (Giddens, 1990, 1991) – the reflexivist response. From
my perspective there is little to chose between them. One way and another
each shows in a hermeneutic of desire the search for security.

Before we elect to subscribe to any answer or mode of answering the
question concerning security or modernity, however, we should first think
about how to pose the question. But because they are so rigorously and
insistently enframed by the metaphysical assumptions of Western thought,
current ways of posing questions about both security and modernity have
already been substantially decided. And, precisely for that reason, so also
have the criteria for determining what proper answers would look like. This
is why I want, initially, to resist being drawn into all the conventional
contemporary debates not only about modernity, but also about what I want
to make my special focus of attention, the means, so to speak, by which I
want to access debates specifically about political modernity, namely

security. For contemporary arguments about security substantially arise
from a shared background, the Western tradition of thought that is
metaphysics. It is that background which first allows security to impress itself
as a self-evident condition for the very existence of life – both individual and
social. One of those impulses which, it is said, appears like an inner
command to be instinctive (in the form, for example, of the instinct for
survival) or axiomatic (in the form of the principle of self-preservation, the
right to life, or the right to self-defence), security is that value which modern
understandings of the political and modern practices of politics put beyond
question.

For a time other than our own, the security of an ecumenic belief offered
by the Christian Church insisted: '*Extra ecclesiam nulla salus*' (No salvation
outside the Church) (Wolin, 1961). The reverse, of course, was equally true.
No Church without salvation. But, and in a way that indicates the continuity
of the metaphysical tradition, that slogan is easily adjusted to furnish the
defining maxim of modern politics: no security outside the state; no state
without security. Security (now advanced under many names in addition to
that of salvation and so thought similarly but differently) is the predicate,
therefore, upon which the architectonic political discourses of modernity
have been constructed; upon which the vernacular architecture of modern
political power exemplified in the state is based; and from which the
institutions and practices of modern politics, *a fortiori* modern democratic
politics whose political imaginary has to be modified to take account of what
I am going to call (in)security, ultimately seek to derive their foundational
legitimacy.

I want to challenge this foundation of politics in security by pursuing a
different line of thought; a line opened up by Heidegger's history of Being as
metaphysics. While allowing me to call into question the very framework of
thought within which the question of the political has been conceived and
pursued as a question of security, namely metaphysics, this strategy has the
additional virtue of nonetheless enabling me to concentrate even more
closely upon the question of security; precisely because metaphysics itself is
so invested with, and by, the appeal to security. As you will see, I think that
this casts a particular light on the questions concerning modernity and the
political as well (Bernasconi, 1985; Hancock, 1989; Llewlyn, 1985; Marx,
1971; Pöggeler, 1990; Rosen, 1989; Sallis, 1970).

Security and genealogy

What is at issue first of all, for me, therefore, is not whether one says yes or
not to our modern regimes of security, but what Foucault would have called
the overall discursive fact that security is spoken about at all, the way in
which it is put into political discourse and how it circulates throughout
politics and other discourses.

Of all recent thinkers, Foucault was amongst the most committed to the task of writing the history of the present in the light of Heidegger's history of Being as metaphysics (Hancock, 1989; Rosen, 1989). That is why, when thinking about security, I have found Foucault's mode of questioning so stimulating. There is a parallel to be drawn, for example, between what he saw the technology of disciplinary power/knowledge doing to the body and what the principle of security does to political human being. What truths about the human condition, he therefore enables us to ask, are thought to be secreted in security? What work does securing security do for and upon us? What power effects issue out of the regime of truth of security? If the truth of security compels us to secure security, how and where is that compulsion grounded? How was it that seeking security became such an insistent and relentless preoccupation for humankind? What sort of project is the pursuit of security and how does it relate to other modern human concerns and enterprises, such as seeking freedom and knowledge through subjectification? Above all, how are we to account – amongst all the manifest contradictions of our current systems of security: which incarcerate rather than liberate; radically endanger rather than make safe; and engender fear rather than create assurance – for that terminal paradox of our modern politics of security which Foucault captured so well in the quotation that heads this piece – a terminal paradox which not only subverts its own predicate of security, most spectacularly by rendering the future of terrestrial existence conditional on the strategies and calculations of its regimes of power/knowledge, but which also seems to furnish a new predicate of global life: the real prospect of human species extinction.

A logical way to pursue this Foucauldian impulse would be to document the discursive facticity of security by discovering how security is spoken about, and who or what does the speaking: to consider historically, again *à la* Foucault, the propositions, viewpoints and assumptions from which they speak; to specify the institutions and detail the various interlocking discursive practices, which produce, store and distribute the bulk of what is said (assembling it in great archives and policing what is true about it); to note as well the tensions and conflicts within the plural regime of security as it weaves the tight international/intertextual (der Derian and Shapiro, 1989) discursive economies which comprise the texture of modern global life, including those, for example, of the state, international organizations, parasitic public media, economic corporations, para-statal research institutions, teaching academies, and medical, informational, communicational, pedagogic and academic disciplines.

Pursuing such a genealogical line of enquiry would enable us to see that security is employable in any and every circumstance, and is invested with a plurality of meanings. It would reveal the extent, too, of the work that security does for and imposes upon us, and serve effectively to excite suspicion about the extraordinary valency which it has in the production and preoccupations of our forms of life. We could not then escape noticing the way security impresses itself upon us as a kind of floating and radically intertextual signifier which, by constant reference to all other signs of the times, transgresses disciplinary, political, corporeal and geographical boundaries as it courses throughout the defining technologically inspired discourses of modernity: state security; national security; political security; global security; regional security; territorial security; economic security; financial security; individual security; collective security; personal security; physical security; psychological security; sexual security; social security; environmental security; food security . . .

These, then, are some of the central considerations to which a genealogy would draw attention. For security, the genealogist (Foucault) would insist, is not a fact of nature but a fact of civilization. It is not a noun that names something, it is a principle of formation that does things. Every concept like 'security', and every periodization like 'modernity', therefore has a story to tell; a story of their own coming to presence. They do so because all concepts and periodizations are, of course, textual articulations and discursive moves which occur in history. The conjunction of language and time is the only place in which they come to presence. That is the only place in which they can appear. Security and modernity are no exception.

But we are not only users of language, we are used, the genealogist would argue further, by the language we use. We are not simply the people who use these words, we are the people who are used by them. Just as there therefore could be no history of security without a history of the political cultures that seek to define, pursue and prosecute order under the various names of security. So also a political culture would manifest its own particular order of fear. Don't ask what a people are, the genealogist of security might say, ask how an order of fear forms a people. And, in particular, bearing the imprint of the way judgements about the political have originated in fear, (s)he would emphasize that security is a principle device for constituting political order and for confining political imagination within the laws of necessity that are invoked by specific discourses of danger.

My first inclination is, therefore, to interpret the defining and now terminal paradox of security genealogically – that is to say, not to respond to it as a call to interpret the 'concept' of security more clearly, as if it somehow existed outside of language and time, nor to extend its range and register so as to make its *telos* more encompassing (Brown, 1977; Brown, 1989; Dyer, 1992; Homer-Dixon, 1991; Mathews, 1989; Pirage, 1991; Renner, 1989; Ullman, 1989). Security does not need a larger domain. It is not my intention, therefore, to argue for an extension of its remit. Nor do I think that we need to recover its 'true' meaning through historical elucidation. This, then, is not an historiographical history of the 'concept' of security in the *begriffsgeschichte* tradition (Ball et al., 1992; Koselleck, 1982; Richter, 1986). Neither am I in the competitive game of salvific metaphysics, the object of which is to decide what is the most accurate and comprehensive security problematic and which is the correct, best or most cost-effective security solution; much less to supply candidates of my own. I respond to it, instead, as a provocation; particularly as a provocation to the thought that governs our understanding of the political.

It follows from all this that security for me is not even an essentially contested (metaphysical) concept. In the thought from which I draw inspiration, the concept does not possess the primacy which it ordinarily enjoys, in virtue of its metaphysical determination, in contemporary political and strategic discourse. I treat security, instead, as a generative principle of formation that has a special place within, and consequently carries an enormous burden of discursive traffic on behalf of, the political tradition and imagination of metaphysics which, because metaphysics is the tradition of thought of the West, is the political tradition of the West. Our politics are metaphysical, and security is their hub.

I do not think that it is a matter, therefore, of overcoming any kind of limitation of seeing, or of broadening the horizons belonging to the scheme in which security appears, so as to thematize a more total and encompassing understanding of it. And so I will not be commending a more total immersion in the conventional world of security in order to help make us even more knowledgeable about security either. Quite the contrary. The very alliance of security and knowledge, so characteristic of modern politics (Dandeker, 1990; Pearton, 1982), is what excites my suspicion most.

'Look', insisted Nietzsche, the philosopher who rejected self-preservation as the essence of life in favour of self-transcendence, 'isn't our need for knowledge precisely this need for the familiar, the will to uncover under everything strange, unusual, and questionable, something that no longer disturbs us?' 'Is it not the *instinct of fear*', he asked – making explicit the crucial connection between the will to truth and the will to secure – 'that bids us to know? . . . And is the jubilation of those who attain knowledge not the jubilation over the restoration of a sense of security?' (Nietzsche, 1974: 355). Since Nietzsche sees the essence of life as 'self-enhancement', all conditions that *simply* aim at life-preservation, such as the will to know, are downgraded to the level of that which hinders or negates life because they preclude in advance the possibility of the 'self-enhancement' which distinguishes its essence. Hence: security as knowledge (certainty); security's reliance upon knowledge (surveillance); security's astonishing production of knowledge in response to its will to know (calculability); the claim of knowledge which gives security its licence to render all aspects of life transparent (totality). All these comprising elements of our contemporary manifold politics of security constitute a monumental enterprise of power/ knowledge whose insatiable maw threatens to consume all thought, and not only that relating to the question of the political. By noting and questioning the already hypertrophic register of security I want, therefore, to call the entire scheme of security into question. For that way lies a modest contribution to making 'our way back from the world to the life already betrayed by knowledge, knowledge that delights in its theme and is absorbed in the object to the point of losing its soul and its name there, of becoming mute and anonymous' (Levinas, 1991a: 215). I consequently argue for a turn in thinking away from present securities – a turn in thinking that refuses to comply with what contemporary politics of security present us

with politically; one that calls into question the structure of its appre-
hensions and the way they have contributed to the political history of the
present; one that contests the very foundation of our politics of security by
calling attention to what security itself actually discloses.

Politics always already entails, of course, a struggle to articulate,
determine and instantiate what the political is to be taken to be. It is always
already a struggle over the very question of the political itself. That struggle,
even when ostensibly concerned with the 'I', in fact most often when
proclaiming the 'I', is also always about the constitution of the 'We'. That is
to say, it is not just about the contingent so-called political, cultural,
ideological and social bonds which bind populations together, but about
what it is to be human – what, because it concerns that problematic being
which we are and which we share that is somehow alike and yet admits of
manifold difference, I want to call our being-in-common (Fraser, 1984;
Ingram, 1988; Nancy, 1988, 1991): being-in-common as a *sensus communis*
that always and continuously bears difference within itself, and how that
very being-in-common is to find concrete material expression in our ways of
being-together.

Contesting our politics of security therefore requires more than a merely
technical engagement over the meaning, range, efficiency, effectiveness,
morality of accountability of conventional and nuclear, military and
political, technologies of security. Neither does it call upon some new
eschatology. (Precisely because these are times so readily filled with
eschatological portent for the human species, the need to resist the closure
of eschatology is as great as that required to resist the closure of teleology;
the interplay between the two being, in any event, characteristic of politics
of security and the way they habitually foreclose the question of the political
– Nietzsche, 1974.) It requires thinking about the very question of the
political itself. But as that also entails thinking about the very location or site
where our being-in-common is at stake it inevitably requires thinking about
Being as well. Thinking the political therefore entails thinking not only
about the Being of the beings we are, but also about the difference between
Being and being; the ontological difference. It consequently shares the same
fate as that thinking, and each is, ineluctably, a form of political inter-
vention. That is why, by appealing to an account of our prolifically
undecidable being-in-common, it is possible to think the 'I' and the 'We'
differently from the way each has emerged in our politics of security.
Possible to think both and to think both together, for example, as an
invitation and not a directive, and as a continuous project of disclosure
rather than of foreclosure determined in advance by the logic of sovereign
identity, however and wherever it finds expression.

Echoing and compacting Foucault, then, my basic and guiding question
concerning security is: *Must we secure security?* (Foucault, 1980). But this is
not one question amongst many others. Neither is it a question that allows us
to confine the response which it demands to genealogy or to the debates
about the status and conditions of modernity. For it is a question that unites

the crisis of modern global politics with that of Western metaphysical thought. That security has a genealogy and that this genealogy reveals how security operates in the production and dissemination of political order is a thought that provokes me. It is, in turn, one of the thoughts which I want to provoke in others. That this genealogy is the political genealogy of the political tradition of the West is, however, a further thought; one, moreover, that points beyond the task of genealogy to that from which the genealogical impulse itself first derives.

Contesting our politics of security presents, therefore, a special challenge which I think moves us beyond even genealogy. It is, moreover, one that is made more urgent and difficult by the character of our time – a time in which recovering the possibility of a future out of the circumstances of the present is increasingly jeopardized in unique ways. Whereas politics has a crucial part to play in this recovery, the recovery and reinvigoration of the question of the political itself is a priority for politics if any future is to remain a recoverable project.

There is, therefore, an additional task which, while it is integral to inciting a genealogical response to security, is nonetheless also prior to it. This task not only requires an exploration of the link between the philosophical and the political in Western thought but also an examination of their current and shared predicament. And it is a task that is first excited by the very radical ambiguity of security itself.

(In)security

All those manifold insistences upon securities of every description, which I referred to earlier, led to an ineluctable but naggingly contradictory conclusion. We live in an age of intensifying and globalizing securities but the very insistence upon security seems, nonetheless, to reveal an increasing sense of insecurity (Lingis, 1989). The more we demand and insist upon security the more manifold become the insecurities which feed the impulse for security.

One obvious indication of this ambivalence is the word itself, which, among other things that I cannot go into here, not only means to be free from danger but also to constrain. Without entering into the fascinating and revealing etymology of security it is evident also, if we pause to think about security for a moment, that any discourse of security must always already, simultaneously and in a plurality of ways, be a discourse of danger too.

For example, because security is engendered by fear (fundamentally aroused by the uncanny, uncertain, different, awesome and incalculable), it must also teach us what to fear when expressing its desire for the secure. (Connolly, 1991: 133, 136). Any appeal to security must also simultaneously be a specification, no matter how inchoate, of the fear which engenders it. But because security is engendered by fear it also calls for counter-measures to deal with the danger which initiates fear, and for the neutralization, elimination or constraint of that person, group, object or condition which engenders fear. Hence, while it teaches us what we are threatened by, it also seeks in its turn to proscribe, sanction, punish, overcome – that is to say, in its turn endanger – that which threatens us.

This radical ambiguity of security – necessarily not only specifying but also generating danger and fear in the very act of identifying them and mobilizing responses to them in the name of security – is brought to mind in a second and equally obvious way. For no age has been as insecure and mortally endangered as this our own insistently secured one. As Foucault pithily pointed out, there has never been as terminal a political prospect as the prospect fashioned by our contemporary politics of security.

Valid as these points are, however, I am going to argue that our politics is a politics which ultimately earns the radically ambiguous title of (in)security less because of the way contemporary forms of life have amplified, extended and intensified the insecurity of life globally – although they have and in related ways, too numerous to catalogue here, which furnish a powerful inducement to doubt the value of security in the way that I want to encourage – but for a more original reason. 'Everything "anti" thinks in the spirit of that against which it is anti' (Heidegger, 1992b: 52–3). Security can, therefore, only be thought by incorporating the trace of insecurity in the very articulation of security itself. That is to say, security only occurs by virtue of the interval between itself and its other. It is whatever it is only by virtue of the way insecurity is always already and simultaneously inscribed within security also.

In short, there is a fundamental belonging together of security and in-security; an indissoluble connection. The radical ambivalence of (in)security is therefore not a paradox. Neither is it a contradiction to be resolved through more careful securing. This ambivalence is inescapable and it provides the very dynamic behind the way in which security operates as a generative principle of formation for the production of political order. It is only because it insecures that security can secure. It is an ambiguity which is essentially tragic.

From out of the unsustainable tragic denials which our manifold politics of security invoke, arise, therefore, the intensifying outbreaks of purificatory violence that characterize our politics. Seeking to establish economies of peace committed to the amelioration, regulation, instrumental manipulation of eventual elimination of violence (wars to end all wars) they install, instead, economies of danger that generate their very own distinctive productions of violence.

Even such modest observations as these indicate that the alliance of security and modernity must launch us upon an enterprise that carries us far beyond either modernity or security; beyond also the tight subjectivist bond, fashioned between the two of them in the political and intellectual revolutions of the sixteenth and seventeenth centuries, that has largely bequeathed us our modern political order. They indicate, too, that we have to be carried beyond a genealogy of security. For to mount such a genealogy requires asking first how security comes to be spoken about at all. And that, in turn, requires a regression to the philosophical assumptions of our politics of security, and to the originary alliance between ontology and the political from which the alliance of security and modernity itself ultimately derives. That entails a regression from what is present in our politics of security, from the history of that present and the way in which what is present currently raises and sets the terms for answering political questions – including not only security, of course, but also the question of the political itself – to whatever governs the present and what makes it present. A regress, in short, to presencing itself. This brings us back, therefore, to the question of Being, the fundamental defining question of Western thought, and to its conjunction with the question of the political. For Western political thought is not only a tradition located within a wider (philosophical) tradition, it shares the essential feature of that tradition – its hermeneutic of desire for a secure *arche* or foundation.

Consequently, if the question of the political is deeply implicated in the question of security, and if the question of the political is also deeply implicated in the question of philosophy, then pursuing the genealogy of security inevitably projects us into considering the relationship between the philosophical and the political and their mutual indebtedness to security. This is the place from which a genealogy of security first discovers its point of departure. We will also discover that the reasons for calling attention to the conjunction of the philosophical and the political are reinforced by the crisis of security that has arisen in the domains of both politics *and* philosophical thought that has arisen in the last hundred years.

In sum, because the very prominence of security suggests that it is an integral part of the fabric and therefore also of the history of the present; because this also suggests that it somehow exceeds our conventional interpretative frameworks of international relations and politics that are so confined within the philosophical horizons of the present, my initial proposition is that while a genealogical approach offers a superior way of understanding the operation of security as a generative principle of formation for the production of political order, in comparison with those supplied by the etiological histories characteristic of politics and international relations, we can only appreciate the profoundly foundational character of security by returning to the very basis of philosophical thought and of the relation of that thought to Western understandings of the political. It is there that the fundamental link between politics and security is grounded. It is there, too, that any genealogy will first pick up the politically constitutive trail of security.

Genealogy to ontology: security and metaphysics

Western metaphysics begins with Plato's separation of the realm of Being (the Forms or Ideas) from the realm of time (becoming, existence)

(Stambaugh, 1972) and the foundation thereby of the view that what is ultimately real is not the constant emerging into presence, coming and going of life as it appears in all its rich temporal mutability, contingency and finitude, but that which is said to exist outside our sensible apprehension of the world (the supra-sensible realms of the Forms or Ideas – hence the meta of meta-physics) or to underlie the shifting properties of things: 'what stands-under (*sub-stantia*) and remains continuously present throughout all change' (Guignon, 1993: 4). Such a view subsequently found expression in *ousia*; *energeia*; Aristotle's primary substance; actuality; the omnipotent creator of Christianity; Descartes' *res cogitans*: Leibniz's monad; Kant's noumena; the primary physical 'stuff' presumed by scientific naturalism; spirit; power, will. And, if we are to subscribe to Heidegger's disputed reading of Nietzsche: the will to power; the will to will; and the eternal recurrence of the same (Guignon, 1993; Muller-Lauter, 1992/1993).

Metaphysics, therefore, comprises a succession of speculative attempts to determine the permanently enduring (secure underlying or supra-sensible) ordering principle that transcends the flux of life in which things are continuously coming to presence and passing away (what the Greeks called *physis*) in order to secure life and our understanding of it. Thought becomes the means of securing some rational foundation upon which we may establish 'the sum total of what is knowable'. Truth becomes a measure of the correspondence between our representation of what appears to be and what is. And acting becomes conforming one's everyday enterprises 'both public and private to the foundation so secured' (Schurmann, 1990: 1). In sum,

> 'Metaphysics' is then the title for that ensemble of speculative efforts with a view to a model, a canon, a *principium* for action. . . . This focal point is continuously displaced throughout history: ideal city; heavenly kingdom; the happiness of the greatest number, noumenal and legislative freedom. . . . But none of these transferences destroys the attributive, participative, and therefore normative, pattern itself. The *arche* always functions in relation to action as substance functions in relation to its accidents, imparting to them sense and *telos*. (Schurmann, 1990: 1)

Now, since the question of the political has been a question posed and answered within the orbit of this kind of thinking (Schurmann, 1990: 87), and since this kind of thinking has also been concerned variously to secure the ground of certain knowledge, the imperative that orders us to order, the means of right reckoning, then the question concerning the political has been construed fundamentally as an architechtonic security project as well. One in which reflection on the question of the political sought to 'translate an ahistorical order, knowable in itself, into public organisation'. An order that further served 'as an a priori model and as a criterion for a posterior legitimation' (Schurmann, 1990: 87). Security, then, is the generic term for the requirement of metaphysics, and of those understandings of politics conceived within the domain of metaphysical thought, to procure for themselves a secure ground, *arche*, or principle, with which to anchor, order and measure life.

The categories for understanding the political – or the essence of politics – were largely derived, therefore, from 'the analysis of sensible bodies and were transposed into practical discourse from speculative or "ontological discourse"' (Schurmann, 1990: 39). Such categories were not *sui generis*, least of all, ironically, in those so-called modern political thinkers, Machiavelli and Hobbes. Celebrated most for their contribution to releasing the question of the political from its bondage to the Church, in the form of the Christian virtues, Aristotelianism and scholasticism, and for discovering the object domain of politics (Heidegger would say regional ontology) in which the rules of the political were to be determined henceforth exclusively by reference to the political alone, these were equally in thrall themselves, though differently, to the metaphysical determination of the political.

Metaphysical thought, I therefore maintain, necessarily issues in a politics of security, while politics of security necessarily draw upon and display the metaphysical impulse to secure thought. 'As Nietzsche had seen very clearly, and as Heidegger shows in ontological terms', Gianni Vattimo writes, 'the metaphysical tradition is the tradition of "violent" thinking. With its prediliction for unifying, sovereign and generalizing categories, and with its cult of the *arche*, it manifests a fundamental insecurity and exaggerated self-importance from which it then reacts into over-defensiveness' (Vattimo, 1993: 5). Consequently the fate of metaphysics and the fate of our politics of security are inextricably intertwined.

There is more than an academic interest at stake, therefore, in this modern conjunction between the philosophical and the political. How we think and what we do, what we think and how we are doing, condition one another. There is clearly more than a coincidence also in relying upon post-Nietzschean thought to argue for that reappraisal of both which requires a recovery of the question of the political. For between Hegel and Heidegger metaphysics exposed itself to its own deconstructive impulses. After Marx, 'one finds Schopehhauer, Kierkegaard, Freud, and Nietzsche turning philosophy upon itself, thereby unmasking its own taboos and twisted roots' (Schmidt, 1991: 442); realizing and exhausting its potential, according to Heidegger, in the advent of the epoch of technology.

The same period also witnessed the exhaustion of the European state system's resolution of the question of the political through the very globalization of the language, forms and practices of the politics of security upon which it was based. The advent of the globalized industrial nuclear age exhibits not only the hollowness of that system's foundational promises to secure order and identity, but also, in the gulf that exists between what its political prospectus offers and what its (inter)national politics provides, the exhaustion of its political imagination (Campbell and Dillon, 1993; Kearney, 1988, 1991). For this was a period in which that politics of security finally realized the full potential of the self-immolative dynamic prefigured in its very inception; the real prospect of human species extinction (Eksteins, 1989).

Consequently, the dependence of our political tradition upon the value of security, and upon its articulation through historically successive discourses of danger, derives directly from the way the philosophical tradition understands and valorizes presence. Presence rigidified and reified as objectness, which in turn arises from metaphysics' understanding of Being as One – that which perdures and subsists, embracing all in unity and identity – rather than as a manifold (simultaneously one and not-one) presencing. These points require the further elucidation, of course, that would come from an enquiry into the fundamental relationship that has obtained between philosophy and politics in the Western tradition: that is to say between the question of Being (Heidegger's fundamental ontology); the question of the Being of beings (metaphysics); and the question of the political (being-in-common).

Fundamental to that axiomatic privileging of security upon which Western understanding of the political relies, fundamental to its common sense, fundamental questions concerning security nonetheless seem never to be pressed. When asked, especially by those branches of the study of politics that currently assert particular disciplinary claims on the world – political philosophy, whose modern inaugural moment occurs with Hobbes, and international relations and strategic studies (currently the popular twin citadels of the metaphysical determination of the political), whose inaugural moment occurs in the global technologization of the political that began once the idea of politics specifically articulated in the post-Westphalian European state system exhausted its prefigured possibilities in global conquest (Campbell and Dillon, 1993; Wright, 1942: 1294–5) – they are never pursued beyond that point where its function as a ground is precisely what is at issue (Buzan, 1991, is a case in point). There is, then, an exquisite paradox at work here. Our politics of security hide what they most depend upon, by making it most obvious. The metaphysical dynamics and demands that determine them are securely secured – locked away and forgotten – by means of the very insistence upon security itself.

The critical conjunction of the philosophical and the political

While philosophy and the *polis* were deeply implicated in one another from the outset of Western thought, therefore, modern philosophy and politics remain implicated in one another; but now differently. During the course of the last hundred years it not only became impossible to continue to subscribe to the metaphysics of presence that has dominated Western thinking, it has become equally impossible to subscribe to an (inter)national politics predicated upon the securing of security (Campbell, 1992; Walker, 1993).

On the one hand, the very lethality and globality, and the potentially terminal paradox, of the modern political condition have not only called into question the specific institutional structures, vocabularies and practices which comprise our contemporary politics of security. The late modern apprehension of danger also calls into question the entire political imagination that underpins our politics of security, the very limits provided by the grounds of its thinking. Our contemporary politics of security drive us back, in other words, to the very presuppositions of the political itself. For this metaphysical politics is at an end in the sense that it is now gathered into its own extreme possibilities (Heidegger, 1972: 57).

On the other hand, post-Nietzschean thought has called into question the metaphysical reserve of philosophy from which our political thinking has traditionally derived its very suppositional support. Consequently, while sensibility to the dangers which our contemporary civilization has engendered demands that we ask how we came to be in the now terminal paradox of security, and whether it was because of the way that we are or have conceived of ourselves to be, post-Nietzschean thought, responding to somewhat different impulses, complements this regress and pushes it one stage further. In asking directly about the Being in virtue of which there are beings at all, and not just the Being of the being that human beings are, it calls into question not simply the vocabulary or institutions of politics as such, but the very metaphysical grammar, or scheme, according to which the political has come to find expression. The provocation for a genealogy of security is, therefore, furnished both by material and philosophical concerns; by the conjunction of an ontic with an ontological crisis in which the one also compounds the other.

In Heidegger's terms the ontic and ontological (like the cognate expressions *existentiel* and existential) are distinguished in that the former term refers to the more immediate everyday level of existence and its concerns, while the latter applies to the understanding of the underlying structures of intelligibility which comprise the conditions of possibility for human being and make human beings the kind of beings that they are: namely, beings that exist in a world and are aware not only of their own existence, by virtue of the fact that they know that they die and are therefore mortal beings, but also, in virtue of this fundamental fact, beings which recognize that there is Being in which their own being occurs.

The ontic crisis refers to the novelty and scale of the global dangers that humankind is fashioning through the devastating complex of its sociopolitical, industrial, scientific and military structures. The ontological crisis not only concerns, however, the way in which the critique of metaphysics has called into question the very way in which human beings have been understood to be the kind of beings that they are. It also concerns the way in which metaphysics has been directly linked to the production and global dissemination of forms of life which generate the burgeoning terrestrial dangers to human and other beings that so distinguish our times.

To put it bluntly, as the real prospect of human species extinction is a function of how human being has come to dwell in the world, then human being has a pressing reason to reconsider, in the most originary way possible and notwithstanding any other motivations that may be advanced for doing so, the derivation of its understanding of what it is to dwell in the world, and how it should comport itself if it is to continue to do so. Such a predicament ineluctably poses this fundamental and inescapable question about philosophy and politics, and of the relation between them: if such is their end, what must their origins have been? (Schurmann, 1990: 25–6).

No matter how much we may want to elide this question, or, alternatively, provide a whole series of edifying answers to it, we cannot settle for either, ironically, if we want to survive. Our present does not allow it. This joint regress of the philosophical and the political to the very limits of their thinking and of their possibility therefore brings the question of Being (which is the question of philosophy) into explicit conjunction with the question of the political once more, and emphasizes the abiding reciprocity that exists between them.

We now know that neither metaphysics nor politics of security can secure the security of truth and of life which was their reciprocating *raison d'être*. More importantly, we now know that the very will to security – the certainty and unadulterated presence and identity which is the requisite ideal of both metaphysics and modern politics – is not only a prime incitement to violence in the Western tradition of thought and politics but also self-defeating, in that it does not in its turn merely endanger, but actually engenders danger in response to its discursive dynamic.

That, then, is why the crisis of Western thought is as much a fundamental crisis of politics, as the crisis of politics is a crisis of thought. Moreover that is why in doubting the value of security, and doubting in a Nietzschean mode rather than a Cartesian one, we are also enjoined by the circumstances of this critical conjunction of the philosophical and the political to doubt metaphysical truth. For the political truth of security is the metaphysical truth of correspondence and adequation in declension to mathesis; mere, but rigorously insistent, calculability. To bring the value of security into question in the radical way required by the way it now, ironically, radically endangers us, correspondingly requires the critique of metaphysics.

This monumental and complementary predicament of both philosophy and politics, therefore, necessarily also invokes a return to the limits of origins (Heidegger, 1975): origins which philosophy and politics share but which are by no means self-evident, instinctual or axiomatic: origins which reveal themselves to be plural and complex, full of shifts, contradictions and conflicts (Schurmann, 1990: 31); origins, too, in intensive amplification, extenuation, pluralification and radical dispersion; origins, in fact, in security – a security now no longer even driven, however, by anthropomorphic or humanistic considerations, a security simply ordering to order.

There is no going back, but there is also no stepping outside of this condition. Humankind has attained a certain limit here in our time and our thinking. And this limit, by virtue of the globalization of Western thought and politics, now increasingly conditions the future of human being. Politics at the end, or rather in the *extremis*, of security consequently confronts the same tasks as philosophy at the end, or in the *extremis*, of metaphysics. Because there is no overcoming this limit, modern thought and modern politics are each an encounter, therefore, with that limit. An encounter that has to be designed to defer both the closure of thought and the end of politics threatened by it (Bernasconi, 1985; Critchley, 1992; Fenves, 1993; Heidegger, 1973; Wood, 1990).

What is most at issue here, then, is the question of the limit and of how to finesse the closure of apocalyptic thinking to which the issue of limits ordinarily gives rise in onto-theological thought: as the authoritative specification of an eschaton; as the invocation of our submission to it; or in terms of the closure of what it is possible for us to say, do and be in virtue of the operation of it. The question of the limit has therefore to be posed in a way that invokes a thinking which not only resists the siren call of fatal philosophers and historians, but also takes heed of the warning that if

> the democratic task of governance ever buries the democratic ethos of disturbance and politicization under the weight of national consensus, historical necessity, and state security, state mechanisms of electoral accountability will be reduced to conduits for the production of internal/external others against whom to wage moral wars of all too familiar sorts. (Connolly, 1991: 153)

It has to be posed, instead, in terms of that which keeps things in play ('[w]here demarcation is lacking nothing can come to presence as it is' (Heidegger, 1992b: 82); exciting a thinking, in particular, which seeks continuously to keep 'open the play of political possibility by subtracting the sense of necessity, completeness, and smugness from established organizations of life' (Connolly, 1991: 153)).

The limits of philosophy and the political

It is important, then, to note that limit bears both a particular meaning and a particular significance here. Giving limits is giving form. It is limit that enables anything to be (the limitless does not appear as such). Limit is consequently not understood as the edge, or end-as-termination, of something. Rather, it is understood to mean the way that something is brought together – becomes present – and so appears to be whatever it is. Limit here, then, means the condition of possibility of anything being that thing which it is. Every object and field of enquiry is, therefore, delimited.

Limit, however, also has a very particular significance in this context. And it does so for a variety of reasons. The first is because both philosophy and politics have an essential relation to the question of limits. Thus, on the one hand, philosophy claims a distinctive competence in addressing the limit conditions (the ontological basis, the boundaries and core concepts) of thought. On the other, politics claims a distinctive competence in addressing the limit conditions (ontological structure, foundational requirements, fundamental passions, basic constitutional arrangements, essential social ordering and so on) of our being-in-common, and of how we realized that being-in-common in how we live together in the world.

Second, the question of limits is peculiarly significant because politics and philosophy each now confront the question of their own limits in new and

fundamentally disturbing ways. Whereas philosophy has become fundamentally preoccupied with its own limits because the critique of metaphysics
positions it at the limit of its own modern thought (Wood, 1990: xiv),
politics, too, finds itself confronting a limit to the scope of its own carefully
considered and violently inscribed limits of political community, political
identity and political rights; in the mass manufacture of global danger,
genocidal conflict and the real prospect of species extinction mundanely
engineered by our forms of political life, and routinely deployed by their
ordering regimes of power/knowledge as strategies integral to the techno-
logized political production and pursuit of community, identity, interests
and rights.

And, finally, the question of the limit is central because in encountering
their own limits in the way that they now do, philosophy and politics
encounter each other again. They encounter each other in ways that are
deeply disturbing and challenging to each of them. Philosophy, for example,
encounters its complicity in the political, politics its complicity in the
philosophical. Each has to address the thing it has often been most
concerned, even designed, to put beyond its thought: philosophy, that it is
political and not only conditioned by the political; politics, that it is a way of
being that indissolubly combines thinking and doing, and is not just a way of
doing. 'Every philosophical colloquium necessarily has a political significance' (Derrida, 1982: 111) wrote, and every politics is indebted, in virtue of
its very grammar and vocabulary, to some philosophical grounding.

By noting this mutual complicity I do not mean to suggest that we know
how it operates, that we can specify how much and in what ways politics
owes its debt to philosophy, or philosophy to politics. Quite the contrary.
The re-excitement of the question of the limit itself indicates that neither the
political nor the philosophical are somehow antecedent to human doing,
demarcated as objects of enquiry, so that we could aspire definitively to
know (Heidegger, 1992b: 6). Indeed, the re-excitement of the question of
the limit itself indicates that it is in the play of the limit that the philosophical
and the political come to be whatever they are.

The political and the philosophical are, therefore, yoked together:
philosophy and the *polis*; technology (understood in the Heideggerian sense
of the term [Lingis, 1989: 1; Loscerbo, 1981]) and the modern (inter)national
state system. The evident fact that they do condition one another does not,
however, resolve the question of how. It merely poses it.

When Heidegger speaks of Being as the defining question of philosophy,
to take the example of a thinker whose thought has a particular if
nonetheless still problematic influence here, he is always also speaking of the
human beings who utter the word 'is'. And when he formulates his account
of human being as 'the there' of Being (*Dasein*) a special instance of the
manifestation of Being where Being shows up in a way that allows it to be
experienced, because it shows up in a being, as far as we know the only
being, namely the beings that we are, that actually notes its appearance and
asks about it. Indeed, it shows up in a being cognizant of its inescapable

mortality for whom Being is an issue in virtue of each human being's knowledge of its mortality. When he thus formulates this account of the *Dasein* that each of us is, that *Dasein* is always already also in a world; is always already *always* in a world.

Despite the 'ontological priority' which Heidegger, therefore, accords to the question of Being (notably in Section 3 of *Being and Time* [Heidegger, 1988; see also Sallis, 1978] and elsewhere, especially in the writings which occur after the so-called turning in his work) nonetheless what he would doubtless call an equiprimordial reciprocity also seems to obtain between the question of Being and the question of the political. For if Being shows up in *Dasein* in a special way – precisely because, according to Heidegger, *Dasein* is so distinctively endowed with Being that it actually poses the question of its own being, and thereby that of Being, to itself – then *Dasein*, particularly that pre-Socratic *Dasein* whose original experience of quicksilver Being, according to Heidegger, so informed and yet was so occluded by the Socratic formulation of the question of the Being of beings, showed up specifically in the *polis*. Hence the clearing of Being materialized in the space of the *polis* just as much as in the sayings of Heraclitus, the poems of Parmenides or the teaching of Socrates, Plato and Aristotle (Caputo, 1987; Wolin, 1990).

Conclusion

Security cannot be taken as an unproblematic ontological predicate of human being precisely because the question of ontology (that of Being, and of the Being of beings) has itself become so problematical since the radical problematization (with Nietzsche and Heidegger) of the very tradition in which it has hitherto been thought. Consequently we cannot understand the institution and operation of politics of security by reference to the expression of that predicate in self-consciousness, the biological individual, the community, or the egotistical subject.

The virtue of approaching security through a philosophy of the limit lies in the way such thinking is concerned not with the discernment of metaphysical truth but the decipherment of value, not with the production of reliable knowledge but the exposure of the processes of valuation and the foreclosure of possibilities effected by regimes of truth as power/knowledge. Such a posture emphasizes that security names a process of valuation and so alerts us to what is being devalued as well. It also stresses that such a process is not a simple monolithic determination of values, but sets in motion a dynamic play of (de)valuation.

While we have no greater provocation than our terminal paradox of security to doubt the truth and the value (the true-value) of security, it is perfectly obvious also that thinking the limit is itself, however, a dangerous game. For to doubt the truth and value of security seems to deny us the very means of survival in the most lethal of circumstances – particularly when it does not come equipped with a promise that we can secure an escape from (in)security, danger, or a final overcoming of the violence associated with it. But what it may do, in the caesura that announces the 'end' of metaphysical politics, is this: first, it may alert us to the inescapable violence and the dogmatic imperatives that are so deeply sequestered within our most foundational valuing practices of political thought as well as political ordering: security itself, of course, but also its offspring – identity, justice and, most neglected of all, love – any love that proclaims an imperial 'Yes' to conceal a violent 'No'; all those loves whose affirmative denials, denying the denials upon which we feed, so form and inform the space of our politics; love of liberty; love of order; love of country; love of church; love of the people; love of the leader; love of the party; love of one's history; love of one's gods; love of the individual; love of the family; love of the self. Security comes crenellated in the form of a host of obligatory denying-loves; loves that mask the spirit of revenge. Pre-eminent amongst them in modern politics is the so-called political realists' narcissistic 'primeval "love"' of the real: 'Every feeling and sensation contains a piece of this old love; and some fantasy, some prejudice, some unreason, some ignorance, some fear, and ever so much else has contributed to it and worked on it' (Nietzsche, 1974: 121).

Second, it may promote the radically hermeneutic application of a critical phenomenology of presencing to the practices and institutions of politics. Third, it could contribute to that continuous recovery of the question of the political which might relax the grip which the insistences and claims of security exercise upon our political imagination. Fourth, it might pursue the invention and exploration of those political strategies, that William Connolly (1991: 138), for example, calls for, capable of folding 'agonistic generosity more deeply into the cultural ethos of a democratic society'. And, in so doing, it may not answer the question 'What is to be done?' according to the way security so rigidly enframes it, with or without 'man', but seek to formulate it differently, perhaps as: 'What could the political practice of mortals, now globally endangered by their politics of security, come to be?'

Other propositions which I would want to advance in respect of our manifold politics of security, include the following. Not only that our traditional philosophical and theoretical resources are inadequate for thinking through the condition of (in)security, a deficiency which occurs primarily in the theorization of the political itself, and that there is in fact a deep complicity between metaphysics and security in the Western political tradition which has itself to be explored instead, but also that it is through our manifold politics of security that the onto-theological imagination is translated into the regimes of truth, institutions and practices which comprise modern political life. Metaphysics becomes material in politics of security because metaphysically determined being has a foundational requirement to secure security. Politics of security are the municipal metaphysics of the Western tradition.

Third, while not denying that modern political discourses and practices have also sought to derive and provide a politics of rights, freedoms and interests out of metaphysics, and that these are in certain ways definitive of the modern condition, all such politics are always already subject to a process of reduction to the determinants of security inasmuch as they remain metaphysically conceived. And this not merely because of the way the exigencies of war and danger always acquire a powerful dynamic and logic of their own (Dillon, 1989), something which Alexander Hamilton noted long before strategic theorists sought to make a political technology out of it via the rubrics of crisis management (Dillon, 1989).

> The violent destruction of life and property incident to war, the continual effect and alarm attendant on a state of continual danger, will compel nations the most attached to liberty to resort for repose and security to institutions which have a tendency to destroy their civil and political rights. To be more safe, they at length become more willing to run the risk of being less free. (Hamilton, quoted in Marshall, 1939).

The politics of security are not merely concerned to note that these exigencies operate. Nor do they merely claim to offer just another picture of political life. They claim to be most true of it.

Why? Referring back to my earlier point about politics and limits, and directly recalling the mathesis that governs the technological mode of being, it is because they claim to articulate the bottom line, the single figures and universal numbers, the final calculus – the limit condition, in short, conceived in terms of calculability – that makes politics possible. They make a determinate claim on the construal and the answering of the question of the political because, in virtue of the moral danger which it is their distinctive competence to articulate, they claim to find the mandate for the political. Politics of security are, therefore, essentially a form of eschatology; politics thought in the light of the last things, the limit situation. But because eschatology is ineluctably linked also, through diverse idioms (essence, cause, *telos* and revelation) to the beginning of things, the limit situation also articulates the natality, the first cause, the ultimate goal, defining essence or revelatory initiation and fulfilment of the political as well. Specifying the end (the limit condition), politics of security claim also to have discerned the advent of the political (Gillespie, 1984; Krell, 1986; Schmidt, 1988). That understanding of the political ultimately construes the political realm as a domain of calculability in which political practices become exercises in the political arithmetic of representation that makes of human being not merely an index of security, but an indice to be secured.

Here, then, the political is always founded in a tight, complex eschatological and, more often than not, vicious circle of genesis and nemesis, which, because it immediately breaches the law of non-contradiction that a thing cannot be at one and the same time its opposite, also immediately offers itself to its own deconstruction. For here you do get the beginning in the end, and the end in the beginning. This horizon of first cause derived from last things is what constitutes the spatio-temporal backdrop that throws political life into high relief, imparting a lucid sense of purpose to, and

providing an imperious principle of formation for, its ordering. Whatever
narrative framework it comes disguised in, the advent of the political in
politics of security is, therefore, always ultimately construed in terms of
ontological, rather than chronological, danger; the Hobbesian state of
nature is the classical but not the only account.

A fourth proposition is that politics of security are always already politics
of identity/difference and desire by virtue of being a politics of fear, because
a discourse of security does not only specify danger and threat (Connolly,
1991). In the process of saying what we are menaced by, and in the course of
harnessing means for dealing with whatever that is said to be, politics of
security, constituting and mobilizing difference, impart form and character
to human being and to its form of life. They specify who we are, and what we
are allowed to be, by teaching us what to fear about what we are not.
Difference is, therefore, integral to what we are. This is by no means a
negative affair, because fear is also an education in what we are not, what we
do not have, what we are supposed to care for and to care about, whose lack,
or the fear of it, is expressed by the articulation of security. A discursive
economy of security is consequently not only a discursive economy of
danger, it is also a discursive economy of the absence that invokes desire.
Through the alliance of *eros* and *thanatos* effected by the politics of
identity/difference integral to security, we are struck by an account of
ontological danger into postures of policing love. Policing love in respect of
who 'we' are thus to be held to be; love distinguished by the how of policing
rather than the celebration of the desire excited by otherness; and of
anathematizing exclusion of those that are thus rendered other. In sum, it is
not only that there can be no politics of security which is not also a politics of
insecurity. There is no politics of security which is not also a politics of
policing love.

A fifth, and final, proposition is that, as the political expression of
onto-theology, our manifold politics of security are most susceptible to
deconstruction and genealogical critique. Because security does things (the
mediation of onto-theology and the political) rather than merely names
things, we have to pose questions about it in the active interrogatory voice of
genealogical critique. From whence does the demand for security arise?
How does security secure? What does security secure? What is securing?
Who is secured? Similarly, because they are alive to the excess of Being over
appearance, as well as concerned with how things come to be rather than
operating upon assumptions about what they are already exhaustively or
determinately supposed to be, genealogy and deconstruction encourage us
to reverse the usual order of political questioning and, in doing so, while
looking for the supplement which security requires but denies in the
ordering of politics, disturb the established truths of a regime of security and
loosen 'the sense of necessity, lawfulness, unity, or intrinsic purpose' which
attaches to them (Connolly, 1991: 138).

This, then, is how I would begin to formulate a new agenda of security
questions. Not asking: 'How effective are our political regimes at satisfying

their foundational claim to legitimacy by furnishing us with security?' but: 'How must the concept of the political be construed, how must the political universe be determined, and what has to be rigorously policed, warred against and excluded, to secure security?' Not: 'What is dangerous?' but: 'What does a representation of danger make of "us" and of those who are not "us"?' Not: 'Who or what is threatened, or what is doing the threatening?' but: 'How does the specification of threat and its discourse of danger determine the "who", the "we" and the "what" that is said on the one hand to be endangered, and on the other to be doing the endangering?' Not: 'What are we endangered by?' but: 'How does a representation of danger make "us" what we are?' And, finally, not: 'What does security secure?' but: 'What is lost and forgotten, and who or what pays the inevitable price, for the way that "we" are thus habited in fear?'

According to these thoughts, security does not reflect what a 'people' are, and seek to protect it. Rather, it discloses how, in tragic denials of the (in)security of mortal life, they are actually formed by attempts to extirpate the 'foreign, strange, uncanny, [and] outlandish' (Nietzsche, 1974), which inevitably comprises their very own mortal existence.

References

Ball, Terence, Farr, James and Hanson, Russell L. (eds) (1992) *Political Innovation and Conceptual Change*. Cambridge: Cambridge University Press.

Bernasconi, Robert (1985) *The Question of Language in Heidegger's History of Being*. Atlantic Highlands, NJ: Humanities Press.

Brown, Lester R. (1977) *Redefining National Security*. Washington, DC: Worldwatch Institute, Paper No. 14.

Brown, Neville (1989) 'Climate ecology and international security', *Survival*, 31 (6): 1–30.

Buzan, Barry (1991) *People, States and Fear*, 2nd edn. Hemel Hempstead: Harvester Wheatsheaf.

Campbell, David (1992) *Writing Security*. Manchester: Manchester University Press.

Campbell, David and Dillon, Michael (eds) (1993) *The Political Subject of Violence*. Manchester: Manchester University Press.

Caputo, John (1987) *Radical Hermeneutics. Repetition, Deconstruction and the Hermeneutic Project*. Bloomington: Indiana University Press.

Connolly, William (1991) *Identity/Difference*. Ithaca: Cornell University Press.

Critchley, Simon (1992) *The Ethics of Deconstruction*. Oxford: Basil Blackwell.

Dandeker, Christopher (1990) *Surveillance, Power and Modernity. Bureaucracy and Discipline from 1700 to the Present Day*. Cambridge: Polity Press.

der Derian, James and Shapiro, Michael J. (eds) (1989) *International/Intertextual. Postmodern Readings of World Politics*. Lexington, MA: Lexington Books.

Derrida, Jacques (1982) 'The ends of man', in *Margins of Philosophy*, trans. Alan Bass. Chicago: University of Chicago Press.

Dillon, Michael (1989) *The Falklands: Politics and War*. London: Macmillan.

Dyer, Hugh (1992) 'Globalisation and environmental change: normative dimensions', paper presented to the British International Studies Association, Annual Conference.

Ekstein, Morris (1989) *Rites of Spring. The Great War and the Birth of the Modern Age*. London: Bantam Press.

Fenves, Peter (1993) *Raising the Tone of Philosophy*. Baltimore: Johns Hopkins University Press.

Foucault, Michel (1980) *Herculine Barbin. Being the Recently Discovered Memoirs of a Nineteenth-Century French Hermaphrodite*. New York: Pantheon Books.

Foucault, Michel (1987a) *The History of Sexuality: Vol. 1. An Introduction*. Harmondsworth: Penguin Books.

Foucault, Michel (1987b) *The History of Sexuality: Vol. 2. The Use of Pleasure*. Harmondsworth: Penguin Books.

Fraser, Nancy (1984) 'The French Derrideans: politicising deconstruction or deconstructing the political?' *New German Critique*, 33 (3): 127–54.

Giddens, Anthony (1990) *The Consequences of Modernity*. Cambridge: Polity Press.

Giddens, Anthony (1991) *Modernity and Self-Identity*. Cambridge: Polity Press.

Gillespie, Michael Allen (1984) *Hegel, Heidegger and the Ground of History*. Chicago: Chicago University Press.

Guignon, Charles (ed.) (1993) *The Cambridge Companion to Heidegger*. Cambridge: Cambridge University Press.

Hancock, Ralph C. (1989) *Calvin and the Foundations of Modern Politics*. Ithaca: Cornell University Press.

Heidegger, Martin (1972) 'The end of philosophy and the task of thinking', *On Time and Being*, trans. Joan Stambaugh. New York: Harper & Row.

Heidegger, Martin (1973) *The End of Philosophy*, trans. Joan Stambaugh. New York: Harper & Row.

Heidegger, Martin (1975) 'The origin of the work of art', in *Poetry, Language and Thought*, trans. Albert Hofstadter. New York: Harper & Row.

Heidegger, Martin (1988) *Being and Time*, trans. John Macquarrie and Edward Robinson. Oxford: Basil Blackwell.

Heidegger, Martin (1992a) *Parmenides*, trans. Andre Schuwer and Richard Rojcewicz. Bloomington: Indiana University Press.

Heidegger, Martin (1992b) *The Metaphysical Foundations of Logic*, trans. Michael Heim. Bloomington: Indiana University Press.

Homer-Dixon, Thomas F. (1991) 'On the threshold: environmental changes as causes of acute conflict', *International Security*, 16 (2).

Ingram, David (1988) 'The retreat of the political in the modern age: Jean-Luc Nancy on totalitarianism and community', *Research in Phenomenology*, 18.

Kearney, Richard (1988) *The Wake of Imagination*. London: Hutchinson.

Kearney, Richard (1991) *Poetics of Imagining: from Husserl to Lyotard*. London: Harper Collins.

Koselleck, Reinhard (1982) '*Begriffsgeschichte* and social history', *Economy and Society*, 11 (4): 409–27.

Krell, David Farrell (1986) *Intimations of Mortality, Time, Truth, and Finitude in Heidegger's Thinking of Being*. University Park Pennsylvania: Pennsylvania State University Press.

Levinas, Emmanuel (1991a) 'Philosophy and awakening', in Eduardo Cadava, Peter Connor and Jean-Luc Nancy (eds), *Who Comes After the Subject*. London: Routledge.

Levinas, Emmanuel (1991b) *Totality and Infinity*, trans. Alfonso Lingis. Dordrecht: Kulwer Academic Publishers.

Lingis, Alphonso (1989) *Deathbound Subjectivity*. Bloomington: Indiana University Press.

Llewlyn, John (1985) *Beyond Metaphysics? The Hermeneutic Circle in Continental Philosophy*. Atlantic Highlands, NJ: Humanities Press.

Loscerbo, John (1981) *Being and Technology. A Study in the Philosophy of Martin Heidegger*. The Hague: Martinus Nijhoff.

Marshall, James (1939) *Swords and Symbols. The Techniques of Sovereignty*. London: Oxford University Press.

Marx, Werner (1971) *Heidegger and the Tradition*. Evanston, IL: Northwestern University Press.

Mathews, Jessica T. (1989) 'Redefining security', *Foreign Affairs*, 68 (2): 162–72.

Muller-Lauter, Wolfgang (1992/1993) 'The spirit of revenge and the eternal recurrence. On Heidegger's later interpretation of Nietzsche', *Journal of Nietzsche Studies*, 4–6: 127–53.

Nancy, Jean-Luc (1988) *L'Experience de la Liberté*. Paris: Editions Galilée.

Nancy, Jean-Luc (1991) *The Inoperative Community*. Minneapolis: University of Minnesota Press.

Nietzsche, F.W. (1974) *The Gay Science*, trans. Walter Kaufmann. New York: Vintage Books.

Oakeshott, Michael (1991) *Rationalism in Politics and Other Essays*. Indianapolis: Liberty Press.

Pearton, Maurice (1982) *The Knowledgable State. Diplomacy, War and Technology Since 1830*. London: Burnett Books.

Pirage, Dennis (1991) 'Environmental security and social evolution', *International Studies Notes*, 16 (1): 8–12.

Pöggeler, Otto (1990) *Martin Heidegger's Path of Thinking*. Atlantic Highlands, NJ: Humanities Press.

Renner, Michael (1989) *National Security. The Economic and Environmental Dimensions*. Washington, DC: Worldwatch Institute, Paper No. 89.

Richter, Melvin (1986) 'Conceptual history *(Begriffsgeschichte)* and political theory', *Political Theory*, 14 (4): 604–37.

Richter, Melvin (1990) 'Reconstructing the history of political languages: Pocock, Skinner, and the *Geschichtliche Grundbegriffe*', *History and Theory. Studies In the Philosophy of History*, 29 (1): 38–70.

Rosen, Stanley (1989) *The Ancients and the Moderns. Rethinking Modernity*. London: Yale University Press.

Sallis, John (ed.) (1970) *Heidegger and the Path of Thinking*. Pittsburgh: Duquesne University Press.

Sallis, John (1978) 'Where does Being and Time begin?' in Frederick Elliston (ed.), *Heidegger's Existential Analytic*. The Hague: Mouton Publishers Ltd.

Schmidt, Dennis J. (1988) *The Ubiquity of the Finite. Hegel, Heidegger and the Entitlements of Philosophy*. Cambridge, MA: MIT Press.

Schmidt, Dennis J. (1991) 'Changing the subject: Heidegger, the National and Epochal', in *Heidegger and the Political. The Graduate Faculty Philosophy Journal*, 14 (2)–15 (1).

Schurmann, Reiner (1990) *Heidegger on Being and Acting: From Principles to Anarchy*. Bloomington: Indiana University Press.

Stambaugh, Joan (1972) *Time and Being*. New York: Harper Torch Books.

Taylor, Charles (1993) 'Engaged agency and background', in Charles Guignon (ed.), *The Cambridge Companion to Heidegger*. Cambridge: Cambridge University Press.

Ullman, Richard H. (1989) 'Redefining security', *International Security*, 8 (1).

Vattimo, Gianni (1993) *The Adventure of Difference. Philosophy after Nietzsche and Heidegger*. Oxford: Polity Press.

Walker, R.B.J. (1993) *Inside Outside: International Relations as Political Theory*. Cambridge: Cambridge University Press.

Wolin, Richard (1990) *The Politics of Being. The Political Thought of Martin Heidegger*. New York: Columbia Press.

Wolin, Sheldon (1961) *Politics and Vision*. London: George Allen & Unwin.

Wood, David (1990) *Philosophy at the Limit*. London: Unwin Hyman.

Wright, Quincy (1942) *A Study Of War, Vol. 2*. Chicago: Chicago University Press.

10

NORMALITY – EXCEPTION – COUNTER-KNOWLEDGE: ON THE HISTORY OF A MODERN FASCINATION

Benno Wagner

In this chapter I shall deal with an epistemic axiom which has managed to survive a series of diachronic and synchronic transformations. It seems to have been the unchallenged wisdom of common sense from pre-Enlightenment times via the classical period of modernity to a present which some observers choose to call postmodern, or post-historical; and it has been incorporated in fields of knowledge as different as medicine, law, sociology, politics, the arts and, inevitably, so-called 'public opinion'. My examination of what at first glance seems to be a 'universal constituent' of modern knowledge seeks to offer a view on the interrelation of modernity and its 'others', counter-projects, etc., that varies not only from older concepts like the 'dialectic of Enlightenment', but also from the more recent models of 'reflexive modernity'. What it shares with them is a strong scepticism towards the idea of a qualitative incision (on whatever level of description) between 'modernity' and 'postmodernity'.

I

'The normal proves nothing, the exception proves everything' (Schmitt, 1922: 22).[1]

When Carl Schmitt first proclaimed this platform for his diagnosis of the times in 1922, he could not possibly have known of the landmark analysis which another 'conservative revolutionary', Arnold Gehlen, first published almost forty years later under the title: 'On cultural crystallization' (Gehlen, 1961).[2] Here Gehlen combines in a striking diagnosis some of the key concepts for the theory of social systems engineered by Niklas Luhmann in the following two decades, with the core findings of J.-F. Lyotard's report on the 'postmodern condition' (Lyotard, 1984). According to Gehlen, the historical process of functional *differentiation* of societies has created a rigid grid of specialized practices and discourses ('technical languages') each of which is formulating its specific sets of problems and solutions and achieving its specific, 'sectoral' kind of progress. Not only is it hardly possible to 'transform' any of the specific developments of technology, social planning, economic management, the arts, etc. into progress in any of the other specialized fields; there is also no hope left of achieving an overall definition of 'progress' as it had been conceived of in the tradition of philosophy of history. While differentiation divides the individual fields of practice and knowledge from each other, the corresponding *specialization* establishes an almost insurmountable bar to unmediated communication between experts and non-experts (the 'public') (Gehlen, 1961: 317). This state of 'cultural crystallization' (1961: 312, 321), Gehlen claims, is marked by the *inclusion* of the traditional meta-discourses like religion, or philosophy, into the various functional fields, and their gradual replacement by a scientific 'culture *encadrée*' of the 'supermachine' (1961: 320). The *traditional*, totalizing codes of identification and orientation which used to be based on a legitimizing exceptional situation (miracle, conquest), *and* their prede-cessors in the programme of Enlightenment (revolution, reason) have become structurally impossible; the 'grand key attitudes', be they religious, philosophical or political, which had accompanied and integrated societies until and throughout the nineteenth century, have survived only as 'empty models' (1961: 315). The premises of Enlightenment are dead, its conse-quences continue, as Gehlen puts it (cf. Habermas, 1988: 11). His analysis anticipates with striking clarity what will reappear in Luhmann's social theory as the impossibility of a totalizing self-description of modern society, of a binding *repraesentatio identitatis* (Luhmann, 1987: 162), and what Lyotard will (re)discover, two decades after Gehlen, as the end of the 'grand récits de légitimation' (Lyotard, 1984).[3]

If we read Carl Schmitt's most disputed treatise it is obvious that his linking of the 'concept of the political' to the exception was already a *reaction* to the state of affairs described by Gehlen and his famous epigones.[4] Under the challenge of relativism and differentiation, Schmitt tries to preserve the 'grand key attitude' by transforming and re-establishing its core element, the *exceptional situation*, as an integrative, 'true' observer position through a shift of focus from the *spatial* to the *temporal* matrix of reference.[5] It is remarkable enough that this project has been exposed to (almost) *unanimous* scientific criticism only after its failure in military, political and moral terms. It is, however, even more remarkable to observe how, despite all these instructions in iron and ink, theorists and practitioners of politics all over the world keep returning to the infamous Schmitt axiom, only to be immediately taught their Gehlenian lesson. In 1977, the terrorist Red Army Faction wanted to tear the 'legalistic mask' off the face of the 'fascist' West German state, but eventually found themselves confronted by a war 'only in a metaphorical sense', as a leading daily paper correctly classified the *symbolic* battle against terrorism and its sympathizers in the public media (Wagner, 1991a: 198; Wellmer, 1979: 269ff). Thirteen years later, Saddam Hussein wanted to demonstrate the true battle line dividing the Islamic from the Western world, but he too was defeated in a war which, according to J. Baudrillard (1991), never took place.[6] Not very much later in the Soviet

Union, Janajew, Pugo and their gang wanted to demonstrate the true state of the national crisis by forcefully imposing a state of emergency on the country, but had to admit after having their soldiers hanging around in tanks for three days, that 'the coup had only happened by mistake'.

II

These observations have led me to ask again those questions about the modern patterns of cultural orientation – which Gehlen had answered so authoritatively – in a more specific way. What happened to the exceptional case? How to explain its transformation from an 'empirical' reality to the 'vampirical' existence of our day with its consumption of so much intellectual, political, cultural and physical energy?[7] If we want to answer this question, we have to develop a point of view which is located beyond the available alternatives of either playing down the significance of exceptionalist strategies of knowledge (as Luhmann has chosen to do),[8] or ascribing their present mode of existence to developments beyond modernity and history, such as 'cultural crystallization' or, in more recent versions, an in-built tendency of any system toward entropy (Hans Magnus Enzensberger)[9] and simulation (Jean Baudrillard).[10] To escape this unsatisfactory choice between neglect and oversimplification, I will focus on the concept of 'normality/normalization' as an organizing cultural principle in order to reconstruct the history of the exceptional case within a model of modernity that is stripped of any unwarranted normative implications right from the start, thus avoiding the 'pseudo-epistemological categories' (Hunter, 1984) of 'crisis' and 'decay' that normally organize the self-description of modernity.

This takes us back to Carl Schmitt's disjunction of the normal and the exception. In Schmitt's model, the exception cannot be anticipated and codified by legal norms. At best, it may 'be characterized as a case of extreme peril, a danger to the existence of the state, or the like. But it cannot be circumscribed factually and made to conform a preformed law' (1985: 6). The highest, unmediated power, that is, sovereignty, is 'he who decides on the exception' (1985: 5), that is 'whether there is an extreme emergency as well as what must be done to eliminate it' (1985: 7). This means that the sovereign decision always has a *cognitive* and a *practical* side, it is practically efficient cognition par excellence. The cognitive distinction between 'normality' and 'exception(al case)' is immediately linked to the practical consequence of normalization.

Sovereignty in this sense had its 'classical period' during the sixteenth and seventeenth centuries, the 'great times of the *jus publicum europaeum*' (Schmitt, 1963: 17). Replacing politics by police, and conflicts between families, tribes and confessions by 'peace, security and order' in the interior, the newly emerging territorial states put an end to medieval feuding. The political decision on friend and foe thus became a state monopoly.

Accordingly, 'war' and 'enemy' became categories of foreign politics, their field of reference being the legally regulated conflicts between (in principle) equal sovereign states: 'Even the enemy has a status; he is not a criminal' (Schmitt, 1963: 10f). The exceptional case was the key to the truth of political power (its legitimacy or illegitimacy).

An *inverse reading* of this 'classical' nexus between exception and knowledge is offered in Michel Foucault's archaeology of power regimes. Here, the observer position shifts from the centre of power to the margins, from the constitution and affirmation of power to its questioning and subversion. Foucault (1986) demonstrates how, with the 'nationalization of war' by the new European states, a discourse emerged which for the first time in occidental history confronted the classical 'Roman' type of history and its narrative of the continuity, universality and magnificence of the sovereign with political-historical knowledge in the modern sense. Like Schmitt's political theology, this counter-history wants to keep alive the memory of the violent and uncontrolled conflicts that precede any established legal order. But while the former aims at the conservation and control[11] of the state of emergency as a constituent of a stable power regime, the latter operates in the opposite direction. It is preoccupied rather with the unearthing and deciphering of those conflicts that had been 'forgotten' *within* or *below* the established political order than with the potential conflicts *between* sovereign states. Like political theology, counter-history questions the universality and the equilibrium, the precondition and focus of philosophico-juridical discourse, by emphasizing the irreducibility of violent conflict to rational and reasonable regulation. This time, however, truth is not connected with the execution of supreme power, but with the suffering that has been caused and concealed in the name of that very power:

> It is the decentred position which enables us to decipher the truth, to do away with all the illusions and errors which want to make us believe that one is living in a world of peace and order. The more I move away from the centre, the more I see the truth. (Foucault, 1986: 15)

The two techniques of exceptionalist epistemology, the centripetal and the centrifugal, have been affected by radical transformations in the fields of politics and of knowledge in the course of the nineteenth century. While Schmitt bemoans the humiliation of the 'classical' state to a mere function of society, Foucault offers a more analytical perspective. A 'dialectically' codified, totalized and rationalized discourse, that is, 'class struggle', replaced the partial, irregular counter-history, that is, in Foucault's terminology, 'race struggle'. At the same time, the *political-historical* dimension of the remaining epistemic corpse of irregular race struggle was substituted by a new *biological-medical* discourse, the strategic form of counter-knowledge was perverted and appropriated by a monistic state racism (Foucault, 1986: 25ff). The figure of the sovereign who is able to perceive and to demonstrate the true political order was replaced by a set of normalizing functions operating beyond the classical distinctions of friend and enemy, war and peace. The classical state turned, as Schmitt has put it, into an 'agnostic state', the distinctions organizing political power were fading out (Schmitt, 1963: 88ff).

III

Here our key concept of 'normality/normalization' moves into focus. In France, this history began with the simultaneous reform of the systems of education and of health after the French Revolution. Taking the state of undisturbed organic health as a model, 'normal' became the official attribute for the French schools of professional teaching, the 'Ecoles normales'. The institutional dissemination of the new term was accompanied by an incisive epistemological transformation emanating from the field of medicine.

With the emergence of the modern axiom: that humanity is not simply opposed to nature, but should subdue and control it, the medical concept of disease as a 'polemic' situation, that is of the struggle of the organism against a foreign, qualitatively different external power, was gradually being undermined. In 1828, this epistemic shift culminated in the famous 'Broussais principle', according to which all diseases can be explained by 'a surplus or lack of irritation of the tissue concerned, as compared to the normal condition' (Canguilhem, 1974: 25). Health and disease, the normal and the exceptional, reappeared at the limiting ends of a continuous, quantitatively differentiated scale. Disease had turned, as Canguilhem puts it, from an object of fear and respect for the healthy person into a scientific research object for the theorist of health (1974: 22). For a variety of reasons reaching from the scientific prestige of medicine to the traditional meta-phorical link between the body and society, the new epistemic figure made a swift career through sociology, demography and economy. Let us now have a closer look at some implications of this epistemic shift.

1. *The exceptional: from gift to given.* The knowledge of that which is normal no longer depended on a pre-discursive instance. Instead, the exceptional was now related to the normal within one identical field of scientific axioms or assumptions. In an essay on the epistemological structure of Foucault's thought, Pierre Macherey (1991) demonstrates how this shift from a transcendent to an *immanent norm* is linked to the *productivity of the norm*. The norm – and we can add: the exception – produces itself simultaneously with and within its own field of application (1991: 186f). As a consequence of this reflexive productivity of the norm, all sorts of exceptions could be caused, analysed and normalized under experimental control. Even many of those exceptions that previously had been 'happening' to individuals or societies (epidemics, economic crises, sudden demographic shifts), could now be considered as 'real life experi-ments' and be evaluated by always already waiting experimental dispo-sitives. (A striking, though only relatively recent example is the tragic role of John F. Kennedy in the theory of mass communication. A heavily staffed

and equipped research team is said to have been waiting for many weeks for an event that would allow them to study 'on the scene' the dissemination of news about a nationally important event when the assassination of the President delivered them the opportunity of the century. This kind of scientific, journalistic, etc. objectivity is, by the way, a striking example of the almost anagrammatical conversion of morality into normality.)

2. *From discontinuity to continuity*. Jürgen Link has described the mode of operation of these dispositives as the 'continuation of fundamental discontinuities' (1992: 65). In order to situate qualitatively different objects (for example, health and disease) in a homogeneous field of relativity, a common medium of comparison has to be found for these objects. In the case of medicine, this was achieved by the introduction of *irritation* as a common term of reference for health and disease. In the same manner, qualitative incisions in the social field such as class differences could be integrated in continuous scales of *income levels* which made it possible to explain the specific position of each individual income holder as the outcome of a random distribution (with randomness, of course, being based on the liberal ideology of 'equal chance') (Link, 1992: 65). The transfer of this technique from physical to social life, however, has some most relevant implications for the epistemic history of the exception.

3. *The priority of the transgression to the rule*. In his attempt to utilize certain elements of philosophy of life for his epistemic criticism, Canguilhem (1974) defines very carefully the differences between the mode of existence that may be ascribed to the normal in the biological organism on the one hand, and the social organization on the other hand. In the organism the rules that guarantee and define normality are immanent, present and unintentional. There is no temporal or spatial difference between rule and regulation. In the social organization the rules have to be established, taught and learned, remembered and applied. There *is* a difference between rule and regulation (Canguilhem, 1974: 172ff). This difference, I suggest, is crucial for the understanding of the mode of reproduction which power assumes in what Foucault has labelled the *normalizing societies*. First of all, this difference implies the priority of the transgression with regard to the rule. If regulation is not coexistent with the rule, it needs transgression as a trigger, so to speak. This also implies that the rule, though logically antecedent, is historically secondary to transgression (1974: 166ff). *The normal needs the exceptional as its supplement*. The exceptional case does not escape normality, but simply serves as a starting signal for procedures of renormalization. If we accept this formal argument, we also have to accept its inversion, that is, the polemic character of the normal.

4. *The polemic character of the normal*.

The normal is not a static and peaceful term, but a dynamic and polemic one. [. . .] To normalize means: To force upon a being or a given a claim which makes appear the multiplicity of that given not only a strange, but a hostile indetermined. The concept is polemic in that it disqualifies that which is not submitted to its authority and at the same time insists on its incorporation. (Canguilhem, 1974: 163)

When Auguste Comte, in adopting the Broussais principle, modified it exactly according to this definition, this was, however, rather due to his sociological point of view than to some power inherent in a concept (Lepenies, 1981: 242f). While sticking to the *methodical* principle of measurable continuity between the normal and the pathological, Comte at the same time dropped the *philosophical* principle of their qualitative homogeneity. His interest in the idea of social control and his belief in the organic convergence of social norms toward self-regulation of the whole made him, philosophically, a partisan of a vitalist axiom established by Xavier Bichat according to whom 'life is the sum of those functions that resist death' (Canguilhem, 1981: 224). Thus, Comte applied a series of supposedly pre-existent 'sane'–'insane' oppositions to various fields of reference such as philosophical methodology, the theory of history and public education. It was this montage of Broussais' gradualism and Bichat's vitalism which gave to the nineteenth century what Lepenies calls its 'new ontology' of disease – biological and social (Lepenies, 1981: 245). However, to speak simply of a 'new ontology' in this context seems somewhat superficial. What we have been resuming here is nothing less than the irreversible transformation of a first order ontology, or *ontology of beings*. The opposition between the normal and the exception was no longer codified and stabilized by traditional knowledge, but had become dynamic, relative to occasion, and highly 'multifunctional', that is easily re-writable and applicable to all sorts of exceptions, from pathological 'abnormalities' via legal 'transgressions' to political 'emergencies'. The identity of this opposition is not grounded on the specific *substance* of its poles, but on the *difference* between them. In this sense, the 'new ontology' may be marked as a second order ontology, or, more exactly, an *ontology of difference*. In other words, the de-ontologized dispositives of normalization had incorporated the polemic capacities of ontological conflicts (health vs. disease, life vs. death, friend vs. enemy), but not the corresponding traditional codes of control. This leads us back to Carl Schmitt's attempt to counter *normalism*[12] by an intensified exceptionalism.

IV

'The normal proves nothing, the exception proves everything'. With this axiomatic disjunction, Schmitt (1922: 22) purports to cut across the network of circular, relative and recursive relations that had been established between normality and exception in the nineteenth century. His aim is the construction of an epistemic frame, or scene, for the reunion of perception and knowledge, a frame to secure the emergence of pre-discursive truth as a concrete possibility. As far as his diagnosis is concerned, his exceptionalism is in line with contemporary observers such as Benjamin, Bloch, Lukacs, etc., all of whom witness the breakdown of humanoid perception in the face of normality culture and all of whom want to regain new a prioris for a totalizing mode of perception.[13] It is specific, however, in view of its relation to the meta-dispositive of normalism, a relation which Schmitt himself might have labelled as 'tragic'. Let me elaborate this in three steps.

1. In his statement 'In the exceptional the power of real life breaks through the crust of a mechanism that has become torpid by repetition' Schmitt (1985: 15) further illustrates his axiom. 'Life', though, has been exactly the signifier by which the evolutionist nineteenth-century normalism has legitimized and organized its multidimensional and multivectoral operations. In Schmitt's narrative, this signifier has radically changed its signified. The very instance which guarantees the convergence of all norms toward self-regulation, in an infinite battle of life against death, is now on the side of death: a torpid mechanism, or, as Schmitt puts it in the third chapter of *Political Theology*: 'the machine now runs by itself' (1985: 48). For what Comte conceives as 'life', a norm-setting instance which itself is nothing but the 'sum of its normalizing functions', is, in Schmitt, nothing but *'Lebensver-hältnis'* (frame of life), not *'wirkliches Leben'* (real life),[14] and therefore, it is but the *medium* of norms, and not their *source*.

> The exceptional [that is real life *sensu Schmitt*] appears in its absolute form when a situation in which legal prescriptions can be valid must first be brought about. Each general norm demands a normal everyday frame of life to which it can be factually applied and which is subjected to its regulations. (1985: 13)

Just like Comte, Schmitt postulates the priority of the transgression to the rule. As opposed to Comte, he distinguishes one specific case in which the continuity and the recursivity between transgression and rule are interrupted. In this case of the 'absolute exception' the medium of interrelation needs an act of creation plus a creator: 'A normal situation must be brought about, and sovereign is he who definitely decides if this normal situation actually exists' (1985: 13). Schmitt, it seems, is not so much concerned about practices and procedures of normalization *per se* as about a regime of normalization left to itself. But why should we depend so much on an intervening sovereignty from time to time?

2. Because 'real life', Schmitt answers, is always 'concrete life', and a genuine philosophy of life is a philosophy of concrete life, a philosophy which 'must not withdraw from the exception and the extreme case, but must be interested in it to the highest degree' (1985: 15). Concrete life, that is the specific life of a people (a people that has been able to form a political unit with a defined territory), a life which cannot be subsumed under universal norms (like humanity, peace, progress) and which is irreducible to the lives of other people. Concrete life is defined by *'Lebensart'* (mode of life), and sovereign is he who is able to grant the homogeneity of *'Lebensart'* and *'Lebensverhältnis''* (of inherited *mode* of life and actual *frame* of life), a homogeneity that is permanently menaced by the *Lebensart* of other peoples. For Schmitt, then, the principle of life is not the *struggle with death*,

but the *fight against life*, hostile life, the life of the enemy, under the risk of one's own, individual, life. The world is a political pluriverse, not a universe on its march for progress (1963: 54ff). Life is not univectoral, but multivectoral. 'Spirit', Schmitt writes against the evolutionist concept of life, 'fights against spirit, life against life, and from the power of an *uncorrupted knowledge* emerges the order of human affairs' (1963: 95, my italics).

3. If Schmitt's anti-normalist modification of the concept of 'life' has been clarified in step 2, the legitimacy, or rather, the operativity of this modification now depends on the nature of that 'uncorrupted knowledge', and especially on its capability to 'conserve and control'[15] hostility, a capability which normalist culture has readily abandoned as an obstacle to its free-style operations of normalization or, if 'inevitable', eradication of the abnormal.

I now refer to a recent article by Friedrich Balke on the question of the 'substance' of a political unit and its 'homogeneity' in Schmitt's political theory (Balke, 1992b: 45ff). As criteria for the specific kind of 'national homogeneity' that has become predominant since the nineteenth century, Schmitt specifies a common language, common traditions and memories, and the common hopes and aims of a people. He is, however, only too conscious of the fact that, in the age of mass media and political propaganda, these resources do not spring from pre-discursive sources of uncorrupted knowledge. Therefore, Schmitt adds one more, decisive, criterion: the conscious will of *the* people to be *a* people. Everything then, we may go on with Schmitt, 'depends on how the will of the people is formed' (1988: 27). Now Schmitt suggests that the nation comes into being in the very moment when the people experience *the* state as *their* state (cf. Balke, 1992b: 46). This identification of the people with their state takes place exactly in the exceptional case in politics, the case of emergency, of actual and immediate confrontation with the enemy. However, if after the integration of the state into the functional grid of society, the state needs the enemy for its re-emergence, how, or from where, should we then define this enemy of the state? At this point, Balke (1992b: 40ff) demonstrates how Schmitt is able to avoid any substantializing definition of the friend–enemy opposition by linking it to the elementary cultural opposition of the familiar and the unfamiliar, as an intensifier. The *enemy* then is the *stranger*, the one who, by definition, cannot be integrated into the concrete life and its specific logic of associations and dissociations, the one who by necessity remains an uncontrolled observer and therefore a permanent menace to a people. Democracy, that is the substantial homogeneity within a political unit, does, as a matter of fact, *presuppose* the stigmatization or annihilation of something substantially different. The people, then, as a substantial political unit, is nothing but the effect of the 'elimination or eradication of heterogeneity' (Schmitt, 1988: 9).[16] At last, we may conclude, it is not a pre-cultural *substance*, but a highly artificial, though now intensified *difference* that is supposed to be the source of

Schmitt's 'uncorrupted knowledge'. The normal proves nothing, the exception proves *any*thing . . .

V

In his attempt to re-ontologize political sovereignty via an intensification of the friend–enemy opposition, Schmitt by necessity ends up with an intensification of the very 'ontology of difference' which he has rightfully interpreted as the end of classical politics and its system of codes for the control of conflict. By claiming the inevitability of existential conflict about concrete life and postulating unrestricted power for the sovereign, Schmitt fails, even in theory, to transform the normalizing nation-state; quite to the contrary, he helps to augment its power and to weaken the ('liberal') mechanisms of self-control. It is an easy move for fascist ideology to put the 'concrete life' of the Aryan people(s) on top of the 'political pluriverse', declare other 'concrete lives' inferior or *'lebensunwert'* and, finally, to re-establish a perverted and, thanks to exceptionalist ventures like the one we have just analysed, intensified 'life–death' opposition.

In principle, the other exceptionalisms of the 1920s and 1930s were caught in the same strategic trap of *integral normality* and its intransgressable field of immanence.[17] However, as far as they had not been grounded on a biopolitical discourse (but on class struggle, chiliasm, aesthetics, etc.) they did not contribute as directly to the intensification and de-regulation of state normalism as Schmitt's exceptionalist venture did.

Although we might have contributed to answering the question of why exceptionalist strategies are not only incapable of producing privileged (counter-)knowledge in and about normality cultures, but quite to the contrary increase their incalculability, we still are confronted with the question of the lasting fascination of these 'fatal strategies'. After all, even our anti-exceptionalist chief witness after turning down all hopes for another 'grand key attitude' in post-Second World War civilization, concluded his analysis by suggesting that the 'Thirty Years' War of our century' (1914–45) 'has inextinguishably burned into the consciousness of mankind, mankind's self-encounter took place in this conflagration, and it is this experience which, I believe, will create a new ethos' (Gehlen, 1961: 327f). Other investments were to follow: Adorno's *Negative Dialectics* (1973) as a radical but vain attempt to immunize the exceptional against the normal by the paradoxical procedure of aestheticizing abstraction; orthodox Marxism (West German Communist Party brand) as a frankensteinesque revival of pre-First World War theories of impoverishment and economic collapse; ecological apocalypses as phantastic bricolages of exceptionalisms of all cultures and (p)ages.[18] It seems as if these post-Second World War exceptionalisms were but another example of the return of the historical tragedy as a farce. This handy formula, however, would underrate their status as 'archaisms with an actual function' (Deleuze and Guattari, 1974:

332). Surrounded by an ever more subtle network of normalizing procedures, counter-cultural projects in the *'Modell Deutschland'* almost
inevitably served as feedback signals within the 'immunology' of the political
system.[19] The most impressive example for such a pragmatic, first-order
analysis of 'useful' and 'disturbing' innovation has no doubt been the
effective symbolic vivisection of the German Green Party into *'Realpo-
litiker'* and *'Fundamentalisten'* exactly along the political borderline of those
ecologist concepts which the *'Modell Deutschland'* was ready and able to
integrate, and those which would have necessitated serious changes to its
socioeconomic construction. This politico-cultural disarmament of the
exceptional situation may be one – paradoxical – reason for its lasting
fascination (the so-called 'playground strategy').[20] Rather than speculating
about further reasons (be they anthropological, psychological, cultural or
whatever) I would like to underline that the 'inflation' of the category of
exception neither means that 'anything goes' nor that our societies have
been swallowed by the regime of simulation. Normalization is still the
business of the day. What no doubt has been submitted to change are the
technical means and the social and cultural environments or settings of their
operation; the *materiality of communication*, as Hans Ulrich Gumbrecht
and K. Ludwig Pfeiffer (1989) have labelled this new field of research.
Instead of discussing the somewhat idle question of whether these changes
justify the label of 'postmodernity', I would suggest systematically looking
for and developing strategies of non-exceptionalist counter-knowledge.
Probably the search for such strategies would have to begin in the boom
period of exceptionalism, the first three decades of our century. And maybe
literature, especially the modern 'avant-garde' novel, should be the
preferred site of exploration, with the writings of Kafka and Musil as the
most promising areas. But here begins a different text.

Notes

1. My translation. Subsequent quotations are from the translation by George Schwab
(Schmitt, 1985). Schwab in this case translates German *'das Normale'* by English 'the rule', thus
reducing the *cultural* concept of normality to a *logical* one.

2. All English quotes from German sources are my translation.

3. For a detailed and well-organized, though obtrusively 'enlightened' history of the focal
concept of *'posthistoire'* see Lutz Niethammer (1989).

4. As far as its purely epistemological implications are concerned, Gehlen's diagnosis of
'cultural crystallization' could have been made well before the Second World War.

5. For a detailed analysis of Schmitt's strategic oscillation between the two poles see
Friedrich Balke (1992a).

6. In his analysis of the 'Gulf War', Baudrillard (1991) obviously – though obviously not
obviously enough for the knights of critical reason – plays with the difference between the literal
and the conventional metaphorical meaning of 'taking place' (*avoir lieu*) and maintains quite
correctly, that this war never offered a classical 'theatre', a spatio-temporal 'situation' for the
clash between the enemies. The 'showdown' between Saddam and Bush happened solely on the
level of media metaphors. This, of course, does not mean to say what some well-meaning critics
seem to have understood: that 'nothing happened' in the Gulf area (and beyond).

7. And not only, as Gehlen (1961) indicates, as a negligable 'empty model'.

8. An attitude which connects early theoretical platforms such as *'Soziologische Aufklärung'* (Luhmann, 1967: 69) to later diagnoses such as *Ökologische Kommunikation*, where Luhmann writes about the analytical achievements of the 'new social movements': 'All we can observe is a resigned commentary on our current decline in the style of Adorno or Gehlen, but it is hardly possible to recur to these positions' (1986: 236).

9. According to Enzensberger, it is due to the 'peculiar dynamic' of exceptionalism that, after its getting in vogue towards the end of the nineteenth century, 'in no time Europe was crowded with supermen [*Übermenschen*]. Millions of leaders by nature [*Führernaturen*] and extremists were competing for a position in the historical vanguard. . . . and tried to win over the silent majority, eventually with diminishing success' (1982: 214).

10. Baudrillard almost literally shares our diagnosis of vampirism when he concludes that in the age of simulation, *any* social substance is stricken with 'leukaemia: the exchange of blood against the white lymph of the mass media' (1982: 104).

11. To describe this specific function of sovereign power, Schmitt (e.g. 1963: 11f) uses the German verb *'hegen'* which combines the meanings of 'conservation' and 'control'. It is therefore a key indicator of Schmitt's ambivalent position in view of commonsense distinctions such as war/peace.

12. Jürgen Link has argued that what Foucault has described as the 'normalizing society' actually deserves the title of 'normalism', or 'normality culture'. By means of a quite original archaeology of discourses reaching from science over politics to literature, Link (1990) demonstrates that normality and normalization in fact are fundamental structures and procedures of 'modern' or 'industrial' cultures that reach far beyond the specialized institutional discourses on which Foucault has concentrated. Thanks to this *interdiscursive* quality, normality serves as an indispensable 'sedative' for the individuals and collectives involved in a highly dynamic social process with exponential growth rates in its most important sectors (economy, knowledge, energy, consumption of resources). Instead of a homogeneous, transcendental, prescriptive *norm*, the project of modernity would then be based on a heterogeneous set of immanent, postscriptive operations of *normalization*, be they operative-effective or rather symbolic-affective in nature. From here, Link (1992) suggests the reformulation of a series of focal concepts of 'modernity', such as 'progress', 'modernization', 'consensus' and 'dialectics'. In this context, it must suffice to point out that the politically contradictory composition of 'anti-democratic thought' in the Weimar Republic (cf. Sontheimer, 1962) appears as a quite consistent phenomenon if one reads the respective projects as *anti-normalist* interventions; without, however, falling back to a trivial understanding of normality as something like a commonsense version of 'reason'.

13. For a cross-reading of these projects see Norbert Bolz (1989).

14. As a matter of fact, Schmitt is rather thinking of 'genuine life' (vs. 'artificial life') than of 'real life' (vs. 'unreal life').

15. Cf. note 11.

16. This analysis has been confirmed with alarming exactitude in the course of the German reunification. When the East German democracy movement changed their platform from 'We are *the* people' to 'We are *a* people' this national identity was only constituted by the common exclusion (and, if 'inevitable', annihilation) of the 'strangers' many of whom used to enjoy the status of invited guests from socialist brother countries in the days of German constitutional schizophrenia. As a matter of fact, the *new* German racism is not so much founded on a substantializing ideology of the otherness of the other (as opposed to the old, Nazi version) as on the *normalizing function* of this artificially intensified difference in view of all sorts of quite material, economic, legal and political discontinuities between the two parts of Germany.

17. I have elaborated this concept of a normality which always already includes the exception in Wagner (1991b: 160ff), with reference to Arnold Gehlen's analysis of the welfare state bureaucracy. For a comprehensive examination of this phenomenon see the study by François Ewald (1993). It should be emphasized that this concept by no means excludes escalations into wars, economic breakdowns and so on, but that these 'crises' cannot simply have been conceived of as 'exceptional' situations as opposed to 'normal' ones. The various dispositives of normalization in our sense must not be mistaken for moralistic 'normalities'. From this point of

view, it may appear less astonishing to find that the staff even of an 'abnormal' place like a Nazi concentration camp consisted to a great extent of quite 'normal' persons from a behaviouralistic or even psychological perspective.

18. For an impressive example of this genre see Rudolf Bahro's second great manifesto of dissidence, *Die Logik der Rettung* (Bahro, 1988).

19. For a systematic elaboration of the concept of immunology see Luhmann (1984: 504ff); for its application to the context of political culture see Wagner (1992: 277ff).

20. After the exceptionalist farce under the title of '1968', Ernst Forsthoff has described this historically new situation as follows:

> The structure of industrial society seals itself against abrupt events, not by preventing them from happening, but by making them inefficient – like the événements in France in May 1968. Under these circumstances, the unconditional trust in the firmness of the preconditions of normality is by no means unfounded. (1971: 167)

References

Adorno, Theodor W. (1973) *Negative Dialectics*. London: Routledge.

Bahro, Rudolf (1988) *Die Logik der Rettung. Wer kann die Apokalypse aufhalten*. Stuttgart: Edition Weitbrecht.

Balke, Friedrich (1992a) 'Aufhalter, Beschleuniger, Normalisierer. Drei Figuren der politischen Theorie Carl Schmitts', in Friedrich Balke, Eric Mechoulan and Benno Wagner (eds), *Zeit des Ereignisses – Ende der Geschichte?* Munich: Fink. pp. 209–32.

Balke, Friedrich (1992b) 'Die Figur des Fremden bei Carl Schmitt und Georg Simmel', *Sociologia Internationalis. International Journal for Sociology, Communication Studies and Cultural Research*, 30 (1): 35–59.

Baudrillard, Jean (1982) *Der symbolische Tausch und der Tod*. Munich: Matthes & Seitz.

Baudrillard, Jean (1991) 'La Guerre du Golfe n'a pas eu lieu', *Libération*, 29 March.

Bolz, Norbert (1989) *Auszug aus der entzauberten Welt. Philosophischer Extremismus zwischen den Weltkriegen*. Munich: Fink.

Canguilhem, Georges (1974) *Das Normale und das Pathologische*. Munich: Hanser.

Canguilhem, Georges (1981) 'Auguste Comtes Philosophie der Biologie und ihr Einfluß im Frankreich des 19. Jahrhunderts', in Wolf Lepenies (ed.), *Geschichte der Soziologie*, vol. 3. Frankfurt: Suhrkamp. pp. 209–26.

Deleuze, Gilles and Guattari, Félix (1974) *Anti-Ödipus. Kapitalismus und Schizophrenie I*. Frankfurt: Suhrkamp.

Enzensberger, Hans Magnus (1982) 'Zur Verteidigung der Normalität', in Hans Magnus Enzensberger (ed.), *Politische Brosamen*. Frankfurt: Suhrkamp. pp. 207–24.

Ewald, François (1993) *Der Vorsorgestaat*. Frankfurt: Suhrkamp.

Forsthoff, Ernst (1971) *Der Staat der Industriegesellschaft*. Munich: Beck.

Foucault, Michel (1986) *Vom Licht des Krieges zur Geburt der Geschichte*, edited by Walter Seitter. Berlin: Merve.

Gehlen, Arnold (1961) 'Über kulturelle Kristallisation', in Arnold Gehlen (ed.), *Studien zur Anthropologie und Soziologie*. Neuwied/Berlin: Luchterhand. pp. 311–28.

Gumbrecht, Hans Ulrich and Pfeiffer, K. Ludwig (1989) *Materialität der Kommunikation*. Frankfurt: Suhrkamp.

Habermas, Jürgen (1988) 'Das Zeitbewusstsein der Moderne und ihr Bedürfnis nach Selbstvergewisserung', in *Der philosophische Diskurs der Moderne*. Frankfurt: SuhrKamp. pp. 9–33.

Hunter, Ian (1984) 'After representation', *Economy and Society* 13 (11): 397–430.

Lepenies, Wolf (1981) 'Normalität und Anormalität. Wechselwirkungen zwischen den Wissenschaften vom Leben und den Sozialwissenschaften im 19. Jahrhundert', in Wolf Lepenies (ed.), *Geschichte der Soziologie*, vol. 3. Frankfurt: Suhrkamp. pp. 227–51.

Link, Jürgen (1990) 'Zahlen Kurven Symbole. Zum Anteil der Kollektivsymbolik an normalisierenden Zahlenspielen', *kultuRRevolution. Zeitschrift für angewandte Diskurstheorie*, 23: 3–9.

Link, Jürgen (1992) 'Normalismus: Konturen eines Konzepts', *kultuRRevolution. Zeitschrift für angewandte Diskurstheorie*, 27: 50–70.

Luhmann, Niklas (1967) 'Soziologische Aufklärung', *Soziale Welt*, 18: 97–123 (quote according to reprint in: Niklas Luhmann (1971), *Soziologische Aufklärung*, vol. 1. Opladen: Westdeutscher Verlag. pp. 66–91.

Luhmann, Niklas (1984) *Soziale Systeme*. Frankfurt: Suhrkamp.

Luhmann, Niklas (1986) *Ökologische Kommunikation. Kann die moderne Gesellschaft sich auf ökologische Gefährdungen einstellen?* Opladen: Westdeutscher Verlag.

Luhmann, Niklas (1987) 'Tautologie und Paradoxie in den Selbstbeschreibungen der modernen Gesellschaft', *Zeitschrift für Soziologie*, 16 (3): 161–74.

Lyotard, Jean-François (1984) *The Postmodern Condition: A Report on Knowledge*. Minneapolis: University of Minnesota Press.

Macherey, Pierre (1991) 'Für eine Naturgeschichte der Normen', in François Ewald and Bernhard Waldenfels (eds), *Spiele der Wahrheit. Michel Foucaults Denken*. Frankfurt: Suhrkamp. pp. 171–92.

Niethammer, Lutz (1989) *Posthistoire. Ist die Geschichte zu Ende?* Reinbek bei Hamburg: Rowohlt.

Schmitt, Carl (1922) *Politische Theologie. Vier Kapital zur Lehre von der Souveränität*. Berlin: Duncker & Humblot.

Schmitt, Carl (1963) *Der Begriff des Politischen*. Text of 1932 with three corollaries and: *Das Zeitalter der Neutralisierungen und Entpolitisierungen*; foreword of 1963. Berlin: Duncker & Humblot.

Schmitt, Carl (1985) *Political Theology. Four Chapters on the Concept of Sovereignty*, translated by George Schwab (originally published 1922, revised edn 1934). Cambridge, MA and London.

Schmitt, Carl (1988) *The Crisis of Parliamentary Democracy*, translated by Ellen Kennedy (originally published in 1923, *Die geistesgeschichtliche Lage des heutigen Parlamentarismus*). Cambridge, MA and London.

Sontheimer, Kurt (1962) *Antidemokratisches Denken in der Weimarer Republik*. Munich: Nymphenburger.

Wagner, Benno (1991a) 'Beobachtungen ohne Selbst. Über Paradoxien, Tautologien und Zuschreibungsprobleme moderner Legitimität', in Hans Ulrich Gumbrecht and K. Ludwig Pfeiffer (eds), *Paradoxien, Dissonanzen, Zusammenbrüche. Situationen offener Epistemologie*. Frankfurt: Suhrkamp. pp. 187–204.

Wagner, Benno (1991b) 'Gelassenheit auf alle Fälle', in Ernst Müller, K. Ludwig Pfeiffer and Benno Wagner (eds), *Geisteswissen. Vom wissenschaftspolitischen Problem zur problemorientierten Wissenschaft*. Frankfurt: VAS. pp. 147–71.

Wagner, Benno (1992) *Im Dickicht der politischen Kultur. Parteiensystem, Mediensymbolik und Alternativen vom 'deutschen Herbst' bis zur 'Wende'*. Munich: Fink.

Wellmer, Albrecht (1979) 'Terrorismus und Gesellschaftskritik', in Jürgen Habermas (ed.), *Stichworte zur geistigen Situation der Zeit*, vol. 1. Frankfurt: Suhrkamp. pp. 265–93.

11

TIME, SPACE, MEMORY, WITH REFERENCE TO BACHELARD

Ann Game

[The reader] will see that the Heraclitean flux is a *concrete* philosophy, a *complete* philosophy. One cannot bathe twice in the same river because already, in his innermost recesses, the human being shares the destiny of flowing water. Water is truly the transitory element. . . . A being dedicated to water is a being in flux.

(Bachelard, 1942/1983: 6)

Sensual representations are in a perpetual flux, they come after each other like the waves of a river, and even during the time that they last they do not remain the same thing.

(Durkheim, 1915/1976: 434)

Water metaphors – sea, river, flow, flux, waves – are prevalent in post-structuralist and feminist accounts of writing and writing the body, the principles of meaning of which are understood to challenge dominant conceptions of knowledge (Cixous, 1986; Irigaray, 1985). This challenge is effected via something of a reversal of philosophy's self-representation as a stable form of reflection removed from the flux of life. 'Writing' is signification understood as transformation, or 'difference in repetition' – every repetition is in a sense 'originary' (Derrida, 1987: 26–7; 1982: 13). A stable form of reflection or representation involves a suppression of the sensual (the body) and movement (the temporal); writing on the other hand is both embodied and temporal. Barthes: 'What is significance? It is meaning, *insofar as it is sensually produced*' (1975: 61). Derrida: 'Differences are the effects of transformations, and from this vantage the theme of *différance* is incompatible with the static, synchronic, taxonomic, ahistoric motifs in the concept of *structure*' (1987: 27). For Bachelard, echoes of whom are very clear in writers such as Barthes, water imagination, reverie, is both fluid, in flux, and material, embodied, sensual (Bachelard, 1942/1983: 8–9).

Durkheim, on the other hand, is making a negative observation in his water metaphors. The context of this quotation is an account of science which provides a particularly clear statement of assumptions in Western knowledge. Since reflection and correspondence metaphors still hold sway in much sociological discourse, it is worth briefly looking at Durkheim.

'We are never sure of again finding a perception such as we experienced it, for if the thing perceived has not changed, it is we who are no longer the same' (Durkheim, 1915/1976: 434). The problem as he sees it is that in the flux and flow of sensuously experienced life, things change, both the subject and the object of knowledge change. Science must attain a form of stability and certainty, over and above this flux; it is counterposed to life as it is lived.

Durkheim says 'the concept' (as presence to consciousness) is 'opposed to sensual representations', it is 'outside of time and change', 'it resists change'. 'It is a manner of thinking that at every moment of time is fixed and crystallized' – solid and stable. In his account, science requires: a suppression of the senses and sensuous life; a suppression of particularity in rhythms of life, differences in duration, experiences of time; and a suppression of particularity in experiences of space. Science, in his view, requires an abstract notion of time and space, that will make possible generalizations and a conception of the whole (1915/1976: 440–1).

The exclusions on which this knowledge is dependent are quite explicit in the text (and I take this to be something positive about the text). The principles of change, in both the subject and object, which Durkheim would suppress, are those which are privileged in post-structuralist writing. (Although not the concern in this paper, it would be possible to demonstrate, with reference to Durkheim's important thesis about the sacred/ profane distinction, that this suppression is not altogether successful.) Whereas, in Durkheim, the subject of knowledge remains outside and distinct from the object, in post-structuralist accounts, there is no outside or before, the subject is constituted in writing, *différance*; and knowledge practices partake of that which they would know. Furthermore, metaphors of fluidity, liquidity, undo a dialectics of outside–inside (Bachelard, 1958/1969: 211–32), opposition and distinction between subject and object. (See particularly Irigaray on fluids [1985: 106–18], which bears comparison with Bachelard on the fluid within–without the subject of water imagination [1942/1983: 117–19, 131–2].) 'A being dedicated to water, is a being in flux'.

My concern in this chapter is with the contribution that Bachelard makes to an understanding of writing the body. With particular reference to *The Poetics of Space* (1958/1969), it will address the principles of knowledge involved in poetic imagination and consider the nature of the subject of this imagination. If time and the body are central to 'writing the body', does Bachelard's phenomenology of space throw any light on time–space relations in this knowledge practice? (Durkheim's suppression of the experience of space, as well as time, draws attention to this issue.) And, how does Bachelard's account of space raise critical questions about the privileging of movement, fluidity over stasis, solidity? In short, does he contribute to a displacement of this opposition?

Bergson: time and the body

Bergson (more or less a contemporary of Durkheim) prefigures many of the concerns in contemporary accounts of writing. His philosophy is almost a direct inversion of Durkheim: a philosophy that is in life rather than one that presumes to stand outside, that deals in 'lifeless abstractions'. He 'dissolves' the distinction between consciousness and the world by taking as his starting point a conception of the world as comprised of 'body-images'. Furthermore, Bergson's critique of the negative oppositional structure of the Hegelian tradition, together with his methodology of multiplicity, prefigures the deconstructive concern with undoing the principle of binary oppositions that structures knowledge. His privileging of movement and the principle of qualitative differentiation over stasis and sameness has a good deal in common with the post-structuralist emphasis on the temporality of signification processes and the critique of the stasis of structure, the synchronic. As deconstructive theorists point out, to privilege the subordinate or repressed term of a binary opposition does not simply entail a reversal, but a displacement of the structure. Movement, the relay of meaning, referral between elements, undoes the very principle of a fixity of elements in separation, present unto themselves. Bergson's philosophy of time and the body (sensuously experienced time that is suppressed by Durkheim, for example), makes trouble for the binary and static structure of knowledge.

For the purposes of this chapter, a brief account of Bergson's conception of time is necessary. For Bergson, time proper is the time of becoming. He makes a distinction between spatialized time and duration, arguing that we commonly and mistakenly think of time in spatial terms: the line of time, marked by discrete moments. We perceive our states of consciousness as one alongside the other; we project time into space. This is abstract, static, homogeneous, quantified, empty time, whereas temporalized time is time lived, in the body, sensuous time characterized by qualitative differentiation (Bergson, 1889/1950). He constantly uses the term 'permeation', to describe the principles in this time. In abstract, static time, each moment is identified as a discrete identity, a presence. In duration there is a permeation of moments: past, present, future melt into each other such that no moment can be identified as a presence, and 'nothing *is* less than the present . . .' (1896/1991: 150). There is, if you like, a process of referral. The present bears traces of the past, such that no element is ever simply present; with each new moment the whole changes, so that everything remains and yet changes – hence the principle of qualitative differentiation and an undoing of sameness. The past can never be repeated, it can never be before us as a presence; memory is not representation of the past, or in the past, but rather, it is the embodiment of time, forward moving (Bergson, 1896/1991). This bears comparison with Freud's account of the operations of psychical processes and memory traces (Freud, 1900/1976: 652–783; 1925/1984), which has been influential in Derridean understandings of the temporality of signification and the deferral of *différance* (Derrida, 1978: 196–231).

The main problem that sympathetic critics, including Merleau-Ponty and Bachelard, point to, is that in his critique of the metaphysical assumption of a priori abstract space, Bergson almost exclusively emphasizes time. Critics claim that he takes on the assumption himself that space is abstract, despite his insistence that this is only how it is commonly thought. While there is evidence of justification of this critique (I will look at Bachelard on this later), and it is certainly the case that Bergson's interest is in time and a critique of spatialized time, it is worth looking again at precisely what he says about the connections between time and space.

Bergson's critique of abstract space in *Matter and Memory* is directly connected with his critique of dualistic thought: mind–body, spirit–matter, subject–object distinctions. The 'mistake' of dualism is that it starts with a spatial point of view: space is 'given *to begin with*' (Bergson, 1896/1991: 231), it is external to the subject, consciousness and sensations, and of a different order. It contains that which is to be known, separate and distinct from consciousness. Thus connections between spirit and matter cannot be 'seen'. Bergson resolves this, as he sees it, epistemological problem by substituting time for space: spirit and matter, subject and object, are not of different orders (all objects have a bodily form), they are marked by different durations. Thus *relations* between them can be understood in terms of different durations. Subject and object are not separate, but interconnected temporally. By starting with time it is possible to come to a conception of relations (spatiality) between elements, *and* an understanding of these relations in terms of 'interpenetration' rather than distinction and opposition. For Bergson, time is constitutive of space insofar as motion produces differentiation. He reverses the notion that abstract space makes motion possible on the grounds that this denies the process of qualitative differentiation in movement, makes movement homogeneous. If he does not precisely reduce space to time, Bergson nevertheless privileges time over space (1896/1991: 179–250). Curiously, in his account, space is left as irretrievably abstract.

Through a reading of Bachelard, I want to suggest that not only does duration displace abstract spatialized time, but that it is dependent upon qualitative space. Bergson is concerned with an account of duration that is embodied. I want to suggest that he falls short of this by not taking sufficient account of space, by excluding it as abstract. My argument here will be that without spatiality, duration remains disembodied and abstract: undifferentiated flow, without limits.[1]

These issues will be addressed with specific reference to memory. The subject of 'writing the body' has a psychical history, and for writers such as Barthes, this subjectivity is disruptive to structure (Barthes, 1986: 43). In contemporary theory, the temporal of memory is emphasized, with reference to Bergson and Freud, as a means of breaking with empiricist notions of correspondence and representation, and the spatial-visual metaphors on which these are based (Arcaya, 1992). I want to take this a step further by suggesting that the embodiment of this temporal, psychical reality is dependent upon qualitative, or lived, space. The question being posed is: what is the relation between time and space in 'the remembering body' (Irigaray, 1985: 215) that 'writes'?

A note on how I came to this: in my writing and teaching on time and memory I realized that all the examples I was giving on duration were focused on space, qualitative experiences of space, space lived temporally through memory. My argument was that time gives space quality (Game, 1991: 148–85). But, despite Bergson, there was something insistent about space and its 'place' in memory. This was confirmed by reading Poulet, *Proustian Space* (1977), who argues that contrary to the common view that Proust is a disciple of Bergson, memory in Proust is spatial, but that this 'space' far from being the abstract given space of metaphysics, is qualitative and heterogeneous. Why did I choose Bachelard to work on closely? He spoke to my experiences of space and memory. I found *The Poetics of Space* an extraordinarily moving book. I was moved to write about it. As we will see, this is crucial to the evaluation of his writing, in his own terms.

Bachelard: a phenomenology of space

Methodology of phenomenology

The introduction to the *Poetics of Space* (1958/1969) is an eloquent methodological essay that sets out what is involved in a phenomenology of space and of the imagination, and the connections between these. It starts with a discussion of *'reverberation'*, the 'very opposite of causality', and, as the editor notes, a metaphor that epitomizes both time and space. Phenomenology is concerned with experiencing an image in its reverberations (1958/1969: xii). Thus, in Bachelard's understanding of phenomenological knowledge, a sound rather than a specular metaphor is privileged, which in turn has implications for an understanding of the subject and the relation between the subject and the object. In this reverberation the poetic image has 'a sonority of being'. The image sets up reverberations in the subject: the self is a sonorous being.

The notion of reverberation, sound waves (sound is wave motion – the sea), points to a movement between the subject and object in a manner that disrupts a neat distinction between these, and a movement within the subject that runs against any notion of an ontological given-ness. There is an immediacy in this reverberation: a poetic image works by taking 'immediate root in me' (1958/1969: xiii). To make sense of this, Bachelard says, we need a phenomenology of the imagination: 'a study of the phenomenon of the poetic image when it emerges into the consciousness as a direct product of the heart, soul and being of man, apprehended in his actuality' (1958/1969: xiv). In the face of such statements one might anticipate critical questions: is there a denial of the mediating processes in talk about immediacy, actuality, the phenomenon in itself? Let me just say that Bachelard is concerned with 'images', and images for him have a reality. Experience consists in images lived. There is little evidence in Bachelard of assumptions about an ontological being that precedes knowledge and is reflected in knowledge. His metaphor for knowledge is reverberation rather than reflection: there is no point of origin, in either the subject or the object (image, phenomenon). (Throughout *Water and Dreams* there is a critique of realism and notions of 'direct knowledge' without mediation [Bachelard, 1942/1983: 135]. Material imagination is distinguished from realism: the sea, for example, is always already metaphorical.)

At this point it might be useful to do some locating, to say a little about the sense in which Bachelard is a phenomenologist (a sense which is to be distinguished from common sociological understandings of this term). Although this chapter is concerned with Bachelard's work on space, it is his phenomenological *approach* to space which is particularly significant. I am both developing an argument about time–space relations and suggesting that phenomenology can contribute to contemporary understandings of knowledge as writing the body. The point of connection with respect to the latter is the phenomenological approach to time–space relations.

The two central ideas in this phenomenological tradition are those of experience (that which is suppressed in Durkheim) and the phenomenon: phenomenology is an experience of the phenomenon. Merleau-Ponty is perhaps the best known figure in this tradition of thought, and both he and Bachelard were writing within a philosophical context in which Bergson's ideas had considerable influence. Thus it is not surprising to find that Merleau-Ponty has a good deal in common with Bergson: for example, in his concern with a philosophy which 'offers an account of space, time and the world as we "live" them', his critique of the mind–body distinction through a privileging of the body, his critique of the notion of a transcendental consciousness and his view that 'there is no thought which embraces all our thought . . . since we are in the world, and our reflections are carried out in the temporal flux onto which we are trying to seize' (Merleau-Ponty, 1962: vii–xiv). For Merleau-Ponty (contrary to, say, Durkheim), we participate in, are connected with the world we would know; we cannot stand outside at a distance. The very formulation 'experiencing the phenomenon' disrupts a distinction between subject and object, pointing instead to a *relation between*.

Experience is regarded with suspicion by various traditions, traditions which in other respects have little in common. For example, social scientists exclude experience, particularly their own, on the grounds that it undermines objectivity. Deconstructive theorists tend to assume that experience involves a notion of an 'a priori' self, a self-presence. For Merleau-Ponty, however, experience is necessarily mediated; there is no self before language, or outside a self–other relation. Being 'situated in language' makes the position of an absolute objective spectator impossible (Merleau-Ponty, 1964: 104–9); it also undermines any notion of a subjective 'a priori' (Merleau-Ponty, 1962: xix). Experience is, then, meaning experienced; Bachelard's version of this is 'images lived'. In the light of contemporary concerns it should be pointed out that for Merleau-Ponty meaning is relational:

> As far as language is concerned, it is the lateral relation of one sign to another which makes each of them significant, so that meaning appears only at the

intersection of and as it were in the interval between words. (Merleau-Ponty, 1964: 42)

It is interesting to note that the metaphor for meaning in this passage – the interval – combines space and time. More generally, it is clear that Merleau-Ponty puts into question the idea of an element being present unto itself: meaning comes of the in between. We will find similar formulations in Bachelard's understanding of space.

Bachelard is outlining a phenomenological approach to poetic images of intimate space; his examples come mainly from poetry, but I think we can take the poetic to be broadly defined. This might be a matter for debate: is Bachelard claiming that this methodology is specific to poetic images? And this question might be asked because Bachelard was a philosopher of science before he became interested in phenomenology. (It is in fact this earlier 'conceptual', rather than 'experiential', Bachelard that tends to be more familiar to English-speaking audiences, particularly those aware of the influence of his approach to science on Althusser and Foucault.) In what might be regarded as his 'transitional work', Bachelard retains a distinction between objective scientific knowledge and subjective knowledge, lived, felt (1942/1983: 7) and in the domain of the poetic (1938/1964: 2). In *The Psychoanalysis of Fire* (1938/1964: 3) he says that he is dealing with the axis of subjectivity having previously dealt with the axis of scientific objectivization in connection with heat. He regards his psychoanalytic study of the subjective elements in the knowledge of fire as itself objective (1938/1964: 4–6). And yet this analysis of the affective basis of scientific metaphors, although assuming the possibility of objective knowledge, could be read as demonstrating the impossibility of knowledge free of metaphor or affect. In the Introduction to *Water and Dreams* Bachelard states that the aim of knowledge is to become rationalistic, something he achieved in connection with fire, but 'to be honest, I must confess that I have not achieved the same result with water. I still live water images . . .' (1942/1983: 7). He goes on to say: 'I always experience the same melancholy in the presence of dormant water . . .' (1942/1983: 7). What is curious about this is the notion of the possibility, and desirability, of feeling no emotion in the presence of water – what is presumably involved in being rationalistic. And indeed in the following study of water imagination this valorization of the rational seems to disappear.

There would seem to be a trajectory in Bachelard towards poetic, material imagination, and the subjective in this. In *The Poetics of Space* there is a positive valorization of affective images, the poetic. (His earlier interest in metaphor was more as a means of critique of scientific pretensions.) The principal concern in this book is with images that have an effect of dream-reading, a creativity on the part of the subject (see also *The Poetics of Reverie*, 1960/1971). The shift towards the poetic is accompanied by the development of an interest in phenomenology, and the rejection of the scientific mode of explanation, including psychoanalytic explanation. Phenomenology works on the same principle as poetic images: if it experiences poetic reverberations, it must also *transmit* them, that is reverberate itself.

Bachelard is concerned with the subjectivity and the trans-subjectivity of an image. Only phenomenology – 'the consideration of the onset of an image in an individual consciousness – can help us to restore the subjectivity of images . . . and to measure their transsubjectivity' (1958/1969: xv). The 'reader of poems is asked to consider an image not as an object and even less as the substitute for an object, but to seize its specific reality'. In this process the duality of subject and object 'shimmers', is 'unceasingly active in its inversions' (1958/1969: xv). The distinction between subjective and objective, apparent in his earlier writings, is displaced here; the concern now is with the combination of the particular and the universal or trans-subjective.

In a number of respects this is very close to Barthes; or at least, the echoes of Bachelard in Barthes are apparent in the concerns with specificity and particularity. Bachelard asks: what is an image in itself, in its specificity? Characteristic of phenomenology, there is a refusal of reductionism of any kind or explanation. Although sympathetic to psychoanalysis (but noticeably less so than in earlier writings), he says that in interpretation and translation it intellectualizes and thus loses the reverberations. Regarding particularity he suggests that 'my' experience is both particular and trans-subjective. We start with our experience of an image in order that might get at something of the trans-subjective of it, without in any sense devaluing the particular. In Barthes' later writings (1984, 1985), he asks of signification systems, such as photography and music: what is it in itself? – a phenomenological question. And, to get at this specificity, he asks a question in terms of particularity: what effect does this have on my body; what is the affect?[2]

Bachelard makes a distinction between resonance and reverberation: in the resonance we hear the poem, in the reverberation we speak it, it is our own (1958/1969: xviii). 'The reverberations bring about a change of being'. The poetic image 'expresses us by making us what it expresses'; this is a becoming of our being (1958/1969: xix). These ideas can be located in a philosophy of becoming and have echoes in post-structuralist conceptions of the writing subject, a subject who is both written and writes. If the image expresses us, the reading process is also a writing, a reverberation, an act of creation. (And here he says that this is a Bergsonian idea, related to '*élan vital*' [1958/1969: xxii].) In the joy of reading we participate in creation. The poetic image 'has a bracing effect on our lives': we are moved. These ideas seem comparable to Barthes' concern with open texts that invoke the desire to write.[3]

Bachelard describes his project of reading images as 'reverberating phenomenologically' (1958/1969: xxi). This raises the issue of forms of writing. Language, specifically poetic language, is language 'that has been lived': 'a fibred space traversed by the simple impetus of words that have been experienced' (1958/1969: xxiv). Where conceptual language would fix, verse has movement, the image flows. He is suggesting that poetic language embodies principles of meaning that are to be valued over conceptual language which embodies traditional knowledge assumptions, and that there is an affinity between the poetic and phenomenology in terms of their principles of meaning. (See also *Water and Dreams: 'liquidity* is . . . the very desire of language. Language needs to flow' [1942/1983: 187].) This suggests the possibility of breaking the limits of genre; Bachelard's writing is both philosophical, conceptual, and also poetic. The two major 'theorists' of 'writing the body', Cixous and Barthes, also disrupt classifications of theory and the poetic in their forms of writing.

Bachelard's choice of object in *The Poetics of Space*, if not precisely an object, is directly connected with the form of knowledge, 'imagining', that he positively values. His concern is with images of 'felicitous space', 'space we love', 'eulogised space', 'images that *"attract"*' (1958/1969: xxxi–xxxii). (Note here, he makes no distinction between material space and images. As in *Water and Dreams*, he is speaking simultaneously of the material, the metaphorical and the psychical.) For Bachelard, it is positive images of the protective, that which is conducive to well-being, that invoke productive imagination. And, he is studying space that has been *lived in* with all the partiality of the imagination, not space in its positivity. Such space, space that has been seized by the imagination, 'cannot remain indifferent space subject to the measure and estimates of the surveyor' (1958/1969: xxxii). In short, his concern is with qualitative space, space that is lived and is transformed by imagination.

The form that imagination takes is a day-dreaming; intimate spaces provide the shelter, the refuge for intimate day-dreaming. And thus the house image has become the topography of our intimate being. Our memories are housed, our soul is an abode; and by remembering houses, rooms, we abide within ourselves. In short, the house image moves in both directions: they are in us, and we in them. This is comparable with what he says about water imagination – the fluid, the sea, that is within–without us. The house is a maternal image for Bachelard (1958/1969: 7) (water is both masculine and feminine [1942/1983: 72–3; 116–32]). However, in terms of feminist debates about the maternal, I do not think that Bachelard's eulogization of intimate space should be read as a desire for wholeness or appropriation of the feminine. Space, including internal space, is always differentiated, an 'originary' differentiation, in his account (see also Derrida, 1982: 22; de Certeau, 1984: 109). His metaphors of flow and breaking of boundaries are comparable with feminist critiques of masculine desire for self-presence.[4]

Bachelard's privileging of intimate space as an object of analysis is connected with the possibilities of creative imagination. In short, there is a direct connection between (images of) intimate space and a particular knowledge, one that is affective and imaginative rather than 'conceptual' and abstract.

The house: space, memory, day-dreaming

'The house is a privileged entity for a phenomenological study of the intimate values of inside space' (Bachelard, 1958/1969: 3). In a study of our images of protected intimacy we cannot consider the house as an object. As opposed to descriptions of ethnographers and geographers, a phenomenologist is concerned with seizing upon the immediate well-being, the inhabiting, a dwelling encloses (1958/1969: 4). Thus, the space of phenomenology is a different space from that of other discourses, it is constituted differently; space is not simply given. Phenomenology is interested in 'concrete evidence of the values of inhabited space', the notion of 'the home'. Phenomenology thus both produces and partakes of space that is experienced as intimate space.

There is a specific subject at issue here: the sheltered, protected being, one who dreams. The house is lived, neither in its positive aspects nor in the passing hour – neither a givenness of space nor quantified time; it is *lived* in the sense that an 'entire past comes to dwell in a new house'. There is no simple narrative, Bachelard says; 'various dwelling places in our lives co-penetrate and retain the treasures of the former days' (1958/1969: 5). The self, in this account, does not consist of a sequence of discrete states. This is very close to Freud's account of memory traces, and Bergson's account of the operations of time. What distinguishes Bachelard is that for memory trace, or moment in time he substitutes 'dwelling place', thus spatializing temporal assumptions in Freud and Bergson. For him, memory *is* 'dwelling place'. Lived time, as opposed to abstract time, is dependent upon spatial specificity, a localization (1958/1969: 8): space is necessary to give quality to time. Space transforms time in such a way that memory is made possible. 'Memory doesn't record concrete duration . . . we can only think of it, in the line of an abstract time, deprived of all thickness' (1958/1969: 9). Bergson's lived time of duration thus becomes abstract time unless there is space; it is space which quickens memory, gives time *life*. Otherwise we are merely left with dates (see Poulet, 1977: 15–16, on the significance of space for a localization of memory in Proust; see also Bakhtin, 1981: 84).

The 'chief benefit of the house is that it shelters daydreaming', 'it protects the dreamer', 'allows one to dream in peace'. It is a (metaphorical) space that makes possible the creative operations of Bergsonian time. And space becomes temporalized in the process: places in which we have experienced day-dreaming reconstitute themselves in new day-dreams; these places live on, in a changed form (1958/1969: 6).[5]

However, it is not simply that temporal principles are governing space; there is another principle operating in space, and thus a dialectic is at work. 'Protection', 'shelter' point to this other principle: integration, binding. While time gives the house different dynamisms, differentiation of duration, the house provides continuity, a counter to dispersion of the subject (1958/1969: 6–7). This touches on current debates around the subject.[6] In connection with these it could be suggested that Bachelard is applying a methodology of multiplicity here. Different principles are operating simultaneously, it is not simply one, to the exclusion of the other: both movement and fixing, discontinuity and continuity. The important point is that shelteredness is the condition for *becoming*; it makes possible an imagining process.

Like Bergson, Bachelard has an embodied understanding of memory. The first house, the house we were born in, is physically and psychically inscribed in us. Despite all other stairways we recapture the reflexes of the 'first stairway', 'we would not stumble on that rather high step'. All other houses are but variations on the first theme. Our bodies do not forget – there is 'a passionate liaison' between the body and that house (1958/1969: 14–15). The body–house metaphor is no *mere* metaphor for Bachelard: the remembering body is housed, and the body houses. Throughout the book Bachelard gives examples of the idea that 'the house is in the body', 'the room is in us' (see for example 1958/1969: 225–6) – this is what living an image is all about. He is insistent on 'the reality of the figurative', something, that is quite enigmatic to 'the reasonable mind' (1958/1969: 226). He quotes Rilke: 'I never saw this strange dwelling again. Indeed, as I see it now, the way it appeared to my child's eye, it is not a building, but is quite dissolved and distributed inside me: here one room, there another . . .' (Bachelard, 1958/1969: 57).

Houses 'live on in us' (1958/1969: 56–7). I have argued elsewhere that Bergson contributes to a Freudian account of memory in his insistence that it is embodied (Game, 1991: 90–111). But Bachelard takes this further with the spatial element of house. Memories are localized, materially; the materiality of place lives, is inscribed in our bodies. The account of this process is close to Freud's understanding of the principles of memory: our experiences are repetitions of childhood experiences, but different, 'variations on a theme'; and, nothing that we have experienced is lost. Bachelard spatializes the temporality of memory: 'the first' is the first house, a dwelling place for memories. (There are echoes of this in Malouf, *12 Edmonstone Street* [1986: 8–10, 64–6].)

In the light of deconstructive critiques of representation there is some debate about the status of childhood experiences and repetition in Freud (see Forrester, 1992). Bachelard is very much concerned with childhood and the child in the adult. For each of us, he says, there is a house of dream-memory 'lost in the shadow of a beyond of the real past' (1958/1969: 15). Beyond interpretation, Bachelard proposes a unity of image and memory, imagination and memory. He wants to go beyond the positivity of geography and psychological history to get at the 'real being of our childhood', 'for childhood is certainly greater than reality' (1958/1969: 16). This strikes me as an important point, and comparable to Derrida's reading of Freud: 'the unconscious makes us concerned with a past that has never been present' (Derrida, 1982: 21). For Bachelard, dream is more powerful than thought, and here we are in the realm of the unconscious, and psychical *reality*. 'It is on the plane of the daydream and not the facts that childhood remains alive. . . . Through this permanent childhood we maintain the poetry of the past' (1958/1969: 16). We might understand 'permanent childhood' as a form of deferred action. In Bachelard's view we remain young late in life in the realm of imagination; we need to grow old to experience youth (1958/1969: 33). This is not youth as it was – nostalgia for youth would be vulgar, he says – but youth transformed by memory and imagination, something greater than the reality of childhood. Whatever 'the facts' of childhood might have been, when we day-dream of childhood, our childhood now, is it not a dream of protection, intimacy, well-being? This is a forward-looking memory, comparable with Bergson's understanding of memory as that which moves the body forward in action. Where Bachelard differs is in his claim that it is space that prompts action. The creative process consists in a play of memory of intimate spaces of solitude and day-dreaming.

In Bachelard's view, phenomenological writing has the potential for provoking such a creative process. He gives an example from his own experience, a memory of smell on opening a cupboard, and says that writing must touch 'the universal' in order to provoke dreaming of the unique in the reader, which in turn is the catalyst for imagination. 'A readers' eyes must leave the page before recollections of my room can become a threshold of memory for him' (1958/1969: 14). (This is precisely the effect that reading Bachelard had on me.) In the reverberation of the reader's soul, a reading becomes a writing. We 'read a room', 'write a room'. As a reader reads a room he leaves off reading and 'starts to think of some place in his own past' – a day-dreaming (see also Barthes, 1986: 29; de Certeau, 1984: xxi). Images reverberate in the reader, setting off a day-dreaming in which memory and imagination are mixed.

Critical questions re Bergson: the space–time relation

Bachelard is in broad sympathy with Bergson's philosophy. Any critique of Bergson, explicit or implicit, is within his own terms. Both are critical of negative philosophy; thus Bachelard takes Bergson to task over *his* negative approach to space. What then does Bachelard's phenomenology of space contribute to a Bergsonian project?

First, Bachelard challenges a notion of space as abstract, static and empty, and he does so in a Bergsonian manner, from the standpoint of how we experience space. For example, the house is not experienced as an inert box (1958/1969: 47), and an empty drawer is unimaginable, 'it can only be thought of' (1958/1969: xxxiii) This is comparable with Merleau-Ponty's critique of abstract a priori space (1962: 243), and his approach to space from the perspective of experience: the body is the 'subject of space' (1962: 98–102, 248–51).

It is from the perspective of lived experience that Bachelard addresses the metaphor of house and body: the house as body (see also Merleau-Ponty, 1962: 68–70, for whom experience is, of course, embodied). To avoid the 'mereness' of metaphor, he prefers the notion of image. Images are lived directly (1962: 47); thus the house as body is not the linguistic imagery of literary critics, nor the object of psychological reductions. It is lived as body, and not as geometrical space. This transposition to the human plane occurs as soon as a house is a space of intimacy: defying rationality, 'the dream-world beckons' (1962: 48). He cites examples from his own experience as well as poetry, of the unity of the mother image and the house image:

> I say Mother. And my thoughts are of you, oh, House.
> House of the lovely dark summers of my childhood.
> (Milosz, in Bachelard, 1958/1969: 45)

There are some important issues here that relate to current debates about metaphor and the body. What is significant in Bachelard's account is that 'image' (metaphor) is lived, embodied, sensuously experienced. Thus, as with Bergson's notion of body-image, a real/representation split is disrupted: metaphor or image is 'real', it is enacted, bodily.

Bergson demonstrates the ways in which time undermines representation; for Bachelard, day-dreaming undermines representation. In the production of meaning that is imagination, the static space of representation becomes mobile space. In the awakening of *feeling* through the reading, in experiencing the image, we *write* space (1958/1969: 49–50). This is very close to post-structuralist concerns with a reading that is also a writing, a practice of the space of meaning, structure, and specifically with Barthes' view that it is the affect that puts structure into movement, invokes a writing, and that significance is meaning sensually produced.

Second, Bachelard has a dynamic dialectical conception of space. For example, with reference to the internal of the house and the external: 'At whatever pole the daydreamer stands, whether in the house or in the universe, the dialectics become dynamic. . . . House and space are not merely two juxtaposed elements of space.' They awaken day-dreams in each other (1958/1969: 42–3). To put this in Derridean terms: two elements do not remain unto themselves, as discrete presences; they bear the trace of each other. Similarly, Poulet says of Proust that, in a multiplicity of relations, places and beings lose their exclusiveness without losing their specificity (1977: 79–81).

These dialectical relations include: 'Dreams that speak both the repose and flight of being', images that condense both; the extreme realities of cottage and manor, retreat and expansion, simplicity and magnificence; and past and present houses. In his discussions of all of these, Bachelard is suggesting something other than a relation of opposition: he speaks of oscillations between, for example, small and large, *reverberations*. In the chapter, 'The dialectics of outside and inside', he undoes this opposition, together with that of open–closed; the yes–no of dialectical division is called into question. (Bachelard uses the term 'dialectical' to refer to both the Hegelian dialectic of which he is clearly presenting a critique and to an alternative conception of relations between terms, spaces.) Reference to the principle of reverberation in this context brings into relief something that I find particularly suggestive about *The Poetics of Space*, namely the shift in registers between psychic, physical, textual space together with the space of knowledge.

Reverberations between spaces suggests that each space changes in the dynamic relation, and certainly that the dreaming subject changes via this relation. It is the effect of these spatial relations, the reverberations, that invokes in the reader a day-dreaming, puts the reader into motion. Through an imagining, a reading becomes a writing, or a rewriting of spaces. Thus the reading process itself is crucial to the transformation of spaces and the subject, which, as for Merleau-Ponty, are inextricably linked. In terms of contemporary debates it could be said that transformation is internal to knowledge systems, that the practice of texts is a transformation.

Third, in connection with the dynamic dialectics of space, Bachelard proposes a rhythmanalysis (1958/1969: 65). His account of rhythms is very close to Bergson on duration – the specificity and differences in rhythms or durations. The difference again is that Bachelard spatializes this process. Different spaces are characterized by different rhythms, between which there are dynamic dialectical relations. There is here a possible significant difference with Bergson, and it relates to the critique of his work that draws attention to the lack of a concept of the other (Derrida, 1978: 93). Although Bergson starts with the premise of bodies moving in relation to each other, acting on each other, any specific duration has the potentiality for creativity within itself, as duration is governed by a principle of qualitative differentiation. For Bachelard, rhythms, or durations *must* be in a relationship; they mean 'in relation to'. It is thinking in terms of space, although not an already given space, that brings the idea of a relation into the picture, and indeed bodily relations. For Bergson, time precedes and makes possible the space of relations. Possibly the issue here is one of thinking the time and space of meaning together, in relation to each other: Derrida's notion of *différance* as the spacing of time and temporalization of space, 'structure and movement' (1982: 27–9). Bachelard's understanding of the dynamics of spatial relations comes close to this.

At the beginning of Chapter 3, 'Drawers, chests and wardrobes', Bachelard presents a critique of Bergson's famous empty drawer metaphor (Bergson, 1907/1913: 5). Bergson frequently uses the metaphor of the drawer together with the notion of 'ready-made garments' in his critiques of 'concept', 'classifications' – the abstractions of lifeless thinking. Bachelard's main point is that through this metaphor, Bergson utilizes the very same form that he would criticize: a lifeless, abstract concept. He discursively produces a space – a drawer – as abstract, empty space. The metaphor hardens and something of the qualitative experience of the image of the drawer is lost through Bergson's abstraction, even if his claim would be that this is how the space of a drawer is commonly understood. Bachelard's point is that this is not how the *image* is *experienced*. Thus he is employing Bergson's own distinction between abstract thought and the experience of life, in connection with space. Space can be abstract, empty, or it can be lived, qualitatively. It is no more given than time is given. Whereas a philosophical tradition has assumed the a priori nature of abstract space, this space is discursively produced, and Bergson, in Bachelard's view, contributes to this through his metaphors.

He gives the example of the wardrobe: 'Bergson did want the faculty of memory to be taken for a wardrobe of recollections' (1958/1969: 79). But Bachelard says this only happens if we operate in the register of ideas, concepts, rather than images. He claims that 'memory is a wardrobe', once we think of memory as something other than mere recollections, and wardrobe as something other than empty space. In short, once we imagine.

Concluding remarks

As with time, it is only thought space that is abstract; lived, experienced, imagined space is qualitative space. Just as lived time undoes thought time, so it is with space. Without lived space, lived time would be impossible, it would remain abstract. Imagined space is the embodiment of time – precisely what Bergson wants. The converse of this is that a quality of space is experienced via a principle of movement or time, that is, a movement between and within spaces. Contrary to Bergson, in Bachelard, movement is both spatial and temporal; if it is a temporal principle, it is made possible by a relation – the spatial. (Again this is comparable with Merleau-Ponty who claims that movement is both spatial and temporal, and that there can be no movement without a moving body, which must change in the process [1962: 267–75].)

For Bachelard, space and time do not neatly map stasis and movement. Where Bergson engages in a simple reversal of oppositions, Bachelard displaces oppositional structures through a series of complex reversals. Unlike Bergson, he does not simply privilege movement to the exclusion of fixity. The principle of movement (displacement, multiplicity) acknowledges the simultaneity of different principles at work. Derrida would put this in terms such as 'différance is no more static than it is genetic' (1982: 12). Bachelard alerts us to this in his discussions of the principle of stability at work in intimate spaces. But this is not a discrete stability so much as one in flow.[7] (In connection with my introductory remarks about metaphors of flow, this suggests that it might be fruitful, as a displacement strategy, to play with metaphors that are anomalous with respect to solid – fluid). To put this in terms of contemporary debates: Bachelard contributes to a displacement of the opposition identity/difference, and an understanding of the simultaneity of specificity and 'contamination'.

Since I have been suggesting that Bachelard's poetics has a good deal in common with writing the body, I will end with a comment on knowledge and the subject. The subject of imagining, dream reading-writing, is an embodied subject of memory, an affective memory that is both temporal and spatial, and forward-looking. Imagined space provides a security, a certainty and even a fixity. In contemporary theory, any talk of 'stability', certainty, is likely to be seized upon as evidence of a desire for self-presence. In fact Bachelard has more in common with the tradition of philosophy that understands the subject as a becoming with no originary presence of being. Certainty is a certainty of becoming, of creative day-dreaming – imagining. In *Water and Dreams* he says: 'This is a specific instance of the law that I wish to repeat on every possible occasion: imagination is a becoming' (1942/1983: 103). Any fixity in the subject is constituted through the dynamic dialectic of spaces, which in turn invokes creative imagination. The 'knowledge' produced is not a reflection of a real self that precedes the imagining process. On the contrary the self is constituted in this process: the reverberation of images.

Notes

I would like to thank Genevieve Lloyd and Andrew Metcalfe for their comments on an earlier draft.

1. This relates to Merleau-Ponty's critique of Bergson's conception of time as continuous: without breaks there is no time (1962: 420). See also his critical remarks about the Heraclitean metaphors of river and flow for time (1962: 411). It is possible to find passages in Bergson where he qualifies a notion of continuous flow. For example, in connection with the 'leap' into water which is knowledge: 'He who throws himself into the water, having known only the resistance of the solid earth, will immediately be drowned if he does not struggle against the fluidity of the new environment: he must perforce cling to that solidity, so to speak, which even water presents. Only on this condition can he get used to the fluid's fluidity' (1907/1913: 203). On precisely the same metaphor see Douglas (1970: 38). This is in the context of a discussion of Sartre on stickiness, and metaphors that are anomalous with respect to the solid–fluid distinction.

2. It might be countered here that in the case of photography, Barthes speaks of the absolute particularity of affect. But is there not something universal, if not trans-subjective, in this: the image might be particular in the case of this system, but can we not recognize the affect he describes? (Barthes, 1984).

3. See Barthes' comments on Bachelard's notion of reading in *The Pleasure of the Text* (1975: 37). He claims that Bachelard's 'dream-reading' falls short of bliss.

4. One of the attractions of Bachelard for me is precisely his positive approach to space, his concern with spaces of well-being. One cannot help but compare his approach to space with that of Foucault, in whose work space is always governed by surveillance.

5. Bachelard distinguishes his concern with day-dreaming from the psychoanalytic focus on dreams. 'The phenomenology of the daydream can untangle the complex of memory and imagination' (1958/1969: 26). This relates to his interest in the creative operations of memory, a mixing of the unconscious and the conscious, as opposed to what he regards as the psychoanalytic interpretation of symbols.

6. On this issue see Harrison: what provides the coherence of the self in the Nietzschean account of becoming? (1991: 198, 215–16). See also Poulet (1977: 60).

7. This bears comparison with Simmel, who speaks of the unity of fixity and wandering embodied in the figure of the stranger; the very potentiality for wandering changes the qualities and boundaries of a space that would be a discrete and fixed identity (1950: 402). Indeed Simmel's writings on space – material, psychic – touch on many of the same issues about borders, frames, and their permeability. While much of this work has not yet been published in English, there are hints of it in 'The Stranger' and 'The Metropolis and Mental Life'. In the latter he compares the permeability of the body with that of the city (1950: 419).

References

Arcaya, J. (1992) 'Why is time not included in modern theories of memory?', *Time and Society*, 1 (2): 301–14.

Bachelard, G. (1938/1964) *The Psychoanalysis of Fire*, trans. A. Ross. Boston: Beacon Press.

Bachelard, G. (1958/1969) *The Poetics of Space*, trans. M. Jolas. Boston: Beacon Press.

Bachelard, G. (1960/1971) *The Poetics of Reverie*, trans. D. Russell. Boston: Beacon Press.

Bachelard, G. (1942/1983) *Water and Dreams: An Essay on the Imagination of Matter*, trans. E. Farrell. Dallas: Pegasus.

Bakhtin, M.M. (1981) *The Dialogic Imagination*, trans. C. Emerson and M. Holquist. Austin: University of Texas Press.

Barthes, R. (1975) *The Pleasure of the Text*, trans. R. Miller. New York: Hill & Wang.

Barthes, R. (1984) *Camera Lucida*. London: Fontana.

Barthes, R. (1985) *The Responsibility of Forms*, trans. R. Howard. New York: Hill & Wang.

Barthes, R. (1986) *The Rustle of Language*, trans. R. Howard. Oxford: Basil Blackwell.

Bergson, H. (1907/1913) *Creative Evolution*, trans. A. Mitchell. London: Macmillan.

Bergson, H. (1889/1950) *Time and Free Will*, trans. F.L. Pogson. London: George Allen & Unwin.

Bergson, H. (1896/1991) *Matter and Memory*, trans. N.M. Paul and W.S. Palmer. New York: Zone Books.

Cixous, H. (1986) 'Sorties: out and out: attacks/ways out/forays', in H. Cixous and C. Clément (eds), *The Newly Born Woman*. Manchester: Manchester University Press.

de Certeau, M. (1984) *The Practice of Everyday Life*, trans. S.F. Rendall. Berkeley and Los Angeles: University of California Press.

Derrida, J. (1978) *Writing and Difference*, trans. A. Bass. Chicago: University of Chicago Press.

Derrida, J. (1982) *Margins of Philosophy*, trans. A. Bass. Brighton: Harvester Press.

Derrida, J. (1987) *Positions*, trans. A. Bass. London: Athlone Press.

Douglas, M. (1970) *Purity and Danger: An Analysis of Concepts of Taboo*. Harmondsworth: Penguin.

Durkheim, E. (1915/1976) *The Elementary Forms of the Religious Life*. London: George Allen & Unwin.

Forrester, J. (1992) 'In the beginning was repetition: on inversions and reversals in psychoanalytic time', *Time and Society* 1 (2): 287–300.

Freud, S. (1900/1976) *The Interpretation of Dreams*. Pelican Freud Library, vol. 4. Harmondsworth: Penguin.

Freud, S. (1925/1984) 'A note upon the "Mystic Writing Pad"', in *On Metapsychology: The Theory of Psychoanalysis*. Pelican Freud Library, vol. 11. Harmondsworth: Penguin.

Game, A. (1991) *Undoing the Social: Towards a Deconstructive Sociology*. Milton Keynes: Open University Press.

Harrison, B. (1991) *Inconvenient Fictions: Literature and the Limits of Theory*. New Haven/London: Yale University Press.

Irigaray, L. (1985) *This Sex Which Is Not One*, trans. C. Porter with C. Burke. Ithaca, NY: Cornell University Press.

Malouf, D. (1986) *12 Edmonstone Street*. Harmondsworth: Penguin.

Merleau-Ponty, M. (1962) *Phenomenology of Perception*, trans. C. Smith. London: Routledge & Kegan Paul.

Merleau-Ponty, M. (1964) *Signs*, trans. R. McCleary. Northwestern University Press.

Poulet, G. (1977) *Proustian Space*, trans. E. Coleman. Baltimore/London: Johns Hopkins University Press.

Simmel, G. (1950) 'The stranger' and 'The metropolis and mental life', in K. Wolff (ed.), *The Sociology of Georg Simmel*. New York: Free Press.

12

THE SOVIET INDIVIDUAL: GENEALOGY OF A DISSIMULATING ANIMAL

Oleg Kharkhordin

In one of the most insightful essays written on Russia over the last twenty years, Ken Jowitt (1992: 80) has suggested that dissimulation, rather than legitimation, is the concept which accounts for the way public and private are tied together in what he calls Leninist regimes. For Jowitt, dissimulation is a central feature of a 'ghetto political culture' in which people retract from an official sphere which means only trouble to them. Instead they try to get as much 'free time and easy life' as possible outside of politics. Dissimulation, then, becomes a model behavioural posture in Leninist regimes, with the help of which one 'minimizes [the] regime's interference in one's private life'. In a later essay Jowitt holds that this mode of integration of public and private spheres is a dangerous Leninist legacy which post-Soviet societies retained from their past. Anti-political privatism precludes an easy transition to Western-type democracies, as private virtues are asserted over and at the expense of public ones (1992: 287–94).

The identification of a dissimulative posture as the means of integrating public and private is Jowitt's genuine theoretical contribution, which singles him out among Western students of Russia who perceive that there is something specific about the way public and private hang together in Communist societies but fail to capture it in a concept. Jowitt managed to pinpoint the central social practice familiar to every Soviet citizen in the 1970s and 1980s: saying something while believing the opposite to be true; participating in social rituals just for the sake of participation; even bringing up children by telling them that a schism exists between what is and what ought to be, a schism not to be mentioned in public statements that should describe the world as if the ideal were real.

However, Jowitt's conception mostly accounts for the 'developed socialist society' of the Brezhnev era. Apparently this society is not only different from pre-revolutionary Russia, but from the society of the first post-revolutionary years as well, because dissimulation was hardly central to both of them. The objective of this study, then, is to trace how dissimulation became so central to the regime, and how it moulded every Soviet citizen into a dissimulating subject.

In other words, if voluntary confession did not become the central practice of Soviet society – as it did in the West, as Michel Foucault (1980) has demonstrated – then how did it happen that dissimulation was increasingly used by people to turn themselves into subjects in Soviet Russia? This question is not a matter of mere curiosity, though. It may happen to be one of the most important questions of the day, as amidst all the flux of the post-Communist world, amidst structures and institutions being changed every day, there is only one relatively stable element of the Communist legacy left. This is the Soviet individual.

To follow the path first trodden by Foucault is a challenging enterprise. He did not leave us a discourse on method but he taught us the art of thinking in the manner one teaches a child the art of walking. But, perhaps, one can be a 'Foucaultian' in the manner he was a 'Nietzschean'. Foucault constantly remoulded Nietzsche to suit his various genealogical purposes, while barely mentioning Nietzsche's name in print. Perhaps, being true to Foucault means forgetting to mention him every time one sets on the way of enquiry in the manner one learned with/from Foucault.

Origins of dissimulation

Peasants constituted the majority of Russia's population before collectivization. A study of their condition may give us a clue to the origins of individual dissimulation which hardly existed in peasant communes. The ancient art of dissimulation was practised, of course, but it was practised collectively, which is tied to the fact that peasants had a predominantly corporate identity. A peasant asked how he or she defined him or herself typically answered: 'We are Orthodox'. Stephen White, one of the most perceptive Sovietologists, presents an excerpt from Chekhov to convey the sense of what it was like to be a Russian peasant:

> In Chekhov's *The Malefactor*, for instance, a peasant brought to court for stealing a nut from a railway track to weigh down his fishing tackle, completely fails to understand his guilt, and in accounting for his activities constantly refers to them in terms of 'we', the people from his locality. 'We make sinkers out of nuts', the peasant explains to the magistrate who is investigating the case. There was nothing as suitable as a nut for a sinker, it being heavy and having a hole in it: and how could one possibly fish without a sinker? The magistrate explained that, because of his action, a train might leave the track and people might be killed. The peasant replied:
>   'God forbid, your honour! Do you think we are wicked heathen? Praise be to God, kind master, not only have we never killed anybody, we have never even thought of it! . . . For how many years has the whole village been unscrewing nuts, and not an accident yet? If I were to carry a rail away, or even to put a log across the track, then perhaps the train might crash, but a nut – pah! . . . We understand, so we don't unscrew them all; we always leave some; we do it carefully; we understand'. (White, 1979: 60)

Chekhov grasped a lot of interesting points here, which parallel nicely the work of latter day anthropologists and sociologists. First, Russian peasants were not individualized and lacked practices to turn themselves into unitary subjects. Moshe Lewin, an expert on traditional Russian culture, asserts that the primary actor in peasant life was not a person, not even a household, but a village (1985: 35). Dorothy Atkinson, describing the rituals of a peasant commune in Russia, notes that though the household was a primary economic unit within the village, all important decisions were always taken by the *skhod*, a village gathering. Though every male head of a household had a voice in the *skhod* and may have resisted a proposed course of action, the decision of the majority was accepted and carried out unanimously, in a manner which Atkinson christens 'democratic centralism writ small' (1983: 374).

Second, dissimulation was a marginal practice for a Russian village. Dissimulation was a collective 'weapon of the weak', used by peasants against the power-holders, be it imperial czarist officials or local tax extractors, as Michael Confino (1991) has shown. Sometimes, though, it was absent even in the face of power, as in the quoted excerpt from Chekhov. On the other hand, dissimulation was virtually impossible in the relations between a household and a village, or within a household. People accepted the *skhod*'s decisions without feigning approval. As Ed Keenan suggests, a constantly repeating situation of a total dependence on the harvest of a given year made it clear that mere preservation was at stake in the commune's sanctions and 'convinced most adult members of the necessity of such sanctions' (1986: 125). Whether it was a matter of persuasion or just obeying a tradition is not important here; what matters is that people did not dissimulate in carrying out decisions of the *skhod*. In the rarest occasions when they tried dissimulation, retribution was harsh and swift, proceeding according to customary law which ruled the Russian village, unrelated to the legality of officialdom, with lynching being the norm for punishment of a transgression.

Even less possibility existed for dissimulation within a household. The Russian language does not have a word for 'privacy'. Peasants of one family lived in the same room, ate from the same pot, and may have even slept on the same stove. The Russian word for dissimulation – *'pritvorstvo'* – is etymologically related with the verb *'pritvoriat'*, meaning 'to close the door' or 'to close oneself off'. Virtually, there was no opportunity to close the door and stay alone in (or to close oneself off from) the peasant family.

How could such a marginal practice become of primary importance for the latter-day Russian society? It is logical to suggest that for individual dissimulation to gain ground, some parts of a totally transparent life of an individual peasant had to be 'closed off'. Now, before we study these practices of closure that made possible the individualization of the majority of the Russian population, we should discuss two general prerequisites of mass individualization in the aftermath of the Russian revolution of 1917.

It seems that the first precondition for this change was the elimination of the condition of 'dual Russia'. Robert C. Tucker describes this condition, following Belinsky and Herzen, as the impenetrability of peasant life to the state. Peasants mostly stayed out of reach of czarist officialdom and its laws and were guided by the common law and by commune decisions. Two worlds literally lived apart from each other before the revolution (Tucker, 1972: 124). The revolution that shook up the old world rendered this separation obsolete.

A huge and rapid influx of peasants into the cities during the industrialization and collectivization drives brought their customs and habits into urban environments. Peasant practices flooded organizations and bureaucracies of Soviet society during the 'ruralization of the cities' in the 1920s and 1930s, so vividly described by Lewin. For example, democratic centralism writ small, that is, the communal mode of unanimous acceptance of majority decisions, was translated into a full-blown organizational pattern of Soviet society. Atkinson describes the crucial event in this translation when communes virtually voted themselves out of existence by a unanimous acceptance of the *kolkhoz* model during village *skhods*: 'The fact that communal assemblies were manipulated and pressured into taking decisions on collectivization did not lessen the traditional responsibility of all members to accept those decisions' (1983: 376). Thus new organizational forms were predicated on age-old peasant practices, which were taken over and remoulded to suit new aims. In a similar fashion, dissimulation was carried over into a new society, but in a drastically remoulded form to satisfy new purposes.

Second, the main saying of 'dual Russia', 'God is high in heaven, and the Czar is far away', was no longer true. Two agents of power, God and Czar, merged together into one single network of saintly power. The Czar was no longer far away because power became proximate and meticulous, concerning itself with the most mundane aspects of its subjects' lives which were left unattended during the long centuries of lazy autocracy. On the other hand, for centuries, 'God is high in heaven' meant that peasants were not harassed with enquiries on the content of their faith insofar as their true Orthodoxy was signified by obedient participation in church rituals. Nobody bothered with the actual content of beliefs. As White notes, Russians did not know the liberal distinction between actions and beliefs (1979: 36). The new Soviet power started to care about beliefs, and not only rituals.

A true inner faith was posited as the essence of a New Soviet individual who – like a lay saint – was supposed to know the discursive content of the Communist doctrine by heart and to consistently demonstrate his/her saintliness in every action. According to Andrei Sinyavsky, three cardinal virtues of the New Soviet individual included fanatical faith in the supreme goal of Communism, an ability to translate this faith into methodical action, and a desire for a common, not personal good. Dzerzhinsky, as canonized by Mayakovsky, was the paradigmatic ethical model of Soviet civilization (Sinyavsky, 1990: 112).

Concomitantly, however, true inner faith could become corrupted. The only practical way to prevent this corruption was controlling certain actions which were treated, consequently, as indicative of this corruption of beliefs. Thus, Soviet power made certain behaviours problematic and ensured that they constantly stayed under its gaze. Why it happened is a matter of historical contingency, and cannot concern us here. How it happened is very important, though, as it defined the whole epoch to come. With the advent of Soviet civilization the whole field of possible free human actions was deployed in that, first, power defined what it made sense to do and, second, what was appropriate among the actions that made sense. But then, dissimulation was brought in among the Soviet people by each individually, to defend themselves against the gaze of power.

Sex and faith

A good example of the discussed developments is the change in the status of sexual practices. Sex, the most 'private' of all spheres of life of a Western individual, may serve as a ground for a discussion of the origins of mass individualization in Russia.

Before, as with most aspects of peasant life, sex was a matter of public concern, not a private affair of an individual. Priests regulated serious sexual crimes, being lenient on misdemeanour when it did not endanger the cohesion of the community. Peasant communes policed themselves, neighbours reporting each other's sexual transgressions when they occurred. However, as Eva Levin writes in her study of Russian sexual practices: 'Orthodox Slavs did not worry about the attitudes and intentions behind behavior. People were made responsible only for controlling their actions, not for controlling their thoughts and feelings' (1989: 301).

Communal regulation of the sexual life of its members was transplanted during the ruralization of the cities into workers' communities also. To a certain degree, it was widespread among the workers who came to the cities before the revolution. As early as 1923 worker-correspondents, writing for the factory newspapers and general mass media, demonstrated that community techniques of sexual surveillance were implanted to such a degree that Trotsky feared the Soviet press would be overwhelmed with 'cant' (Trotsky, 1973: 65). Correspondents produced narratives that used real names, without any doubt of their right to expose the excesses of other workers' sexual lives – which were obviously visible with all their transgressions. Trotsky lamented this and asked that some stories modelling good behaviour be presented and that fictitious names be used to provide some examples of a 'positive' everyday life. Contemporary sources echo Trotsky's concerns. For instance, William Chase describes barracks of industrial enterprises in Moscow in the 1920s, where up to 200 families lived in a single space, one bed housing one family. 'Privacy' in sexual intercourse was achieved by putting a blanket over one's head; the rest of the barrack's inhabitants being witness to reproductive activities' (Chase, 1986: 191).

How could privacy originate in this milieu? To repeat the question that was posed earlier, how could an individual close him or herself off from the community? Elsewhere I have suggested that the private sphere initially grew not among workers and peasants as such, but only among those of them who became party members, as an unintended consequence of the party's self-examination to root out the contaminating influences on its purity (Kharkhordin, 1994). The argument is as follows.

If the original Bolshevik revolutionaries were mostly ardent believers, who had individually experienced something similar to religious conversion that William James described in his classic work (1902), and therefore did not need to dissimulate in adhering to the saintly ideal, latecomers were individualized in different conditions. In the 1920s the 'party ethics' campaign and the spectacular 'sex' trials over those workers and peasants who, having become party members and Soviet officials, still engaged in sexual licentiousness, marked a watershed in two respects. First, communal vigilance was introduced into the party itself, which lacked it beforehand. This was done in order to ruthlessly stamp out certain doctrinally unacceptable behaviours, which some party members could demonstrate in the aftermath of chaotic years of Revolution and Civil War. As a result of this, the party was becoming structured not as the Panopticon but as the Abbey of Thélème so picturesquely described by Rabelais (Glucksmann, 1980: 20) – where everybody watched everybody. Certain mutual checking techniques were used to find out what was 'lurking' in one's sexual life as it became indicative of the broader issue of the corruption of the inner integrity of a Communist.

Second, the introduction of collective surveillance into party life led to the unintended consequence of the formation of spheres of dangerous behaviour, which had to be cordoned off from the gaze of power by an 'individual', who was formed by this 'concealment'. These spheres were generally not hidden from mutual surveillance in other communities, as the Chase and Trotsky examples indicate, but became no longer tolerated by power once communal surveillance was applied to a new object: it was not a worker/peasant but a 'new believer', whose integrity of inner faith was put into question by dangerous inclinations. Thus, *latter-day 'individualization' occurred first in those party members who had to individually withdraw (or better, retract) dubious behaviour from the omnipresent gaze of their fellow comrades*. In other words, in opposition to former Bolshevik converts, latecomers simply dissimulated adherence to the saintly code, which was now enforced by mutual vigilance. The same happened with other saintly creatures, like Young Communist League and Young Pioneers' members. Workers and peasants, who were not Communists, initially did not have to dissimulate: the sex behaviour was largely irrelevant to power concerns.

Now, some parallels with the developments in the West may be drawn. According to Foucault, in the West individualization occurred via the merger of confessional practices with the discursive fiction of an inner essence called 'sex':

> . . . one confesses one's sins, one confesses one's thoughts and desires . . . one sets about telling with the greatest precision what is most difficult to tell; one confesses in public and in private, to one's parents, to one's teachers, to one's doctor, to those one loves; one confesses to oneself, in pleasure and in pain, things

that it would be impossible to tell anyone else . . . Western man has become a confessing animal. (Foucault, 1980: 56)

One can likewise suggest that in Soviet Russia individualization occurred via the merger of practices of dissimulation with the discursive fiction of an inner essence called 'the Communist faith'. People formed themselves as Western subjects by confessing constantly on the matters of sex, while in Russia they became Soviet subjects by dissimulating Communist faith. In both cultures individualization proceeded from top to bottom. In the West the bourgeoisie was individualized first, with the working classes acquiring 'subjectivity' later, when confession spread its net far and wide. In Soviet Russia the initial 'subjects' to appear were party members who had to dissimulate first and foremost. Later dissimulation individualized the rest of society.

The differences are striking also. 'Sex' was not posited in Communist Party discourse as the essentially important set of behaviours; and Soviet subjects did not intensely question their sexuality to learn the truth of themselves. Rather, sexual licence was one of several political sins which endangered the everyday existence of the new lay saint. The seven primary sins, which testified to the corruption of the saintly conscience, were initially formulated in 1924 by the Party Control Commission. This Commission had to employ neologisms to name some phenomena in question. The primary sins included: careerism and quarrelling with the objective of getting rid of obstacles to one's career (*sklochnichestvo*); marrying or getting in close personal contact with members of the petit bourgeoisie (*oNEPivanie*); expanding one's land plots and other primary economic factor possessions (*khozobrastanie*); excessive luxury in dress or spending habits (*izlishestva*); alcoholism; sexual licence; participating in religious rites (Iaroslavkii, 1924/1989: 157).

Disparate behaviours, desires and attitudes were grouped here under one general name of 'corrupting influences'; but 'sex' was never singled out as having a specific significance among them. Neither did this signifier subsume all other behaviours which would be grouped as 'sexual' in the West. Some of those were discussed on *ad hoc* basis and with different emphases. For example, duelling over a woman was strongly denounced not because of the desire component but because of the possessive attitude it demonstrated towards a woman and the non-comradely attitudes it evoked among males. Male masturbation and homosexuality were left to the Aristotelian sense of appropriateness of each local party cell: if the party could not do without the 'sinner', then it could retain him in a current position, accepting full responsibility for the consequences of his actions (Iaroslavskii, 1924/1989: 168–9). Of course, categories of Western medical classifications were used to point at the cases discussed, but they were immersed in completely different systems of signifiers. Only after the spectacular sex trials of the late 1920s, all linked to dismemberment, rape or murder (for details see Naiman, 1991), did sex become specifically suspect; what mattered, however, was the linkage of saintly behaviour to ghastly crimes, not sex *per se*.

Dissimulation spreading downwards

The initial result of individualization by means of dissimulation is described by Steven White in his conception of 'consequences of Stalinism' (1979: 111). The Stalinist legacy included total secrecy as a characteristic of personal life, a feeling of complete powerlessness in the face of power, and the double nature of an individual. The visible obedient participant in Communist rituals and the invisible truth-teller and gain-seeker shared the same body. However, as White ingeniously put it, it was not obvious what part of this double individual was more 'real'. A Soviet citizen kept oscillating between the two, seemingly real in both incarnations.

This oscillation is also nicely captured in the concept of the 'modal schizophrenia' that Katerina Clark ascribes to the literature of Socialist Realism. Strikingly reminiscent of what White writes about the double individual, 'modal schizophrenia' is a combination of 'what is' and 'what ought to be' in a single novel, that is, a 'combination of the most matter of fact, everyday reality and the most heroic prospects', in Zhdanov's words (Clark, 1986: 37). In everyday life Soviet people oscillated like the hero of a Socialist Realist novel, from the most mundane privacy of one's bed to the heroism of one's public person. This oscillation soon gave way to a more pointed and blatant dissimulation, where gain-seeking became predominant.

From the 1930s on, the number of dissimulating individuals, that is, people individualized by dissimulation, grew steadily. The years of Stalinist terror made this process pervasive, but equally invisible to registration: inept dissimulators, together with other victims of the machinery of terror, finished their days in the *gulag*. However, one may suggest that an indirect first sign of the overall increase in the number of dissimulators was the appearance of the literary figure of the successful careerist dissimulator, sometimes depicted in what Vera Dunham has called the 'middlebrow fiction' of Socialist Realism. Novels seem to distinguish two different types of dissimulators: the intellectual from the old days, who is bound to lose out, and the new upwardly mobile careerist.

The former, for example, appears in Ehrenburg's novel *Out Of Chaos* (1933, quoted in Brown, 1982: 201), which depicts the construction of the famous Kuznetsk metal works. The main hero, manager Safonov, is an individualist who strongly detests the human ant-hill he has to supervise during this construction. However, he confines his criticisms to his private diary, and delivers loyal speeches in public. Ehrenburg's verdict on such a split intellectual personality is obvious: Safonov commits suicide. Intellectuals cannot survive the dissimulatory posture imposed on them by the new circumstances.

Latter-day dissimulators are radically different from the intellectual Safonov. They are formed as individuals by the practice of dissimulation. Their double-faced life is not a painful split forced upon their heretofore unitary self; on the contrary, this split is normal for them because they originate as individuals by means of this split. From time to time, in the utmost secrecy, they can even confide to their lovers their 'innermost secrets' (which they posited by such confessions!); they can let their zealous self-control go – at least, in the novels which strove to exhort the people to vigilant denunciations of such 'double-facers'. For instance, in one of the narratives Dunham finds a careerist who reveals his true intimate heart to a mistress:

> 'Soon we will finish our work here. . . . I shall receive a sizeable bonus. And on to Moscow. . . . You and I, we will have a Bluthner piano, a Telefunken set, and crystal, real French crystal. . . . So that all these things should come alive, we need the poetry of an electric push-button behind which stands the charm of the French word *comfort* and the convenience of the American word *service*.'

Oddly enough, the spoiled and idle belle cuts him down to size:

> 'May I ask you one more intimate question? . . . Why are you in the party? A petite bourgeois (*meshchanka*) is asking you that! . . . You are even worse than I am. . . . You are a slave of possessions, you are a shell, which does not contain any pearl but dirt.' (quoted in Dunham, 1976: 50)

The poor dissimulator, having revealed some of his most intimate dreams, elicits nothing more but an adequate characterization of the structure of his self: he is a shell, which hides only dirt under normal appearance. The shells are normatively denounced.

Another post-war novel, however, hints at a newer reality: if you are not a shell, you cannot survive. Not only because of 'the purifying terror' which eliminates unskilful dissimulators or non-dissimulators, but also because a new dynamic has been recently set into motion: dissimulators, having become the dominant type of Soviet individual, force everyone to become one. Those who did not learn to dissimulate 'naturally' will be made to learn dissimulation by force. Even the residual Bolshevik saintly converts are forced to adopt a dissimulative posture.

A novel called *First and Last*, implying the first in knowledge and the last in citizenship, tells the story of a young ensign of the naval academy. He is a diesel engine addict, spends all his time working on the engine, and forgets about serving the community. When forced by his superiors and peers to care about something other than technical tasks, the ensign defends his right to serve the socialist motherland the way he sees fit. This does not work very well. A sly villain, the insidious friend of the ensign, who occupies a powerful position at the top:

> proffers advice, the kind that oils the wheels of any deal. He leans confidently over and whispers: 'You know what? Don't argue against these truths. They say all these things. Well, let them. You should agree with them. It isn't difficult, is it? That way it will be much more peaceful. It's only a conditional agreement. It does not bind you to anything serious'. (quoted in Dunham, 1976: 201–3)

The secrets of the trade of dissimulation are laid out perfectly. The ensign rejects them. The result is quick to follow: the ensign is the only one to graduate as merely a lieutenant junior grade; his peers turn away from him and the head of the academy refuses to shake hands with him. The story ends with public punishment of the deviant. But now, this is a strange deviance! In the late Stalinist society the refusal to play by the unwritten rules of dissimulation is an abnormality to be punished. The ultimate judge of what is normal is no longer some doctrinal ideal, but the community that imposes standard norms of behaviour, the saintly congregation that covertly admonishes its members to dissimulate in order to fit into these norms!

This novel seems to be one of the first to foretell the future of the Soviet society: the collective of saints is replaced by the collective of accomplices, who present saintly images in public, and consistently demand the display of loyalty to these images both at work and at home. Later, in the 1960s and 1970s, these images are somehow to be corrected according to 'realistic' assumptions of what can be expected from the members of the congregation. *Blat*, the use of connections for minor personal profit within the saintly system, will become a joint practice of subverting the saintly ideals and being lenient to comrades for minor subversions. These minor subversions do not matter so long as the primary loyalty holds, and this is the loyalty to the mechanism of collective vigilance – which ensures the preponderance of the collective in establishing what should be obeyed and how it should be obeyed. With the development of Soviet society in the 1950s–1970s the acuteness of substantive demands will subside; finally the collective will not demand much more than loyalty to the procedure of display of loyalty itself – an ultimate ritualization of life.

In the late 1940s and early 1950s, at the initial stage of this transformation of substantive loyalty to the professed ideals into procedural loyalty to the shared practice of dissimulation, the collective only took the first step. It tried to wrestle the power to decide what should be dissimulated from the hands of the leaders. Hence, in 1954 Ehrenburg's novel *The Thaw* opened up the period which acquired its name from the book's title. This novel by the renowned Laureate of the Stalin Prize for literature, which was read all over the Soviet Union, called for the 'warming up' of human relations. The substantive constraints of the definition of the saintly conduct were to be made more flexible, more 'humane'. 'Nobody's perfect' was the message; everybody should have the right to make mistakes, or at least a chance to correct them (Brown, 1982: 198).

However, the essential mechanism of mutual surveillance, which Stalin's terror sought to impose on all those areas of society where it was not yet practised, was not called into question. In fact, it was lauded as an achievement. People should care more about each other, said the novel. They should be friendly and not as 'cold' as during Stalin's macabre days, when they denounced their friends to the leaders for the smallest deviation from saintly standards. Now they can settle all these matters between themselves, in a comradely manner.

Ehrenburg's was also the first attempt to give an artistic insight into the hidden 'inner life' of the heroes. The secret of universally practised dissimulation was, if not made public, then at least asserted as the core insight of the coming new wave of literature. The positive heroes of *The*

Thaw are not drawn as hagiographic saints, whose outward appearance coincides with their true selves (which was typical of Socialist Realism); on the contrary, each character has some intricate inner life, which is not to be seen from the outside. The novel followed the methodological stricture that Ehrenburg formulated in the later essay 'On Writers' Work' (Brown, 1982: 202–3). Supposing that the hero of a novel is a neighbour of the worker who will read the novel, wrote Ehrenburg, what new discoveries will the reading bring? The answer was obvious: none, if the novel does not depict a hidden inner life. Both the personal and the social life of an ordinary worker are already open to the neighbourly gaze. Therefore, the novel had to pay attention to this hidden psychology in order to be interesting and engaging (Brown, 1982: 198). 'The secret inner self' was finally discovered in the Soviet individual; the mechanisms by which this inner self originated stayed in the background.

The 'warming up' of the Thaw after 1954 put the ability of the Soviet society to police itself to its first full test. The *styliagi* scare was the first action of mutual surveillance on the scale of the whole country, which demonstrated its power, and imposed the necessity to dissimulate on virtually every citizen. *Styliagi* was a derogatory name for upper-class youth, who dressed in stylish clothes, presenting a challenge to the gray and faceless public. A *styliagi*, according to newspaper descriptions, and according to the interviews with a few surviving genuine *styliagi*, wore 'outrageous clothes': thick-soled shoes, tight trousers, a striped shirt with a bright tie and a stylish jacket. The unlikely model was Johnny Weissmuller from the film *Tarzan in New York*, which somehow managed to pass Soviet censorship in 1951. (One is tempted to add: it passed censorship precisely because nobody could conceive anything scandalous about this film.) Little groups of *styliagi* would walk down what they called 'Broadway', that is, the right side of Gorky Street, between Red and Pushkin Squares in Moscow, displaying themselves in full gear, and end up in some restaurant where they would stay till 3 or 4 in the morning.

One surprising thing about the *styliagi* is that they were better off before Stalin's death in 1953 than after. They were under solid protection, because many of them were sons and daughters of the few families of the top Soviet elite. Fred Starr, who documented the merger of *styliagi* with jazz culture in the 1950s, notes that:

> . . . many elite children adopted the upbeat new mode of behavior and dress to flaunt their privileges. Nikita Khrushchev's children were arguably the founders of the 'style hunting' in 1940, but soon after the war the new cult of youthful assertiveness spread to Gromykos and other prominent families. . . . What had began as a fad among children of the elite before the death of Stalin had burgeoned into a full-scale revolt by alienated Soviet youths . . . (Starr, 1983: 238–9)

With the new emphasis on egalitarianism and the downgrading of leaders officially approved, the masses threw themselves into regulating the 'scum', as *styliagi* were popularly called. A campaign against *styliagi* started to rage in the pages of the Soviet press. A novel phenomenon was the mechanism of repression by the masses which almost spontaneously set itself into motion. With the appearance of 'voluntary people's guards' – which were supposed, according to Khrushchev, gradually to replace the withering state apparatus – street patrols started to check on clothes. The initiative came from the bottom. The Soviet people cared.

Alexei Kozlov, a future leader of the best Soviet jazz-rock group Arsenal, and at the time a devoted *styliagi* (which meant that he was one of the few who wore their stylish outfits seven days a week) recalled the way he was initially treated in public transport on the way to 'Broadway'. People would call him a parakeet, or a monkey, and shame him all the time. For that reason, said Kozlov, there were few women among *styliagi*; it was unbelievably more difficult for a woman to withstand the popular assault (Troitsky, 1988: 10). The popular pressure grew as the Thaw progressed. The baggy-trousered crowds would now not only shame a *styliagi* on the street, but approach him to cut his tight trousers into stripes ('no joke!', adds journalist Artemy Troitsky, who first recounted this common event for Western audiences [1988: 13]) and cut off the bulging part of his Tarzan-like haircut. Street patrols only institutionalized this practice.

After the whole commonwealth started to wage war on *styliagi*, the latter had to adopt a dissimulatory retreat. From time to time they would reappear in public spaces for a moment, as guerrilla fighters against uniformity, only to retreat immediately afterwards into safe privacy. However, the phenomenon of *styliagi* was more a product of Soviet moral panic than a real movement. Kozlov says that he knew no more than fifty people who were as devoted as he was. Others put on their flashy clothes only once a week. These few strangely dressed people, showing up on Gorky Street in Moscow, served as a referent for a huge public campaign which raged all over the Soviet Union.

The mechanism of this campaign is described in an article 'Who Of Them Is Styliaga?' which appeared in *Komsomolskaya Pravda* in 1956, at the height of moral panic. A Komsomol activist named Antonov was designated as a *styliagi* by his fellow comrades in a provincial town of Batyriovo. He demonstrated a 'somehow abnormal behavior among the club youth. He differed from the rest in everything: in haircut, in his suit and in his raised collar'. The dispute between Antonov and the local satirical journal, which ridiculed his appearance, could not be resolved at a local level. The district Komsomol committee sent a photo of Antonov to *Komsomolskaya Pravda* to figure out whether he was a *styliagi*. The newspaper ruled that he was not, and lamented the avalanche of letters which described the excessive collective zeal demonstrated during this campaign. For example, in Odessa some Komsomol members were purged for having moustaches. The head of the Odessa Komsomol rationalized the purge: first a moustache, then a bright tie and you get a *styliagi* (Rusakova, 1956).

By 1960 the campaign against *styliagi* subsided; apparently, they were all exterminated, at least in public. *Styliagi* became the first victims of conformism as enforced by the masses, and they were not non-conformists by any means. When they appeared, the mechanism of conformity was not yet set into full motion; the terror waged still allowed for some spaces which escaped the grid of mutual surveillance. During the Thaw these spaces were successfully eliminated. The dinosaurs of the Stalinist society, *styliagi* simply had to learn to dissimulate to survive. And many did.

The new generation of style-conscious youth appeared as full-blown dissimulators. Dissimulation had flowed down from the top to the very bottom; now it individualized not only the party or Komsomol members, but every single working youth. The new breed of style-seekers, called 'crown princes' or 'grand dukes', was predominantly recruited from working-class families. They engaged in black market deals or illegal foreign currency exchange to get money and clothes. They met all the requirements for model Soviet youth. They were model dissimulators also; in fact, one of the dealers caught was the head of the Komsomol bureau of some enterprise (Kassof, 1965: 133). Vassily Aksionov, later to become a renowned *émigré* writer, but still a dedicated Communist at the time, wrote a piece in 1960 which seems to be the closest Soviet Russia ever got to *Verstehende Soziologie*. If a *styliagi* lurked within every working-class youth, the problem was not punishment, the problem was understanding for subsequent correction:

> How did . . . the sons of ordinary working families come to lead such a life? . . . [The struggle against them] cannot be reduced to what used to be done several years ago when every young fellow with welted pockets and every girl with dyed hair was hauled off to a patrol post. We must proceed differently and we must first of all understand why moths, flying towards the dangerous flame of an attractive life appear among our serious, intelligent, young people. (quoted in Kassof, 1965: 158–9)

Dissimulation and resistance

Pierre Bourdieu (1990) has described the mechanism of 'collective misre-cognition' with the help of which rural societies or tightly knit religious communities maintain themselves. This mechanism is strikingly reminiscent of the Soviet society of the 1960s. Bourdieu argues that a group united by mores necessarily misrecognizes the objective conditions of its own exist-ence, and this misrecognition is enforced and supported by practices of what he calls 'serial constraint' or 'cross-censorship'. In other words, everybody watches everybody else, immediately inflicting punishment for even a minimal violation of the professed beliefs of the group.

As it was already pointed out, the unanimity of the 1960s was achieved in the USSR through the imposition of exactly this kind of serial constraint. 'There is nothing that groups demand more insistently and reward more generously than this reverence of what they claim to revere' (Bourdieu, 1990: 109). Even if many did not believe in Communist ideals in their hearts by the early 1970s, they continued to engage in cross-censorship that each suffered reluctantly but without failing to impose on others. Virtually all helped to impose on others the constraints they themselves experienced from others, and breaking off was unimaginable.

The *kollektiv*, that is a collective of the people united by work at a given organization, became the founding unit of the Soviet society. The *kollektiv* became the site where mutual surveillance functioned to the fullest. A network of *kollektivy* constituted the whole social terrain of Soviet life. The decisive monopoly of social power enjoyed by these *kollektivy* after Stalin's death was shaken only by developments which followed the non-conformist trials of the mid-1960s. First, future Nobel Prize winner Joseph Brodsky, a poet, was put on trial in 1964 on the basis of allegations of 'idleness'; and a year later the Sinyavsky–Daniel process inaugurated the new era of liberal dissent in the USSR.

Following these trials of genuine artistic non-conformists two new ways of living in private, frequently protected by profound dissimulation, emerged. If the first one, the dissent movement, challenged the content of what the Soviet commonwealth claimed to revere, the second, the counter-culture, challenged the mechanism of mutual surveillance itself. If the first one attacked the misrecognized representation (and therefore, was forcefully suppressed by the members of the commonwealth, as it openly put the existence of the commonwealth in question), then the second attacked the mechanism of serial constraint that supported and enforced the misrecognized representation. The second did not have any alternative discursive ideals to offer; thus, it was rather more effective, because it did not elicit the strong counter-reaction from the masses who were eager to defend their professed ideal 'to the last drop of blood'.

Dissent in Russia was always predicated on moral grounds, and dissenters who opposed a post-Stalinist regime were no exception to this general rule. All post-war dissidents shared one characteristic – an intense inner belief, which caused them to act according to the professed ideals. Hence the intense moral tonale of the movement, though beliefs varied. The majority of the dissenters of the first wave of the late 1960s were 'children of the Thaw', that is, espoused Communist ideals (Zhitnikov, 1977). One could say that their profile was very close to that of the Huguenots in sixteenth-century France. Both groups were dissatisfied with ritualized reality and strove to live according to the Cause, as gathered from individual reading of the Word: the Bible in the Huguenot case and the texts of Marx and Lenin in the Soviet case. Both attempted to use their positions as citizens and magistrates to reform the ritualized system from within: people like Roy Medvedev were the de Mornays of the USSR. Both were repressed; but if the Huguenots were eliminated as a problem in one night (of St Bartholomew), Communist dissenters in post-war Russia were straightened up by the series of demonstrative trials. In the face of mounting repression many returned to whole-hearted dissimulation. Others were converted to liberal truths which revealed for them the 'true' character of the Soviet regime as a system violating essential human rights. Some lapsed into religious mysticism.

The important achievement of the dissident movement was establishing the sphere of the critical public (in the Habermasian sense) through interpersonal contacts among the dissidents. This sphere of *samizdat* literature grew out of the informal network of literary distribution in the late 1950s, when millions of people copied popular poems by hand. The appearance of *samizdat* followed the Habermasian model, which holds that the bourgeois public sphere starts as a family discussion forum, develops into an inter-family sphere of letters, and gets politicized by discussing political questions (Habermas, 1989). Accordingly, when the literary communities in the USSR had to discuss the consequences and repercussions of the Sinyavsky–Daniel trial, they became political. Some discussants chose to sustain this public sphere opposed to and critical of the regime. The critical public sphere, thus conceived, was crushed by KGB repression twice, in the mid-1970s and again in the early 1980s, but easily re-emerged each time because of the steady supply of dissimulating individuals who contributed to it in their unseen lives. Those dissidents who decided to go public were eliminated quickly and efficiently without any reaction from the majority of the population and, in some cases, with popular support.

The distance of dissenters from 'ordinary people', which effectively precluded them from gaining in influence, stemmed from their quasi-religious profile. They were closer to a Bolshevik saint than to a person on the street. Religious zeal was the driving force of these few Soviet citizens turned into liberal saints. The irony of the moment consisted in the fact that the masses were more inclined to sin than to strive for righteous living. A ritualized support of the system allowed more and more freedom in private, including the freedom from conscience.

The counter-culture, by contrast, was close and understandable to ordinary people. 'The system' (*sistema*) – as the hippie community was known, though it sounds paradoxical to the Western ear – was all about clothes and fun; it had nothing to do with dangerous transgressions or ideological fervour. Nevertheless, 'the system' challenged the Soviet system in a profound manner. The counter-culture hardly had any discursive ideals to profess: it just chose not to fit into the mechanism of the mutual enforcement of conformity. Hippies did not offer a new Higher Cause to be supported by the same mechanism of mutual surveillance; they defied this mutual surveillance itself as the mechanism of social cohesion. Therefore, repressions against the counter-culture were simultaneously less tangible and more massive. Hippies did not risk ending up in jail, as a rule, but could be bullied in every city of the USSR for their looks. For them, however, and in contradistinction to *styliagi*, it was a conscious choice.

The hippie 'system' was an extreme case. Not many were ready to take on this style of life in a feat of total sacrifice. It required heroism as impressive as that of open dissenters. A majority of counter-culture adherents employed their dissimulatory techniques to hide their private adhesion to it, and also tried to minimize social interference in their personal lives. The essence of this youth *intifada* against mutual surveillance is best captured by a phrase by Boris Grebenshchikov, the leader of the most popular rock group Aquarium: young people were becoming 'the generation of street cleaners and night watchmen'. These professions were in high demand because they allowed escape from imprisonment on the charges of idleness and guaranteed little interference from the *kollektiv*. These professions also supplied lots of free time.

The defiance of the mechanism of mutual surveillance, as a professed positive value of the rock culture, lessened the grip of this mechanism even on average dissimulators. As a result, subsequent younger generations also grew more and more unaffected by the regime's substantive values. Alternative values of the free and easy life, of good clothes as expressive of personality, of meaningful sex as a means of personal fulfilment were developed by the rock culture. Every Komsomol member, having performed the necessary ritualized actions at school or worksite, changed into jeans and listened to rock at home. Rock also supplied a real charisma, a perception of a totally alien reality. Led Zeppelin records served as the functional equivalents of bits of the stone of Mecca brought home by rare pilgrims to the sacred place. One might say that if rock culture never lived up to its revolutionary promise in the West, it did in the USSR. Millions of dissimulating Soviet citizens pledged their allegiance to a different life by secretly worshipping Deep Purple. Rock culture left the official dogma bereft of its remaining charisma, and eroded emotional support for the system among the young. In other words, rock was one of the primary forces which prepared 1985 among the young.

The result was the avalanche-like collapse of officialdom in the *perestroika* years. To quote Bourdieu once again:

> The fact that the primary belief of the strongly integrated communities is the product of serial constraint that the group applies to itself, which may be suffered with great impatience . . . but without ever being able to spark off a revolt that could call them into question [explains why the break of 1987–89 occurs] in a sudden, collective form, with circular control losing its efficacy as soon as there is a glimpse of the real possibility of breaking it. (Bourdieu, 1990: 111)

A legacy of dissimulation

One wonders whether *perestroika* was capable of eliminating the dissimulative split between public and private life that was constitutive of the Soviet individual. Present-day Russians may have inherited it and still engage in ritualized support of some ideals, offered by the powers that be, with a full-blown intention of reverting to an almost unrestrained personalism or privatism once the minimal requirement of participation in the public ritual of consent is fulfilled. If dissimulation persists, and helps to support some myth, be it the myth of 'democracy' or 'Great Russia' – then it may still ruin any attempt to unite the crumbling country with the help of some positive ideology.

All discursive programmes of current political actors, centring just on the content of the message of political ideology, fail to change this condition. At best they may replace the current sustaining myth with another one, commanding no more allegiance than the one they will have just replaced. On the contrary, a programme, taking into account the form in which the message of political ideology should be articulated, will have more success if this form complies with the fundamental structure of dissimulation. The question is, then, what can elicit not only ritualized support, but also mobilize the profound energies inherent in the post-Soviet system? Looking for an answer to this question seems hopeless as privatism alone is the deep moving force, while all non-personal or impersonal frameworks fail to cope with its omnivorousness.

But perhaps, the solution to the current predicament may be paradoxical: there, where lies the greatest threat, hope is also contained. Perhaps, if nobody is able to really believe in any positive discursive doctrine after decades of dissimulation, then everybody may have a sort of a negative belief, namely *the belief that there are no more beliefs* capable of moving people. If some government names this belief shared by a majority of Russians, it will become the first government to articulate groundlessness as its foundation.

Can Russia become a postmodern community – with a shared belief in the decline of metanarratives as its ground? Perhaps, Russia is even closer in this respect to the postmodern condition than the West. This does not seem strange at all, if one remembers that Nietzsche borrowed the term 'nihilism' from a Russian novel.

References

Atkinson, Dorothy (1983) *The End of the Russian Land Commune, 1905–1930*. Stanford, CA: Stanford University Press.

Bourdieu, Pierre (1990) *The Logic of Practice*. Stanford, CA: Stanford University Press.

Brown, E. (1982) *Russian Literature since the Revolution*. Cambridge, MA: Harvard University Press.

Chase, William (1986) *Workers, Society and the Soviet State. Labor and Life in Moscow, 1918–1929*. Urbana-Champaign, IL: University of Illinois Press.

Clark, Katerina (1986) *The Soviet Novel: History as Ritual*. Chicago: University of Chicago Press.

Confino, Michael (1991) *Société et Mentalités Collectives en Russie sous l'Ancien Régime*. Paris: Institut d'Etudes Slaves.

Dunham, Vera (1976) *In Stalin's Time. Middleclass Values in Soviet Fiction*. Cambridge: Cambridge University Press.

Foucault, Michel (1980) *The History of Sexuality. Volume I: An Introduction*. New York: Vintage Books.

Glucksmann, Andre (1980) *The Master Thinkers*. New York: Harper & Row.

Habermas, Jürgen (1989) *The Structural Transformation of the Public Sphere*. Cambridge, MA: MIT Press.

Iaroslavskii, Emelian (1924/1989) 'O Partetike' (On party ethics), in A.A. Guseinov, M.V. Iskrov and R.V. Petropavlovskii (eds), *Partiinaia Etika. Dokumenty i Materialy Diskussii Dvadtsatykh Godov* (Party Ethics. Documents and Materials of the Party Discussion of the 1920s). Moscow: Politizdat. pp. 170–96.

James, William (1902) *The Varieties of Religious Experience: A Study in Human Nature.* New York: Longmans, Green & Co.

Jowitt, Kenneth (1992) *New World Disorder: The Leninist Extinction.* Berkeley: University of California Press.

Kassof, Allen (1965) *The Soviet Youth Program. Regimentation and Rebellion.* Cambridge, MA: Harvard Universitiy Press.

Keenan, Edward L. (1986) 'Muscovite political folkways', *Russian Review*, 45 (1): 115–81.

Kharkhordin, Oleg (1994) 'Reveal and dissimulate: a genealogy of private life in Soviet Russia', in Jeff Weintraub and Krishan Kumar (eds), *Public and Private in Thought and Practice.* Chicago: University of Chicago Press.

Levin, Eva (1989) *Sex and Society in the World of Orthodox Slavs, 900–1700.* Ithaca, NY: Cornell University Press.

Lewin, Moshe (1985) *The Making of the Soviet System.* New York: Pantheon.

Naiman, Eric (1991) '*Sexuality and Utopia. The debate in the Soviet 1920s*', unpublished dissertation, Department of English, University of California, Berkeley.

Rusakova, E. (1956) 'Kto Iz Nikh Styliaga?' (Who is *styliaga*?), *Komsomolskaia Pravda*, 11 August.

Sinyavsky, Andrei (1990) *Soviet Civilization: A Cultural History.* New York: Norton.

Starr, Frederick S. (1983) *Red and Hot. The Fate of Jazz in the Soviet Union, 1917–1980.* Oxford: Oxford University Press.

Troitsky, Artemy (1988) *Back in the USSR: The True Story of Rock in Russia.* Boston and London: Faber & Faber.

Trotsky, Leon (1973) *Problems of Everyday Life.* New York: Monad Press.

Tucker, Robert C. (1972) *The Soviet Political Mind.* London: Macmillan.

White, Stephen (1979) *Political Culture and Soviet Politics.* New York: St Martin's Press.

Zhitnikov, K. (1977) 'The decline of the democratic movement', in M. Meerson-Aksenov and B. Shragin (eds), *The Political, Social, and Religious Thought of Russian Samizdat.* Belmont, MA: Nordland.

13

BIO-POLITICS AND THE SPECTRE OF INCEST: SEXUALITY AND/IN THE FAMILY

Vikki Bell

Modern man is an animal whose politics places his existence as a living
being in question.

(Foucault, 1981: 143)

Foucault once remarked that no-one wanted to talk about the end of *The
History of Sexuality: An Introduction (1981)*, henceforth *THS*, where he
details the operations of bio-politics, where he makes rare comment on
racism and Hitler, and where he considers the movement from a 'symbolics
of blood' to an 'analytics of sexuality'.[1] The central argument of this last
section is that the development of capitalism was accompanied by the 'entry
of life into history' (1981: 141). The 'menace of death' was no longer the
threat it had been, and that relief enabled and was enabled by, a relative
control over life. The concept of bio-politics that Foucault introduces here
refers to a politics that centres around bodies as living beings and as
populations; it is a politics that 'assumed responsibility for the life processes
and undertook to control and modify them' (1981: 142). Gaining velocity in
the nineteenth century, new forms of knowledge focused on births and
deaths, health, life expectancy and longevity, with statistical models
encouraging assessment and prediction. As a result, people were no longer
simply legal subjects who were controlled with reference to the sword, and
ultimately death; rather, bio-politics makes them 'living beings', possessing
'a body, conditions of existence, probabilities of life, an individual and
collective welfare, forces that could be modified and a space in which they
could be distributed in an optimal manner' (1981: 142).

We do not have much evidence of Foucault's ruminations on the various
regulatory techniques of bio-power, although the concept of population
which they create and on which they depend, and the construction of various
populations, is central to the thesis of *THS*.[2] In the lecture on governmentality, he argues that the middle of the eighteenth century saw a shift from
the family as the model for government to the family as a privileged segment
of the 'population' which became the principle focus and purpose of
government (1979: 17). It is clear that bio-politics incorporates the
disciplinary aspects of power that Foucault outlined in *Discipline and Punish*

(1977), and gathers these techniques of power into strategies which are not so much about individual bodies but about aggregates. Furthermore, sex occupies a peculiar place within this history, for sex is not simply an *example* of the operations of bio-power, but is an especially crucial target due to its pivotal place between the two 'ends' of the bio-political spectrum. The control over life depends upon strategies mobilized at the level of the population, but its deployment is dependent on encouraging people to behave in a disciplined mode with regard to their bodies and sexual habits. That is (voluntary, domestic) population control is effected by the disciplinary response of individuals to deployed knowledge about populations.[3] This chapter considers the tension that results when the deployment of sexuality as a mechanism of simultaneous regulation and incitement is considered in relation to 'the family' as the principle place at which, and vehicle through which, bio-politics works. That tension is the point at which 'the family' and 'sex' come together: the spectre of incest.

I

The paradox is this: that the family is on the one hand regarded as the institution *par excellence* of the private sphere, a sheltered space of personal freedom, on the other it is the place where the one law that must not be traversed, lest the very basis of civilization fall, is said to operate; that whilst the most conservatively inclined agree that the family implies sexual relations – that, indeed, the family is the proper home of sexuality – it is also the place at which sexual relations are supposedly the most strongly circumscribed. 'The family' and sexuality are held together by sexuality and apart by the incest prohibition, the rule on which the maintenance of civilization supposedly rests. Foucault alerted us to this tension that haunts discussion of 'the family': 'incest . . . occupies a central place; it is being constantly solicited and refused; it is an object of obsession and attraction, a dreadful secret and an indispensable pivot' (1981: 109).

Why does Foucault suggest that incest is *indispensable*? The answer concerns the mode in which 'the family' has come to be governed within bio-politics; and that government is intimately related to the knowledges that have been formed through, for and around it. Sociological knowledge is interconnected with bio-political government, then, not as an antagonistic analysis, although that might sometimes be the case, but as a tool and a product of its operations.

The understanding of the family propounded by the sociology that has its roots at the end of the nineteenth century is a collection of stories about the incest prohibition. Repeatedly, the incest prohibition has been elevated as fundamental, crucial, pivotal: it is the foundation of all that differentiates 'now' from 'then'. Perhaps this is at its most clear in the work of Lévi-Strauss (1949/1969), where the incest prohibition is elevated to a gate-way position signalling the very transition from nature to culture, a position paralleling on the societal level the importance of the incest prohibition in Freud's theorizing of the individual's transition through the Oedipus complex. Everything universal in man, Lévi-Strauss insisted, relates to the natural order; but where there were rules 'we know for certain that the cultural stage has been reached' (1949/1969: 8). Accepting the universality of an incest prohibition, Lévi-Strauss regarded this rule as a contradictory social fact, a peculiar phenomenon which has 'the distinctive characteristics of nature [that is, its universality] and of its theoretical contradiction, culture [that is, it is a rule]' (1949/1969: 10).[4] In his exploration of this paradox, he theorized the incest prohibition as 'the fundamental step *because of* which and *by* which, but, above all, *in* which, the transition from nature to culture is accomplished' (1949/1969: 24). In Freud's more grandiose stories of the origin of culture and civilization, a similar importance is accorded the incest taboo. In *Civilization and its Discontents* (1930/1985) sexual desire is posited as *the* principle reason for the founding of the family:

> One may suppose that the founding of families was connected with the fact that a moment came when the need for genital satisfaction no longer made its appearance like a guest who drops in suddenly, and, after his departure, is heard of no more for a long time, but instead took up its quarters as a permanent lodger. (Freud, 1930/1985: 288)

The necessity to work and to have one's helpers nearby may have led to the formation of primitive families, Freud argues, but the desire for sexual satisfaction is the precipitating factor in the establishment of the 'civilized' family. Sexual desire thus grouped individuals into units, and there was now just 'one essential feature of civilization' lacking: 'the arbitrary will of its head, the father, was unrestricted' (1930/1985: 289). Referring back to *Totem and Taboo* (1913/1985), in which he had attempted to bring together contemporary anthropological work on totemism, studies of folklore, and his own clinical observations in a search for the origin of the incest taboo, Freud states that 'the taboo-observances were the first "right" or "law"' (1913/1985: 290). The totem as described by anthropologists such as Durkheim (1898/1963),[5] could be thought of as representing the father as it did for Little Hans[6] and as totemic groups suggest when they describe the totem as a common ancestor and primal father, Freud reasoned, so that, substituting the father for the totem reveals that the two ordinances of totemism – not to kill the totem and not to have sexual relations with a woman of the same totem – correspond to the two crimes of Oedipus, who unwittingly killed his father and married his mother, and with the two primal wishes of children (1913/1983: 130). Whilst Freud stated that it was 'unfair to insist on certainty' and 'foolish to aim at exactitude' in the timing and dates of his hypothesis (1913/1983: 143) he postulated nonetheless the following explanation of the origin of the incest taboo. At some point in our past, he suggested, a patriarchal father cast out his sons so that he would have sole power and sole access to the women of the group. These brothers came together, killed and devoured their father, accomplishing in that act the ultimate identification with him. After exercising the negative part of their ambivalent feelings toward the father, however, the dead father became stronger than the living, such that they practised 'deferred obedience': what had been prevented by him now became prohibited by the sons themselves. The totem became the father substitute, giving the sons a second chance:

> [The totemic system was a] covenant with their father in which he promised them everything that a childish imagination may expect from a father – protection, care, indulgence – while on their side they undertook to respect his life, that is to say, not to repeat the deed which had brought destruction on their real father. (1913/1983: 144)

Thus the sons revoked their deed by forbidding the killing of the totem, the father substitute, and they renounced its fruits by resigning their claim to the women to whom they had gained access: the incest taboo was thereby instituted.

For Lévi-Strauss, as for Freud, therefore, the incest prohibition required explanation, and the explanations they developed gave it a most, *the* most, fundamental position in the attainment of civilization. For the former it is 'at once on the threshold of culture, in culture, and in one sense . . . culture itself' (1949/1969: 12); for the latter, it is not only the key to and result of the attainment of an essential feature of civilization (the check on paternal omnipotence), but the necessary obstacle in the development of the individual's very individuality. The period 'before the rule' is painted as a time of unrestricted sexual access, of following instincts; after the rule, there is a 'sacrifice of instincts' as civilization imposes restrictions on the liberty, empty as it was, of primitive life (Freud, 1930/1985: 284).

If one were to approach the work of such theorists with a Foucauldian scepticism, it is their timing as opposed to their accuracy which becomes of interest. Why did anthropological and sociological interest in the incest taboo blossom in the twentieth century? For although Lévi-Strauss and Freud both purport to detail a foundational movement from a state of nature (or primitivism) to one of civilization (or culture), their analyses have the concerns of the twentieth century written all over them. Ruminations on incest had not previously been in the same register of moralizing and theorizing as these, Foucault argued. Of course the myth of Oedipus had incest as its dominant theme, but at the time, incest was 'of little interest to philosophers and moralists, compared with the overriding concern with retaining self control . . . this serious important prohibition could be at the heart of a tragedy. It is not, however, at the centre of moral reflection' (1988: 262). Antiquity may have known philosophical reflection on incest, as in Artemidorus' analyses of dreams of incest (see Foucault, 1986: 21–3), but the practice of incest itself was not problematized as a moral practice. The theorization of the prohibition needs to be linked, Foucault argued, to the accompanying problematization of incest as a social problem at the end of the nineteenth century.

> Incest was a popular practice, and I mean by this, widely practised among the populace, for a very long time. It was towards the end of the 19th century that various social pressures were directed against it. And it is clear that the great

interdiction against incest is an invention of the intellectuals. . . . . If you look for studies by sociologists or anthropologists of the 19th century on incest you won't find any. Sure, there were some scattered medical reports and the like, but the practice of incest didn't really seem to pose a problem at the time. (1988: 302)

It is clear that for twentieth-century social theorists, by contrast, at least into the reign of sociological functionalism, the incest prohibition became and remained a necessary piece of the social puzzle under investigation. The practice of incest signalled chaos, and the taboo had been instituted in order to avoid that chaos. Parsons (1954), as the classic example, made a link between the structural theory of Lévi-Strauss and Freud's psychoanalytic theory, arguing that to practise incest would be to give membership of the lower level structure, the nuclear family, priority over that of the higher level structure, society as a whole. Because society requires that individuals (here Parsons is referring only to men) participate in the higher level structure of society, in non-familial roles, the incest prohibition fulfils this need by 'propelling' the individual out of the nuclear family of origin and into these non-familial roles. It simultaneously propels him out of the family of origin and into a new nuclear family.[7]

Foucault suggested that the twentieth-century interest in incest, and the insistence on the universality and fundamental importance of the incest prohibition has to be approached as constituted within the deployment of sexuality as he details it in *The History of Sexuality: An Introduction* (1981). However, the deployment of sexuality, as has been well rehearsed, is about the expansion and the explosion of a discursive complex 'power-knowledge-pleasure' through confession, through bio-political knowledges, and through the various practices these ways of speaking initiate and sustain. And yet the question of incest has been 'put into discourse' in a qualitatively different manner, as has already been suggested; contemporary with the incitement to speak about pleasures – and incestuous desires were included here – is the development of a discourse on the universal and fundamental prohibition of incest, exactly the juridical mode of speaking about sex that *The History of Sexuality* seemed to argue had been superseded. Thus there is a tension between an incitement to speak and excavate pleasures and a taboo that categorically forbids. From the same pen, even, we have inherited both the most fantastical theory on the origin of the incest taboo and the analyses that interpreted the talk of the bourgeoisie as incestuous fantasies. One begins to see the sense in which Foucault declared incest both incited and forbidden.

To speak of the taboo is, of course, still to speak about sex. To repeat over and over how much this sexual act is forbidden is still to bring the idea of incest into the discursive space that the deployment of sexuality opened up. This is exactly the question at issue and the peculiarity of incest. The explosion of discourses on sexuality did not simply incite people to give commentaries on their sexual pleasures and desires, to worry and police others' sexual practices, but it created stories about sexual practice that were extended backwards and elevated as foundational truths. Lévi-Strauss' and

Freud's theories of the origin of the taboo were gestures to the past, backward-looking theories that were ignited by present concerns. And this insistence on the taboo was and is a *contemporary* way of sustaining what is essentially a juridical mode of control over sexual practices that operates by exclusion: 'it speaks, and that is the law'.

But *why* would a juridical mode of speaking about sex be created within a society that was more generally moving into a period of confessing pleasures? One might suggest that these theorists were shocked at the scale of incestuous practice that nineteenth-century surveys of working class life and housing were uncovering, or at the number of dreams and commentaries that could be regarded as incestuous, and were attempting to insist on the incest prohibition as a way of halting this practice. However, rather than reduce this sociological outburst to the offended sexual morality of the writers concerned, the 'tension' that exists around the question of incest might be seen as arising from the way in which 'the family' and the population have been governed; that is, it is a consequence of the privileged place 'the family' occupies within bio-politics. In short, the argument is that the incest prohibition was continually reiterated as a fundamental rule because the prohibition sustains 'the family' that was needed as a central political target and mechanism. The reiteration was in response to the threat that was being posed by the deployment of sexuality; its efficacy, however, is another question.

II

Let us backtrack a little in order to look more closely at this complex situation, for the argument developed here relies on a particular reading of the thesis of *The History of Sexuality: An Introduction*, one which is unusual, at least for those who have fallen prey to the portrayal of Foucault's thesis as it has become generalized within sociological debates. For whilst the thesis of *THS* has frequently been characterized with a few broad strokes – a change in the way we speak about sexuality, a challenge to the way we conceive of power, and so on – the latter section of the book on which we are focusing here, challenges such a reading. This reading picks up upon the distinction between the system of alliances and the deployment of sexuality.

If 'sexuality' is the name accorded the result of the strategies and techniques that constitute the current regulation of bodies and sexual practices, what came *before* sexuality? For clearly Foucault could not be arguing that sexual practices and pleasures did not take place prior to the eighteenth century? 'What came before' can be characterized by one word: blood. Before the entry of 'life itself', Foucault argues, power operated with reference to bloodshed and to death; its focus was not so much on the practices of the people as on the will of the sovereign and the fear of famine. The sovereign with his sword, however, is just one aspect of this 'symbolics of blood' (1981: 148). Society was ordered around the sign of blood – 'being a certain blood, to be of the same blood, to be prepared to risk one's blood' – controlled via warfare – 'the ability to shed blood' – and wrong-doers were punished in bloody fashion – by execution and torture (1981: 147). Sexual practices too were understood and controlled through the notion of blood, in relation to the lines of descent – the family tree – by which one's station was conferred: this is what Foucault terms the 'deployment of alliance' or alternatively the 'system of alliance'. Its aim was not the bewildering proliferation that was to come but dependable repetition. The system of alliance is homeostatic, seeking to reproduce and maintain relations and hierarchies through its predominantly *legal* system of marriage, property, names and inheritance (1981: 106–7). Sexual relations and practices were accepted or punished according to the threat they posed to the juridical system of alliance; those that clearly stood in opposition to it – such as bigamy, parricide, adultery and incest – were severely punished. The enforcement of obedience to such laws, and the punishment of those who contravene them, is the primary task and mode of power.

However, Foucault suggests, as it began to falter as an instrument and support of the economic and political processes that were taking place in Western societies, the system of alliance began to be supplanted (1981: 106). The juridico-discursive mode of power that had controlled sexual relations with reference to the statutes, backed up with the threat of death, gave way in the eighteenth century to a mode of power that replaced the licit/illicit divide with the measurements of degrees of variation from 'the norm'. The punishment of illicit sexual practices is replaced with a pressure to seek out and measure pleasure, for the alliance concern with 'link between partners and the definite statutes' is now subordinated to the deployment of sexuality's attention on 'the sensations of the body and the quality of pleasures' (1981: 106). The symbol of blood is replaced with the statistics and study of sexuality.

The argument is not that the deployment of sexuality has completely supplanted the operations of the system of alliances. Partly because the transition has been muddied by the ways in which sexuality has taken up the symbol of blood for its own purposes – by, for example, the eugenicists or, especially, de Sade, who managed to retain blood within practices within the deployment of sexuality; for them, blood 'flowed through the whole dimension of pleasure' (1981: 148). But also because the period since these changes has seen the proliferation of discourses around blood that are, albeit frequently *through* sexuality, still connected to death: 'biologistic' racism, for example, contemporary with the changes as they extended their disciplinary techniques, is understood by Foucault as a bio-political appropriation of the 'historical weight' of blood, with Nazism as 'the most cunning and most naive . . . combination of the fantasies of blood and the paroxysms of a disciplinary power' (1981: 149).[8]

The incomplete transition between the deployment of alliance and the system of sexuality that concerns us here, however, is that which occurs around 'the family'. Foucault suggests that the system of alliances was focused on kinship ties and their legal ramifications; it has the legal family as its principle target and its ultimate purpose. That is, its purpose is to preserve 'the family' as an eternal and inevitable unit, predominantly in terms of law and, within that, predominantly in terms of the transfer of property. The deployment of sexuality is 'anchored' in this system of alliance that preceded it and is built upon the institution which the deployment of alliance explicitly sanctified. But the deployment of sexuality has instead its focus on the quality of family life, and its construction of sexual relations is one which assesses not how acts relate to statutes but how the pleasures (and displeasures) of acts relate to the actor's constitution as a feeling subject (1981: 106). These knowledges and techniques of sexuality are (at least initially) gathered around and reliant upon the family, for they employ its structure to deploy their new ways of speaking about sex. The utility of parents, and especially mothers, in the disciplinary techniques of the deployment of sexuality, for example, was crucial to the creation of new approaches to sex because they became the 'agents' whose co-operation was required in order to root the new concerns and areas of knowledge. By encouraging parents to supervise such things as childhood masturbation or their own fertility, in light of knowledge about their respective potentially deleterious effects – both individual and at the level of the population (or even 'the race') – meant that through the vehicle of 'the family' these strategies created the conception of sexuality to which they seemed to respond. The family behaved as 'a crystal', seemingly the source of sexuality but actually reflecting and refracting the activity that the deployment of sexuality set in place all around it (1981: 111). Later, there would be greater institutional supports for such knowledge, with the focus remaining predominantly on 'the family', even as that notion was allowed to change its form. Thus the cornerstone of *both* the system of alliance and the deployment of sexuality is therefore 'the family', but differently constituted. For one it is a reproductive unity forming the infrastructure of a dependable society, for the other it is a sexualized and a dangerous domain.

If the family was therefore 'one of the most valuable tactical components of the deployment of sexuality' (1981: 111), sexuality is 'incestuous from the start', constituted through the practices of those around and 'within' the family. It is clear, then, why the spectre of incest haunts the period in which those ways of speaking about sexuality collectively termed 'the deployment of sexuality' predominate. The incitement of sexuality around the family sexualizes that domain. Nineteenth-century instructions to parents about 'parenting' might appear to entail demands to reduce or eliminate childhood sexuality, and one might add, twentieth-century instructions might seem to suggest the use of signals of acceptance of 'appropriate' exploration; but the *effect* of such instructions to parents was, according to Foucault, to problematize children's sexual activities:

> and this had the consequence of sexually exciting the bodies of children while at the same time fixing the parental gaze and vigilance on the perils of infantile

sexuality. The result was the sexualising of the infantile body, a sexualising of the relationship between parent and child, a sexualising of the familial domain. (1980: 120)

The incitement of sexuality around the family brought sex and the family so close that incest might well have been regarded as too horrifically logical; if the social reformers' accounts were to be believed, it was in danger of becoming the least remarkable sexual encounter. And yet because the deployment of sexuality requires the family, it also requires that the incest so incited *not* take place. Herein lies the point of tension: the activities of the deployment of sexuality threaten its own most precious site of activity, and relies as a consequence on the retention of the incest prohibition, a prohibition 'belonging' to an order of talking about sex that is a classic juridical rule of the system of alliance.

Foucault's suggestion that the 'affective intensification of familial space' overwhelms the system of alliance, and that the insistence on the universality and foundational quality of the incest prohibition might be explained as the 'response' to the activities of the deployment of sexuality (1981: 109) seems to paint a picture of two societal formations in conflict: the deployment of sexuality battles with the system of alliance it supersedes but cannot surrender. However, if the interpretation sketched in the section above is correct, one can develop the more convincing argument that the deployment of sexuality's tactics recreate *versions* of those aspects of the system of alliance that are the most politically useful or (even) necessary to them. This would make sense of Foucault's point that the 'comparative safety' of legal formulations are nostalgically sought after. The 'incest prohibition' as it has been articulated in the late nineteenth and twentieth centuries cannot be understood as the same 'incest prohibition' as it had taken its form as a juridical, predominantly religious, rule. Although the elements of sanction and the lines of licit and illicit remain within its contemporary inflection, they are now translated into bio-political mode. The psychoanalytic imperative to give voice to one's desires within the 'Oedipal triangle', for example, institutes the incest prohibition, now 'saturated with desire' (1981: 113) as the very key to understanding sexuality. In this sense, then, the deployment of sexuality remains 'coupled' to the system of alliance (1981: 113), and 'the family' remains the fraught vehicle and site of regulatory techniques.

Once it has been noted that, in contrast to a thesis about a complete change in the way in which power operates around sex, Foucault's thesis is that some aspects of government more akin to the system of alliance are held onto from 'within' the deployment of sexuality, it is clear why the spectre of incest is located exactly at that pivot:

> it is manifested as a thing that is strictly forbidden in the family insofar as the latter functions as a deployment of alliance; but it is also a thing that is continuously demanded in order for the family to be a hotbed of constant sexual incitement. (1981: 109)

III

The tension surrounding the family with the deployment of sexuality is erased from the particular and highly sociological reading of Foucault that enters debates on modernity and postmodernity. There are undoubtedly other routes by which to make the point, but the 'rise' of the incest prohibition in anthropological and sociological literature within a twentieth century in which the power-knowledge-pleasure discourses of the deployment of sexuality have come of age, expresses the fact that the system of alliance and, therefore, the seemingly archaic legal formulations, are not simply aspects that 'linger on' or are clung onto within a changing pattern of relations, but are part and parcel of *this* moment of government. In other words, a 'former' system of control around sexual practice is created and deployed within the current bio-political strategies. This fold of the old within the new renders misguided those attempts to incorporate Foucault's bio-political (or, as is more usual, disciplinary techniques) into debates on new epochs. For although Foucault's genealogies were histories of the present, such that he was commenting on contemporary processes, he did not have a conception of a totalized present. Charting historical processes of normalization was not, for Foucault, about charting the birth of a qualitatively different period of history so much as a tracing of the tactics and strategies that have informed specific present truths. Thus whilst in Foucault's earlier work the notion of 'episteme' contained a sense of historical discontinuities and change, the notion of a current qualitative and complete change inadequately depicts Foucault work, and imposing umbrella terms loses the dynamics of the historical processes he described. Extracting an argument about complete sea changes in his theses has to collapse details and smooth over the tensions in the historical processes and formations he described. But the crime is not mere inaccuracy, but a failure to elucidate the *politically useful* ambivalences and tensions contained in the *dispositifs* he made the objects of his (later) studies.

The quotation that heads this article, the lecture on governmentality (with family-as-model giving way to family-as-vehicle) and the contrasts that animate *Discipline and Punish* (such as the oft-quoted opening torture versus timetable contrast), are all examples of the ways in which Foucault presented his arguments as though he were focusing upon a stark and striking change. However, the tendency to enlarge these images into full-blown theories of stages, is to transpose Foucault on to the terrain of sociological theories of social change. The complexities of the argument about the role of the family in government exemplifies the sense in which his argumentation resists that attempt. In the section on 'right of death and power over life' that has been discussed above, he argues

> I do not mean to say that a substitution of sex for blood was by itself responsible for all the transformations that marked the threshold of our modernity. *It is not the soul of two civilizations or the organizing principle of two cultural forms that I am attempting to express.* (1981: 148, my emphasis)

This rebuttal of a potential reading of his argument is the one I am seeking to foreground here. It is an anticipation that he also addresses, perhaps more clearly, in the lecture on governmentality, where he states

> We must consequently see things not in terms of the substitution for a society of sovereignty a disciplinary society and the subsequent replacement of a disciplinary society for a governmental one; *in reality we have a triangle: sovereignty-discipline-government.* (1979: 19, my emphasis)

A certain reading of the thesis of *The History of Sexuality: An Introduction* has taken exactly this form of substitution; removing the sense in which the system of alliance continues to operate as a political tool amongst more recent modes of government. Or, to put the point differently, the system of alliance is *made operative* in the present, for the argument is that one has to take the discursivity of the notions of historical periods seriously. The way in which we articulate the present might be the better focus of study; the Foucauldian question is not so much 'What is this present and how is it different from the past?' as 'How are we invited to go about attempting to understand this present – and in doing so how do we create that present in opposition to a creation of the past (and/or of the future)?'

The insistence on the universality and foundational quality of 'the incest taboo' was not perpetuated by government officials but by social theorists, psychologists, anthropologists and so on, who were, to use Foucault's phrase, 'without hypocrisy'. To Minson's argument that 'the traditional family' is a 'retrospective construct originating in the family reform movement' (1985: 202), then, one can add that the eternal and universal incest-avoiding family is a retrospective and universalized concept of twentieth-century social science.[9] The extension and elevation of these theories has meant the institution of a truth which has dovetailed with political ends, for the retention of 'the family' as both necessary and as dangerous has become a useful tool within bio-political government of the population. This is, of course, the argument as Donzelot (1980) develops it; the state governs not against but *through* the family. The state has an interest in maintaining the desire on the part of 'the family' to be a self-sufficient and private site, and therefore in drawing support from the multitude of voices that continue in their various ways to posit the family as the only safe and stable place at which individuals can develop and 'be themselves', whilst at the same time the state can justify its right to enter that site through the equally multitudinous arguments that the family is the most dangerous and damaging place.

And yet in the present midst of such a scenario the incest taboo is in crisis, and in a way that it was not when Foucault was writing. It is being pushed and pulled in several directions by several groups with different interests – feminists, social workers, conservatives – as the new terminology of child sexual, familial, emotional and ritual abuse threatens the clarity anthropology and sociology had accorded it: the taboo, it is declared, is non-existent, one-sided, failing, irrelevant, too narrow, too weak, unfitting for the contemporary family. But this 'crisis' is not to be understood as simply a new epoch in which sexuality is no longer referred to rules but spirals throughout the social domain, the final triumph of the deployment of sexuality over the system of alliance. For however the status of 'the incest prohibition' is figured in these debates – it is rarely abandoned completely – sexuality and the family are ever a question of a morality of rules. The call for a solution is continually posed in terms of boundaries – age boundaries, 'appropriate boundaries' – by both 'progressive' and 'reactionary', so that even where 'the incest prohibition' is regarded as an outmoded term, sexuality and the family continue to be articulated as a question of knowing and following rules in the juridico-discursive form of licit/illicit. And where ethics is understood as a response to such rules, the breakdown of rules is understood as the impossibility of ethical behaviour, or rather, the impossibility of recognizing ethical behaviour. In a moment when that 'family', which remains an object of political knowledge and a vehicle of political strategies, is no longer 'the family' as understood in the biblical list of forbidden relatives, what could be more convenient for bio-politics than these 'confused' debates? On the one hand the non-specified nature of the rules is maintained; on the other, simultaneously and just as loudly, is their possibility and necessity. Thus the sexualization of the familial domain continues contemporaneously and in the same discursive space as, say, the pitiful pleas of those held up as victims of rigid politically correct systems; and thus the call for more detailed and better knowledge with experts to communicate that knowledge.

The argument begins perhaps to become too neat, and there is the danger that it becomes teleological. Bio-politics cannot be posited as an actor with intentions nor even can a strategy be understood *of its own accord* as the creator of the family on the basis that it can be shown to need or rely upon the family. Bio-politics is only the *name* the observer can give to the strategies which use the notion of the family as it is articulated from various enunciative points, and which use it not so much in its actuality as in its potentiality. The reiteration of that potential is part of a strategy which disciplines the ways in which people organize their lifes; the reiteration of its impossibility fuels the demand for better ways.

The question of ethics looms at the edge of this discussion. For if bio-political strategies make, and make use of, a situation in which the rule book is unclear whilst at the same time that rule book is sincerely sought after, the very notion of ethics as obedience to universal moral rules comes under scrutiny. But even if this is the mode in which a popular understanding of acting ethically is formulated, it is an impossible demand. As Bernauer has put it in a discussion of Foucault's ethics, in the search for a moral code 'like Oedipus, we become victims of our own self-knowledge' (1992: 268), articulating our 'selves' through the language and categories of bio-political knowledges. These knowledges offer up conceptions of the self that in their different ways direct our search to the attempt to think the 'unthought', and are, as such, profoundly 'modern' as the Foucault of *The Order of Things* described them (1970: 328). The ways in which our selves are articulated in the attempt to quieten the discursive noise that threatens our sense of even the possibility of a safe morality *in themselves* remove that possibility. 'For modern thought, no morality is possible' (Foucault, 1970: 328). The 'unthought' is lodged within and born alongside humanity: 'the shadow cast by man as he emerged in the field of knowledge; [and] . . . the blind stain by which it is possible to know him' (1970: 326). It is the 'space' which has been theorized as alienated humanity in Marx, the *an sich* in Hegel, the unconscious in Freud and so on: 'the whole of modern thought is imbued with the necessity of thinking the unthought' (1970: 327). (This is not the 'modernity' that is opposed to an historical period of 'postmodernity'; but it is a commentary on the history of a way of posing questions, a commentary on the genealogy of an attitude to one's present.)

If in this tangled present we seek the 'comparative safety' of legal formulations as moral codes, we seem obliged to seek them through bio-political knowledges. In the arena of sexual abuse, is this not the impetus behind those scientific articles that attempt to inform us *at what age* sexual intercourse with a family member is no longer psychologically disturbing, *to what extent* this particular familial relationship is more harmful than a relationship with an unrelated partner, how widespread, how long, etc., etc.? But, as Foucault puts it in *The History of Sexuality*, life 'constantly escapes' the techniques that govern and administer it (1981: 143) and this at their own admission. The promise and terror of the 'unthought' always guarantees that answers are never offered nor accepted as the ultimate answers. The dream of complete self-transparency and the incessant striving toward pure self-knowledge are modes of articulating the self which are fuelled by bio-political knowledge and which lead to the proliferation of such knowledges.

It is at this point, or at some point analagous to it, that Bernauer suggests Foucault's later work on sexuality becomes relevant. For in these works, he is attempting to think through an ethics which is not obliged to proceed via true knowledges [savoirs] of the self. Bernauer suggests that 'Foucault's effort to liberate ethical reflection from its modern dependence upon knowledge makes his work a counter-ethic to that "ethic of knowledge" [*connaissance*] which promised "truth only to the desire for truth itself and the power to think it"' (1992: 268). The notion of morality as obedience to truths formulated as rules was not the morality of Antiquity. In the second and third volumes of the history of sexuality his interest was in laying out an ethics of existence that did not engage in a search for truths on which to found rules, but was about a practice of one's own liberty:

> the will to be a moral subject and the search for an ethics of existence were, in Antiquity, mainly an attempt to affirm one's liberty and to give one's own life a certain form in which one would recognize oneself, be recognized by others, and which even posterity might take as an example. (1988: 49)

In *The Use of Pleasure* Foucault explored the classical Greek notion of *enkrateia*, the domination of oneself by oneself and the tensions that were associated with the ongoing effort involved in avoiding the shame of being defeated in that struggle (1986: 69). Such a morality may have obeyed certain canons, but the meticulous attention to monitoring one's self made central to that morality a notion of one's life 'as a work of art' (1988: 49). It is intriguing that Foucault explained his interest in these different ways of 'acting ethically' in relation to a perception of his present as a time in which morality as obedience to rules had disappeared:

> for a whole series of reasons, the idea of morality as obedience to a code of rules is now disappearing, has already disappeared. And to this absence of morality corresponds, must correspond, the search for an aesthetics of existence. (1988: 49)

In his attempt to think beyond a morality of rules of the form licit/illicit, Foucault's work suggests a mode by which one might begin to interrogate the power of that formulation. But how are Foucault's comments on ethics relevant to the situation sketched above, one in which the rule of the incest prohibition has passed from being a juridical statement with biblical weight to a truth 'invented' and kept alive by the social science of the twentieth century, a truth which has, moreover, been utilized by a bio-politics focused around the family? In some senses, Foucault's work on ethics seems to have left the complexity of the situation of bio-political government in order to detail some distant prior situation, but if his interview comments on that work are taken seriously, there must be some connection to a diagnosis of the present.

There is a temptation to suggest that the two arguments weave together into the following position: the incest prohibition is losing credibility because it belongs to a different way of speaking about sexuality; attempts to maintain the prohibition through bio-political knowledges are weak because they cannot yield stable commands of the licit/illicit form, and are suspect because they are used to maintain 'the family' which is an oppressive institution; as a consequence, those discussing sexual abuse must attempt to articulate a morality based not upon rules but upon an ethics of existence. This would be an ethics of liberty, and seems to be the position that Foucault and some others set out in a debate on adult–child sexuality (1988; see Bell, 1993, for comment). It would be a position that gives up the importance of the family and that is suspicious of formalized 'knowledges' of sexuality, making the negotiation of consent the sole important aspect of sexual encounters, not age nor sexual acts nor familial relation.

My hesitation is that, although there are arguably flickers of such an approach in feminist campaigns around sexual abuse,[10] the attempt to move Foucault's work into an imperative programme of action is fraught with difficulties. Having illuminated a relationship between political government, social scientific knowledge, the family and changes in the articulation of sexual behaviour, there is a sense that one must offer an escape route out of these connections. His comments on the disappearance of rules notwithstanding, it seems preferable to regard Foucault's contribution not as presenting a solution but as a muddying of the relationships as they are often posed (in social science, in feminism, in law, in anthropology and so on) *without* attempting to step 'outside' the present complexity in a search for a better way to proceed. The connections might be useful to a present bio-political situation, but this is not the same as arguing that the component parts are categorically bad and should henceforth be abandoned; the point is to disrupt the logical purity of those analyses which do promote themselves as solutions.[11] The concept of bio-politics is to remind us that the search for happiness through (scientific) truths may invite us into a constellation of power rather than a future utopia.

Notes

1. Foucault's comment is in an interview translated in Foucault (1980) as 'The confession of the flesh'.

2. As Donnelly notes (in Armstrong, 1992: 199).

3. What is new about this mode of government is not its 'form', that is, it is not the reflexively that it involves, as some have suggested. For people no doubt have responded to other forms of 'knowledge' reflexively prior to these developments. Rather it is the 'content' that is new; the contrast between life and death.

4. Lévi-Strauss refused to accept any of the arguments of his day which suggested that the genetic consequences of inbreeding in offspring were a conscious factor in promoting the prohibition. That is, that humankind noted that related couples were more likely to have children with malformations and therefore instituted the incest prohibition (a theory that is still held by some commentators, see, for example, Ember, 1983). He argued that this would require 'eugenic second sight' in individuals (1949/1969: 13).

5. In *Incest: The Nature and Origin of the Taboo* (1898/1963) Durkheim had argued that exogamy was the consequence of the totemism practised by traditional societies, and studied by several anthropologists at that time. Totemism was the precursor, Durkheim believed, of present religious practices of industrialized societies. It involves a group of people (a tribe) taking and worshipping a class of objects in the material world (such as an animal or a plant) as its totem. Each individual in the totemic group is regarded as having a special relationship to the totem, and the totem was thought to be of the same blood as those within the totem group. Durkheim's thesis was that the totem functioned to maintain group solidarity since the totem is the sign of the group, the group effectively worships themselves. (Later the totem would no longer take a physical shape: that is, it would become thought of as a non-corporeal God.) The totem was sacred, and there was a taboo on shedding the blood of the totem (animal or plant) or harming it in any way. By extension, Durkheim argues, there was a taboo on sexual intercourse with a woman of the same totem group because this would risk coming into contact with her blood which was the blood of the totem. (A later commentator argued that there was no need to pose the intermediary blood taboo; there was a general totem taboo – Lang, 1905, quoted in Freud, 1913/1983).

6. Psychoanalysis had shown, Freud argued, that the hypothesis of an innate incest prohibition was 'totally untenable' since the 'earliest sexual excitations of youthful human beings are invariably of an incestuous character' (1913/1983: 24). In the case of 'Little Hans' he saw parallels with anthropological work on totemism. Freud argued that Little Hans had displaced his ambivalent feelings toward his father – attraction/love, hate (because his father was a competitor for his mother's love) and fear (of his father leaving/dying and of castrating him) – onto horses. This resulted in a desire to see and be near horses, but also a tremendous fear of them, a situation which parallels the relationship of the totemic tribe to the totem which was both feared and revered.

7. Drawing on Freud, Parsons argued that the child is erotically attached to the mother and

gave the example of breast-feeding as the most obvious example of the child gaining oral-erotic gratification (as well as hunger gratification). A general attachment is necessary for socialization to take place; however, because the child has to be socialized and operate as an independent personality, the erotic attachment has to be repressed and the mother, as the primary socializing agent, must frustrate the chid's erotic attachment to her. Thus incestuous wishes, for Parsons as for Freud, are a necessary part of a child's development. The incest prohibition forces the child to repress and/or displace its incestuous wishes not only for the mother but also for the family in general, thereby avoiding the social disruption that the occurrence of incest would cause.

8. Foucault's mode of argument has been criticized by Bhabha (1991) who has pointed out the sense in which race is posited here as within a time-lag, and racism as 'historical retroversion'. Whilst the point that Bhabha is making in his paper is a sound one, if my reading of Foucault contained in the third section of this chapter is adopted, he misses his target in taking Foucault as the example, for Foucault is discussing the *creation* of the 'old' ways of speaking within the new as a political tactic of a present which it is not possible to periodize via historical temporalities. There is only a 'time lag' in Bhabha's sense if we read Foucault as attempting to make such a periodization.

9. Perhaps it is necessary to stress that this argument does not *necessarily* mean that 'the family' does not avoid incest and has not avoided incest – the issue is how we describe and understand that avoidance.

10. For feminism is the place where the incest prohibition has been most clearly attacked as a discursive problem. But more than this because there are definitions of sexual abuse such as that sometimes articulated within feminist discourse which links the definition to the sense, feeling, suspicion – none of these words is sufficient – of needing to keep the abuse secret. If he asks you (child) to keep it secret, if you (parent) feel you need to keep it secret, then it was, in all probability, sexual abuse. What is interesting about this is its potential refusal of juridical models and its attention to the sensations and one's sense of the self; it is internal, monitoring, reflexive, meditative. It is of a different register from the psychological models that attempt to approximate an idea of science and that are frequently deployed in the court room, social work, etc. But it is also a definition which one cannot immediately see as useful as a replacement definition in those settings.

11. Such as those who suggest less family, more family, new prohibitions, old prohibitions, etc.

References

Armstrong, T. (ed.) (1992) *Michel Foucault: Philosopher*. Brighton: Harvester Wheatsheaf.

Bell, V. (1993) *Interrogating Incest: Feminism, Foucault and the Law*. London: Routledge.

Bernauer, J. (1992) 'Beyond life and death', in T. Armstrong (ed.), *Michel Foucault: Philosopher*. Brighton: Harvester Wheatsheaf.

Bhabha, H. (1991) ' "Race", time and modernity', *Oxford Literary Review*, 13: 160.

Donzelot, J. (1980) *The Policing of Families*. London: Hutchinson.

Durkheim, E. (1898/1963) *Incest: The Nature and Origin of the Taboo*. New York: Lyle & Stuart.

Ember (1983) 'On the origin and extension of the incest taboo', in M. Ember and C.R. Ember (eds) *Marriage, Family and Kinship: Comparative Studies of Social Organization*. New-haven, Connecticut: Human Relations Area Files.

Foucault, M. (1970) *The Order of Things*. London: Tavistock.

Foucault, M. (1977) *Discipline and Punish*. Harmondsworth: Penguin.

Foucault, M. (1979) 'Governmentality', *Ideology and Consciousness*.

Foucault, M. (1980) *Power/Knowledge: Selected Interviews and Other Writings 1972–77*, edited by C. Gordon. Brighton: Harvester Press.

Foucault, M. (1981) *The History of Sexuality: An Introduction*. Harmondsworth: Penguin.

Foucault, M. (1986) *The Use of Pleasure: The History of Sexuality Volume Two*, trans. R. Hurley. Harmondsworth: Viking.

Foucault, M. (1988) *Politics, Philosophy, Culture: Interviews and Other Writings 1977–84*, edited by L. Kritzman. New York: Routledge.

Freud, S. (1913/1983) *Totem and Taboo*. London: Routledge & Kegan Paul.

Freud, S. (1930/1985) *Civilization and its Discontents*. Harmondsworth: Penguin.

Lévi-Strauss, C. (1949/1969) *The Elementary Structure of Kinship*. London: Eyre & Spottiswoode.

Minson, J. (1985) *Genealogies of Morals: Nietzsche, Foucault, Donzelot and the Eccentricity of Ethics*. Basingstoke: Macmillan.

Parsons, T. (1954) 'The incest taboo in relation to social structure and the socialisation of the child', *British Journal of Sociology*, 5.

14

THE BIRTH OF IDENTITY POLITICS IN THE 1960s: PSYCHOANALYSIS AND THE PUBLIC/PRIVATE DIVISION

Eli Zaretsky

Sparked by the African-American and other freedom struggles, and by the women's liberation movement, a new type of politics emerged in the United States, Canada and Europe in the 1960s. 'Multiculturalism', 'class, race and gender', 'identity politics' and the 'politics of difference' are among the concepts and slogans it has generated. Its defining idea is that no superordinate group appellation, such as 'man', 'humanity', 'the working class' or 'the American people', should be used without recognizing the *differences* that exist within the aggregate – such differences as male and female, abled and disabled, native born and immigrant, and so forth. The term 'identity' is associated with emphasis on the particular as opposed to the general. 'Difference' connotes the refusal to homogenize or aggregate.

The politics of identity and difference is generally associated with a rejection of universalizing philosophies descending from the Enlightenment, such as liberalism and Marxism. These philosophies recognized that the local or particular community of identity, such as lesbianism or the African-American community, could be the central point of identification for the self. But they insisted that in the political sphere the 'larger' interest – universal justice, class standpoint – prevail. The newer politics, by contrast, refused to subordinate group identity to a larger framework or relegate it to the 'private' sphere. Identity politics questioned not only Marxism but also the liberal emphasis on 'rights'. 'Black power' sought to surpass civil rights, women's liberation went beyond equal-rights feminism.

Accompanying the emergence of identity politics, national, religious, linguistic and racial conflicts intensified everywhere, especially after the collapse of the Soviet Union in 1989. Older ideas of a struggle between the 'people' and vested interests, oppressed and oppressor, socialism and capitalism gave way to a proliferation of claims based on national, racial or linguistic identity (Serbia, Croatia, the Northern League of Italy, Palestine, Rwanda, Azerbaijan, Armenia, the Kurds). The ending of the Cold War increased the number of movements that sought self-determination in the form of separate states (such as the Baltic states or the Ukraine), or in the form of confederations (as in Canada, Spain or the British Isles). In addition, it gave renewed impetus to movements that insisted on cultural separation or 'multiculturalism' while situating themselves within a universalistic polity. These latter movements are the main subject of this paper.

Though born at a moment of revolutionary upheaval, the politics of multiculturalism, identity and difference grew up when many other progressive forces were in retreat. By the 1980s, world capitalism was largely unrestrained as an economic system, as a form of state policy and as a set of values. Communism collapsed, and most ideas associated with it were discredited. The new politics, however, brought forth a whole new set of political initiatives, largely, though not entirely, focused on culture. In understanding these initiatives the most important question we want to ask is how to distinguish its progressive and reactionary forms. To ask that we must consider its relation to the progressive politics of the past.

The standard view is that the politics of difference is best understood as a repudiation of Marxism. Class, race and gender, understood as components of identity, replace a universal and structurally defined proletariat. This chapter is an argument against that view. I argue that there is an important line of continuity between Marxism and the politics of difference which can best be appreciated when a third term, psychoanalysis, is also considered. I shall make this argument in two parts.

First I shall show that in the period before the 1960s, when Marxism was the dominant critical outlook, there was a tacit division of labour between Marxism and psychoanalysis. This division was based on an assumed division between the 'public' and the 'private', where the 'public' was understood by Marxists as the capitalist economic realm and the 'private' was the realm of gender relations, sexuality and the family. But, in another sense, the 'private' realm also referred to ethnicity, culture and national, racial or religious identity. Psychoanalysis developed theories that applied to both meanings of the private realm. It did so by reducing both of them to the question of how individuals construct their identity – their identity as female or as homosexual, for example, but also their identity as Chinese or French or working class. Freud's most important insight was that the social determinations of identity, such as race, class and gender, have no effect until they have been remade by individuals in a way that is unique and personal to each of them. This insight could be, and was, used both critically and ideologically. I will trace these usages in Freud, and in later theorists in the Freudian tradition, such as Erik Erikson, who originated the analytic-theoretical use of the term 'identity', and Herbert Marcuse, who sought to develop the critical dimension of psychoanalysis. I will show that all efforts to develop the critical dimension in psychoanalysis had limited success so long as the division between the public and the private remained culturally hegemonic.

In the second part, I will show how a tendency to define identity in terms of culture challenged the hegemony of the public/private split. This shift reflects a change in the nature of capitalism as fundamental as the rise of the welfare state in the twentieth century. The crucial event was the coming together of two movements that had hitherto been separate: national movements based on race and ethnicity and movements based upon gender and sexuality. The link was the emphasis on identity. The result was a realignment or reorganization of the division between the public and the private, which brought the private sphere, the sphere of culture but also the sphere of the family, to the fore in a new way. What had previously been the taken-for-granted background of political life, the process of identity creation, now became foreground and was politicized.

The amalgamation of the themes of gender and sexuality with those of nationhood had explosive power. After 1968, it was as if what had heretofore been private became public. The issues that Freud had described as intrapsychic and familial were acted out on a social scale and on a political stage. The actors, however, were no longer individuals but sharply defined identity-based groupings whose relations to one another became increasingly problematic.

The division between the public and the private

The liberal conception of politics that has been hegemonic in the West since the Enlightenment was based on the assumption of a division between the public and the private. According to this assumption, individuals' private ties, beliefs and values cannot be the basis of public life. In public or political life, so the theory held, we are dealing with free, autonomous, rational, self-determining individuals, individuals who are able to stand at some distance from their own immediate situation. The organizing principle of public life is justice, as represented by such principles as rights, due process and equality before the law. These principles apply to individuals of any culture, faith or belief. Cultural background or religious belief is a 'private' matter. Politics is the realm of the 'right', not the good. Politics respects the autonomy of the 'private' sphere by standing at a distance from it.

The Marxist criticism of the liberal distinction between the public and the private focused on the relation between the *bourgeois* and the *citoyen*. Marx argued that the formal equality of the political sphere belied the social inequality, the relations of domination and subordination, that organized economic life. Marx's critique of liberal politics was a logical extension of his critique of capitalism, namely that the formal equality of the market, in which individuals exchanged the products of their labour with one another according to their value, was belied by the reality of the sphere of production, in which *surplus* value was appropriated. Equality was real but abstract. The *citoyen* was always already a *bourgeois* or *prolétaire*.

However, there were two other aspects of the public/private division that Marxism did not challenge. The first was the distinction between *ethnos* and *demos*, where *ethnos* refers to national or cultural identity and *demos* refers to the liberal conception of the political sphere. In the nineteenth century, Marxists judged national questions by whether they served the interests of the 'international working class'. Thus Poland was supported against Russia and Ireland against England. In the twentieth century, 'nation' was frequently posed against 'class' in Western Europe, while the theory of imperialism permitted Marxists to integrate Communist and nationalist themes in Cuba, Vietnam and China. In neither case, though, was the need to be part of a particular group, and the demand that that group be recognized in its particularity, acknowledged as an irreducible need in its own right.

In addition, Marxism failed to problematize another version of the public/private division, that between the 'economic' sphere and the family (Zaretsky, 1976). This division, like the distinction between *bourgeois* and *citoyen* arose from the contradictory character of capitalist society. Although the family is a key site of socially necessary labour, it is not a site in which surplus value is produced and appropriated. In pre-industrial societies, the 'economic' role of the family was clear. But in the course of *capitalist* industrialization, economic activity was removed from the home. Marxists focused on the 'official' economy, the sphere in which value was produced and exchanged, and lost sight of the place of the family in the system of production. For Marxists the 'public' sphere was the sphere of the economy, and of politics insofar as politics was tied to economics. As a result, questions of identity and personal life, insofar as they were questions of sexuality and gender, were left out of Marxism.

In this context, the privileged discourse of group identity, as of personal identity, became psychoanalysis. From the psychoanalytic perspective, questions of group and national identity are inseparable from questions of family, sexuality and gender. 'Identity' is the term that brings the two discourses together.[1]

Psychoanalysis became important to Western thought around the same time that Marxism began to become obsolescent, during the shift from competitive to corporate capitalism which occurred in the early twentieth century. Still earlier, from the beginnings of industrialization, there had been a tendency for working-class men and women to draw their identity from cultural images rather than from workplace experience. Nineteenth-century workers, especially young workers, saw themselves as working class, but many were still more emphatic in defining themselves through dress, slang, sexual stance, music and leisure time activities (Stansell, 1987: 91) Many of those with stigmatized identities such as African-Americans, gay men, Asians or immigrants, also considered their class position less important than race or sexual orientation as a component of identity. For nineteenth-century white women, the waged workplace was a temporary arena of action; many of them, too, defined their identities in such terms as 'daughter', 'wife', 'mother' and 'woman'.

Three developments of the early twentieth century encouraged the tendency to define identity in cultural terms and to marginalize workplace experience. First, there was a vastly increased role assigned to consciousness, knowledge and science, along with a vast increase in the productive power of labour. This encouraged a sense that the economic sphere was limited and could be brought within human control. Second, there was a shift from an emphasis on saving, thrift and sacrifice to an emphasis on expanding consumption. Mass consumption and mass culture emerged as basic spheres for the formation of personal identity. Finally, there was a shift from a conflict model of society centred on the capital/labour relation to a co-operation model, associated in the United States with the term 'progressive era'. This shift, taken along with the emergence of mass culture, encouraged the emergence of a new imaginary, focused on transcending conflict, both personal and social, through mental means.

Nineteenth-century culture or 'Victorianism' had been organized around the dichotomy between public and private – work and family. In the early twentieth century this dichotomy remained important but the private sphere of the family was increasingly subsumed in a larger context of 'personal life' – forms of life which saw themselves as cut off from and no longer defined by the sphere of production. Adolescence, youth and the issues important to youth, especially sexuality and identity, emerged as new, and by the 1920s, dominant concerns. Familial repressiveness, which had served a function in an era of scarcity and competition, seemed antiquated and idiosyncratic. Gender distinction, which for the Victorians had meant distinctive male and female traits, expectations, physiologies, sexualities and social spaces (the public and the private) gave way to 'similarity' except for one, new, all-important difference: sexual object-choice.

The publication of *The Interpretation of Dreams* in 1899 profoundly altered the modern understanding of identity. There Freud demonstrated that everything social and interpersonal dissolves and is remade within individuals to take a personal form. That is, we give the social codes that make us white or black, English or French, working class or bourgeois, a personal meaning before they become effective. In Freud's theory, this was most importantly the case with gender. Whereas nineteenth-century psychologies alternated between emphasizing heredity and emphasizing the environment, Freud's theories, though leaving room for constitutional and environmental factors, emphasized motivation. Motivation tended to derive from Freud's extended conception of sexuality, what he called each person's 'special individuality in the exercise of the capacity to love' (Freud, 1912). On the basis of a person's internal needs, social messages could be restructured in ways entirely unintended by their senders.

Given Freud's account of the dissolution of external social codes and their reformulation as internal or psychological, it is significant that he did not use the term 'identity'. Freud's term was 'identification'. He began to use this term, along with the closely related term 'narcissism', in his attempts to rebut the essentially affirmative psychologies of the self propounded by Alfred Adler and Carl Jung. In contrast to Freud, these psychologists sought to bolster defective images of the self, rather than to question apparently acceptable ones. In Freud's theory, identification always involved *desexualization*. The 'ego', he speculated, develops through inducing the 'id' to give up its desire for the parents. It does so by *identifying* with the parents, saying, in effect, to the 'id': 'Look, you can love me too – I am so like the object.' Identification establishes the 'self-respect' from which repression proceeds: parental identifications are the kernel of the ego-ideal from which the superego will develop.

Identification is also the means by which groups form. In 'On narcissism', Freud wrote that the ego-ideal also 'has a social side; it is . . . the common ideal of a family, a class or a nation'. 'That which [the individual] projects ahead of him [sic] as his ideal is merely his substitute for . . . the time when he was his own ideal' (Freud, 1914/1955: vol. 14, 88, 91, 95–7). In *Group Psychology and the Analysis of the Ego*, Freud defined a group as 'a number of individuals who have put one and the same object in the place of their ego-ideal and have consequently identified themselves with one another' (Freud, 1921/1955: vol. 18, 116). The fact that each member of the group substitutes an idealized image for their own defective ego-ideal sustains them in a common ideology of 'self-mastery'. 'Each individual . . . feels within himself the strength of the whole group' (Abraham, 1926). The power of the leader comes from the fact that 'his' suggestions seem to come from within the individual members. *Civilization and its Discontents* (1930/1955) elaborated. Restricting aggression within such groups as nations, religions or political movements raises the self-esteem of its members. It is always possible to bind together 'people in love', Freud wrote, 'so long as there are other people left over to receive the manifestations of their aggressiveness' (Freud, 1930/1955: vol. 21, 114–16).

Thus, Freud's concept of identification was a critical one. The construction of both personal and group identity, for Freud, invariably contained a defensive moment. In contrast to contemporary post-structuralist interpretations of Freud, such as those of Elizabeth Grosz (1990) and Eugene Holland (1993), Freud did not value the dissolution of identity over its construction. He did, however, see identification as partial and tentative and, in today's language, used his understanding of its constructed nature to limit and problematize identity claims.

The decline of Freud's critical perspective in the course of the history of psychoanalysis can be seen in Erik Erikson's term 'identity'. Erikson originated the psychoanalytic use of the term in the United States in the 1940s, a place and time which represented the fulfilment of the promise unleashed by early twentieth-century mass production. On one hand, 'Keynesianism', the release of mass consumption, the beginnings of the 'baby boom', the expansion of higher education, science and technology all seemed to presage a society moving beyond the limits imposed by relations of production. On the other hand, the effort to maintain those relations produced the repressive, Cold War focus on identity.

Erikson's purpose was to get beyond what he regarded as Freud's intrapsychic focus. Erikson defined identity as 'the ability to maintain inner sameness and continuity', and explained it as the outcome of 'the selective repudiation and mutual assimilation of childhood identifications, and their absorption in a new configuration'. Identity, he explained, was the product of an interaction between self and society. Rather than societal norms being grafted upon the individual as a vulgar Marxist or 'social control' perspective might suggest, Erikson argued that the society influenced individuals primarily by making available to them the resources by which they solve internal, developmental tasks (Erikson, 1956). Such resources are essentially cultural and include such institutions as religion, economics and politics, all understood as spheres of identity creation.

Erikson's goals were cultural and political rather than technically analytical. The problem of identity, he held, was as strategic to his time as sexuality was to Freud's. Erikson situated the problem in relation to a particular group, youth, and a particular stage of the life cycle, adolescence. Youth is characterized by the fact that it is *not* defined by its place in the system of production. Erikson developed such concepts as 'moratorium', aimed at elucidating the freedom individuals have in the formulation of their identities. He also grasped the group meaning of identity. He saw identity as a special problem in America due to its disparate class and racial composition, its immigrants and native Americans. He wrote of the difficulty in sustaining 'ego-ideals' in a land 'characterised by expanding identifications and by great fears of losing hard-won identities' (Erikson, 1964: 647; 1950: 282–3, 412–13).[2] Writing at a time when key terms included 'alienation', 'anxiety', 'stranger', 'authenticity' and the 'Invisible Man', Erikson's broadest influence was on the theory of mass society and the theme of the threat to individual identity that underlay that theory.

The impact of Erikson's writing, however, was to encourage the Cold War focus on primary institutions such as the family, schools and health. In part this was because he presupposed a holistic view of culture that denied the antagonistic character of society. In the period in which he wrote, psychoanalysis had largely gained control of a vast network of satellite institutions in such fields as counselling, testing, welfare, education, personnel, law (especially new branches such as juvenile and domestic relations) (Peter Berger, 1965: 27–8). The 'psychoanalytic tradition of moral safeguarding' (Lewes, 1988: 137) that developed encouraged a monolithic and repressive conception of a single normative or 'correct' identity. Analysts argued that 'every homosexual is a latent heterosexual' (Rado, 1940), that 'the anatomical equipment of the female child puts her at a disadvantage in relation to the possessor of the phallus' (Young-Bruehl, 1988: 428–9) and that Kinsey's 'erroneous conclusion in regard to homosexuality' will be 'used against the United States abroad, stigmatizing the nation as a whole in a whisper campaign' (Bayer, 1981: 28, 30; Bergler, 1954). As for politics, according to Norman Podhoretz (1979: 48), Freud supplied 'the most persuasive and authoritative theoretical foundation for believing that . . . human nature was fixed and given and not, as the 'liberal imagination' would have it, infinitely malleable'.

During the years in which psychoanalysis was greatly influential, there was also an attempt to 'synthesize' Marx and Freud. Probably the most important work in this tradition, Herbert Marcuse's (1955) *Eros and Civilization*, was contemporary with Erikson. In contrast to Erikson, Marcuse saw modern mass culture as an administered system of domination, but unlike Erikson, Marcuse was not able to formulate the concept of identity. In *Eros and Civilization* we can see both the strengths and the limitations of twentieth-century Marxism.

Whereas earlier analytic radicals, especially Wilhelm Reich, understood 'sexuality' as a kind of suppressed force which, once released, could threaten social domination, Marcuse criticized Reich for viewing sexuality as a 'panacea' and turned instead to the concept of narcissism (Marcuse, 1955: 21). His vision was based on his awareness of the productive potential of advanced capitalism. According to Marcuse, insofar as Freud suggested that the ego was involved in a project of mastery, control and acquisition, this was a later, defensive development. This aspect of the ego, Marcuse argued, was 'antagonistic to those faculties and attitudes which are receptive rather than productive, which tend toward gratification rather than transcendence' (1955: 101). The foundation of the self, Marcuse insisted, was an originary narcissism which survives as 'the oceanic feeling'. Although often misunderstood as egotistic withdrawal from reality, Marcuse maintained, this feeling constitutes 'a fundamental relatedness to reality [a] libidinal cathexis of the objective world'.

Whether or not Marcuse's reading of Freud was accurate is not so important as the fact that by 1955 a conception of human nature had begun to develop within Freudo-Marxism that shared important ideas with subsequent feminist, gay liberation and ecology movements: a critique of instrumental rationality, a desire for a new connectedness with nature, a redefinition of sexuality beyond its genital, heterosexual limits, a rejection of the centrality of the industrial working class and its values, and a search for new agents of change. In spite of the conservatism of institutional psychoanalysis, Marcuse grasped that Freud had as much or more to offer the critique of late capitalism as Marx. Just as Norman O. Brown, who read Freud at Marcuse's suggestion, wrote of 'the superannuation of the political categories' of the 1930s, so Marcuse criticized the Marxist assumption of a 'nature-dominating, rational ego' (Brown, 1959: ix). The Marxist elevation of labour, Max Horkheimer had already written, made Marxism into an 'ascetic ideology' which turned socialists 'into carriers of capitalist propaganda' (Jay, 1973: 57, 129).

But neither Marcuse, nor any other critical thinker of the period, was able to appreciate the discovery of identity and difference that was about to emerge. Without this appreciation, Marcuse was limited to seeing the relation between the individual and the culture in either harmonious or antagonistic terms. A whole new understanding of culture – as a set of institutions and practices, rather than as a 'reflection' of society – intervened before Marcuse's insights could be used.

The politics of identity and difference

The politics of identity and difference that began in the late 1960s, like the emergence of personal life in the early twentieth century, resulted from a global shift in the character of capitalism. In 1843, Marx defined critical theory as 'the self-clarification of the wishes and struggles of the age' (quoted in Fraser, 1989: 113). The shift in the character of capitalism has brought about an epoch whose wishes and struggles are dominated by issues of identity, gender and nationality: in a word, by issues of difference.

'Difference' emerged socially through two related processes: the development of a diversified proletariat and the globalization of capital. Of course the industrial proletariat was only putatively homogeneous. It was divided through factors such as race, skill, seniority, ethnicity and gender. However, the relative weight and centrality of large-scale industry gave apparent plausibility to the Marxist claim that these divisions were 'secondary contradictions' or 'contradictions among the people'. Since the Second World War, however, 'post-industrialism', the rise of service and part-time work, along with the increasing significance of educated labour, gave industry far less weight in a complex technical and social division of labour.

Accompanying this shift was the globalization of capital. After the Second World War, the old colonial system, which fostered nationalism in both the metropole and the colonies, gave way first to decolonization and then to a new world system characterized by large-scale and continuous emigration flows, subaltern and transient cultures, and stateless corporations as well as peoples. Globalization, like 'post-industrialism', encouraged the entry of previously marginal groups – women, racial minorities and new immigrants, previously peripheral nations – into the metropolitan labour force. Both tendencies came together in the 1980s, as services supplanted goods production as the driving force of internationalization.

The diversification and the decentralization that accompanied the global division of labour made the Marxist assumption of working-class homogeneity untenable and brought the category of difference to the fore. Technological changes, along with the increased significance of knowledge, information and communication in production, gave the category of difference a new sphere in which to operate. This was the sphere of culture.

In the advanced capitalist countries in the late twentieth century, the role of culture (including the media, advertising, tourism, education, the 'public sphere', psychotherapy, music, leisure, sports) changed exponentially so that the culture could be said to help organize social life, rather than merely representing it. Political parties and other modes of participation that had mediated between the liberal public realm and the private declined in significance. TV and the 'newer' media, such as talk shows and direct mailing, became more important. Commodity culture, 'civil society' and the media became increasingly important as the terrain of identity creation.

As the cultural sphere emerged with a new kind of force and autonomy, the meaning of the division between the public and the private changed.

Both Marxist and Freudian theories, because they presupposed that division, treated culture as if it had no independent existence but instead functioned as a 'mask' covering the truths of the public (Marxist) or private (Freudian) realm. These theories could now be seen as reductionist because the two spheres – 'public' and 'private' – that they pretended to analyse, were now dissolving into a third, that of culture. Hence the host of new theoretical paradigms, discourse analysis, cultural studies, deconstruction, postmodernism, and new theorists, such as Michel Foucault, who rejected the earlier Marxo-Freudian tradition, and sought to replace it.

Changes in capitalism had already thrown into question the social democratic politics of the trade union movement and of Western Marxism: the politics of the 'family wage' which had been the mediation between the public and the private. Globalization further eroded the social democratic idea that the nation-state could serve as a counterweight to the private economy. The New Left had recognized the obsolescence of the older politics but had been unable to generate an alternative. Nonetheless, the powerful 'surrealist' and counter-cultural elements of the 1960s began the process of externalizing what had earlier been private and repressed: sexuality, family, gender. Hence their enormous performative dimension. As the identity fragments of the 1970s and 1980s crystallized, the tendency toward the construction of politicized group identities around formerly 'private' characteristics accelerated.

The crucial change occurred with the convergence of movements defined by national or ethnic identity, such as the Black Power movements, the Brown Berets, the Young Lords, AIM (the American Indian Movement), with movements concerned with the politics of 'personal' life, especially the women's and gay movements. For both types of movement, an entrenched imaginary centred on a synechdocal white, male, Western, heterosexual, ethno- and androcentric identity functioned as part of a hegemonic logic of domination. Both sought to reclaim stigmatized identities, to revalue the devalued pole of dichotomized hierarchies such as white/black, male/female or straight/queer. But a special symbiosis occurred when 'ethnicity', that is, cultural and national identity within a multicultural framework, became the model for women's and gay politics (Fraser, manuscript). This brought together two different types of demand – recognition of ethnic or national particularities in the cultural sphere and liberation of suppressed wishes in the private. The result was a uniquely new politics.

The birth of identity politics began with an intense rejection of psycho-analysis, which gay activists termed in the early 1970s the 'enemy incarnate' (Bayer, 1981: 105). The 1973 American Psychiatric Association meetings which dropped the classification of homosexuality as a disease were filled with gay activists shouting such remarks as 'Where did you take your residency, Auschwitz?' When the heroine in Erica Jong's *Fear of Flying*, published in the same year, left her analyst, she told him:

> Don't you see that men have *always* defined femininity as a means of keeping women in line? Why should I listen to *you* about what it means to be a woman.

Are you a woman? Why shouldn't I listen to myself for once? And to other women? (Jong, 1973: 20–2)[3]

Dramatic incidents such as these effectively obscured an earlier history in which psychoanalysis had already been configured as a theory of oppressed national, racial or ethnic groups. This reconfiguration began in the 1950s and replaced the earlier Freudian emphasis on sexuality with an emphasis on self-esteem. In this regard it resembled Erikson's contemporaneous introduction of the concept 'identity' but, unlike Erikson, it conceptualized society as a sphere of domination.

The key theory developed in France where the main issue for the left was decolonization. Several theorists, especially Octave Mannoni and Frantz Fanon, combined existentialism, with its agonistic conception of the relation of self and other, and psychoanalysis, with its theory of transference, to reconceptualize the colonist/colonial relation. The question that concerned both of them was how to free a national group from the psychological effects of a previous situation of subordination.

Octave Mannoni's *Prospero and Caliban* (1990) prefigured the shift from economics to culture. Mannoni argued that the key issue raised by colonialism was not merely economic inequality but rather how economic inequality was 'embodied in struggles for prestige, in alienation, in bargaining positions and debt of gratitude, and in the invention of new myths and the creation of new personality types'. The inability of the French Communists to think at this level, Mannoni argued, meant they played little role in French decolonization (Mannoni, 1990: 8, 46–7, 63). Fanon, Mannoni's critic, went further. Recognition, he argued, could not be 'given', but had to be taken, violently, as the prelude to genuine democratization. So devastating was the colonial assault on the colonial's self-esteem, insisted Fanon (1986), that only collective violence could recuperate the damage.

When American feminists, two decades later, began to re-examine the relevance of psychoanalysis after their initial rejection of it, their reading of it was similar to that of Mannoni and Fanon. Juliet Mitchell's *Psychoanalysis and Feminism* (1974) was the first work of the period to redirect feminists' attention to psychoanalysis. But because Mitchell's book defended Freud's original theory, even while reinterpreting it as a theory of women's subordination under patriarchy, it was received with a great deal of ambivalence by its intended audience.

Far more popular, at least at first, was Nancy Chodorow's *The Reproduction of Mothering* (1978). Chodorow took the book's key term, 'gender identity', from Robert Stoller's *Sex and Gender* (1968) where it referred to the cognitive sense of femaleness or maleness. But Chodorow transformed Stoller's usage in order to characterize men and women in terms of different psychic structure, values and orientations to the world – that is, as identities. *The Reproduction of Mothering* restated Freud's psychology in gynocentric and matricentric terms aimed at raising women's self-esteem as a male-centred discourse had lowered it. Females, Chodorow argued, achieve 'an unambiguous and unquestioned gender identity' while the psychology of men depended upon an endless series of displacements and divisions (Chodorow, 1978: 142, 158, 163, 166–70, 214; Stoller, 1968).

The new post-1968 focus on identity and difference supplied the social basis Marcuse's utopian *Eros and Civilization* had lacked. Marcuse's work was crucial to Dennis Altman's early writings on gay identity which argued that 'procreative sexuality' buttressed Marcuse's 'performance principle' and that the 'perversions' were actually incipient rebellions. Altman also captured the main thrust of the new politics by describing the linguistic shift from the use of 'homosexual' as an adjective – implying there is a 'neutral' 'person' who had a particular sexual orientation – to its use as a noun, implying that being gay was constitutive of identity. For several reasons, gay theorists played a leading role in the emergence of identity politics.

As Fanon went beyond Mannoni, so Adrienne Rich and other advocates of radical lesbianism went beyond early 1970s feminism. Whereas Chodorow defined women in relation to the men who oppress them, and in that sense as part of a totality, radical lesbians sought to assert women's identity without regard to men, as suggested by the phrase 'the woman-identified-woman'. While 'freedom' or 'tolerance' for lesbians had been an important feminist demand, Adrienne Rich's 'Compulsory heterosexuality' (1980), perhaps the key text in developing a radical lesbian perspective, was directed against works such as Chodorow's that linked women's identity to heterosexual marriage and childrearing. Rich argued that support for lesbianism as a 'sexual preference' was merely liberal, a matter of individual rights. Lesbianism, she maintained, is not a matter of sexual preference any more than race is a matter of skin colour. In both cases what is at stake is *identity*. In contrast to the psychoanalytic emphasis on sexuality, which reflected its heavy freighting of the private sphere, Rich and others saw lesbianism as membership in a community based on shared experiences, that is, on identification. Thus for Blanche Cook, lesbians are 'women who love women, who choose women to nurture. . . . Lesbians cannot be defined simply as women who practice certain physical rites together' (quoted in Phelan, 1989: 73–4).

Although Rich posed her politics against Chodorow's, she was actually bringing to the surface the identity component in Chodorow's work. The break in the early 1970s between women's liberation and the New Left has generally been explained as the result of the sexism of New Left men, but 1970s feminism was no mere reaction. Radical lesbianism and cultural feminism – women's identity politics – constituted the emotional basis of much of 1970s feminism, even when it was rejected in the realm of politics and theory. Chodorow, after all, had defined men and women as identity groups and minimized the element of sexuality in psychoanalysis before Rich wrote. Chodorow had also framed her theory in terms of the idea that society had 'dual systems' – economics and sex-gender. This theory is best understood as a compromise formation, the last version of the Marxo-Freudian, public/private critical politics that existed before its collapse.

The politics that has prevailed since the 1970s has pivoted on the question of how to define identity. Under the rubric of 'anti-essentialism', a series of theorists has argued that no-one can be represented by a single identity (Spelman, 1986). The break-up of identity communities, such as that of 'women' in the 1970s, at first took place in the name of opposing identity formulations such as 'lesbian' or 'women of colour'. But the break-up of identity groups also occurred because these groups sometimes imposed conceptions of identity as oppressive as those against which the groups had originally protested.

At that juncture, 'the linguistic turn' – the idea that language shapes and does not merely represent reality – led to the stress on ambiguity and indeterminacy. Advocates of 'difference' urged a politics aimed less at establishing viable identities than at destabilizing identity claims, a politics that eschewed such terms as groups and rights in favour of such terms as places, spaces, alterity and subject positions, a politics that aimed to operate on the margins of the society and in the interstices of the culture rather than at society's supposed centre. In contrast to earlier Hegelian/Marxist theorists, for whom the crucial task was mediation, some theorists of 'non-identity' of the 1970s and 1980s, such as Liz Grosz, sought to describe what Deleuze and Guattari have called 'fragments that are related to one another only in that each of them is different, without having recourse to any sort of original or subsequent totality' (Deleuze and Guattari, 1983: 42). Others, however, such as Miriam Hansen, urged a language of community that knew 'itself as rhetoric, as a trope of impossible authenticity' and which therefore could admit 'difference and differentiation within its own borders' (Hansen, 1993).[4]

But debates concerning identity and difference, essentialism and social constructionism, the politics of cultural studies and the politics of decon-struction, though important are nonetheless *internal* to the politics that characterize our time. They presuppose identity as the central content of politics and do not historicize it. Therefore, these debates do not provide a means to situate and evaluate the politics of the present, as only an historical perspective can.

Conclusion

From this survey we conclude that the standard view, according to which the politics of identity and difference is best understood as a repudiation of Marxism, is wrong. During the epoch when Marxism was hegemonic over the Western left, psychoanalysis served as a locus for questions of group and individual identity elided by Marxism. As a result, an important line of continuity between Marxism and the politics of identity can be appreciated when the history of psychoanalysis is brought into relation with the transition from Marxism to identity politics.

We have seen that identity politics resulted from the convergence of two types of social demands avoided or minimized by classical Marxism: ethnic or racially based movements that have demanded *recognition*, especially in the sphere of culture, and movements concerned with gender and sexuality that have demanded *liberation* and that have been based on the sphere of personal life. Both of these types of demands were anticipated within psychoanalysis but were also avoided and minimized.

We have also seen that questions of personal identity, gender and sexuality were defined in terms of the conventional understandings of the public and the private. They were cast as private and, ultimately, intra-psychic. The content of psychoanalysis, Freud wrote, is 'what is most intimate in mental life, everything that a socially independent person must conceal' (Freud, 1966: 18). Analysis thus became a major source of support for the characteristically modernist idea that the basis of life is to be found in the private sphere and that 'social' was secondary, derived and essentially false. Questions of group identity were equally minimized. An article from the 1950s explained that in the analytic setting cultural difference should be minimized by restricting it to 'reality involvements and ego interests', a minor sphere according to the authors (Hartmann et al., 1951: 23, 31).[5]

The emergence of the politics of identity, difference and multiculturalism made it possible for concerns that had previously been considered 'private', individual or intrapsychic to present themselves as 'public'. The new politics is based on the new role of culture and the decline of the salience of the earlier division between the public and the private. This politics reflects the fact that in modern society identity is created, not given, and that culture is the sphere of identity creation. It has now become possible to see that many of the issues of modern society were essentially issues of identity.

The crucial characteristic of identity thinking, which bore the mark of its lineage within analysis, was the focus on motivation or 'agency'. A recent example is David R. Roediger's *The Wages of Whiteness* (1991). Roediger addresses a classic problem, unsolvable in the epoch in which Marxism dominated critical theory: the problem of white workers' racism. Marxists, of necessity, explained workers' racism in reductive terms: racial prejudice was a mask for economic advantage. Those who opposed this reductionism, such as W.E.B. DuBois, argued that racial prejudice was an 'independent' factor, but it then became unclear why whites adopted it. Roediger solved this problem by pointing to 'whiteness' as an essential component of white workers' identity. Workers manoeuvred for economic position in the course of the same process in which they constructed their personal and group identity. 'Whiteness' was as important to their identity as their class and gender.

The value of situating the politics of identity historically, is in bringing out its continuity with the older politics of Marxism and Marxo-Freudianism or critical theory. This returns us to our original question: how are we to distinguish progressive from reactionary forms of identity politics? The argument presented here does not supply a full or definitive answer to this question but it does suggest a part of the story.

One distinguishing mark of progressive identity politics today lies in the ability to be aware of one's own history, and to use that history self-critically. Invariably that history would lead the identity impulse simultaneously in two different directions. First, it would lead outward, to see the ties to other identities, other forms of difference and to building larger and more comprehensive forms of solidarity but in forms that respect difference. This is the legacy of a Marxism that has not been abstractly negated but has been genuinely transcended, *aufgehoben*.

But second, such a history would also lead identity politics in another direction, inward, to the ultimately irreducible if indefinable sphere of the individual, from whose needs all forms of identity are constructed. This is the legacy of psychoanalysis, which, like Marxism, has not lost its relevance.

Notes

1. For a geneaology of the term 'identity' within psychoanalysis see Zaretsky (1994).
2. 'We live in a country', Erikson wrote, 'which attempts to make a superidentity out of all the identities imported by its constituent immigrants' (1950: 412–13).
3. The passage continues: 'And then: As in a dream (I never would have believed myself capable of it) I got up from the couch (how many years had I been lying there?) picked up my pocketbook, and walked . . . out. . . . No more arguing with Kolner like a movement leader! I was free!'
4. Hansen continues: 'The admission of discursive struggle into the process of subordinate groups . . . is the condition of the possibility of different counter publics to overlap and form alliances'.
5. 'Analytic' knowledge, they write, 'tends to *enlarge* the cultural area or the number of groups to which one feels responsible. . . . To interpret one's own actions predominantly in terms of national character seems to contradict the lessons implicit in psychoanalytic psychology'.

References

Abraham, Karl (1926) 'Psychoanalytic notes on Coué's system of self-mastery', *International Journal of Psychoanalysis*, 7.
Bayer, Ronald (1981) *Homosexuality and American Psychiatry: The Politics of Diagnosis*. New York: Basic Books.
Berger, Peter (1965) 'Towards a sociological understanding of psychoanalysis', *Social Research*, 32.
Bergler, E. (1954) 'Homosexuality and the Kinsey Report', in A. Krich (ed.), *The Homosexuals as Seen by Themselves and 30 Authorities*. New York: Citadel Press.
Brown, Norman O. (1959) *Life against Death*. Middletown, CT: Wesleyan University Press.
Chodorow, Nancy (1978) *The Reproduction of Mothering*. Berkeley, CA: University of California Press.
Deleuze, Gilles and Guattari, Felix (1983) *Anti-Oedipus: Capitalism and Schizophrenia*. Minneapolis: University of Minnesota Press.
Erikson, Erik (1950) *Childhood and Society*. New York: Norton.
Erikson, Erik (1956) 'The problem of ego identity', *Journal of the American Psychoanalytic Association*, 4.
Erikson, Erik (1964) 'A memorandum on identity and negro youth', in Stephen Schlein (ed.), *A Way of Looking at Things: Selected Papers from 1930–1980*. New York: Norton.

Fanon, F. (1986) *Black Skin, White Masks*. London: Pluto Press.

Fraser, Nancy (1989) 'What is critical about critical theory?', *Unruly Practices: Power, Discourse, and Gender in Contemporary Social Theory*. Minneapolis: University of Minnesota Press.

Fraser, Nancy, 'From Redistribution to Recognition', unpublished manuscript.

Freud, Sigmund (1955) *The Standard Edition of the Complete Psychological Works of Sigmund Freud*, translated from the German under the general editorship of James Strachey, in collaboration with Anna Freud, assisted by Alix Strachey and Alan Tyson. New York: International Universities Press.

Freud, Sigmund (1966) *Complete Introductory Lectures*. New York: Norton.

Grosz, Elizabeth A. (1990) *Jacques Lacan: A Feminist Introduction*. New York: Routledge.

Hansen, Miriam (1993) 'Foreword' to Oskar Negt and Alexander Kluge, *Public Sphere and Experience: Toward an Analysis of the Bourgeois and Proletarian Public Sphere*. Minneapolis: University of Minnesota Press.

Hartmann, Heinz, Kris, Ernst and Loewenstein, Rudolph M. (1951) 'Some psychoanalytic comments on "culture and personality"', in George B. Wilbur and Warner Muensterburger, *Psychoanalysis and Culture*. New York: International University Press.

Holland, Eugene W. (1993) *Baudelaire and Schizoanalysis: The Sociopoetics of Modernism*. Cambridge: Cambridge University Press.

Jay, Martin (1973) *The Dialectical Imagination: A History of the Frankfurt School and the Institute of Social Research, 1923–1950*. Boston: Little Brown.

Jong, Erica (1973) *Fear of Flying: A Novel*. New York: Holt, Rinehart & Winston.

Lewes, Kenneth (1988) *The Psychoanalytic Theory of Male Homosexuality*. New York: Simon & Schuster.

Mannoni, Octave (1990) *Prospero and Caliban*. Ann Arbor: University of Michigan.

Marcuse, Herbert (1955) *Eros and Civilization*. Boston: Beacon Press.

Mitchell, J. (1974) *Psychoanalysis and Feminism*. Harmondsworth: Penguin.

Phelan, Shane (1989) *Identity Politics: Lesbian Feminism and the Limits of Community*. Philadelphia: Temple University Press.

Podhoretz, Norman (1979) *Breaking Ranks: A Political Memoir*. New York: Harper & Row.

Rado, Sandor (1940) 'A critical examination of the concept of bisexuality', *Psychosomatic Medicine*, 2 (4).

Rich, Adrienne (1980) 'Compulsory heterosexuality and lesbian existence', *Signs: Journal of Women in Culture and Society*, 5 (4).

Roediger, David R. (1991) *The Wages of Whiteness: Race and the Making of the American Working Class*. London/New York: Verso.

Spelman, Elisabeth (1986) *Inessential Woman*. Boston: Beacon Press.

Stansell, Christine (1987) *City of Women: Sex and Class in New York, 1789–1860*. Urbana, IL: University of Illinois Press.

Stoller, Robert (1968) *Sex and Gender: On the Development of Masculinity and Femininity*. New York: Science House.

Young-Bruehl, Elizabeth (1988) *Anna Freud: A Biography*. New York: Summit Books.

Zaretsky, Eli (1976) *Capitalism, the Family and Personal Life*. New York: Harper & Row.

Zaretsky, Eli (1994) 'Identity politics: its roots in romanticism, psychoanalysis and the Enlightenment', in Craig Calhoun (ed.), *Social Theory and the Politics of Identity: From Persons to Nations*. New York: Blackwell.

15

THE MODERN ERROR: OR, THE UNBEARABLE ENLIGHTENMENT OF BEING

Eugene Halton

It seems to me that man has what we call a human heart, but that he also has something of the baboon within him. The modern age treats the heart as a pump and denies the presence of the baboon within us. And so again and again, this officially non-existent baboon, unobserved, goes on the rampage.

(Vaclav Havel, 1986)

In order to convey what I mean by 'the modern error', let us consider what is meant by the term 'the modern era'. By the word 'modern' most people mean the twentieth century, especially when talking about art. Take, for example, the Museum of Modern Art in New York, which is renowned for its twentieth-century collection. 'Modern' in this sense used to function as a synonym for the term 'contemporary' in the first half of the twentieth century, but now connotes the art of the first two-thirds of the twentieth century.

A broader chronological sense of what is meant by 'the modern era' would include the industrial era, basically the development of mechanized industry in the nineteenth and twentieth centuries. Broader again would be the Age of Enlightenment, especially the rise of revolutionary governments, democracy and the Western project of 'liberty, fraternity and equality'. The theme of the Enlightenment is most often connected with the goal of a society ruled by reason and its laws, rather than by royal decree, caprice or irrational upsurges.

We can take a yet longer view of the modern era as synonymous with the rise of capitalism, or with the rise of scientific materialism in the West, and its establishment of a mechanical universe ruled by mechanical, physical law.

We can also take a sceptical view, as postmodernists have done, of the modern era as a delusionary culture which 'privileged' such concepts as individualism, progress, science and being, among others. In 'privileging' being, according to postmodernists, modernity falsely accorded 'essential' and 'natural' characteristics to what were merely the dominant conventions of the culture. Being, say the postmods, is insignificant, and significance, or signification, is either a convention rooted in the arbitrariness of linguistic communication or a transgression of convention. In my view this supposedly 'postmodern' view simply extends the modern tendency to denigrate being – the passional relation to existence – in favour of knowing. Hence by my lights postmodernism is more a sign of the exhaustion of modernism than a genuinely new and non-modern outlook.

This brings me to my peculiar title: 'The Modern Error: Or, The Unbearable Enlightenment of Being'. I aim to suggest that the underlying premises of the modern era – e-r-a – are false in a way that carries catastrophic consequences. Despite the many genuine achievements of the modern world – which I for one would not want to live without – the spirit of modernity has been one which denigrated the basic conditions of human being.

The comedians Mike Nichols and Elaine May used to have a routine going back to their days with the Second City Comedy Club in Chicago, in which they would toss words back and forth which would qualify as 'cleans' and 'dirties'. For example, the term 'Lake Michigan' is a clean, while 'Lake Titicaca' – enunciated very slowly – is a dirty. 'Sword' is a clean, while 'rapier' is a dirty. Are you with me, dear reader? We can apply the same method to a number of terms in intellectual life today. The term 'public intellectual' is clearly a clean, while for many, the term 'tenured radical' is a dirty. Philosophy is regarded by many today as a dirty, while social theory is a clean.

There is, of course, a long tradition, going back at least to Marx's last thesis on Feuerbach, to call for the end of philosophy. But today anti-philosophical philosophers, such as Richard Rorty, to take a notorious example, gloatingly decry the very idea of the love of wisdom – philo-sophia – and the quest toward a comprehensive understanding which the term connotes, as obsolete. In this general mind-set, contingency, pluralism and social constructionism are cleans, while essences, foundations, experience and universals are all dirties. 'Reality' is a dirty while 'fiction' is a clean. The 'I' is a dirty, and so is 'we'. An 'author' is a dirty, while a 'text' is a clean. 'The body', formerly a dirty, can be redefined as a 'text', and made into a clean. 'Local cultures' are clean, while 'humanity' is a dirty. 'Privileging' and 'valorizing' something is a dirty, while using the terms 'privilege' and 'valorize' as verbs is a clean. 'Postmodernism' is a clean, while 'modernism' is a dirty. 'Non-hierarchical multiculturalism' is a clean, while a 'canon' is a dirty. Both those who characterize certain people as 'politically correct' and those who are so characterized agree that it is a dirty. John Dewey used to be a dirty for most post-Second World War academic philosophers, but now that the 'public intellectual' has become a clean, Dewey has become a clean. Even more remarkably, Dewey, the philosopher who lamented what he termed 'the eclipse of community', has become a clean for many who also regard community as a dirty. Figure that one out!

Central to contemporary intellectual life is the assumption that 'the big picture', traditionally sought by philosophy, is a dirty, while 'little pictures' are clean. I wish to claim that fallible big pictures are not only still possible but are requisite for confronting the modern and postmodern world. Also central to intellectual life today, although more problematically, is the assumption that organic nature is a dirty, while culture is a clean.

When the term 'nature' is used in the context of ecology it can be put safely within a political context, and then regarded as a clean. But the idea that organic biology may have some direct and inward influence on persons, institutions, societies and civilizations, that human conduct cannot be completely reduced to socio-historical cultural constructions categorically distinct from nature – such an idea is a dirty, even if John Dewey, the newly reconstructed clean public intellectual, might have sought such a naturalistic basis for human conduct. That side of Dewey is declared a dirty, and consigned to the dungheap of history.

As Marshall Berman has noted in his wide ranging and provocative book, *All That is Solid Melts into Air* (1982), the terms 'modernity', 'moderniz- ation' and 'modernism' have different meanings and values associated with them. 'Modernization' is usually associated with the view that science, technology and rational values promote progress. 'Modernism' is usually associated with the kinds of art which erupted in the twentieth century, which seemed to fly in the face of the Western achievements of represen- tation and perspective in painting, of tonality in music, of ornament in architecture.

Modernism is usually associated with the concept of the 'avant-garde', which links it with the idea of progress associated with modernization, even though many avant-garde movements were reactions against rationaliz- ation. Artistic modernism is generally acknowledged to have lost its grip on the arts. When we consider the emergence of twentieth-century modernism, it seems at first glance to be primarily a European phenomenon, at least up until the Second World War. We think of Picasso and Paris, and more recently, of Klimt, Kokoschka, Schiele, Schoenberg, Wittgenstein and others in Vienna, of Russian constructivism and the Bauhaus. These revolutionary movements emanated out of Europe rather than America, in my opinion, because the sheer weight of the past had become oppressive in Europe. This was not the case in America, for one thing, because there was much less of a past to discard. Serious art and serious, original thought also tended not to be supported in ways that valued artists and philosophers. Hence we have the phenomenon of the American 'isolato', as Melville called it, in contrast with European artists' circles.

This said, Melville himself is a remarkably early contributor to modernist literature, with *Moby Dick* penetrating as deeply into the modern heart of darkness as Dostoyevsky's *The Brothers Karamazov* and, almost one hundred years after *Moby Dick*, Thomas Mann's *Dr Faustus*. One can also argue that modern architecture was begun in Chicago, by architects such as Sullivan and Wright. But it really only emerged in a modernist movement in Europe: Chicago kissed its baby goodbye, in effect, and it returned as the monster of the 'international style' in the person of Mies van der Rohe years later, a rational system applicable anywhere, delocalized in its cosmopolitan aspirations, institutionalizing itself in gigantic ascetic skyscrapers of glass and steel.

But there is also an opposite tendency in the modernist movement against rationality and formalism, signalled by primitivism, Dadaism and other currents. Form-breaking, mercurial and transient qualities have been key elements of the modern experience, and remain entrenched in characterizations of postmodernism. In his 1918 essay, 'The conflict in modern culture', Simmel pointed out the significance of the form-breaking concept of life for twentieth-century culture. He saw in the rise of artistic expressionism and in the prevalence of *Lebensphilosophie* itself, especially philosophical pragmatism, a new cultural paradox. In Simmel's view human cultures are marked by an ever-present dialectical tension between form and life. Yet this dialectic between form and fluid vitality had reached a peculiar turning point by the turn of the century: the form of the twentieth century was revealing itself as formless life itself. Simmel drew attention to the paradox that life, inherently formless, was becoming the form of the age – a formless form. His examples included expressionism in art and pragmatism in philosophy. In Kandinsky's works of the period in which Simmel was writing, colour is liberated from form to become expressive in its own right. Jamesian pragmatism, with its elevation of vital existence over immovable truth, struck Simmel as a key indicator of the paradoxical transposition of life to form. One might add that Simmel himself, though still a formalist, drew from the same spirit of the time in turning to *Lebensphilosophie*. Unfortunately he did not see the other half of the paradox, the formalization of life itself, resulting in lifeless life. Instead of a dialectical tension between life and form, a strange inversion was occurring, eventually producing lifeless life and formless form, each, in effect, cancelling the other out instead of transforming it.

It is instructive to consider the ways the ethos of modernism sought a cleansing break with the past, one which was to uncover universal principles (for example, in international architecture, positivism and 12-tone music) and, freed from the dead hand of the past, also was to produce a radically original, brave new world. When we consider this ethos and how it was able to institutionalize itself in America after the war, we begin to find dim outlines of a larger narrative at work, one which is, in my opinion, only continued in postmodernism. That narrative is the dream of a purely rational world of freedom and equality and unlimited progress, a world in which increasingly automatic contrivances spun from the head of science and technology secure human autonomy. As that dream unfolded it released great and terrible energies and ideas. But as it came to its culmination in our time, it realized its diabolic inversion, which was present from its inception: a radical alienation of the human soul, body and mind from the organic conditions of being. This is what I mean to suggest by 'the modern error' and 'the unbearable enlightenment of being' (my apologies to Milan Kundera). Of special note is that the American institutionalization of modernism took place primarily through universities, where thinkers and artists could work securely in a protected environment, yet an environment increasingly dominated by the rational intellect, and its tendencies for specialized knowledge and technique.

The term 'modernization' has usually been more associated with the level of industrialization in the economy, as an index of progress, yet, like modernism in the arts, it has fallen into disfavour with the rise of potentially catastrophic ecological problems due, precisely, to 'modernization'. With these senses of the word 'modern' as a starting point, let us turn briefly to some of the ways the modern experience has been conceptualized by social theorists.

We can understand the modern era as the rise of capitalism and its consequences. Though Karl Marx seems to have become a downright dirty recently, and not only for the right, we can still view, with Marx and critical theory, the rise of capitalism as associated with the rise of individualism and the breakdown of traditions as binding forces in society. Robert Bellah, William Sullivan and their co-authors of *The Good Society* (1991) lucidly depict how John Locke's conception of primal individuals inherently separate from the institutions of the societies into which they are born, live out their lives and die, has fostered a culture in contemporary America which surrenders both individual autonomy and democratic institutions to automatism and unchecked corporate power and greed.

We can, with Max Weber, view the rise of a new ethos of rationality, associated with the capitalistic spirit but not limited to it. As opposed to Marx's optimism that capitalism would give way to socialism and communism in the inevitable unfolding of history, Weber foresaw the withering effects of bureaucracy which the modern ethos and its rationalism was leading toward, effects which the downfall of Communism has dramatized and which the immense social problems of the United States reflect.

We can also see the modern era from the unique perspective developed by Lewis Mumford, who saw modernity as the 'myth of the machine', the story of the successful rise and domination by the 'megamachine', a cultural belief system which developed a mechanical world view in its physical science, which eventually was taken to be the basis on which culture was constructed. What is unique in Mumford's perspective is that the modern megamachine, though idiosyncratic in world perspective, is not unique, but corresponds to the re-establishment of the ancient megamachine which was formed in the advent of civilizational structures. There, one saw the rise of centralized bureaucracies, of standing military organizations and mass killing warfare, and of the exalting of the king to divine or semi-divine status, as, for example, in Egypt, where the Pharoah was an incarnation of the Sun God.

With the rise of these civilizational structures, new energies crystallized in the establishment of centrally organized power, ranging from economic, political and religious bureaucracies to the harnessing of large-scale organized human labour. Civilized humanity discovered the secret of the ants and bees: how a division of labour could produce a populous and efficient social life. The great dream of civilizational life might be expressed as how an increase in forms of automata could create living conditions which might enlarge autonomy. Thus was born the spectre of human reason, the emanation to outward institutional form of the rational capacity, which increasingly displaced the non-rational but reasonable sources of institutions. And thus too, if we listen to William Blake and Mumford, was born the power of the human machine world, of mechanized order and stochastic contingency, which is completing itself – realizing its entelechy or perfection – in our time.

As Blake said almost two hundred years ago, 'The Spectre is the Reasoning Power in Man, and when separated from Imagination and closing itself as in steel in a Ratio of the things of Memory, It thence frames Laws & Moralities to destroy Imagination, the Divine Body, by Martyrdoms & Wars' (from 'Jerusalem'). Those who live by conceptual reason often devalue Blake by consigning him to the category of a 'romantic', meaning by romanticism some combination of excessive sentimentalism, individualism or nature mysticism. Yet he poses a serious critique of *homo sapiens* in the previous quotation and throughout his work. He is saying that Imagination is a deeper human capacity – poetically expressed as 'the Divine Body' – than rational reasoning – poetically expressed as a secondary emanation or 'Spectre' – and that rational reasoning depends upon a living continuity with Imagination.

The separation of rational reasoning from Imagination – 'closing itself as in steel in a Ratio of the Things of Memory' – is expressed in a way similar to the metaphor used by Weber to describe the developmental logic of instrumental rationality in modern culture: a steel-hard casing or 'iron cage'. But where Weber's negative metaphor served to depict the consequences of what he took to be the inherent closed-ended logic of modern rationality, Blake's poetic expression explicitly denies that rationality is a fully autonomous capacity, and shows the way to conceive of rationality as an open-ended capacity which depends upon something greater than itself – Imagination – in order to function reasonably. To a modern or even postmodern rationalist, however, the idea that something as wispy sounding as 'Poetic Imagination' can be foundational to rationality must seem like a fanciful delusion. Perhaps it is. And yet I beg the reader's patience, for I am claiming that Blake's words derive from an anthropology that resonates with the scientific philosophy of Charles Peirce, the founder of pragmatism no less, and the social philosophy of Mumford, one which could contribute to a transformation of social theory today. It is an anthropology which allows that intelligence is projective before it is reflective, and that conjecturing remains a more basic capacity than criticism, a capacity which is the very ground on which criticism stands.

These views, especially Mumford's, have much still to say about the modern predicament, and the postmodern post-predicament. Let me also suggest another angle on viewing the modern era, which I believe offers some insights into postmodernity. My own approach is to view the modern era as cultural nominalism, a split world view in which only individual things are regarded as real and thoughts are regarded as conventions. I am not claiming that the philosophy of nominalism opened up by William of Ockham – which was known as the *via moderna* – caused the modern era, but simply that it was the intellectual manifestation of the emerging modern era. By looking at the modern era as cultural nominalism certain seemingly opposed views coalesce into an image of modernity as 'the ghost in the machine'.

Weber assumed this split of 'the ghost in the machine', the inherited legacy of Descartes and Kant, as a progressive development, and it pervaded his own thinking on political life and the social sciences. The mechanical world picture may have been a historical reality, but it was by no means historically necessary for the rise of sophisticated science. In its false materializing of the object and false etherealizing of the subject, the mechanical world represents a progressive abdication of human autonomy to the automaton. It must ignore generative, incarnating mind in favour of either objective mechanism or subjective, incorporeal spirit.

Weber claimed that action has to do with subjectively intended meaning; yet one need not begin with isolate subjects subjectively 'intending' meaning, nor is human conduct exhausted by intentions. An alternative view is to see conduct as fundamentally social and derivatively 'subjectively intended'. One can still champion the subjective as an ineradicable element of human conduct and institutions, but the subjective expressions and intentions of the human personality are not divorced from the social medium, as Weber thought. The passionate and 'intending' self is continuous with the communicative signs of the social medium, no matter how autonomous it may be.

One of the consequences of the neo-Kantian perspective shared by Weber and Simmel, as well as many contemporary theorists, is a view of meaning as a human faculty conferred on the chaos of experience. As Weber (1904/ 1949: 81) said: '"Culture" is a finite segment of the meaningless infinity of the world process, a segment on which *human beings* confer meaning and significance'. Simmel sounds even more contemporary in his 1911 essay, 'On the concept and tragedy of culture' (1911/1968: 33) where he says:

> Ocean and flowers, alpine mountains and the stars in the sky derive what we call their value entirely from their reflections in subjective souls. As soon as we disregard the mystic and fantastic anthropomorphizing of nature, it appears as a continuous contiguous whole, whose undifferentiated character denies its individual parts any special emphasis, any existence which is objectively delimited from others. It is only human categories, that cut out individual parts, to which we ascribe meaning and value. Ironically, we then construct poetic fictions which create a natural beauty that is holy within itself. In reality, however, nature has no other holiness than the one which it evokes in us.

Simmel's Kantianism, beautifully expressed here, assumes the modern ghost-in-the-machine perspective in denying that nature possesses qualitative differentiation (or form, in Kant's language) independent of human categories. Clearly humans do construct 'poetic fictions' of nature, given that being human means being inescapably anthropomorphic to at least some degree. But admitting this does not rule out the possibility that human life, so rooted in the fantastic symboling processes of dreaming, ritual life and language, may not itself be a 'poetic fiction' evoked by nature. Nor does it rule out the possibility that Kant's dualistic view of nature and knowledge may itself be a poetic fiction of the modern mind.

From my perspective, the Lockean/Kantian view that all natural beauty is but a 'secondary quality' of subjective human perception rather than a genuine transaction between a quality of nature and a human perceiver, that faculties of knowledge spring unevolved and full-blown from human heads alone, rather than as tempered achievements of creatures who evolved in transaction with the inherent forms of nature, strikes me as the modern fantastic anthropomorphizing of nature into the ghost in the machine. Though Simmel, and more particularly Weber, saw more deeply into the ever-darkening consequences of modern rationalization than many of their more optimistic contemporaries, neither saw the possibility that the very process of rationalization was itself responsible for conferring meaninglessness on the world process, thereby reducing it to a sensory manifold. That is, they could not see that the Kantian perspective might itself be a product of faulty and by no means inevitable development of rationalization.

Simmel, standing within the Kantian orbit, noted the parallel emergence of objective nature and subjective freedom over the past few hundred years:

> Thus we can observe the distinctive parallel movement during the last three hundred years, namely that on the one hand the laws of nature, the material order of things, the objective necessity of events emerge more clearly and distinctly, while on the other we see the emphasis upon the independent individuality, upon personal freedom, upon independence [*Fürsichsein*] in relation to all external and natural forces becoming more and more acute and increasingly stronger. . . . Whatever difficulties metaphysics may find in the relationship between the objective determination of things and the subjective determination of the individual, as aspects of culture their development runs parallel and the accentuation of the one seems to require the accentuation of the other in order to preserve the equipoise of inner life. (Simmel, 1900/1978)[1]

With characteristic perspicacity, Simmel reveals an unexpected correlation in the making of the modern world, one which released previously undisclosed human potentials.

Yet although these are distinctive achievements of the modern era – the mechanical view of nature and the release of the personality (exemplified, as Milan Kundera points out, in the emergence of the novel), they came at what we must now realize was a terrible cost. What Simmel was celebrating as a modern epiphany might also be characterized as the manifestation of the split-brain world of a mechanized nature severed from organic purpose and a spectral world of subjectivity sundered from nature. The legacy of the bifurcated worlds of Descartes and Kant culminated in extreme forms of

objectivism and subjectivism in the twentieth century, with deadly consequences which we can no longer ignore. The Kantian view that 'facts' are
objective and values are subjective, which both Simmel and Weber
inherited, ultimately gave licence to the diabolical release and massive
expansion of powers which exceeded human purpose or limitation: let us not
forget that the atomic bomb is one of the great epiphanies of the modern
world, and that German *Innerlichkeit* and *Kultur* could easily turn into the
god-like view that I can do whatever I feel inside, apart from otherness, a
view which reached its extreme terminus in Adolph Hitler.

This dark side of the modern epiphany was expressed quite clearly by
H.G. Wells in his book *The World Set Free*, which detailed a world nuclear
war which involved what Wells called 'atomic bombs'. That book was
published in 1913, before the first outbreak of world war!

Progress, modernity and disintegration anxiety

The final downfall of most of the European Marxist-Leninist regimes at the
close of 1989 signalled the death-knell of the nineteenth-century modernist
dream of communism. Though Stalinism and its predecessor, Leninism,
represent crucial breaks from Marx's critical programme – most fundamentally in their ruthless repression of Marx's call for 'relentless criticism of
all existing institutions' – Marx himself is by no means immune from the
failures of Marxism. His view of an inevitable grand march of history, his
allowance of a transitional 'dictatorship of the proletariat' phase, his
relatively uncritical attitude toward centralized state power and machinery,
all left great gaps through which gross tyranny could and did march.

Yet despite the obvious failings of Marxism, Marx remains an astute social
critic and historian, and many aspects of his critique of capitalism, the
machine and modern life, as well as his rooting of human life in experience
or practice, when shorn from the vision of an inevitably progressing history
and an all-powerful state, will remain valuable resources to social thought.
One can see Mumford's concept of the megamachine, for example, as a
more refined development of the critiques of the machine given by Marx,
Samuel Butler and others, freed from the unnecessary utilitarian restrictions
of Marx's materialism.

If Marx had been able to rid himself of an inevitable conception of history
and an overly materialized conception of human conduct, 'historical
materialism' might have provided a much needed corrective to the reified
views of nature and etherealized views of mind which characterize the
Kant-dominated tradition of social theory, including Weber, Durkheim,
Simmel, Parsons, Habermas and others. Yet its faith in inevitable and
revolutionary progress appears as a quaint utopian fantasy after the
catastrophic destruction of lives, cities and the moral fabric of Western
civilization and world culture witnessed in the revolutionary twentieth
century. For we have witnessed what Henry Adams sensed so accurately in

his remarkable letter to Henry Osborn Taylor in 1905. Note that this letter was written within about a year in which Einstein discovered relativity, Picasso and Braque invented cubism and Stravinsky released the daemonic energies of *The Rites of Spring*. This historian and humanist and descendant of American Presidents said:

> The assumption of unity which was the mark of human thought in the middle-ages has yielded very slowly to the proofs of complexity. The stupor of science before radium is a proof of it. Yet it is quite sure, according to my score of ratios and curves, that, at the accelerated rate of progression shown since 1600, it will not need another century or half century to tip thought upside down. Law, in that case, would disappear as theory or *a priori* principle, and give place to force. Morality would become police. Explosives would reach cosmic violence. Disintegration would overcome integration. (Adams, 1905)

Adams sensed the revolutionary social implications of the increasing release of power brought about by modern materialism. In the course of the 'century of progress', law did give way to force, in the name of 'Realpolitik' and technological progress. Morality did become police as police states proliferated throughout the world, employing huge armies and centralized secret police institutions, and ever more sophisticated weaponry, all done frequently behind the facade of a 'democratic' republic. Explosives did reach cosmic violence, with all the implications that 'dreamers' such as Adams or H.G. Wells predicted and that 'realistic' scientists and politicians were not prepared to meet. Disintegration did overcome integration, as the very 'successes' of modern societies created disastrous consequences which we have yet fully to face. Consider the denial involved in Mikhail Gorbachev's statement in 1992 *after* the Soviet Union was dissolved:

> I am entirely certain that its death [Stalinism] does not affect socialism itself. The idea of socialism lives on, and it is my feeling that the quest – the desire to experiment and to find a new form for putting the socialist idea into practice – is ongoing . . . this quest affects not only our country (where a phase of history well known to us all took its start and ran its course) but the entire world, including the capitalist countries. (Gorbachev, 1992)

A 'phase of history' which 'ran its course': what bloodless euphemism. Communism was a deadly phase of the era of dehumanizing materialism in which we are still living, and it was that materialism and its tendency to elevate power over purpose which was the root of the problem, not simply bad Stalinism versus good socialism.

In America alone, the birth of the atomic age coincided with the creation of an arrogant military welfare state whose relentless test detonations of 'bombs of cosmic violence' up through the early 1960s will have killed more Americans – current estimates are at least 300,000 deaths due to radioactive fallout – than the Korean and Vietnam wars combined, not counting the scores of thousands of contaminated military personnel, uranium miners and American families who lived near the bomb-making plants. Deliberate deception was employed by the US government against the American public and any scientists courageous enough to release information showing the deadly probabilities.

A flood of materials was released around 1990, corresponding to the end of the Cold War, which demonstrated conclusively the ways American Cold War policy, in the name of 'national security', subverted the requirements of public criticism for a viable democracy. Thousands of American families living near bomb-making factories and reactors, such as those in Fernald, Ohio, and Hanford, Washington, were exposed to appallingly high levels of radiation while the government of the US officially employed deception by claiming that there was no health hazard – even though it very well knew the dangers (see Halton, 1990). Likewise, the USSR probably killed at least as many of its citizens before Chernobyl through infantile handling of cosmic energies as the US military-industrial-academic complex did, not even counting its lethal attitude toward other forms of environmental pollution.

In his remarkable New Year's Day, 1990 speech, Vaclav Havel, who went from being a prisoner to becoming the President of Czechoslovakia in a matter of months, decried the way that Communism had turned people into 'the means of production'. He went on to say that 'we', the Czech people, are not simply victims, but have also participated in the little lies which allowed the 'monstrous, smelly machine' of Communism to keep on rolling. In other words, it is not sufficient to point the finger at the other; one must also include the possibility of self-criticism. Clearly the Communist machine was a slave state in contrast to America. Yet the evil Communist machine did not exhaust the evil of machine-like ways of thinking, despite the gloating of those in the West who celebrated the 'victory' of democracy and capitalism over Communism. Havel's words also carry a universal significance beyond their immediate context which are directly applicable to America and its arrogant national security military machine.

Despite the end of the Cold War, there has been little serious consideration of the proper limited context of what Dwight Eisenhower called the 'military-industrial complex' in a democratic republic. The irresponsible little Dr Strangeloves and their minions continue to dictate vital decisions affecting public life, immunized from public criticism. The reification and deification of nuclear power by the US and the USSR in the Cold War era, as well as the specific targeting of whole civilian populations by all of the great 'enlightened' modern superpowers, are key symbols of the descent into rational barbarism which Adams forewarned. As Nietzsche said, 'We moderns, we half-barbarians. We are in the midst of our bliss only when we are most in danger. The only stimulus that tickles us is the infinite, the immeasurable.' What better symbol of immeasurable power, what better materialization of the infinite has the modern world produced than the cult of nuclear bombs. In the bowels of the deadly military bureaucracies of the superpowers, under pure and total rational control, sat the tens of thousands of mechanical nuclear Calibans, ready at the push of a button to wreak the extermination of the biosphere if 'rationality' required it of them. 'We moderns, we half-barbarians.'

Though we humans possess rationality, we are not rational beings and cannot become rational beings. Or let me modify that. The moment we truly become rational creatures is the moment when Ahab is lashed to the whale, when he, as the rational isolato subject, attains a final unity with the narcissistic object of his rationalization, his death. It is the moment of Raskolnikov's rational murder. That moment of the realization of the rational creature is the 'interesting age' in which we now are living.

We humans are passionate beings, whether we are modern workers in a rationalized factory or computer terminal, or Realpolitik calculators planning how to maximize our individual strategic interests, or scientists enquiring into the origins of the physical universe, or philosophers enquiring into the sources and ends of public life. We are beings of passion currently possessed by a singular passion for being rational. This rational passion, having exalted itself above creation in the name of 'God', 'Science', 'Reason', 'Critical theory', 'Modernity' and even, in unconscious self-alienation, 'Postmodernity', has blinded its adherents to the inner community of passions which are necessary to human sanity, and to the passional relation to the outer world of nature and experience. In the quest to attain universal intellect at any expense, we have committed the 'Unpardonable Sin', as Hawthorne put it in his short story *Ethan Brand*, of rationally possessed hubris, and have become severed from the universal 'heart-throb' of humanity. We moderns have become the fiendish Frankenstein monsters, Ethan Brands, Ahabs, Raskolnikovs, Mr Kurtzs and Adrian Leverkühns, presciently felt and imagined by those writers sensitive to the drift of modern culture.

The contemporary intellectual landscape is still dominated by those who believe that all we need to do is improve our critical rationality, science or technology, or to include multiple 'modes of authority' in our methods and theories. Yet, as Coleridge said, 'deep thinking is attainable only by a man of deep feeling' – today, of course, we would say 'by a man or woman of deep feeling' – and those who, living from the head alone, have lost the capacity to feel deeply are not likely to point the way toward a renewal of thought and culture.

Let me emphasize that I am not rejecting rationality *per se*, but simply the dominant tendencies of modern culture toward an ever more rational world. One of my basic premises is that the progressive development and release of rational capacities in modern culture and its institutions was only possible because of the legacy of the many forms of non-rational reasonableness embedded in Western civilization, a legacy by no means obsolete. In its ever greater expansion the rational mind increasingly devalued that which was not rational, and claimed that reason was synonymous with the rational. It was only able to do so, in my opinion, because of the rich, hybrid compost of organic intelligence on which it was based and which fuelled it, a reasonableness developed out of pre-Western, non-Western and pre-civilizational, even prehistoric sources. Those patterns of ritual expression and forms of feeling in the human constitution, such as dreaming, play and intense mother–infant bonding, reach back to deeply embedded biological sources – to pre-human and ecstatic mammalian sources – which were pivotal to the emergence of human beings and which continue to animate human conduct at the highest levels as well as the lowest (Halton, 1992, 1995).

The casting off of archaic culture, of traditional customs, mores and beliefs, of localized community, in the development of modern culture not only produced positive energies in the development of the modern autonomous self, but also had the unenlightening consequence of jettisoning the checks and balances of the human person, leaving the individual much more dependent on singular sources of socialization. 'Enlightenment' was supposed to replace the chaotic dark regions of the mythologizing psyche with sober modern reason, a project which neglected the possibility that mythic narratives might be expressions of a deeper relatedness with the powers that move humans than rational consciousness can touch. As Havel has put it:

> Yes, when traditional myth was laid to rest, a kind of 'order' in the dark region of our being was buried along with it. And what modern reason has attempted to substitute for this order, has consistently proved erroneous, false, and disastrous, because it is always in some way deceitful, artificial, rootless, lacking in both ontology and morality. It may even border on the ludicrous, like the cult of the 'Supreme Being' during the French Revolution, the collectivist folklore of totalitarian systems, or their 'realist', self-celebrating art. It seems to me that with the burial of myth, the barn in which the mysterious animals of the human unconscious were housed over thousands of years has been abandoned and the animals turned loose – on the tragically mistaken assumption that they were phantoms – and that now they are devastating the countryside. They devastate it, and at the same time they make themselves at home where we least expect them to – in the secretariats of modern political parties, for example. These sanctuaries of modern reason lend them their tools and their authority so that ultimately the plunder is sanctioned by the most scientific of world views. (Havel, 1986: 160–1)

Consumer culture today is the chief socializing agent of the modern ghost in the machine, promising freedom and autonomy and immediate gratification while relentlessly colonizing both the civic community and the very structure of the self, from infancy on, like a retro-virus: a retro-virus which says, 'Buy me, drink me, eat me, dream me, desire me, and you will be yourself'. In the virtual reality of consumption culture anything goes if people will buy it, only the real cost for the delusion of endless possession is a loss of self-possession. The endless parade of consumptive fantasies becomes a way of life: the self can be endlessly redescribed, like new clothing. Between the Big System and pure chance contingencies stands the hollow self, with its glorious hypertrophied freedoms to choose and idealize, unburdened by its organic needs and limitations, by spontaneous empathy, or by purposes or commitments which transcend its singular existence. If, as Marshall Berman (1982) points out so well, Faust was the embodiment of the myth of development and modernization, postmodern Post-Faustian Person, driven by the irrational march of rational images and fantasies instead of the Grand March of history, is perhaps the logical terminus of the Faustian myth: the complete colonization of the inner life of humanity and the 'wide world outside' by the ghost in the machine.

Re-attuning humankind

Berman has claimed that we need to live the modern project more fully to realize its potentials, but I disagree. People did not fail modernism, as Berman seems to imply, modernism failed people, because of its unbalanced premises. The modern era has indeed bequeathed many valid potentials for human life, but to realize them a new civilizational context is required.

The future of human development at this point in history does not hinge on becoming more rational or, in the name of pluralism, more arbitrary, or on the blank postmodern carnival of all-purpose contingency, but on reharnessing rationality to its humane and cosmic moorings. In the fallible big picture I am suggesting, critical consciousness, which it was the virtual task of the modern era to cultivate – and perhaps the axial age up to the present – is fused with those deeper, tempered forms of reasonableness, the biosemiotic capacities through which we became human in the first place. The seemingly scientific term 'homo sapiens' becomes revealed as an artefact of the age of knowledge, for being human involves feeling, dreaming, experiencing, remembering and forgetting, and not simply knowing. Humans became human, in my view, by transmuting feeling into communicable form, by transforming those ancient biological mammal characteristics of mother–infant nurturance, play and rapid eye movement (REM) dreaming into social forms. Through such forms – dramatic ritual, the art of language, the languages of art and myth – emerging humans learned to become humans by communicatively comprehending the joys and sufferings of life. The ritualized expression of these capacities not only helped turn us into humans, with all of our fantastic diversities, visions and destructiveness, but remains, in personal, institutional and civilizational forms, the basis for the further development of the most sophisticated human endeavours. Emotions can develop or atrophy, both individually and institutionally, and can range from fleeting sensations to instinctive procli-vities whose forms, however variously expressed, remain deeply engrained aspects of being human. The biological need of an infant to bond with its mother is one part of our primate heritage which is crucial for the emergence and development of the self. No matter how conventionally social and gender roles may be constructed, the stubborn fact remains that infants and toddlers require empathic mothering, however a mother may be defined.

The claim that there are influences and limitations upon human conduct which transcend current norms, local traditions and even human history, is an idea which does not find much favour in the contemporary atmosphere of rampant relativism, with its Rortys and Lyotards, its deification of contingency, its narcissistic scorn for experience as an irreducible mode of being. Charles Peirce's view that rationality remains an immature capacity whose further development involves its dependence upon, and ultimately its coalescence into, the extra-rational biosemiotic sources of concrete reasonableness, is utterly at odds with Habermas' vision of human development as the perfection of rationality, and with the pervasive, uncritical biophobia of contemporary thought. Why is it that supposedly critical thinkers fear critically reconstructing the received mechanical picture of nature, which remains inadequate to account for the rise of human purpose?

In his theory of 'communicative rationality' Habermas, supposedly a 'critical theorist', never thinks to criticize the assumption that rationality must be pre-eminent in human development. The acknowledgement of deep human passions, of the spontaneity of the human soul in its diverse expressions, flies in the face of most leading contemporary theories, with their effete disparagement of feelings, sentiments and passions as reducible to conceptual forms of legitimation or convention. These theories reify the emotions as supposedly outside of mediation, and then recite the litany of how everything is socially mediated. These theorists refuse to consider the possibility that passions or emotions are themselves inherently social modalities of signification embedded in, but not reducible to, conventionalized signification. Thus, in postmodern dress, they mindlessly repeat the basic premises of cultural nominalism which are traceable to the rise of philosophical nominalism: all meaning is either a convention or a contingency. This neat dichotomy, with the extreme relativism which usually accompanies it, is simply too narrow.

When seen in this light, the seemingly benign postmodern, post-factual, post-rational world where there are no truths or facts but only conventions and language games, reveals its corrupt consequences. When a Stanley Fish or Richard Rorty says that everything, including truth and goodness and beauty is a matter of 'socialization', taking, I might add, the process of socialization in the most *banal* sense of automatic internalization of norms, when they or James Clifford or other postpeople say that experience is but a 'mode of authority', the possibility of a public life, wherein fallible standards of discrimination, judgement, excellence and justice form the fabric of the good life, must give way sooner or later to direct power: morality becomes police, and integration gives way to disintegration. Contemporary theory and philosophy provides the groundwork for such a postworld.

The nominalistic premises of the modern age, which remain uncritically assumed by both Habermas and Rorty, and by those who believe that human social life is solely a conventional construction, urgently need to be overhauled through an imaginative realignment of humanity's place in the cosmos. Such a realignment involves opening social theory and philosophy to the public dimension, but it also involves opening the public dimension of social thought to the roots and limits of nature and world culture. Whether we will it or not, we are in the midst of making a world civilization, and the contemporary litany that theory can only be local, though not without its merit, is also a form of nearsightedness which remains blind to the significance of translocal norms and the bearing of those norms on local culture (not to mention that the assertion that theory must be local is itself not locally grounded and seems to claim the status of a universal).

The time has come to find a new way of renewing reason, a project requiring a transformation of values and outlook as vast as those which took place in the axial age or the modern age.[2] The renewal of reason will involve opening the gates to the entire historical and prehistorical heritage of humankind, to renew the archaic values of family, household, neighbourhood and local community and the sympathetic relations they engender, to renew those organic and communicative essences of play, dreaming and mother–infant nurturance which are our human-mammalian legacy and crucial for the development of the spontaneous self, and also making a life-sustaining world culture with self-critical institutions capable of supporting and protecting the vitality of local ways. By actively cultivating such a 'big picture', we undercut the one already in place, in order to recontextualize rationality and to reactivate the precious roots of reason which the modern age claimed to have outgrown.

It is no exaggeration to say that the dominant contemporary theories of meaning advocate a thoroughly post-biological image of humankind (some, such as Derrida, even callowly terming themselves anti-humanist, seemingly oblivious to the positive virtues of the humanist tradition). And in our 'post-rational', 'postmodern', 'post-' culture, post-biological is taken to be a positive achievement, instead of the extreme form of self-alienation that it really is. Those who break the great taboo against mixing nature with culture tend to be looked upon with scorn and perhaps embarrassment by the majority of contemporary theorists. In this scorn and embarrassment, I claim, one sees the effete rational intellect, unwilling to confront critically its own extra-rational context.

With shrunken hearts and swollen, talking heads, the weird parade of anti-naturalists – the Stanley Fishes and Richard Rortys, Jürgen Habermases and Arnold Gehlens, radical feminists and conservative rational choice theorists, multiculturalists and defenders of the Western Civilizational Enlightenment – march in unquestioned lockstep unison. Because of these uncritical attitudes toward the received mechanical picture of nature by supposedly critical theorists, a social theory rooted in organic life and human passion, such as that which I am proposing, would undoubtedly be seen as obsolete by those leading theorists who have proudly and arrogantly severed the possibility of connections between their theories and biological life. Yet a biosemiotic social theory, capable of encompassing both the varieties and contingencies of human signification and the organic needs, limits and transformative possibilities of the living human being in his and her social, political and economic worlds, forms a profound critique of contemporary theory and contemporary life, and of the spirit of mechanized, depersonalized subjectivism which informs both.

We can pity poor modern man or woman, who conceives the universe to be a machine or a cybernetic system, or an unreal convention, who conceives his or her own mind and brain to be a machine. The human personality *can* be reduced to a mechanical or material basis, only all that is most human must be denied or bleached out. We can pity poor postmodern person, who can at best conceive of himself or herself as a broken machine, or as a 'text', or as an electronic component of a 'virtual reality'. These postmodern versions bespeak the realization of a thoroughly dehumanized world, in which all human attributes, especially emotional warmth and empathy, have vanished. But more than pity is required, for we are all of us implicated in the tragedy of modern life. Without a deep empathy for fellow moderns and postmoderns, ranging from our immediate life-situations to the large panorama of modern civilization in all of its diverse forms, and without self-empathy for our inescapable participation in this tragedy, we can too easily stand aloof while pretending to simply wipe the slate of history clean again. The myth of the machine, realizing its perfection in the electronic 'virtual reality' that is contemporary life, resonates ominously with the description of the anxiety of the disintegration of the self given by psychoanalyst Heinz Kohut:

> What leads to the human self's extinction . . . is its exposure to the coldness, the indifference of the nonhuman, the nonempathically responding world. It is in this sense, and in this sense only, that we may say that disintegration anxiety is closer to the fear of death than to what Freud designated the fear of loss of love. It is not physical extinction that is feared, however, but the ascendency of a nonhuman environment (e.g., of an inorganic surrounding) in which our humanness would permanently come to an end. (Kohut, 1984: 18)

We must find the means to correct the mistaken premises which form the modern error. In my view this task requires a fundamental transformation of the modern world view rather than piecemeal change, because piecemeal change will amount to too little, too late. In the name of freedom and knowledge, the modern era gave birth precisely to the non-empathically responding world Kohut describes, the schizoid ghost in the machine which now threatens to dissolve our humanity and the natural world. It is time to begin to body forth a new world view and world civilization, new ways of living both locally and globally in harmony both with outer nature and the nature within us, while preserving the genuine achievements of modern civilization, such as human rights, and private and public freedoms, as well as rediscovering the lost resources of the human past and new ways of joining them to the present. Without the hope of such a thoroughgoing transformation, we are likely to continue to go the way of the earth's ozone shield into corrosive self-extinction.

Notes

1. See also Gianfranco Poggi's *Money and the Modern Mind: Simmel's Philosophie des Geldes* (1993), where he argues that Simmel views modernity as an epiphany. Poggi quite accurately analyses Simmel's Kantian idea that truth is relative, that is, is a relation of representations, and why this should be taken as another manifestation of the superiority of modern over pre-modern thinking. He ignores the dark side of the modern 'epiphany', such as

the simultaneous emergence of the Absolutist state, from the Baroque kings to the 'Big Men' of twentieth-century totalitarianism. In celebrating the modern over the premodern, one must ask how the modern police state is superior to the ancient Greek *polis*. Similarly, positivism is especially characteristic of the last century and must be reckoned with as a modern achievement which punctures the presumed superiority of modern thought.

2. The axial age, a time period beginning roughly around 600 BC, marked the emergence of the universal religions, such as Zoroastrianism and Buddhism and, later, others such as Christianity, Mithraism, Manichaeism and Islam, and also the development of a new kind of person and a new kind of community. The term 'axial age' is associated with Karl Jaspers, but Lewis Mumford also formulated the concept independently at about the same time, in the late 1940s, and claims that both were preceeded by J. Stuart Glennie about fifty years earlier. As Mumford says in his book, *The Transformations of Man* (1956):

> The central change brought in by axial religions is the redefinition – in fact the recasting – of the human personality. In that act, values that emerge only in the personality replace those that belonged to institutions and institutional roles. The new feelings, emotional attachments, sentiments are now incarnated in a living image, that of the prophet.

In Mumford's view the rise of the axial personality marked an opposition to and compensation for the bureaucratic civilizational structures.

References

Adams, Henry (1905) 'Letter to Henry Osborn Taylor, January 17, 1905', in *The Letters of Henry Adams, Vol. 5: 1899–1905*, edited by J.C. Levenson, Ernest Samuels, Charles Vandersee and Viola Hopkins Wimmer. Cambridge: Belknap Press, 1988, pp. 627.

Bellah, Robert, Madsen, Richard, Sullivan, William M., Swidler, Ann and Tipton, Steven M. (1991) *The Good Society*. New York: Alfred A. Knopf.

Berman, Marshall (1982) *All That is Solid Melts into Air*. New York: Simon & Schuster.

Gorbachev, Mikhail S. (1992) 'No time for stereotypes', op-editorial, *New York Times*, 24 February.

Halton, Eugene (1990) 'Cold War's victims deserve a memorial', op-editorial, *New York Times*, 10 March.

Halton, Eugene (1992) 'The reality of dreaming', *Theory, Culture & Society* 9: 119–39.

Halton, Eugene (1995) 'The cultic roots of culture', in *Bereft of Reason*. Chicago: University of Chicago Press.

Havel, Vaclav (1986) 'Thriller', in *Vaclav Havel or Living in Truth*. London: Faber & Faber.

Kohut, Heinz (1984) *How Does Analysis Cure?* edited by Arnold Goldberg with Paul E. Stepansky. Chicago: University of Chicago Press.

Mumford, Lewis (1956) *The Transformations of Man*. New York: Harper & Row.

Poggi, Gianfranco (1993) *Money and the Modern Mind: Simmel's Philosophie des Geldes*. Berkeley: University of California Press.

Simmel, Georg (1911/1968) 'On the concept and tragedy of culture', in *Georg Simmel: The Conflict in Modern Culture and Other Essays*, translated and edited by Peter Etzkorn. New York: Teacher's College Press.

Simmel, Georg (1900/1978) *The Philosophy of Money*, translated by Tom Bottomore and David Frisby. London: Routledge & Kegan Paul.

Weber, Max (1904/1949) 'Objectivity in social science and social policy', in *The Methodology of the Social Sciences: Max Weber*, translated and edited by Edward A. Shils and Henry A. Finch. New York: Free Press.

INDEX

Abraham, Karl 249
Abu-Lughod, Lila 39
accumulation
  local 84
  and modernization 11, 48, 130
  and space-time compression 70
Achebe, Chinua 133
action
  associative 135–7
  and belief 17, 18, 212–13
  collective 57–9
  global 59
  individualist 135–7, 150–1
  in sociological theory 128, 135–6
  in Weber 21, 266
Adams, Henry 268–9, 270
Adler, Alfred 248
Adorno, Theodore 19, 20, 129, 187
aestheticization of everyday life 23
Ahmad, Aijiz 117
Aksionov, Vassily 221
Albrow, M. 45
alienation 56, 239, 263
alliances, and incest taboo 18–19, 232–8
alterity
  and anthropology 78–9, 81
  and self-identification 88
Altman, Denis 19, 255
ambivalence, and contingency and
    systemness 11–12
Americanization 3
Anderson, Benedict 6, 7
anthropology
  and cosmopolitanism 7, 78–9
  and cultural specificity 81
  global systemic 84–5
  reflexive 4, 7
Anzaldúa, G. 56
Appadurai, A. 84, 119
Appiah, K.A. 37–8
architecture, modernist 112, 262–3
Ariès, Philippe 145
Aristotle, and being 164
Arnason, J.P. 47

Asad, Talal 121 n.5
assimilation
  and global processes 87
  and hybridization 56–7, 78
  and modernization 133, 148
association, and collectivism 131, 135–7
Atkinson, Dorothy 211, 212
Avneri, Uri 52
awareness, global 72–3, 77, 79, 118, 119

Bachelard, Gaston
  and imagination 15–16, 192, 193
  and phenomenology 196–9
  and rhythm 205
  and space 193, 196–206
  and time 194–5
Bairoch, Paul 129, 130
Baker, Houston Jr 56
Bakhtin, M. 56
Balibar, E. 39
balkanization, as global phenomenon 33, 73,
    75
Balke, Friedrich 186
banks, regional investment 59
Barber, B.R. 32
Barthes, Roland 192, 195, 199–200, 204
Bateson, G. 55
Baudelaire, Charles Pierre 111, 125
Baudrillard, Jean 8, 16, 96–8, 149, 179, 180
Bauman, Zygmunt 3, 10, 11–12, 20, 47,
    140–53
Bayer, Ronald 250
being see ontology
being-in-common 160, 166, 169
belief
  and action 17, 18, 212–13
  and security 156
Bell, Daniel 6, 23
Bell, Vikki 3, 16, 18–19, 20, 227–41
Bellah, Robert 264
Benjamin, Walter 184
Berger, Peter 11, 140–2, 148, 150
Bergson, Henri 14, 15, 193–6, 197, 201–2,
    203–6

Berman, M. 20–1, 46, 111, 125, 262, 272–3
Bernauer, J. 238, 239
Bérubé, Michael 56
Bhabha, Homi K.
  and Foucault 242 n.8
  and heterogenization 4, 6
  and hybridization 56
  and temporality of modernity 113, 116, 117
Bichat, Xavier 14, 184
Billington, M. 38
bio-politics 187, 227–41
Black, Cyril 115, 133
Blake, William 265
Bloch 184
blood, and power 232–3, 236
body
  and bio-politics 227–8, 232
  and house image 202, 203–4
  and space 203
  and time 193–6
  writing 192, 193, 195, 197, 200, 206, 261
Booth, Ken 49
Bor, J. 62
boundaries
  and global flows 11, 99–102
  national 34, 93–4, 99–102, 105
  transgressing 144, 149
Bourdieu, Pierre 81, 221–2, 224
Brazilianization 3
Brodsky, Joseph 222
Broussais principle 182, 184
Brown, Norman O. 251
Butler, Samuel 268

Canevacci, M. 55
Canguilhem, Georges 14–15, 182, 183–4
capital, cultural 10, 29
capitalism
  dependent 51, 55
  disorganized 8, 23, 92
  entrepreneurial 102
  'fast' 99
  and globalization 6, 112, 125, 252
  as Great Unifier 129
  and modernity 48, 96, 110, 264
  transnational, and neo-worlds 9, 91–2, 101, 102–3
  and world-system theory 4, 33
Castells, M. 9, 92–3, 100
centralism, democratic 17, 211, 212
change
  as defensive 11
  and global flows 1–2

change, cont.
  and modernity 47, 127, 135, 140
  and nation-state 97–9
  in post-structuralism 192–3
  and postmodernism 32
  and society 2
Chase, William 213, 214
Chase-Dunn, C. 65 n.2
Chekhov, Anton 210, 211
childhood
  and experience 15, 202–3
  and indeterminacy 145
  and sexuality 234–5
Chodorow, Nancy 254–5
choice, and identity 140–50
city
  global 10, 51, 89 n.7, 119, 120
  modern 109, 110–12, 114, 118–20
  traditional 112, 120
civil society 58, 252
civilization
  and culture 29
  and globalization 6, 29
  and modernization 17, 27, 264–5
  Western 23, 144, 271, 275
Cixous, H. 200
Clark, Katerina 216
Clark, T.J. 111
class
  global structure 79–80
  and identity 247
  and polarization 129
Clifford, J. 4, 6, 7, 274
CocaColonization 45, 70
Coleridge, S.T. 271
collectivism
  dissimulating 17
  and individualism 131, 148–51
collectivization, and modernization 11
colonialism
  and identity politics 254
  and modernity 10–11, 27, 110–12, 116, 133
  and postcolonialism 117–18
commerce, as Great Unifier 129, 130
communalism
  and being-in-common 160
  and modernity 147, 150
communication
  and globalization 36, 45, 49–50, 79, 103, 137
  intercultural 31
communism
  downfall 245, 268–9
  faith in 212, 214–15
  and modernity 148

communism, *cont.*
  and privacy 16–18, 209, 211, 213–15
Communist Manifesto, and modernity 125
community
  as cultural formation 151
  fortress 29–30, 31
  glocal 102
  imagined 7
  international 101
  moral 152
  in postmodernism 12
  return to 150–3
  virtual 7, 9–10
Comte, Auguste
  and Great Unifier 129
  and Broussais principle 184, 185
Condorcet, Marie Jean Antoine Nicolas
    Caritat, marquis de 127, 129
confession, and sexuality 210, 214–15
Confino, Michael 211
conflict
  in counter-history 181
  in modernity 8, 128–33, 135–6, 148
  and normality 187
  and unity 52–3
Connolly, William 169, 172
constructionism, social 21, 256
consumption
  glocal 29, 101–2, 103
  and identity 248
  and socialization 272–3
contingency
  of human existence 11–12
  and postmodernism 21
continuity, and discontinuity 15, 183, 184,
    185, 201
control
  cultural 13, 16
  social, and normality 184
convergence
  and cultural hybridization 60
  in world system theory 4
Cook, Blanche 255
core-periphery
  and attribution of meaning 6, 7, 74
  and education 32
  and global flows 2, 100–1
  and global system 75
  and historical/post-historical worlds
    91–2
  and modern city 114
  and routes to modernization 10–11
  semiperiphery 51
  and Western hegemony 23, 126
  and wild zones 92, 100–1, 105

corporation, multi-national
  and globalism 46, 75–6
  and imperialism 59
  and nation-state 152
  and nationality 93
  and power 3
cosmopolitanism
  disillusioned 7, 10, 78–9, 82
  and localism 29, 32, 73, 78–9, 153
Cox, R.W. 45, 50
creolization 105, 137
  as confused essentialism 82–4
  and hybridization 5, 6, 7, 39–40, 53–4, 62,
    86
critical theory 252, 257, 264, 274–5
crystallization, cultural 72, 178–9, 180, 264–5
culture
  and belonging 128, 148
  and civilization 29
  and community 151
  counter-culture 188, 222–3, 253
  crossover 5, 53–4, 56, 60
  and cultural imperialism 37–40, 70
  and diversity 39–40, 117
  dominant 148
  and effects of technology 63
  and globalization 33, 45, 53, 76–8, 80–9
  and hybridization 5, 23, 39–40, 41, 60–4,
    86–7
  local 29, 31, 39, 61–3, 78–9
  and mass media 105
  and modernity 80–1, 85, 119–20
  and nationalism 41
  and nature 61, 262, 266–7
  and postmodernity 100, 120–1
  as process 7
  and public/private spheres 252–3
  rock 224
  as substance 7, 82, 84–5, 86, 88
  and system theory 6–7, 76–8
  temporal progression 85
  as text 82–4
  traditional 11
  translocal 61–4
  and universalism 20
  in world system theories 69
  see also hegemony, cultural; identity
culture, global 2, 31, 38–9, 52, 53, 60, 79
  and diasporas 63–4
  and nation-states 72
cyberspace, and neo-world order 8, 91, 93

decentralization
  and the global 137
  and nation-state 97–9, 100–1, 104

decolonization
  and identity politics 254
  ideological 37–8
  and nation-state 98, 100
deconstruction
  and difference 194
  and global technology 13
  and representation 202
  and security 174
Deleuze, Gilles 15, 20, 21, 187, 256
democracy
  and centralism 17, 211–12
  and the exceptional 186
  global 58, 59
dependency theory
  and globality 4
  and Marxism 5
  and structural hybridization 51, 55
Derrida, Jacques 20, 21, 170, 194, 202, 275
  and *différance* 192, 205, 206
Descartes, René 144–5, 164, 266, 267
destabilization, and hybridization 57
determinism, and freedom 140–7
Dewey, John 21, 261–2
difference
  and differentiated markets 28–9, 38
  and essentialism 80–4, 88
  and the exceptional 186–7
  and global systems 75
  and hybridization 60
  and locality 29–30, 87
  and modernity 120
  and nationality 41
  politics of 19, 20, 49, 174, 244–5, 252–8
  and postmodernism 178–9
  and relativization 71–2
  as right 5
  simulated 99
  and spatialization 200, 205, 206
  and temporality 194–5
  and transformation 192–3
Dillon, Michael 3, 12–13, 16, 155–75
Dilthey, Wilhelm 14
discontinuity, and continuity 15, 183, 185, 201
discourse
  minority 33
  reverse 37–8
  of security 156–7, 161
disease, as the exceptional 14, 182, 184
disjuncture, globalization as 84–5
dissent, Soviet 222–3
dissimulation 16–18, 209–25
  downwards spread 216–21
  legacy 224–5
  origins 210–13

dissimulation, *cont.*
  and resistance 221–4
diversity
  and hybridization 52
  and locality 29–31, 34, 39–41
  and modernity 126, 137
  and modernization 48–9, 126
Donzelot, J. 237
DuBois, W.E.B. 257
Dunham, Vera 216–17
durée/duration 15, 194–6, 201, 205
Durkheim, Emile 12, 14
  and change 192–3
  and time and space 15, 193, 194, 197
  and totem 229

ecology, transnational 104–5
economy
  and conflict 135
  cultural 120
  dual 50–1
  and family 247
  global 2, 45, 46, 49, 96, 110, 118, 129
  and nation-state 152
Egypt, and route to modernity 133, 137
Ehrenburg, Ilya Grigorievich 216, 218–19
Eisenhower, Dwight 270
elite
  and cosmopolitanism 7
  global 79–80, 95
  and modernity 110, 147–9
  Russian 17, 219
Ellington, Duke 54
Elvin, Mark 112–13
emotion, and reason 21–2, 273–4
enemies
  and cultural hybridity 5
  and normality 180–2, 185–7
Engels, Friedrich, *Communist Manifesto*
  125–6
Enlightenment
  and modernity 21, 110, 113, 127, 179, 244,
    260, 272, 275
  Scottish 127, 129
Enzensberger, Hans Magnus 180
equivalence 6, 8–9, 13
Erikson, Erik 19, 245, 249–51, 254
essence, as prior to existence 142
essentialism
  and creolization 82–4
  and culture 80–1, 85–6, 88
  and hybridization 55, 57–8, 64
  and identity 19, 55, 256
  of modernism 260–1
  strategic 41

ethnicity, and identity 49, 253
ethnoscapes, global 2, 50, 84, 119
Eurocentrism, of modernity 47–8, 110–15, 119, 120, 262–3
European Court of Human Rights 5
European Union, and regionalism 50, 59
Europeanization 3
exceptionalism
    and disease 14, 182–4
    and individualism 20
    and normality 14–15, 178, 179, 180, 184–7
    and politics 178–9, 180–2, 185–8
existence
    and essence 142
    in Lyotard 142–3
experience
    in Bachelard 196–203, 206
    childhood 15, 202–3
    in Durkheim 197
    in Halton 273–4
    in Marx 268
    in Merleau-Ponty 197

faith, in communism 212, 214–15
family
    and conflict 135
    and economy 247
    and public/private spheres 246, 247–8
    and sexuality 18, 228–9, 231–40
    and the state 227, 237, 250
Fanon, Frantz 254, 255
fascism, and modernity 132, 148, 187
Featherstone, Mike 1–23
Feddema, R. 56
feminism
    and essentialism 19–20
    and identity politics 254–5
    and sexual abuse 240
Ferguson, M. 25
Fish, Stanley 274, 275
flow, global 2, 23, 84, 93
    and global cities 10
    and neo-world orders 7–8, 104–5
    as signal 16
    and simulation 97
    as unbounded 99–102
    and 'wild zones' 92, 100–1, 105
form, and life 263
Forsthoff, Ernst 190 n.20
Foucault, Michel
    and confession 210, 214–15
    and identity 20, 253
    and individualization 214–15
    and modernity 113, 155
    and morality 239–41

Foucault, Michel, *cont.*
    and normality 14, 181, 183, 189 n.12, 236
    and politics 227–8
    and security 156–8, 160, 162
    and sexuality 18, 228, 230–1, 232–6, 238–9
    and space 207 n.4
    and state and society 11, 15
Fourth World movements 73
fragmentation, global 19, 49, 80, 82, 84–5, 119
France
    and identity politics 254
    and normality 182
Frankfurt School, and individuality 19, 20
freedom, and determinism 140–7, 150, 153, 267
Freud, Sigmund
    and identity 245, 246, 248–51, 253–4, 257
    and incest prohibition 229–30, 231–2, 239
    and memory 195, 201, 202
Friedman, Jonathan 3, 5–7, 10, 12, 16, 69–89
Fukuyama, Francis 91–2
functionalism
    and modernization 5
    and sociology 63, 231
fundamentalism, and globalization 73, 84
future
    and modernity 126–8, 130, 149
    and security 161

Game, Ann 3, 13–16, 192–207
Geertz, C. 39, 79, 81, 89 n.8
Gehlen, Arnold 275
    and cultural crystallization 178–9, 180
    and exceptionalism 14–15, 187, 189 n.17
    and the individual 145–6
    and *Instinktarmut* 11, 20, 22, 141–2
genealogy
    and Foucault 210, 236
    and ontology 160, 163–6
    and security 156–61, 162–3, 167, 174
geopolitics, and nation-state 8, 93–4, 100–1, 104
Giddens, Anthony 7
    and Great Unifier 129
    and history 32–3, 192–207
    and individuality 146–7
    and instrumental rationality 30
    and modernity and globalization 47, 48
    and time-space 3, 4, 26–7
Glennie, J. Stuart 277 n.2
globalism
    critical 59
    definition 46

globality
   as condition of globalization 73–4
   as condition of modernization 3, 27
   and locality 29, 32–7, 40–1, 49
   and modernity 27, 48
globalization
   as condition of modernization 3–4, 5
   as consequence of modernity 2, 3, 29, 30,
      47
   as disjuncture 84–5
   form 40, 41
   and global arena 73–4
   and globalizations 45–6
   history of 35–6
   as hybridization 5–6, 7, 45–64
   and imperialism 59
   and institutional process 75–6
   and modernization theory 47, 115
   as policy/unintended consequence 46
   and regionalism 50
   and spatialization 1, 3–4, 26, 32–4
   strong/weak 77–8
   theory 3, 69–73, 88
   timing 47–8
   as Westernization 45, 47–8, 52, 63, 124,
      168
   see also culture; heterogenization;
      homogenization; modernity; system,
      global
glocality
   and cyberspace 91, 93
   and nation state 95, 97–8, 101–2
   and world orders 91–6, 102–6
glocalization 4–5, 26, 28–41, 49
   business usage 28–9, 30–1, 40
   and cultural imperialism 37–40
   and universalism/particularism 28, 30–7,
      38, 72
Gobineau, Joseph Arthur, comte de 54
Gorbachev, Mikhail 269
Great Unifier, in sociological metanarrative
   129–31, 137
Grebenshchikov, Boris 224
Greenfeld, L. 30, 34
Grosz, Elizabeth 249, 256
Guattari, Félix 15, 187, 256
Gumbrecht, Hans Ulrich 188

Habermas, Jürgen 42 n.4, 46, 129, 274, 275
Hall, Stuart, and heterogenization 4, 6
Hall, T.D. 65 n.2
Halton, Eugene 3, 16, 20–2, 23, 260–76
Hamedah, Shirine 112
Hamilton, Alexander 173
Hannerz, U. 29, 32, 62, 64, 69, 82

Hansen, Miriam 256
Hartmann, Heinz et al. 257
Harvey, D. 6, 7, 48, 70, 110
Hashimoto, Akiko 41 n.1
Havel, Vaclav 22, 260, 270, 272
Hawthorne, Nathaniel 271
Hegel, G.W.F. 165, 239
hegemony
   classificatory 6–7, 83, 85
   cultural 70, 117, 148
   decline 79
   and hybridization 57
Heidegger, Martin 8, 22
   and security 156–7, 162, 164–5,
      169–71
Held, D. 50, 59
heterogeneity
   and micromarketing 29
   and normality 186
heterogenization 4, 5–6, 7, 26–7, 84
   and hybridization 62
   and locality 31, 36, 40
Hirschman, Albert 152
historicity, of modernization 48
history
   and counter-history 181
   'end of' 1, 91–2
   global 45, 47–8, 124
   of globality 52–3
   and histories 32–3
   and Marxism 1, 268
Hobbes, Thomas 92, 165, 166, 174
Holland, Eugene 249
Holocaust, and modernity 20
home, and globalization 30, 35, 39
homogeneity, and normality 19, 185–6
homogenization 84
   and attribution of meaning 77–8
   hegemonic 80
   and hybridization 58, 62, 63
   and locality 31, 35–6, 38–40, 78
   and modernization 4, 25–7
   and proletariat 252
   and Western culture 33–4, 53
homosexuality, and politics of identity 250,
      253, 255
Horkheimer, Max 20, 251
Hösle, V. 51
house, imagery 15, 200–4
household, and dissimulation 211
humanities
   and modernity 109–10, 114–15, 126
   and postmodernism 117
Hunter, Ian 180
Hutcheon, Linda 117

hybridization
  continuum 56–7
  critique 7
  and culture 5, 23, 39–40, 41, 60–4, 86–7
  globalization as 5–6, 7, 45, 49–64
  and nation-state 40–1
  and politics 54–9
  and post-hybridity 60–3
  and postmodernism 117
  structural 49–53, 63–4
  theory 55
hyperrealism 7–10, 12, 91, 96–105
hyperspace 16, 51, 96–7, 105–6

identity
  collective 19, 22, 99, 148–50, 210–11, 247,
    249, 257
  construction 245, 249, 256–7
  crisis of 148
  and culture 81–2, 83–4, 86–9, 117, 128,
    131, 152, 245–8, 251–2, 257
  ethnic 49, 253
  gender 254–5
  and global systems 74, 79
  and globalization 33
  and homosexuality 250, 253, 255
  identity-space 6–7, 69, 71, 75, 80, 86, 88
  individual 145–6, 148–50, 250
  loss 2, 6, 149
  multiple 5, 52, 57–8, 84, 256
  national 12, 26, 30, 34, 74, 95, 133, 153,
    186, 247, 253
  neutralized 99
  politics of 19–20, 49, 174–5, 244–58
  transnational 73, 78
imagination
  and house image 15, 200–4
  and knowledge 3, 15–16, 22, 196–200,
    206–7
  phenomenology of 15, 196, 198–9
  and reason 265
  and water image 192–3, 198, 200
IMF, and imperialism 59
imperialism
  cultural 37–40, 70, 119
  and global political theory 58–9
  and globalization 70
  linguistic 111
  and modernity 47, 113
incest
  and bio-politics 228–38
  and deployment of alliances 18–19, 232–8
  and rules 240
individual
  and culture 86

individual, cont.
  and security 155–6
  and society 250
  Soviet 209–25
individualism
  and collectivism 131, 148–51
  dissimulating 16–18, 209–25
  and hubris 20–1
  and modernity 135, 137, 145–8, 264
  and the nation-state 12, 46, 153
  permissive 105
  and psychoanalysis 19
  Western/Eastern 17
industry
  and globalization 165
  as Great Unifier 129, 130
inequalities, and globalization 129–30, 147
informationalization 7
  and aestheticization 23
  and disorganized capitalism 92–3
  and global flows 2, 96–7, 99–101
  and loss of identity 2
instinktarmut 11–12, 20, 22, 141–2
institutionalization
  in Berger 140–1
  global 75–6, 79–80
  of locality 4–5
institutions, national
  and international organizations 2
  and politics of security 166
intentionality, and meaning 21, 266
interconnectedness, and modernity 118–19
interculturalism 4, 5, 55, 61
interdependence, global 70, 101–2, 114, 137
interest, national 94–5, 101
internationalization
  economic 45, 46, 120, 252
  and locality 36–7
  of sociology 25–6
  of the state 50
intimacy
  and memory 15, 16, 52
  and space 200–3, 204, 206
  see also privacy
Irigaray, Luce 20, 193

James, William 21, 214
Jameson, Frederic 48, 92, 100, 102, 110
Japan
  and glocalization 28–9, 40
  and hybridization 41
  influence on European painting 60
  modernization 132–3, 137
Japanization 3
Jaspers, Karl 277 n.2

Jencks, Charles 117–18, 119
Johnson, P. 36
Jong, Erica 253–4
Jowitt, Ken 209
Jung, Carl 248

Kandinsky, Vasily 263
Kant, Immanuel 164, 266–8
Keenan, Edward L. 211
Kern, S. 36
Kharkhordin, Oleg 3, 16–18, 20, 209–25
King, Anthony 3, 10, 32, 108–21
Kinsey, Alfred Charles 250
knowledge
  bio-political 231, 234, 238–40
  and counter-knowledge 13–14, 15, 181–8,
    192
  and exception 180–1, 182–7
  and imagination 3, 15–16, 22, 196–200,
    206–7
  and memory traces 15
  and modernity 109–10, 113, 179, 181
  and ontology 196, 206–7, 260–1
  and perception 184–5, 267
  phenomenological 196, 198
  in post-structuralism 192–3
  and security 12–13, 159, 164, 170, 171
  social construction 131
  spatialization 12–16
  and temporality 194
Kohut, Heinz 276
Kozlov, Alexei 220
Kundera, Milan 263, 277

Labie, Smadar 56
labour division
  and colonial mode of production 10,
    111–12
  global 252
  and modernization 264–5
Labov, W. 89 n.6
Lacan, Jacques 20
language
  in Bachelard 199–200
  and genealogy 158
  and identity politics 256
  natural/creole 83
Lash, Scott 1–23
Lebensphilosophie 14, 15, 263
Leibniz, G.W. 164
Lepenies, Wolf 184
lesbianism, radical 255
Lévi-Strauss, C. 228–9, 230, 231–2
Levin, Eve 213
Levinas, Emmanuel 159

Levy, Marion J. 115–16
Lewes, Kenneth 250
Lewin, Moshe 211, 212
liberalism
  and modernity 147, 244
  and public/private spheres 246
  and social action 136
Link, Jürgen 183, 189 n.12
Lipschutz, R.D. 58
locality
  and cosmopolitanism 29, 32, 78–9
  and culture 29, 31, 39, 61–3, 77–8
  global creation 4–5, 26, 31, 35
  and globality 29, 32–7, 40–1, 49, 72–4, 80,
    84–5, 87
  and nationalism 4, 26
  see also glocalization
location, structural 128
Locke, John 264, 267
Luhmann, Niklas 9, 178, 179, 180
Lukács, Georg 129, 184
Luke, Timothy W. 3, 5, 13, 16
  and world orders 7–10, 12, 91–106
Lyotard, Jean-François
  and humanity 142–3
  and postmodernism 110, 178, 179

McDonaldization 45, 99
Mcgrew, A. 50
Macherey, Pierre 182
Machiavelli, N. 165
MacIntyre, Alasdair 21
McNeill, W.H. 35
McWorld 4, 33–4
Maine, Sir Henry 145
Manchester, as modern city 111
Mann, Michael 50
Mannoni, Octave 254, 255
Mânouchkine, Ariane 53, 60
Marcus, G. 4, 6
Marcuse, Herbert 19, 245, 251, 255
Maritain, Jacques 144–5
markets
  expansion 102–3
  global 28–9, 48
Marx, Karl
  and alienation 239
  and capitalism 129, 246, 264, 268
  Communist Manifesto 125–6
  and community 151
  and critical theory 252, 268
  and philosophy 261
  and polarization 138 n.3
Marxism
  and dependency theory 5

Marxism, *cont*.
  and identity 244, 245, 247, 251, 256–8
  and public/private spheres 246–7, 253
  and temporality 1
  Western 129, 253
  and world market 46–7
Massey, Doreen 61
May, Elaine 261
meaning
  attribution 6, 77–8, 81, 86, 88
  in Bachelard 199–200, 204, 205
  and constructionism 21, 85–6
  and creolization 82
  flows 82, 86
  globalization 2, 73, 87, 89
  in Merleau-Ponty 197–8
  and social action 21, 266
mechanization, and modernity 14, 264–8,
    275–6
media, mass
  and culture 105, 252
  and globalization 97, 125, 131
medicine, and normal/exceptional 182–3
Medvedev, Roy 222
megamachine, in Mumford 264–5, 268
mélange, global 49, 51–4, 55–7, 60
  and migration 56
Melucci, A. 59
Melville, Herman 262
memory
  collective 57–8
  global 5, 52
  and imagination 15, 202–3
  and knowledge 15, 194
  and space 15, 196, 201–2, 206
  and temporality 15, 195–6, 201
mercantilism, and global systems 76
Merleau-Ponty, M. 194, 197–8, 203, 205–6,
    207 n.1
mestizaje 54
metanarratives, in postmodernism 1, 32,
    124–6, 129, 137, 225
metaphysics
  and limits 169–71
  of presence 1, 12–13, 163, 164, 166, 168,
    172
  and security 155–6, 159, 163–6, 172
  see also ontology; philosophy
Meyer, W.J. 35
micro-regionalism 50
micromarketing 28–9
migration
  and global city 119, 120
  and hybridity 49, 56
militarization 269–70

Minson, J. 237
misrecognition, collective 221–2
Mitchell, Juliet 254
mobilization, political, and hybridization
    57–8
models, as systems of signs 9
modern, definition 108–9, 111
modernism
  aesthetic 21, 112, 262–4
  definitions 108–10, 262
  and homogenization 4, 6
  in humanities 109–10, 114–15, 126
  nationalized 72
  and temporality 4, 10, 109–11
modernity
  and *Communist Manifesto* 125
  crisis 6–7, 23
  criteria 109
  and culture 80–1, 85, 119–20
  definitions 108–11, 112–13, 126–7, 260, 262
  and freedom and order 140–6, 149
  and the future 126–8, 130, 149
  and global modernities 3
  and globality 27
  and globalization 5–6, 10–12, 45, 46–9, 52,
    63
  and globalization as condition 3–4, 5, 47,
    71
  and globalization as consequence 2, 3, 27,
    30, 47
  and identity 145–6
  as identity-space 71, 80, 86, 88
  and individualism 16–21
  and interconnectedness 118–19
  and the modern error 260–76
  and normality 180–2, 189 n.12
  parameters 69–89
  routes to 10–11, 27, 124–35
  and security 155–75
  in sociology 110
  structural/cultural dialectics 128–31
  and temporality 6, 10, 27, 108–11, 113–15
  vehicles of 135–7
  and the West 111–15, 119, 133, 137, 143–4
modernization
  civilizational route 17
  and colonial zone 11, 27, 133–4
  definitions 108–9, 115–16, 118, 262, 264
  divergent 3–4, 10–11, 48–9
  European route 10–11, 131–2, 133–4
  and external threat 11, 17, 27, 132–3
  and functionalism 5, 63
  and the future 126
  globalization as condition of 3, 27
  historicity 48

modernization, *cont.*
  New World route 10–11, 27, 132, 133
  and spatialization 6, 10–11, 23, 109–21,
    133–5
  theory 47, 63, 114–18
morality
  and bio-politics 238–41
  and moral community 152
  and normality 183
multiculturalism 117, 120, 244–5, 257
  and interculturalism 5, 61
Mumford, Lewis 264–5, 268, 277 n.2
myth, and emotions 22, 23, 272

Naipaul, V.S. 57
narcissism, and sexuality 248, 251
nation-state
  decentring 97–9, 100–1, 104
  and diversity 40–1
  and global system 75
  and globalization 2, 23, 34, 49, 51–2, 71–2,
    74, 75
  and historical/post-historical worlds 91–2,
    99
  and identity 12
  as illustrator 8
  increase in 97–8
  internationalization 50
  and modernity 5, 46, 94–5, 97, 134
  new world order 7–9, 12–13, 91, 96–8,
    104–6
  and normality and exception 180–2, 186,
    187
  and order/disorder 94–6
  and politics 165–6, 170
  and power 3, 93–4, 97
  and public/private spheres 253
  and society 150–1
  and spatialization 100
  and transnationality 97
  and universality 152, 153
  see also sovereignty
nationalism
  as agent of modernization 11
  cultural 41, 63, 87
  globalization 84, 101, 129–30
  and identity 12, 30, 153
  and localization 4, 26, 34, 72–3
  long-distance 49
  and social action 136
nationality
  and nation-state 93, 97, 99, 152
  and transnationality 102, 103
nature
  and culture 61, 262, 266–7, 274–6

nature, *cont.*
  as systems of equivalence 13
Nelson, Benjamin 48, 140, 146
neo-Marxism, and structural hybridization
    51
neo-modernization theory 47
neo-realism, in international relations theory
    58
neo-worlds 7–10, 102–6
neocolonialism 59
Nettl, J.P. 115
networks
  global 49, 80, 93, 101–2
  social 16, 63
New York, as modern city 118
Nichols, Mike 261
Nietzsche, Friedrich 14, 210, 225, 270
  and security and politics 159, 164, 165,
    171, 172, 175
nihonjinron 41
nominalism, Enlightenment 21, 266, 274
normality
  and exceptionalism 178, 180–8, 236
  as polemic 183–4
  and rule 140, 183, 185
nuclear weapons
  and modernity 268, 270–1
  and nation-states 98–9, 105

ontology
  and knowledge 196, 206–7, 260–1
  and normality 184, 187
  and security 160, 163–6, 167–71, 174
order, and modernity 11–12, 144–6, 148
organization, international
  globalized 75–6, 79–80
  and nation-state 2
  and power 3
orientalization
  global 54
  and hybridization 5

Pan-Africanism, and globalization 5, 37
Paris, as modern city 10, 110–11
Parsons, Talcott 17, 71, 231
particularization
  in Bachelard 199
  and globalization 72–3
  and identity politics 253
  and lebanonization 33
  and locality 26, 28, 30–7, 38, 72
  and nation-state 71–2
  and spatialization 26
  and universalism 4–5, 12, 49, 71
patriotism, decline 49

peasantry, Russian, and collective
    identity 17, 210–12, 213
Peirce, Charles S. 16, 21–2, 265, 274
perception, and knowledge 184–5, 192–3,
    267
perestroika, and dissimulation 224–5
Perkin, Harold 152
Pfeiffer, K. Ludwig 188
phenomenology
    methodology 196–200
    and space 15, 201, 203
philosophy
    as obsolete 261
    and politics 163–5, 166–71, 172–3
    see also metaphysics; ontology
pidgins 83
Pieterse, Jan Nederveen 3, 5–6, 45–64, 110
Plato, and being 163–4
pluralism
    cultural 31, 61
    geographical 31
Podhoretz, Norman 250
poetics, and the imagination 15–16, 22, 193,
    198–207
Poggi, Gianfranco 276 n.1
polarization, global 10, 120, 129–30
politics
    and bio-politics 187, 227–41
    and dissimulation 209
    and eschatology 160, 169, 173
    and the exceptional 178–9, 180–2, 185–8
    global 45
    global theory 58–9
    and hybridization 54–9
    hyperreal 7–8
    of identity 19–20, 49, 174–5, 244–58
    and limits 169–71, 173
    and modern knowledge 12–13
    and modernization 115
    and nation-state 93–4, 165
    and philosophy 163–5, 166–71, 172–3
    postinternational 50, 58
    and public/private spheres 246–7
    of security 155–75
Pomian, Krysztof 144
populism 136
post-industrialism 2, 252
post-structuralism
    and change 192–3
    and Freud 249
    and politics of difference 20, 194
    and the subject 199
    and writing 204
postmodernism
    and community 12

postmodernism, *cont.*
    and contingency 21
    critique of modernity 260–1, 263
    and culture 100
    definition 117, 120–1
    and differentiation 178–9
    and exceptionalism 188
    and globalization 5–6, 48, 118
    and heterogenization 4
    as hypermodernity 7
    and nation-state 95, 102, 106, 153
    and nature 275–6
    and spatialization 1, 32, 110, 116–17, 119
    and technology 8–9
    and temporality 1, 26
    and universality 151–2
Poulet, G. 196, 204
power
    and hybridity 56, 57
    and knowledge 13–14, 157, 170, 171, 181
    and modernity 47, 113
    and nation-states 3, 93–4, 97, 100–2, 104,
        180–1
    in neo-world orders 9–10
    and sexuality 18, 227–8, 231–3, 236
pragmatism, in Halton 21, 263, 265
Pratt, Mary Louise 65 n.6
presence
    and globalization 26–7
    in philosophy 4, 12–13, 163, 164, 166, 168,
        172
present
    in Bergson 194
    in Foucault 236–7
    and the future 126–7
    and past 276
    and politics of security 163, 168
privacy
    and the family 228
    and individualism 16–17
    in Russia 17–18, 209, 211, 213–16, 220
    see also intimacy; public/private spheres
production
    and articulation of modes 50–1
    colonial mode 10
    globalization 45, 87, 114
    and glocal modes 101, 103
    informational mode 9, 91, 92, 96
    and neo-worlds 102
    postmodern 117–18
progress
    and differentiation 178–9
    and Marxism 268–9
    and modernization 131, 262, 263
property, intellectual 10, 104

Proust, Marcel 196, 204
psychoanalysis
    in Bachelard 16, 198–9
    object-relations 15
    and politics of identity 19, 245, 247–51,
        253–5, 256–8
public/private spheres 51
    and culture 252–3
    and politics of identity 245–51, 255–6, 257
    in Russia 209–25

racism
    of state 181, 189 n.16
    working class 257
Rado, Sandor 250
rationality
    communicative 274
    and emotion 21–2, 23
    as Great Unifier 129, 130, 152
    instrumental 19, 30–1, 34, 129, 251, 264–5
    and mechanization 264–6
    and modernity 20, 96–7, 155, 264–7, 270–5
    see also Enlightenment
rationalization, bureaucratic 14, 20
reading, as writing 203, 204–5
realism
    hyperrealism 7–10, 12, 91–2, 96–102
    and modernization 4, 102
    and nationality 93–6
    and neo-world orders 7–9, 13, 92, 97–8,
        102, 105
    political 172
    Socialist 216, 219
reason see rationality
recolonization 59
reflexivity
    and globalization 53, 79
    and modernity 155
reform, and the future 127
regionalism
    and globalization 50, 59
    and technoregions 103–5
Reich, Robert B. 93
Reich, Wilhelm 251
relations, international
    and nationality 93–4
    and security 163, 166
    theory 45, 58, 64
relations, social
    and culture 81
    intensification 48
relativism, cultural 61, 79, 85–6
relativization, and globalization 71
religion
    and modernity 134, 136–7

religion, cont.
    and security 156
    and syncretism 56
religions, world, and history of globality 53,
        73, 277 n.2
representation
    and deconstruction 202
    misrecognized 222
    and realism 8–9, 13, 92, 96
    and space 204
    and time 204
resistance
    collective 57–8
    and dissimulation 221–4
    global sites 97
    to modernization 132
resonance, and reverberation 199
reverberation, and time and space 16, 196,
        199, 203, 204–5, 207
revolution, and the future 127
Rich, Adrienne 255
rights, and identity politics 244
Rilke, Rainer Maria 202
Robbins, B. 32, 42 n.3
Robertson, Roland
    and awareness of the globe 118, 119
    and civilization 6
    framework of globalization 71–2, 88–9
    and globality 53, 70–1
    and glocalization 4–5, 25–41, 49, 76
    and homogenization/heterogenization 4, 26
    and locality 72–3
    and modernization 3, 115
    and nationalism 138 n.2
    and spationalization 23
    and West-centredness 47, 124
    and world system theories 69
Rodó, José Enrique 138 n.6
Roedinger, David R. 257
Rokkan, Stein 134
Ronan 14
Rorty, Richard 21, 261, 274, 275
Rosenau, J.N. 50
Rowe, W. 49, 53
rule
    and incest 227–40
    and transgression 14, 140, 183, 185
Rushdie, Salman 57
Russia
    dual 17, 18, 211–12
    and individualism 16–18, 209–25
    and postmodernism 225
    and route to modernity 133–4, 137
    and working class as agent of moderniz-
        ation 11

Said, Edward 4, 57, 117
Saint-Simon, Claude Henri de Rouvroy,
    comte de, and Great Unifier 127–9
samizdat 223
sape, la 87
Sartre, Jean-Paul 39, 149
Sassen, Saskia 120
Schelling, V. 49, 53
schizophrenia, modal 216
Schmidt, Dennis J. 165
Schmitt, Carl 14–15, 178–9, 180–2, 184–7
Schurmann, Reiner 164–5
Schwab, George 188 n.1
science, as Great Unifier 129
security
    and genealogy 156–61, 162–3, 167, 174
    and (in)security 13, 156, 161–3, 172, 175
    and intellectual property 10, 104
    as knowledge 12–13, 159, 164
    and metaphysics 155–6, 159, 163–7
    and modernity 155–6
    physical 105
    politics of 155–75
Seed, John 111
self *see* identity; individual; individualism
sexuality
    and bio-politics 227–39
    and childhood 234–5, 240
    and identity politics 19, 248–51
    and power 18–19, 231–3
    and privacy 17–18, 213–15
    and public/private spheres 246–8
Sharabi, Hisham 55
Shohat, Ella 55, 57
sign, economy of 120
signal, and global flows 16
similarity
    and hybridization 60, 62
    localized 72
Simmel, Georg 21, 207 n.7, 263, 266–8
simulation
    and Baudrillard 96–8, 180
    and exceptionalism 180, 188
    in hyperrealism 9, 12, 92, 96–9, 106
Sinyavsky, Andrei 212
Smith, A.D. 52
socialism, and social action 136
socialization, and culture 81, 83, 86, 272, 274
society
    biosemiotic theory 275–6
    as central focus of sociology 2, 63, 150–1
    global 2, 36, 45, 58, 63, 118
    and individual 250
    industrial 2, 110
    mass 250

society, *cont.*
    as necessary 141–2
    normalizing 183, 189 n.12
    postindustrial 110
    and state 2, 14
    transnational 103
    two-tier 147–9
    see also civil society
sociology
    cultural 69, 70
    and the family 228–9
    global 25–6, 63–4
    indigenous 25–6
    and metanarrative 124–6, 129, 137
    and modernism 110, 114–15, 126, 128
    positivist 14
    and society 2, 63, 150–1
    and the state 150–1
    and temporality 128, 140
    and world society 45
sovereignty
    and the exceptional 180–1, 185–6, 187
    and neo-world order 8, 104–5
    and the state 14, 93–6, 98, 100–1, 152
spaces
    hybrid 51
    intimate 106, 200–3, 204
spatialization
    and the body 193, 196–206
    and globalization in social theory 1, 3–4,
        26, 32–4
    and hyperspace 16, 51, 96–7, 105–6
    and knowledge 15–16
    and locality 26–7, 32–3, 41
    and memory 15, 196, 202–3
    and modernity 6, 10–11, 23, 109–21, 133–5
    and nation-state 100–1
    and postmodernism 1, 32, 110, 116–17
    and space-time compression 48, 70, 106
    standardization 36
    and temporality 1, 4, 11, 23, 26–7, 194–5,
        201, 205–6
specialization, and differentiation 52, 179
specificity
    in Bachelard 199, 204, 205
    cultural 69, 81, 88, 99
Spencer, Herbert, and Great Unifier 129
Spivak, Gayatri 57, 113, 117
Stalin, Joseph 95, 216, 218, 268–9
standards of living, and collective identity 99
Starr, Fred 219
state
    and the family 227, 237
    and security 156
    and society 14, 150–1

state, *cont.*
  and subjectivity/objectivity 8
  see also nation-state; sovereignty
Stoller, Robert 254
stranger, and normality 186
structures, social
  and modernity 130–1, 133–6
  need for 140–2
styliagi, Russia 219–21, 223
subjectivity, and objectivity 8, 198–9, 267–8
suburbanization, and localization 4
Sullivan, William 264
surveillance
  collective, in Russia 18, 212–14, 218–24
  and nation-state 105, 130
Sweden, and working class as agent of
    modernization 11
symbolism, collective 57–8
syncretism 137
  and global system 74
  and hybridization 55, 56
system, global 5–6, 22–3, 69, 73–80
  commercial 88
  as condition of globalization 73–4, 77, 79,
    80
  and disjuncture 84–5
  and global institutions 75–6, 79–80
  and global processes 74–80
  and identity 74, 75, 86–9
systemness, of human existence 11–12, 15

technology
  and culture 63
  and Heidegger 8
  and individual 20
  and power 9–10
  and security 104
  as system of equivalences 8–9, 13
  and technoregions 9, 103–5
temporality
  and being 163–4
  and the body 193–6
  and culture 85
  and the future 126–8
  and hybridization 64
  and knowledge-creation 15
  and modernity 6, 10, 27, 108–10, 113–15
  in sociology 128, 140
  and space-time compression 48, 70, 106
  and spatialization 1, 4, 11, 23, 26–7, 111,
    194–5, 201, 205–6
  standardization 36
textualization
  of culture 82–4
  see also writing

Therborn, Göran 3, 10–11, 17, 27, 124–37
Third World
  and nation-states 94
  and postmodernism 117–18
time
  as *durée*/duration 15, 194–6, 201, 205
  mixed 51
Tomlinson, J. 39, 47–8, 59
totemism, and incest 229–30
Toulmin, Stephen 94
tourist industry 29, 76, 120
tradition
  breakdown 264
  construction 12, 35, 39, 131
  and modernity 3
  and nation-state 95
  return to 150, 153
transgression, urge to 14, 144–5
tribalism, and globalism 33
Troitsky, Artemy 220
Trotsky, Leon 213, 214
Tucker, Robert C. 211–12

Ukiyo school of painting 60
UN
  Declaration of Human Rights 59
  and new world order 91
unity, and conflict 52–3
universalism
  and culture 20
  and globalization 2, 46, 125
  and hybridization 5, 6
  and identity politics 244–5
  and liberation 153
  and locality 28, 30–7
  and particularizations 4–5, 12, 27–8, 49,
    71–2
  and postmodernism 151–2
  and spatialization 26
urbanization
  opposition to 29–30
  and structural hybridization 51
Urry, J. 6
USA
  and effects of Cold War 269–70
  and modernism 262–4

vampirism 180
Van der Rohe, Mies 262
Vattimo, G. 1, 165
Vienna Congress, and world society 36
vitalism, friend/foe 14–15, 184

Wagner, Benno 3, 13–14, 20, 178–88
Wallerstein, I. 4, 6, 33, 34, 73

water, as image of flux 192–3, 198, 200
Weber, Max
    Economic Ethics of the World Religions
        125–6, 128
    and globalization 30
    and meaning 21
    and modernization 131, 134, 266
    and rationalization 14, 129, 264–5, 267–8
    and society 2, 14
Weiner, Myron 115, 116
Wells, H.G. 268, 269
Westney, D.E. 41
White, Stephen 210, 212, 216
Wiener, Norbert 141–2
William of Ockham 266
Williams, Raymond 108–9, 119
Wolff, Janet 111
working class
    as agent of modernization 11, 251
    as homogeneous 251, 252
    and identity 247
world, situated 22–3
World Bank
    and global awareness 79, 80
    and imperialism 59
    and polarization 129, 130
world orders
    and glocality 91–6, 100–2
    and homogenization 33–4, 40

world orders, *cont.*
    and nation-state 7–9, 12–13, 91, 96–8
    neo-world 7–10, 13, 22, 102–6
world systems theories
    and culture 69, 80
    and Friedman 6
    and homogenization 4, 33
    and King 10
    and Luke 7–8, 13
    and Marxism 46
    and modernity 2, 109–10, 115, 118–19, 126
    and nation-state 99, 102
    in Therborn 11
world-space 39
writing
    in Bachelard 199–200, 203
    the body 192, 193, 195, 197, 200, 206, 261
    and reading 203, 204–5
    as transformation 192–3, 205

Yeats, W.B. 133
Yoshino, K. 41
Young, I.M. 58
Young-Bruehl, Elizabeth 250

Zaretsky, Eli 3, 16, 19–20, 244–58
Zea, Leopoldo 138 n.6
Zukin, Sharon 120